MORMON PASSAGE

MORMON PASSAGE

∾

A Missionary Chronicle

∾

Gary Shepherd
and
Gordon Shepherd

University of Illinois Press
Urbana and Chicago

© 1998 by the Board of Trustees of the University of Illinois
Manufactured in the United States of America
1   2   3   4   5   C   P   5   4   3   2   1

This book is printed on acid-free paper.

Library of Congress Cataloging-in-Publication Data

Shepherd, Gary, 1943–
Mormon passage : a missionary chronicle /
Gary Shepherd and Gordon Shepherd.
p.   cm.
Includes bibliographical references and index.
ISBN 0-252-02356-0 (alk. paper). —
ISBN 0-252-06662-6 (pbk. : alk. paper)
1. Church of Jesus Christ of Latter-Day Saints—Missions.
2. Mormon Church—Missions.
3. Shepherd, Gary, 1943–   .
4. Shepherd, Gordon, 1943–   .
5. Missionaries—United States—Biography.
6. Church of Jesus Christ of Latter-Day Saints—Missions—Mexico.
7. Mormon Church—Missions—Mexico.
I. Shepherd, Gordon, 1943–   .
II. Title.
BX8661.S54   1998
266'.9332—dc21
97-4789
CIP

To our old companions in Mexico.
And to Beckie Jones Shepherd and Lauren Snow Shepherd,
our companions in marriage.

Contents

Preface

Writing in 1983 on the emerging prospects of a distinctive Mormon literature, Brigham Young University English professor Eugene England observed that surprisingly little attention had been given by contemporary Mormon writers to the Mormon missionary experience—surprising, that is, because of the centrality of lay missionary service in Mormon culture. In England's judgment, "One place that can stimulate an authentic search for self, one that can be true to our theology as well as our deepest reality and needs, is the mission field. . . . With such a focus, the missionary experience, as reality and archetype, can do more for Mormon life and letters than serve as an exotic area for exploring religious identity crises . . . what I am suggesting has already been done remarkably well in some missionary diaries" (1983, 125).

Most recently, in his bibliographic guide to Mormon missions and missionaries, David Whittaker remarks on the "surprisingly few studies" by historians or social scientists who have taken for their theme the paradigmatic shaping experiences of Mormon society as lay members (primarily youths or young adults between the ages of nineteen and twenty-three) prepare for, enter into, and return from their mission field assignments (1993, 31).

These Mormon scholars are not alone in commenting on the paucity of serious scholarly attention paid to the missionary experience or to the role of missions and missionary movements in modern world history. Dana L. Robert, a historian and Protestant missiologist at Boston University School of Theology, observes that "until the 1980s missionary thought and activity was seldom studied in its own right, nor was the role of the missionary as transmitter of cross-cultural information to America taken seriously. . . . Popular piety was ignored in favor of formal theological and political pronouncements. Intellectual sources superseded other forms of documentation, with the social biography of the missionary force seldom examined" (1994, 148, 149). Robert identifies studies of evangelical work "in the field" as among those topics "in the greatest need of future research. . . . Historians are realizing that missionary biography is not necessarily hagiography; critically done, it can illuminate aspects of American identity, cross-cultural relations, and theological development. . . . The lives of 'ordinary' missionaries should

be mined. . . . These first person accounts are the primary sources of twentieth-century missions" (152, 154).

Through this book we hope to make a contribution to Mormon studies
in precisely those areas of relative neglect that England, Whittaker, and Robert
have identified. Based on an edited integration of our journals and correspondence as youthful missionaries in Mexico during the mid-1960s, we offer a
documentary case description of Mormon missionary life. Our account is
supplemented by a set of more detached, analytical essays on the structure,
historical context, and significance of the LDS missionary enterprise from
our current perspectives as academic sociologists. The multiple narrative,
case study approach we employ is similar in method and intent to that used
by Oscar Lewis in such works as *Five Families: Mexican Case Studies in the
Culture of Poverty, The Children of Sanchez: Autobiography of a Mexican Family,* and *Pedro Martinez: A Mexican Peasant and His Family.*[1]

Like Lewis, we were not guided by the objective of organizing our material into a discrete set of topical problems, nor did we attempt to formulate
a rigorous set of hypotheses to be systematically tested against the documentary data. Rather, our primary intention is to portray the LDS missionary
experience as realistically and authentically as possible—as a complex social
process. Through our chronological narratives we want to convey what it
means to be a young Mormon missionary, following the developmental path
prescribed by Mormon society, and struggling to adjust to the exigencies of
missionary life in a foreign culture.

The potential defects of relying on mission field diaries and correspondence—as a way of conveying an insider's perspective of missionary life—
are as apparent as some of their virtues. Such documents can either be exceedingly banal or overbearingly pompous. Much of what is written in the
mission field may be calculated to impress an intended or imaginary audience with the diligent, if not heroic, efforts of the author and with the ultimately triumphal progress of the work. This is not invariably the case, however. Idealized conceptions of missionary work officially promoted by the
sponsoring organization may be punctured from time to time by a more
balanced, realistic assessment of events in the private musings of a personal
journal or letters to selected confidants. Such documents can provide a hu-
manizing glimpse into the daily routines of those who compose the rank and
file of a religion's missionary force.

As we began to explore the possibility of organizing our personal documents for a study of Mormon missionary life we struggled, however briefly,
with questions of appropriate modesty and objectivity in flaunting our deeds.
Of much greater initial concern was the embarrassment that we anticipated

would follow from a revelation of how our minds worked at an age when we were scarcely past adolescence and the fact that some of our deeds would have to be reassessed as causes of dismay rather than as sources of pride. Upon reviewing our materials we discovered that the writing had its share of problems yet showed what we thought were certain strengths. There is neither a great deal of introspection nor are there many attempts at amateur analysis to be found in our missionary documents; for the most part they are observational and descriptive. And, although often naive, our mission field writings do not seem excessively burdened with pious platitudes, as we had feared they might. Indeed, some who have read the manuscript have expressed surprise at the relative lack of deep religious feeling or spirituality in our writing. Our apparent idealism and enthusiasm were often clothed in youthful irreverence and were occasionally articulated in vernacular crudities.

Our accounts of missionary experience were often egocentric on the one hand and ethnocentric on the other. We are, at this later date, mortified by the occasional outbursts of anti-Catholic sentiment in our missionary writings and our disdainful dismissal of various Protestant groups we encountered, by our casual insensitivity toward many of the traditions of Mexican culture, and our ignorance of the world in general. But these personal failings were nevertheless true reflections of a narrowly focused missionary experience in a foreign land where, as callow youths, our essential objective was to win converts to a new religious faith—circumstances that almost inevitably fostered a certain amount of self-righteousness, defensiveness, and dogmatism. Also offensive but revealing were the many harsh judgments we made of other missionaries who failed to meet our notions of proper missionary character or conduct. In contrast, we were quite willing to be self-congratulatory of our own performances (often expressed through vicarious exchanges of pride in one another's accomplishments). We were pleased to discover in retrospect, however, that such lapses into narrow-mindedness and personal aggrandizement in our writing were relieved from time to time by a certain appreciation for the absurd and occasional self-deprecating humor.

One may question, of course, how generalizable our accounts are as portraits of the missionary experience. And one can also question whether events recorded several decades ago have much relevance to current Mormon missionary practice. We cannot claim, in fact, that our missionary experiences were perfectly typical, much less our interpretation and description of them. In some respects we were not typical at all. For one thing we are twins: twin brothers who were called to missionary service at the same time and place, enacting missionary roles in the same sorts of circumstances and replicating one another's missionary development—a relatively rare occurrence in the LDS proselyting system. In many ways our relationship transcended the restrictions of missionary rules and was a countervailing force to the shaping pressures of missionary socialization. We participated in a certain amount of mutually condoned deviance from missionary regulations, especially during the training phase of our experience. Paradoxically, however, our relationship also became a powerful factor in reinforcing compliance with essential standards of diligence and dedication to the missionary role.

Although Mormon missionary work has undergone a fair amount of organizational change since our day (which we will try to indicate in later parts of the book), we are confident that the basic experience for current missionaries in the field is much the same as it was for us. We believe that even though they may be unique in their particulars, our accounts contain some universal elements of the missionary experience that should be recognizable to all who have served missions for the LDS Church.

Disclosed in our diaries and correspondence is a picture of the religious "plausibility structure" of the mission organization. Plausibility structures are the creation of every subculture.[2] They consist of integrated networks of individuals who share common assumptions, traditions, understandings, and sources of authority, which, in turn, shape their values and perceptions of reality. These networks maintain adherence to a particular belief system, reinforce commitment to group norms of conduct, unify participants in a common cause, and insulate them against the often dispiriting antagonism and incredulity of the outside world. What emerges in the description of our Mexican missionary experiences is the portrayal of a developmental process in which careers of faith are forged and tested and then cracked and solidified anew at various stages of missionary growth—from neophytes struggling to learn both a new language and the requisite skills of the missionary role, to increasing levels of self-confidence and the gradual assumption of leadership responsibilities.

It is perfectly obvious that the Mormon missionary system not only recruits new members into the faith but also, of equal importance, serves as a kind of prolonged rite of passage and training ground for Mormon youths, especially young males. The mission field becomes a place where many young Mormons consolidate their faith for the first time. It is a place that prepares and equips them for life-long careers of service in the lay structure of the LDS Church. Historically, the majority of Mormonism's most prominent officials have commenced their advancement through the ecclesiastical ranks after completing a period of missionary labor.

At the same time, it would be a distortion to picture missionary social-ization as being invariably successful in its intended consequences. A majority (approximately two-thirds) of U.S. Mormon males who are age-eligible at nineteen do not serve proselyting missions for the church, a fact that con-tinues to frustrate Mormon leaders.[3] Among those who do serve, there is a wide range of experiential outcomes. Although most called to missionary service quickly seem to conform to an institutionally idealized image of the devout missionary, some struggle constantly with their religious faith. Some learn to suspend any nagging doubts about the value of their efforts and become dedicated workers. But others are overwhelmed with the sacrificial demands of missionary life and become discouraged, losing their desire to do much more than maintain appearances until their missionary assignments have expired. While the enthusiasm and commitment of some waxes and wanes over time, only a small minority requests that their missions be ter-minated or are sent home for serious breaches of mission rules.[4] These vari-ations in missionary commitment and morale should become abundantly clear through descriptions given in our journals and correspondence.

In short, Mormon missionary enculturation is not so different from that which is sponsored by similar organizations in other institutional contexts. Human socialization, even when imposed under highly structured condi-tions, is seldom a perfectly uniform process (Goffman 1961; Wrong 1961). It affects different individuals in different ways, with a variety of ultimate organizational consequences. Some idea of the day-to-day functioning of the Mormon missionary system and of the diversity of responses by Mormon youth to the missionary experience is, we think, captured in this book.

We have taken certain editorial liberties. To enhance readability we have corrected spelling, punctuation, and some of the more egregious errors of grammar and syntax in the original documents. Most important, we have exercised editorial selectivity. We eliminated a number of our journal entries (or portions thereof) if, in our judgment, they offered only redundant, rou-tine information that did not advance the development of basic themes or story lines or did not contribute some insight into our missionary experi-ence in Mexico. On similar grounds, we also deleted portions of our corre-spondence. At the same time, we have attempted to remedy an occasional hiatus in our journal records by incorporating some supplementary mate-rials drawn from personal recollections as well as letters to our parents and other correspondents.

We have elected not to burden the text with expositions of Mormon doc-trine. For readers unfamiliar with or puzzled by the tenets of Mormonism, there is an ample supply of Mormon exegeses, apologetics, and general historical works to be found elsewhere.[5] We have also altered the names of a number of former missionary companions and other friends mentioned in our writing. We have done this out of concern for the feelings of certain individuals and respect for their privacy. Some might be pleased by our descriptions, but others would be seriously offended and would, no doubt, vigorously wish to dispute our characterizations.

The organizational format of the book integrates both of our accounts in a chronology that moves from one story to the other. There are occasional gaps in the record, but a narrative thread emerges that provides coherence to the numerous events recorded. The bulk of the narrative is carried through journal entries complemented by the insertion of our letters to one another, written throughout the time we were in Mexico. We have divided the book into sections on the basis of major chronological transitions in missionary status. Following an introductory chapter on the structure of Mormon growth and Mormon missions in the modern world, Part 1 deals with the concept of LDS missionary callings as a rite of passage and focuses on the missionary farewell service preceding our induction into missionary life. Part 2 is concerned with patterns of formal LDS missionary training and covers the three months we spent studying Spanish at what was then called the Language Training Mission (LTM) on the campus of Brigham Young University. In Part 3, we discuss Mormon recruitment success and growth in Mexico and record our lengthy apprenticeships as junior companions. Part 4 describes the mission's promotion and mobility structure and deals with our experiences as senior missionary companions. And finally, in Part 5, we consider the consequences of lay missionary service for Mormonism as we end our assignments to Mexico in mission leadership positions.

We struggled for several years trying to devise a workable combination of seemingly disparate elements to produce this book. What portions of our voluminous field journal entries and personal correspondence to eliminate? How to organize the remainder of these materials into a coherent account of our separate but simultaneous activities? How to integrate our youthful narration of missionary experiences with our current detached analysis as sociologists in such a way that the reader is provided a meaningful framework for understanding the Mormon missionary system without being jerked back and forth between excessively dissonant voices? We cannot claim to have finally found ideal solutions to these and other substantive and organizational questions. But whatever success we may have achieved in dealing with these problems owes much to a number of readers who have helped guide us to a clearer understanding of what needed to be done at various stages during the evolutionary development of this project.

Preeminent among those who made significant contributions is Lavina Fielding Anderson. She patiently and assiduously read through a succession of manuscript drafts, each time offering sharp criticisms, wonderfully constructive suggestions, and much needed encouragement concerning the ultimate worth of the project. Patrick McNamara also provided several careful readings that yielded perceptive advice and valuable support at critical junctures. Rod Stark perceived merit in what we were attempting, and his enthusiastic endorsement mattered a great deal. Armand Mauss forced us to reexamine very carefully the fundamental premises of our work. Linda Knight Newell, Kendall White, Jacqueline Scherer, Conrad Shumaker, Ken Mackintosh, Lisa Hansen, and Philip Davis all read various manuscript versions and were generous with their helpful comments. Brooks Green contributed both interest and the finely crafted map of Mexico, locating cites of missionary headquarters. Kathy Barrett generously toiled to "transliterate" page numbers for our index. Finally, the staff of the University of Illinois Press has been unfailingly cooperative and professional. Liz Dulany was particularly effective in seeing our manuscript through the maze of publication review, and Mary Giles copyedited our work with a laser eye. We are grateful to all.

Notes

1. Based on extensive tape-recorded interviews (subsequently edited to create seamless narratives), Lewis attempted in these books to produce a "literature of social realism" by portraying, in the context of a particular cultural milieu, the inner lives of ordinary people expressed in their own words. In *Children of Sanchez,* Lewis advocated and defended what he called the "method of multiple autobiographies" in which individuals relate, in serial format, their separate accounts of the same events that conjointly shape their lives (1961, xi). This method intentionally produces reiteration and chronological repetitions in the narrative but does so from a different set of changing perspectives. The consequences are not necessarily tedious and redundant but rather, if done effectively, can generate "a cumulative, multifaceted, panoramic view" for readers that is true to the complexity of everyday life. "Independent versions of the same incidents . . . provide a built-in check upon the reliability and validity of much of the data, and thereby partially offset the subjectivity inherent in a single autobiography."

2. The concept of a plausibility structure is developed in Berger (1967) and Berger and Luckmann (1967).

3. See for example, *Church News:* "More Missionaries Needed Urges President Benson" (March 9, 1986), "President Benson: We Can Do Better" (April 13, 1986), and "More Missionaries Called, More Needed to Serve" (May 18, 1986); see also *The Ensign:* "Proclaim My Gospel from Land to Land" (May 1989, 13), "Called to Serve" (May 1991, 39), and "But the Laborers Are Few" (May 1992, 23).

4. The LDS missionary department will not release figures on the number of missionaries who fail to complete their designated terms of service in the field. We cannot specify a precise number, yet based on anecdotal accounts, haphazard observation of numerous Mormon youths over the years, and direct experience with our missionary cohorts in Mexico we are confident in concluding that the majority of Mormon missionaries—certainly more than 90 percent—complete their missionary assignments.

5. For reference articles on Mormon history and theology, see Ludlow (1992); for a comprehensive bibliography of scholarly works on Mormonism, see Allen et al. (forthcoming).

Introduction: Mormon Growth and
Mormon Missions in the Modern World

Mormonism is far from being the first religion to confidently pursue the evangelization of the world. In certain respects, however, its organized contemporary efforts to do so may be unique, if not unparalleled, in modern religious history. The Church of Jesus Christ of Latter-day Saints (the official name of the Mormon or LDS Church) has grown from an isolated American sect in the nineteenth century to an international church with a world membership rapidly approaching ten million people—a membership that continues to grow at an impressive rate not only in the United States but also in Latin America, the West Indies, the Philippines, and West Africa.[1] LDS growth has attracted the attention of religious leaders, politicians, journalists, and scholars alike who have begun to contemplate the emerging portents of a "new religious tradition."

Non-Mormon observers have increasingly perceived that modern Mormonism is in the process of becoming an unusually important contemporary movement. For example, Jan Shipps, a historian and religious scholar, has observed that

> Without fully and consciously realizing that they were doing so, the followers
> of Jesus established a new religious tradition. This book [*Mormonism: The Story
> of a New Religious Tradition*] tells the story of yet another assembly of saints
> whose history, I believe, is in many respects analogous to the history of those
> early Christians who thought at first that they had found the only proper way
> to be Jews. . . . Mormonism is a form of *corporate* Christianity. While it per-
> ceives itself as Christian, Mormonism differs from traditional Christianity in
> much the same fashion that traditional Christianity, in its ultimate emphasis
> on the individual, came to differ from Judaism. . . . Nomenclature notwith-
> standing, Mormonism is a new religious tradition. (1985, ix, 148, 149)

The religious historian Martin E. Marty has noted that "often overlooked in assessments of American religious demography, this 'new religious tradition' [Mormonism] increasingly demands separate analysis. . . . Historians cannot all avoid the story of the social past of a movement of up to five million people [in 1982]. It would be inconceivable that they escape the notice of non-Mormons" (1987, 303, 305). Moreover, Harold Bloom, a literary critic and religious scholar, reminds us that

> Missionary zeal is not uncommon among American sects and denominations, but the Mormons abound in it to a unique degree. . . . Their future is immense. . . . No other American religious movement is so ambitious, and no rival even remotely approaches the spiritual audacity that drives endlessly towards accomplishing a titanic design. The Mormons fully intend to convert the nation and the world; to go from some ten million souls to six billion. This is sublimely insane. . . . Yet the Mormons will not falter; they will take the entire twentieth-first century as their span, if need be. . . . The more deeply I study the Mormons . . . the more I become convinced that someday soon they will be the Established Church of the American West. (1992, 93, 94, 113, 263)

Journalists Robert Gottlieb and Peter Wiley have written that "almost overnight, this small Utah church became an international church, with an international missionary program beyond the dreams of any other church in the world. . . . The Mormon church is an institution that in the coming decades will more and more occupy center stage in American society. It will be important as this county's fastest growing religion, a growing economic power, and a political influence" (1984, 14, 18). And, in the opinion of Rodney Stark, a sociologist, "It is possible today to study that incredibly rare event: the rise of a new world religion. I shall attempt to demonstrate that the Church of Jesus Christ of Latter-day Saints, the Mormons, will soon achieve a worldwide following comparable to that of Islam, Buddhism, Christianity, Hinduism, and the other dominant world faiths. . . . Today [1983] there are five million Mormons on earth. How many will there be in the near future? Projections require assumptions. If growth during the next century is like that of the past, the Mormons will become a major world faith. . . . Mormon success makes them the single most important case on the agenda of the social scientific study of religion" (1984, 18, 23, 26). Although other interested observers might be more cautious than Stark in their projections of Mormon growth into the next century (Bennion 1995; Bennion and Young 1996), it is clear that the LDS Church already has become a major religious movement to be reckoned with.

Sources of Mormon Growth

Religious organizations grow either through birth rates that exceed death rates and member defections (natural increase) or through recruitment of new members (Finke and Stark 1992; Hoge and Roozen, eds. 1979; Stark and Bainbridge 1985). Historically, both natural increase and the systematic recruitment of new members have been essential sources of Mormon growth.

Mormonism is a pronatalist religion that also requires its members to abide by a health code, including abstinence from alcohol, drugs, and tobacco products, which is statistically correlated with lower mortality rates (Heaton 1992, 1525). According to Tim Heaton, a Mormon demographer, "High birth rates have been an important source of growth throughout LDS history. In the frontier era, high fertility was necessary to fuel population expansion. After 1900, conversion rates for several decades were relatively low, and fertility was the major source of growth. . . . In the twentieth century, the LDS and Utah birthrates generally have been parallel with, but substantially higher than, birthrates in the United States" (1992, 1522, 1524). The Mormon fertility rate is about one and a half times the national U.S. average (Heaton 1986).

Since World War II, the Mormon birth rate, relatively low mortality rates, and, in particular, intensive proselyting efforts have produced a growth rate of 58 percent a decade, with the greatest proportional increases occurring during the 1960s and 1980s (table 1).

If predictions about Mormonism's imminent rise as a major world faith eventually prove to be true, what do growth rates indicate about the potential number of Mormons in the twenty-first century? To quote Stark,

> If we assume they will grow by 30 percent per decade, then in 2080 there will be more than 60 million Mormons. But since World War II, the Mormon

Table 1. Fifty Years of Mormon Growth: Decade Comparisons, 1945–95

Year	Members	Absolute Increase	Increase
1945	979,454	—	—
1955	1,357,274	377,820	38.6%
1965	2,395,932	1,038,658	76.5
1975	3,572,202	1,176,270	49.1
1985	5,919,483	2,347,281	65.7
1995	9,341,000	3,421,517	57.8
50-year totals		8,361,546	853.6
Mean percentage increase per decade			57.5

Source: *Deseret News Church Almanac, 1997–1998.*

growth rate has been far higher than 30 percent per decade. If we set the rate at 50 percent, then in 2080 there will be 265 million Mormons. Admittedly, straight-line projections are risky; they assume the future will be like the past. There is no way to be sure that Mormon growth won't suddenly begin to decline. But . . . I can find no reason to expect the Mormons suddenly to lose their ability to gain converts. In historical terms, they must lose their conversion capacity very quickly if they are *not* to become a major world faith. (1984, 23, 24)[2]

As Stark recognizes, Mormon growth projections hinge most importantly on the LDS Church's continuing ability to win converts through missionary efforts. Perhaps the best way to measure LDS growth through conversions is to compute the ratio of convert baptisms to eight-year-old baptisms. (Births are counted by LDS recording procedures in yearly membership totals and are referred to as "children of record.") Children's names are removed from the rolls of the church if their parents fail to have them baptized at age eight, the doctrinally established age of accountability. Beginning in the early 1960s, as organized proselyting efforts accelerated, the number of Mormon converts began to exceed the number of Mormon children baptized into the church (table 2). For every child baptized in 1960 there were 1.15 Mormon converts; subsequently, that ratio has increased substantially, and since 1990 it has averaged approximately four converts per child baptism.

Table 2. LDS Converts Compared to Child Baptisms for Selected Years, 1940–95

Year	Convert Baptisms	Child Baptisms	Ratio of Convert to Child Baptisms	Converts as Percent of Total Baptisms
1940	7,877	14,412	0.55	35
1945	4,957	16,106	0.31	24
1950	14,700	22,808	0.64	39
1955	21,669	32,807	0.66	40
1960	48,586	42,189	1.15	53
1965	82,455	49,413	1.67	63
1970	79,126	55,210	1.43	60
1975	95,412	50,263	1.90	65
1980	211,000	65,000	3.25	76
1985	197,640	70,000	2.82	74
1990	330,877	78,000	4.24	81
1991	297,770	75,000	3.97	80
1992	274,477	77,380	3.55	78
1993	304,808	76,312	3.99	80
1994	300,730	72,538	4.15	81
1995	304,330	71,139	4.28	81

Sources: LDS Conference Reports, 1940–96; *Deseret News Church Almanac, 1997–1998.*

Clearly, it is recruitment, significantly more so at present than natural increase, that is fueling Mormon expansion. Thus, to comprehend the rapid rise of Mormonism as a religious force in the modern world, it is essential to comprehend the missionary ideology and practices of the Latter-day Saints. We offer four guiding propositions to be elaborated on throughout this book as the bases for making sense of Mormon expansion. First, an apparent market exists in many parts of the world for the kind of religious life that Latter-day Saints advocate; second, LDS expansion in the world religious economy is primarily a function of an unusually large and highly organized missionary force; third, LDS recruitment success through its missionary force is a function of the willingness of the church and its members to invest unusually high levels of their material and personal resources to support the missionary enterprise; and, fourth, the large-scale mobilization of human resources devoted to LDS missionary work is, in turn, a function of intensive religious socialization of the lay membership.

By "religious economy" we mean the marketplace of competing faiths in a society where individuals exercise personal preferences in deciding about religious affiliation. Where religious choice is possible and competition among different denominations for adherents is allowed by political authorities, we may speak of a "religious market." As in other market economies, action in a religious market is shaped by both supply and demand. Competing denominations must mobilize their resources in a simultaneous attempt to shape and cater to individual religious preferences. The structure of the world's religious economy defines the historical context in which the LDS Church has developed and continues to expand through missionary recruitment.[3]

The Social and Historical Context of Mormon Missionary Success

The growing success of Mormonism as a missionary religion in the modern world cannot be understood adequately without placing it in the larger social and historical context in which it originated and developed. Founded in a frontier setting within two generations after the American Revolutionary War, Mormonism emerged at a time of great national expansion and social change in a fledgling nation still struggling to define its national political character and build its economic infrastructure. It was also a time of great religious ferment and utopian experimentation, of numerous new religious movements, and of intense evangelical competition, revivals, and Christian sectarianism (Cross 1950; Hughes and Allen 1988; McLoughlin 1978). From its inception, Mormonism was a committed missionary religion in the evangelical mode of nineteenth-century American Protestantism. Its early expansion was almost entirely a result of proselyting religious seekers in New England and the Eastern Seaboard states, the Midwest and Canada, and especially segments of the industrial working class in Great Britain and Scandinavia, the great majority of whom migrated to Mormon centers in the United States following their conversions (Ellsworth 1951; Sonne 1987; Thorp 1977; Vogel 1988; Yorgason 1970).

The Mormons were not alone in their evangelizing success, of course. Some Protestant missiologists (Latourette 1953) have called the nineteenth century the "great century of missions," an era in which a zealous religious movement was launched through the innovation of an extensive network of Protestant voluntary societies to Christianize the world (Hutchison 1987; Neill 1964). According to Andrew Walls, a religious historian, the "century's greatest missionary achievement was the Christianization of the United States" (1991, 149). In turn, the United States quickly came to dominate and transform the overseas missionary movement through the systematic implementation of characteristically pragmatic, American methods.

> The Christianization of America reached its climax as American industrial enterprise and capacity took on a world significance. This combined with the frontier antecedents to give American missions a distinctive style only partly modified by the immense theological divergences, which American missions display. The style is innovative, entrepreneurial, and problem solving. It is marked by a stress on organization and efficient business methods, including a readiness to invest in what might crudely be called product development and market research. (Walls 1991, 156, 158)

For those familiar with Mormon missionary practices, it should be clear that Walls's characterization of the American approach to evangelism in general is simultaneously a fair description of the Mormon approach in particular. A good case could be made that the LDS Church has "Americanized" its missionary strategies and procedures to a far greater extent than most, if not all, of its contemporary competitors in the world religious economy. The strengths as well as the problems associated with an American, business-oriented approach to missions will be alluded to throughout this book.

American missionary ideology has undergone some major historical divisions and transformations. Most nineteenth-century evangelism was characterized by urgent, apocalyptic preaching (Sandeen 1970; Sweet 1979, 1984; Tuveson 1968). That was true of the Mormons, who were intensely preoccupied with the imminent end of time, the gathering of the elect to an American Zion in the Rocky Mountains of Utah, and with what they believed was a divine mandate to establish the literal Kingdom of God on earth in preparation for the destruction of worldly governments and the advent of the millennium (Hansen 1967; Hill 1989; Underwood 1982, 1994). Mormons shared with other nineteenth-century missionary denominations the belief that the principal duty of faithful Christians was to testify unapologetically to the unconverted and that the sincere enunciation of verbal statements alone, transmitted through the "power of the Holy Spirit," would be sufficient to convince the pure in heart to reform their lives drastically in conformity to doctrinaire religious ideals (Walls 1991, 160).

In the latter nineteenth and early twentieth centuries, however, the Social Gospel movement became a major force in mainline, urban denominations attempting to adapt to the growing ethnic inequities and social problems of American cities (Marty 1979; Olmstead 1961). Verbal evangelism alone seemed to many missiologists to be a superficial solution to material human misery. The Social Gospel approach to Christian evangelism shifted energy and resources away from the exclusive mission of converting souls to that of social and political reform—to the development of medical, educational, and social service programs for the needy and disadvantaged. The Social Gospel movement was associated with what Burdick and Hammond call "revisionist thinking" about missions, an increasingly critical stance taken by prominent Protestant theologians toward traditional assumptions about the inherent superiority of Christian theology and culture (1991, 199). Instead, many mission theorists advocated a new Christian agenda, sensitive to the values of religious and cultural pluralism, which would stress ecumenical cooperation over aggressive soul-winning campaigns. Such an approach contrasted sharply with the older and most prominent missiology theory of traditional Christendom, which proclaimed the "ultimate supremacy of Christ as described in the New Testament. . . . All other religions, philosophies, and teaching are false. . . . Exclusivist missiologies deny outright the validity of competing truth claims and stress active gospel proselyting" (King 1983, 44, 43).

By the first quarter of the twentieth century, their once prominent position in the world religious economy undermined by their increasingly moderate and relativistic mission theories, mainline dominance (e.g., Presbyterians, Methodists, Episcopalians, and Lutherans) of Protestant overseas missions peaked and then went into precipitous decline (Schlesinger 1974). Attrition in missionary ranks and leadership by mainline dominations left a vacuum in Christian evangelizing that was soon filled by nonestablishment evangelicals, Protestant fundamentalists, and pentecostals. Relative to "establishment Protestantism's systematic dismantling of its foreign missions,

beginning in the 1920s . . . the missionary thrust by nonestablishment Protestants offers an astonishing contrast . . . evangelicals adhered to older theological priorities: the primacy of the supernatural, a definitive social orientation, an open hostility to modernity, and thus a continued conviction that
conversion of others to Christianity was their chief objective" (Burdick and
Hammond 1991, 202).

Since World War II, American evangelicals (and, more recently, pentecostals) have been the dominant force in Protestant Christian missions, both
domestically and overseas (Robert 1994). Burdick and Hammond's data
show that by 1985 evangelical foreign missionary personnel overwhelmingly outnumbered their establishment counterparts 14 to 1. It is these same
modern sectarians, with their uncompromising moral strictures and fundamentalist faith, traditional approaches to Christian proselyting, and emphasis
on church growth, who are increasing in number while most historic denominations of the Protestant establishment struggle to maintain the active allegiance of membership at home, let alone expand through recruitment in
foreign missions (Hoge and Roozen, eds. 1979; Roof and McKinney 1987).

In the context of shifting patterns in American missionary history and ideology, Mormonism has followed essentially the same path as the more growth-
oriented Protestant evangelicals and fundamentalist sects. Although the LDS
Church has toned down its nineteenth-century apocalyptic rhetoric (Shepherd
and Shepherd 1984a, 1984b, 1984c, 1986) and invested considerable institutional resources into humanitarian outreach programs (Mauss 1996), its absolutism and self-confidence in its ultimate millenarian mission have never
wavered.[4] While making numerous policy accommodations over the years, the
LDS Church persists in representing itself as the only true church recognized
and guided through revelation by God and as possessing the only complete (i.e.,
restored) gospel and authority of Jesus Christ necessary for salvation. It remains
committed to the goal of converting every living soul who will listen to its
message, regardless of any cultural constraints of place or time, and continues
to prepare for a ruling role in the still-anticipated millennial Kingdom of God.[5]
That is the traditional Christian approach to conversion, and, for the Mormons,
it has worked spectacularly well since World War II in increasing the international growth of the LDS Church.

Resource Mobilization: Size, Distribution, and Organization of the LDS Missionary Force

What makes it possible for a relatively new religion like Mormonism to convert more than three hundred thousand people annually? The most parsi-

monious answer appears to be that the number of LDS converts is a direct function of the number of LDS missionaries laboring in the field. The best single predictor of the annual Mormon conversion rate is the size of its world-wide missionary force (Irving 1976; Thomas 1986). There is no other religious denomination in the world—Catholic, Protestant, or non-Christian—whose full-time proselyting force is even close in size to that recruited, trained, and supported by the LDS Church. Approximately fifty thousand Mormon missionaries, stationed in more than three hundred missions in Latin and North America, Oceana and the South Pacific, Europe, parts of Asia, and sub-Saharan Africa, proselytize six to seven days a week, fifty-two weeks a year.[6] In contrast, according to figures published in the Missions Advanced Research and Communication Center (MARK) *Mission Handbook,* eighty-five thousand full-time Protestant missionaries served worldwide in 1992 (Siewert and Kenyon 1993), many of them on furlough at any given time (an estimated 20 percent) or functioning as staff in "enabling," humanitarian agencies rather than engaging in active proselyting (Wilson and Siewert, eds. 1987, 650). The single largest Protestant sending agency was the Southern Baptist Convention Foreign Mission Board, which supported 3,660 overseas career missionaries in 1992 and an additional 329 "short-termers" serving two-month to four-year assignments. At the same time, U.S. Catholic missionaries (mostly religious order priests and nuns) serving abroad numbered 5,441 (Siewert and Kenyon 1993, 60, 493).

Because the typical LDS missionary stint is a temporary assignment of eighteen to twenty-four months' duration, simply to maintain a force of fifty thousand requires that approximately thirty thousand new missionaries be set apart every year to replace those who return home. Mormon officials review from five hundred to eight hundred missionary applications a week, according to *The Ensign,* a LDS periodical (May 1993, 32). More than six hundred thousand Mormons have served full-time missions for the LDS Church since its founding in 1830.[7] In fact, the Mormon missionary force does not remain static; it continues to grow. Figures from selected years since 1960 (table 3) show that the Mormon missionary force more than quadrupled in size between 1960 and 1995. For most of that period, approximately one-third of the Mormon males in the United States between the ages of nineteen and twenty-one (the church's principal recruiting pool for new missionaries) served missions.[8] If the percentage who accepts missionary assignments stays more or less constant while church membership continues to grow exponentially, the size of the missionary force will also continue to increase dramatically.[9] That seems to be what LDS ecclesiastical authorities want and are planning for. Church officials constantly emphasize the need

Table 3. Size of LDS Missionary Force and Convert Baptisms for Selected Years, 1960–95

Year Ending	Missions	Missionaries in the Field	Converts Baptized	Ratio of Converts to Missionaries
1960	58	9,097	48,586	5.3
1965	76	12,585	82,455	6.6
1970	92	14,387	79,126	5.5
1975	134	22,492	95,412	4.2
1980	188	29,953	211,000	7.0
1985	188	29,265	197,640	6.8
1990	256	43,651	330,877	7.6
1991	267	43,395	297,770	6.9
1992	276	46,025	274,477	6.0
1993	295	48,708	304,808	6.3
1994	303	47,311	300,730	6.4
1995	307	48,631	304,330	6.3

Sources: LDS Conference Reports, 1960–96; Deseret News Church Almanac, 1997–1998.

for more missionaries and an increase of missionary effort.[10] In their public statements at least, they have seldom indicated any willingness to limit church commitment to expand the missionary enterprise, despite a looming "capital crunch" for the institutional church anticipated in the mid-1980s by some outside observers (Gottlieb and Wiley 1984, 124–28). It is possible that the Mormon missionary force could, within another generation, well exceed a hundred thousand full-time missionaries.

Conversions do not come easily. The average number of LDS convert baptisms worldwide per missionary in the field ranges between six and seven a year. That may seem like a paltry payoff for so many personnel hours invested in preparation and constant effort. But, when tens of thousands of missionaries can all convert a few individuals annually, it adds up to hundreds of thousands of new members. To reinforce that point, consider the following statistical projections. The zero-order correlation between increases in the LDS missionary force and the number of convert baptisms every year since 1960 is .96. If that degree of correlation remained constant, and if the current number of approximately 50,000 Mormon missionaries was doubled, then LDS convert baptisms would increase to more than 672,000 a year.[11]

Of equal importance to the size of the missionary force for explaining and predicting the number of conversions is Mormonism's worldwide geographical distribution (table 4). As Andrew Walls and other missiologists have long perceived,

> The present phase of Christianity has seen another dramatic shift in its center of gravity. Not long ago Christianity was the religion of nearly all the peoples of Europe and their New World descendants, and of few others.

Today it is a faith distributed throughout the world, is specially characteristic of the southern continents and appears to be receding only among the peoples of European origin. . . . The only safe prediction appears to be that its [Christianity's] southern populations in Africa, Latin America, Asia and the Pacific, which provide its present centers of significance, hold the key to its future. (1984, 70, 73)

As recently as 1960, 90 percent of all Mormons lived in the United States, largely in Utah and the Great Basin region of the Rocky Mountains (Heaton 1992, 1520). By 1996 less than half of all Mormons worldwide resided in the United States (and only 16 percent in Utah), whereas approximately 44 percent of the world's Latter-day Saints were distributed in the southern regions of the world that Walls has identified as the twentieth century's emerging geographical center of Christianity.

Mormon missions are proliferating in countries of the southern continents, especially in those of Latin America, and convert baptism rates in these countries are much higher than in most regions of the United States or Europe. Thus, for example, in 1991 the LDS Italy and French missions averaged only a little more than one baptism per missionary per year, whereas in that same year Mexico averaged more than thirteen baptisms per missionary, resulting in approximately nineteen thousand Mexican converts in a six-month period.[12] According to Heaton,

membership projections based on the assumption that each area will continue at the same rate observed between 1980 and 1989 indicate that geographic shifts may become even more dramatic. The membership in the

Table 4. Distribution of LDS Membership and Missions by World Geographical Areas (Estimated as of February 29, 1996)

	Missions	Members	Total Membership
United States			
(excluding Utah)	87	3,228,000	34.6%
Utah	3	1,484,000	15.9
Canada	7	143,000	1.5
Mexico	18	728,000	7.8
Central America	11	349,000	3.7
South America	61	1,948,000	20.9
Caribbean	7	85,000	0.1
South Pacific	13	317,000	3.4
Asia	35	593,000	6.3
Europe	53	371,000	4.0
Africa	11	95,000	1.0
	306	9,341,000	100

Source: Deseret News Church Almanac, 1997–1998.

United States, Canada, and Europe is growing at a relatively slow pace, such that their percentage would drop to 40 percent in the year 2000, to 22 percent in 2010, and to about 11 percent by 2020. Although the African membership is growing at a high rate (14 percent annually), it has such a small base that it would constitute less than 3 percent by 2020. Asia would grow to more than 13 percent of the membership by 2020. But the biggest gains would be in Mexico and Central and South America. Collectively, these areas would increase their share to 46 percent in 2000, to 62 percent in 2010, and to 71 percent in 2020. (1992, 1521)

One additional, critical consideration linked to Mormon proselyting success is its centralized organizational and funding structure. Most Christian missionary-sending denominations finance their work through a wide variety of self-supporting mission agencies: "Some agencies concentrate their efforts geographically or functionally; others are widely diversified. There are independent missionaries who have no affiliation with any organization. Some agencies are little more than groups of people who have loosely banded together to carry out a particular ministry. Still others have formalized organizations with a constitution, by-laws, a statement of faith and a board of directors. Some have developed large organizational structures and support staffs, while others are little more than individual ministries" (Wilson and Siewert, eds. 1987, 558). While the bulk of Protestant missions consists of many small agencies, 40 percent of all career and short-term missionary personnel are concentrated in only ten agencies that tend to dominate Protestant missionary activity (Wilson and Siewert, eds. 1987, 560).

In contrast, Mormon missionary work is organized and directed through the missionary department of the LDS Church. The missionary department is not an autonomous mission agency of the conventional Protestant type; it is a department of the LDS administrative headquarters in Salt Lake City, Utah, and its functioning is closely monitored by Mormon general authorities, especially that body of men in the Mormon hierarchy known as the Council of the Twelve Apostles. As summarized by Jay Jensen, a long-time missionary department staff member and current general authority, "The leaders of the Missionary Department of the Church of Jesus Christ of Latter-day Saints . . . have three principal goals: (1) to increase the number of convert baptisms, (2) to keep new converts active and involved in the LDS Church, and (3) to increase the number of missionaries serving" (1988, 1).

The activities the missionary department sponsors in pursuit of its goals are deeply embedded in and coordinated with the programs of other church departments. Almost every LDS auxiliary organization is conceptualized as having a missionary component. Although various policy differences are known to exist among Mormon general authorities, program decisions, once made, can be implemented rapidly throughout the entire church.[13] The relatively recent organizational innovation of on-site area presidencies throughout the world presumably has increased the flexibility of institutional responses to local conditions, but the LDS hierarchy, through the agency of its centrally controlled missionary department, is able to impose a rigorous level of uniformity on missionary preparation programs, doctrinal exposition, proselyting strategies and techniques, missionary financing, and mission field governance.[14] The finance office of the missionary department, for example, formulates and sets the budget for every LDS mission in the world. Mission budgets must be approved by the Council of the Twelve, who keep close watch over mission expenditures and will not tolerate careless overspending of the appropriated budget.

LDS missionaries do not choose their fields of labor, as is commonly the case in Protestant missions, but accept callings to go wherever the missionary department assigns them. This not only includes proselyting missionaries but also those laymen called as mission presidents to administer the daily affairs of every LDS mission for three years. Mission presidents are appointed through a recommendation process that originates with local bishops, stake presidents, and LDS area authorities. Recommendations are forwarded to Salt Lake City and reviewed by members of the Council of the Twelve, who select and make the calls, frequently disrupting or suspending the secular careers of those who voluntarily accept their appointments when called upon to serve. The ability to mobilize personnel and quickly shift resources from one area of missionary operation to another based on calculations of institutional need and growth potential rather than idiosyncratic personal preferences is a fundamental advantage of the Mormons' centrally controlled organizational structure.

In all of this it should be understood that Mormons do not consider it necessary to receive an "inner call" in order to forsake worldly pursuits and render full-time missionary service to their church. Mormonism's insistence that all members (but especially young men as they enter the lay order of the Melchizedek priesthood) have missionary obligations gives the LDS Church a decisive, missionary force recruiting advantage over many of its proselyting competitors. While "short-term" missionary service (the Mormon norm) is becoming more and more common for Christian missionaries generally, most continue to think of their status as a lifetime religious calling, a type of occupational career (Siewert and Kenyon 1993, 57). For many career missionaries, obtaining financial backing and remuneration is potentially problematic:

> Overseas personnel receive their support in a wide variety of patterns. Some
> of the major agencies which are related to denominations undertake the pro-

vision for missionary salaries and the missionary is only indirectly involved in how or from where those (their) funds are derived. Other denominations arrange for their missionaries to present the mission fields to local churches where pledged or budgeted support to the agency may or may not be designated to specific missionaries. At the other end of the scale are missionaries who are completely responsible for raising their own support. In some agencies one of the first tasks of a missionary is to make known his support needs to friends or churches and his ability to accept his assignment is dependent upon whether such support is raised. (Wilson and Siewert, eds. 1987, 614)

In fact, the majority of Protestant missionaries (66 percent who were surveyed in 1985) are responsible for raising their own support. Doing so typically involves more than just personal living expenses; it also includes salary and, in many cases, retirement benefits (Wilson and Siewert, eds. 1987, 604).

Full-time Mormon missionaries do not receive salaries or retirement benefits. To the extent possible, they are expected to pay their own living expenses, and the majority do so in compliance with what they consider to be their religious duty. Before accepting mission calls to serve, Mormon youths are expected to earn money for anticipated expenses. Mormon parents often establish missionary savings accounts for their children or, in some cases, take on part-time jobs themselves in order to bring in extra income. Those with financial means not only help support their own children's missionary expenses but also often donate financial help to the missionary sons and daughters of others in their local congregations who are less well-off than themselves. In addition to a doctrinally established 10 percent tithe required of all members of the church, individuals are encouraged to make regular contributions to the General Missionary Fund, money from which is used primarily to support the growing number of missionaries originating in developing countries, who otherwise could never hope to pay for their own upkeep. Currently, about one-quarter of the Mormon missionary force is made up of missionaries called from outside the United States and Canada, a majority of whom are financed through the General Missionary Fund (Hart 1993a, 5). In the final analysis, it is this deeply rooted missionary ethos, expressed in the organized willingness of Mormon lay members to commit financial and personal resources continually to the church, that makes possible the annual maintenance of an unusually large (and growing) centrally supervised LDS missionary force.

Because living costs varied so widely from mission to mission throughout the world, placing many Mormon families at a huge financial disadvantage, the First Presidency declared in the February 1991 issue of *The Ensign* a new policy to equalize contributions required to maintain missionaries in the field.

Currently, the standard amount required of North American missionaries or their families is $375 per month, regardless of where the missionary may be assigned to serve. Monthly payments are funneled through local ward bishoprics to the missionary department, which then disperses the funds as needed throughout the LDS missionary system worldwide. If $375 represents a worldwide monthly average, it is possible to estimate the yearly cost of supporting a single, full-time missionary to be $4,500. At this rate the annual cost to church members for maintaining a missionary force of fifty thousand would be $225 million. Although that is a relatively large sum of money, it does not begin to account for the total dollar amount, directly or indirectly, that the LDS Church expends on its missionary activities. That figure—which includes missionary department costs, construction, staffing and operating expenses of missionary training centers worldwide, mission field offices, residential quarters and living allowances for mission presidents, literature publication and distribution, videos and films, visitors centers, television and radio programming, and a variety of different types of advertising and public relations events—is simply not reported by church officials but surely amounts to tens of millions of additional dollars annually.

Other Christian denominations also spend considerable sums in support of their missionary efforts—more than $2 billion for all U.S. overseas ministries in 1992 (Siewert and Kenyon 1993, 56). The lack of any published data on total LDS missionary expenditures, however, makes it impossible to formulate precise cost-effectiveness comparisons of LDS proselyting success with that of other missionary organizations. We do know, however, that a large fraction of mission income reported by most Protestant agencies is expended on fund-raising and administrative costs, salaries, retirement benefits, and humanitarian supplies and services rather than on financing the living expenses of those engaged in direct and regular contact with potential converts (Wilson and Siewert, eds. 1987, 609–14). It is likely that a much larger proportion of LDS resources is channeled directly into proselyting rather than being used up in collateral costs. Mormon missions are relatively cost-effective because the majority of LDS missionaries are willing and able to be self-supporting, live Spartan lives, and concentrate almost exclusively on searching for and instructing potential converts. And, after two years of full-time service, the eroding consequences of career burnout (a problem in Protestant missions) are curtailed by the induction of eager new replacements who are a constant source of rejuvenation to the missionary enterprise. These are all features of Mormon missionary work that contribute to the LDS Church's competitive advantages and relative proselyting success in the world. religious economy.

Although essential to understanding the scale of Mormon proselyting activity, an emphasis on centralized resource mobilization alone cannot explain fully their missionary success.[15] We must also take into account the nature of Mormonism's appeal to different segments of the world religious economy and understand the idealization of the missionary role in Mormon culture, especially for young men as they approach adulthood.

NOTES

1. For summary vignettes of LDS growth in these and other regions of the world, see the *Deseret News Church Almanac, 1997–1998.*

2. In a reassessment essay, Stark stands by his initial projections, stressing once again his "full awareness of the perils of straight-line projections. At the very least, however, these projections offer us a glimpse of future possibilities based on current realities, not on hunches or hopes. More than that, unless there are substantial shifts in trends that have been stable for a considerable time, the future must conform to these projections—for arithmetic is an exact science" (1994, 22). Bennion and Young, whose more conservative statistical projections for Mormon growth in the twenty-first century are tempered by their analysis of the "complex dynamics of Mormon expansion," estimate an LDS world population of "no more than about 35 million members" by 2020 (1996, 29, 30).

3. For applications of the concept of religious economies, see Berger (1967); Finke and Stark (1988, 1992); Iannaccone (1990, 1992, 1994); Sherkat (1995); Sherkat and Wilson (1995); and Stark and Bainbridge (1985). In a competitive religious economy the counterpoint to member recruitment is member defections. Like other growth-oriented missionary religions, Mormonism must not only be concerned with recruiting new members but also with keeping the loyalty of those it already claims, especially that of converts prone to drop out of active participation after joining the church (chapter 16).

4. According to Mauss, the LDS Church, in part for humanitarian motives and also to gain entrance into non-Western countries, "has been funding an enormous program in various countries of medical, agricultural, technical, educational, and social service programs of all kinds. These efforts are indispensable to the eventual establishment of the church in such countries; for most of them have made clear to *all* foreign churches that they will not be welcome until they have shown a willingness to help with modern development . . . which is the top priority in most of those countries today" (1996, 242).

5. Writing on the Mormon missionary approach, Lanier Britsch, an LDS spokesperson, stated (perhaps overstated) that "Latter-day Saints generally have little use for what might be called mission theory. They pursue the work of preaching the gospel in a matter-of-fact manner, worrying little about cultural adaptation and other related problems" (1979, 24).

6. Information on new LDS mission openings and numbers of missionaries serv-

ing in the field is published periodically in the *Church News* and *The Ensign*, particularly following the annual LDS general conference in April. Every two years these data are published in the *Deseret News Church Almanac*.

7. This figure is estimated from data given in the *Deseret News Church Almanac, 1993–1994*, 400.

8. Personal communication through LDS Communications Department spokesperson; also see Thomas (1986, 102–3); and Thomas, Olsen, and Weed (1989, 17).

9. A declining birth rate among the core North American membership could have a significant impact on LDS missionary force enlistments. To the extent that this occurs, a relative decline in the number of young men eligible for missionary assignments in U.S. and Canadian congregations would have to be offset by a corresponding increase in the percentage of non-North Americans and young women in order for the size of the LDS missionary force to continue expanding.

10. The following quotations are from addresses given by LDS general authorities and published in *The Ensign:* "We will not rest until every able-bodied young man is made worthy and desires to receive a call to a mission" (Boyd K. Packer [March 3, 1985, 10]); "Still, many of our young men, young women, and couples have not heeded the prophet's call to serve. . . . Why have we been so reluctant to catch the spirit of this work?" (L. Tom Perry [May 1989, 13]); "The demand for increased numbers of full-time missionaries is greater than ever before. And again we issue the call for every young man to heed the voice of the prophet to serve as a full-time missionary" (May 1992, 23); "The call to missionary service rarely comes when it is convenient or easy to serve. . . . Is it possible for a young man in this church not to think about a mission? . . . Nobody asked any of the early missionaries of the church whether they would like to serve, or if it would be convenient" (Gardner H. Russel [November 1992, 83]); "Let there be no mistake about it, the opportunity of a lifetime is yours. . . . To those of you who have the Aaronic Priesthood [males between the ages of twelve and nineteen] I say, *prepare for your full-time missions*" (Thomas S. Monson [May 1995, 49, emphasis in the original]); and "I testify there is no more majestic call. . . . I pray that every young man, and every able couple, will join those who have paid the price to serve a full-time mission" (Harold G. Hillam [November 1995, 42]).

11. The closer a statistical correlation is to 1.00, the stronger the relationship between the variables under consideration. As correlations approach 0.00, the weaker the relationship. A zero-order correlation means that only the relationship between two variables is being measured without taking into account other related factors. For example, factors in conversion success other than the number of missionaries in the field would include such things as the degree of peoples' attachments to competing religions in different mission areas and regional variations in the density of LDS membership. In areas where people are attached strongly to their religious traditions, and/or where there are few Latter-day Saint communities, conversion rates to Mormonism would be predictably low, independent of the number of missionaries proselyting in those areas.

12. These figures were obtained from a copy of the LDS Church's *World Mission Statistical Report* (1991).

13. See, for example, Quinn's (1993) summary of general authority disputes over an aggressive sales approach strategy to boost conversions of teenagers in the early 1960s. In a related vein, see Gottlieb and Wiley's (1984, 95–102) account of the upper-echelon struggle among church officials to control how church funds would be invested in LDS building programs during the same era.

14. According to a church press release, "Each of the areas is presided over by a presidency, consisting of a president and two counselors, from the First Quorum of the Seventy. The presidencies are accountable to the First Presidency and the Council of the Twelve for building up the Church and regulating its affairs in their respective areas. This organization lends strength to administration . . . and provides flexibility in meeting challenges of growth" (*Deseret News Church Almanac, 1985,* 296). "Area authorities" (local leaders) have been appointed to assist in the administrative tasks of area presidencies throughout the world (*Church News,* August 5, 1995, 3). In 1996 there were twenty-three LDS administrative areas worldwide, fifteen of them outside the boundaries of North America (*Church News,* June 15, 1996, 8–9), constituting what church officials often refer to as the "International Church." When membership statistics and infrastructure reach a certain point within world areas, they are subdivided into smaller geographic units. Multiplication of local administrative units through subdivision in response to member growth has always been the basic pattern for generating new stakes, wards, and missions under centralized planning and supervision.

15. For summaries of the merits and limitations of a resource mobilization approach to understanding social movement success, see Marx and McAdam (1994); McCarthy and Zald (1977); and Turner and Killian (1987).

PART ONE

❧

Rite of Passage

Introduction:
Religious Socialization for the LDS Missionary Role

To understand Mormonism one must understand the lay character of the LDS Church. One must also understand the extent to which the Mormon missionary ethic, nourished and reinforced from one generation to the next, creates a dynamic within Mormonism that lies at the heart of its members' active lay participation and the church's ongoing vitality.

From its inception, Mormonism shared with the radical wing of the Protestant Reformation a rejection of any ecclesiastical distinctions between laity and the ordained clergy (Hughes and Allen 1988; Kraemer 1994 [1958]; Troeltsch 1960, vol. 2; Widstoe 1939). Over time, however, the centralized administration of the LDS Church has evolved into a professional bureaucracy of considerable size and complexity (Gottlieb and Wiley 1984; Heinerman and Shupe 1985; Quinn 1997; Woodworth 1987). In many respects, contemporary Mormon general authorities have acquired characteristics similar to those of prelates in vocational clergies. But the type of religion officially advocated by and practiced in the modern LDS Church continues to presuppose a high degree of member commitment and active lay participation. Ordinary members are expected to staff completely, without remuneration, the ecclesiastical structure of local ward and stake organizations and administer as well as participate in the priesthood and auxiliary programs of the church. Programmed lay activities constitute the essence of the Mormon religious community.

The Mormon ideal is for all members to not only be actively situated in the ecclesiastical role structure of the church but also to pursue lay careers of active religious involvement, resulting over time in an extensive repertoire of church assignments for every member and, for males, progressive advancements in the offices of the lay priesthood. To be a faithful Latter-day Saint means that one's personal resources are at the disposal of the church whenever and however one is called upon to serve. All church callings are equated with what Mormons believe is their over-riding, divinely sanctioned mandate to spread the restored gospel and build the Kingdom of God on earth. For both women and men, faithful lay careers in the Mormon church are taken as true signs of their enduring moral character and are believed to be a reliable indicator of their spiritual standing, under God's judgment, in the life to come. Conversely, persistent unwillingness to accept church callings, or refusal to discharge lay obligations to participate actively in church programs, typically results in some degree of stigmatization in LDS communities. Actively committed Mormons believe the ultimate salvation of recalcitrant members to be seriously jeopardized.

When people persistently devote themselves to a set of exclusive commitments in a pluralistic society like the United States, especially in concert as a group, they risk being perceived by outsiders as odd or fanatical. In a pluralistic environment, voluntary organizations with demanding and relatively exclusive membership requirements, such as the LDS Church, tend to be the exception and often find themselves in conflict with other groups. Exclusive organizations must develop systematic ways to attenuate the influence of competing social commitments while maximizing the investment of member resources in their own programs (Iannaccone 1990; Kanter, 1972). This is never easy. The wide range of alternative life-styles and career paths available in modern life is compelling, especially to the young. In addition, the dominating contemporary ethics of individualism and materialism prompt widespread resistance toward attempts at limiting personal choices in the pursuit of self-gratification.

How does the LDS Church manage to flourish in such an environment? How does modern Mormonism not only recruit new members by the tens of thousands but also hold onto the active loyalty of a substantial proportion of its young from one generation to the next? Arguably, the single most important cultural practice for maintaining the generational continuity of Mormon society, especially for young males, is the lay system of LDS missionary service.

Anticipatory Socialization for Missionary Service

Although lay missionary work for the LDS Church is performed by both males and females, it has been traditionally emphasized as the primary religious duty of LDS males. Consequently, Mormon socialization for missionary service is overwhelmingly focused on the preparation of young men to accept missionary callings. At the same time, however, missionary enlistment rates for young women also have increased significantly since the 1980s.[1] The causes and consequences of this trend have not yet been adequately studied. Here, we will emphasize the socialization of males for missionary service, which is still the Mormon norm. In subsequent chapters we will discuss the implications of increased female missionary participation for the LDS Church.

In order to maintain (or increase) the rate of lay missionary participation by its young men in a secular, pluralistic society, the LDS Church must continually socialize them to regard fulfillment of a church proselyting mission as one of the great priorities of their lives. That goal cannot effectively be accomplished on a large scale by merely admonishing children in religious meetings. It requires that parents, other family members, peers, and local ward youth leaders share similar missionary attitudes, provide convincing role models, and consistently reinforce the expectation of missionary service in their relationships with young people. The LDS Church is successful in its missionary efforts because it makes strenuous efforts to involve its entire lay membership—youths as well as adults—in the propagation of missionary ideals through a complex of church organizations, programs, campaigns, publications, and service opportunities, all of which are institutionally linked to Mormon family life.[2] In short, a "plausibility structure" is created for active LDS youths in which missionary service comes to be taken for granted as a normative feature of the Mormon community.

Gender Emphases

Through fulfillment of missionary callings, young men are groomed to exercise lay priesthood authority in future church roles and assignments as adults. In contrast, females are not ordained to officiate in the LDS priesthood and are not formally encouraged to regard fulfillment of a full-time missionary assignment as one of their great priorities in life. Even though many young women do serve proselyting missions for the LDS Church, their institutionally prescribed status sequence continues to emphasize Victorian ideals of marriage, motherhood, and homemaking (Elliott 1991; Foster 1979). In particular, it is the anticipated status of an LDS temple marriage in which they are to be sealed eternally to worthy Melchizedek priesthood holders, subsequently support their husbands' priesthood callings, and faithfully raise their children in the temple covenant that LDS Church authorities continue to emphasize as the primary responsibility of young women. Thus, although Mormon officials acknowledge the contributions that sister missionaries make and concede that missionary work can be a valuable learning experience for young women to have, they do not consider missionary service to be an essential step in their religious development (Kimball 1981, 30).[3]

Not surprisingly, studies of the U.S. membership by LDS Church researchers show that the level of religiosity at home and parental influence (including parents' temple marriage and missionary service by one or both parents, regular family home evenings, prayer, and scripture reading) are the strongest predictors of young men's intentions to serve Mormon missions. In turn, intention to serve a mission is by far the best indicator of whether young men actually accept and fulfill a missionary calling: "By age sixteen to eighteen most young men have made a fairly firm decision about missionary service" (Thomas, Olsen, and Weed 1989, 8). By the time they graduate from high school, 75 percent of Mormon males in the United States have a fairly good idea about whether they want to serve a mission for the church and, "in fact, carry through on that decision. . . . Those young men who definitely intend to serve a mission, and in fact, serve, make that decision relatively early in life. . . . The decision to go on a mission seems to result from a general lifestyle wherein family and friends reinforce the notion that a mission is the expected behavior. Many of the respondents indicated that they could never remember when they had not planned to go on a mission" (1989, 9, 10).

Much of the religious teaching to which Mormon children are exposed, both in the church and at home, is clearly a form of "anticipatory socialization."[4] Anticipatory socialization can be defined as a learning process in which individuals come to identify with the values and role requirements attached to social statuses that they do not currently possess but to which they aspire. The task of the lay church is to channel member aspirations toward the acquisition of statuses within its organizational structure. Indeed, among the many social positions one is bound to accumulate in society over the course of a lifetime, the lay religious organization typically attempts to establish membership in the church as a "master status"—the single most important status for defining one's social identity. Consequently, the church can assume priority claim on its members' commitment and personal resources. In Mormonism this priority claim is dramatically articulated in a temple endowment ceremony as the law of consecration, which devoted lay members covenant to obey throughout their lives.[5]

Anticipatory socialization is facilitated when groups develop typical career paths, or "status sequences," for their members to follow (Merton 1968, 319). Within Mormonism certain status sequences are normatively prescribed, especially for children and youths through the young adult years.

Particularly for males, it is the anticipation of a missionary call that represents a turning point in the sequence. In addition to the critically important influence of parental teaching and example, religious socialization in the LDS Church is institutionally organized through age cohort groups. Children and youths receive weekly indoctrination in a variety of cohort organizations and classes taught by local lay members. Instruction in these classes conforms to a standardized, centrally correlated curriculum and frequently includes emphasis on the theme of missionary service.

Anticipatory socialization for the missionary role intensifies for Mormon males once they are inducted into the lay priesthood structure of the LDS Church at the age of twelve and begin their advancement through the ranks of the Aaronic priesthood (i.e., deacon, teacher, and priest). Local officials—particularly the ward bishop and Aaronic priesthood advisors—collaborate with parents to reinforce missionary preparation through a series of regular interviews and goal-setting programs that increasingly emphasize the importance of a missionary calling. At the age of nineteen, Mormon males are eligible for induction into the higher Melchizedek order of the priesthood and may be ordained to the office of elder. At this stage of their advancement they are also eligible to be considered for a missionary calling, and the normative pressures exerted by family, peers, and religious officials to fulfill missionary obligations often become acute. The longer they postpone making a missionary commitment, the greater the likelihood that eligible young men will become encumbered with interfering educational, financial, occupational, or marital obligations. LDS youths are no different in this regard than their non-Mormon contemporaries. In general, the "biographical availability" of postadolescent youths in the United States has made them an important source of energetic volunteers for contemporary political and social reform movements, as well as attracting their involvement in the development of new religions (McAdam 1988).

Age Eligibility

As Mormon missionary efforts escalated following World War II, the average age of missionaries called to service gradually began to decline. "Through the 1950s, young men generally served missions in their early twenties. Age of eligibility for missionary service was changed from twenty to nineteen in March, 1960. Since the mid 1960s most young men who have served have gone on their missions at age nineteen. A smaller group start their missions at age twenty or twenty-one, with very few after this age. . . . Rates of missionary service have remained quite stable, particularly for nineteen year olds" (Thomas, Olsen, and Weed 1989, 18).[6]

In many respects the adolescent religious development of Mormon youths is a winnowing process that reflects the limits of effective anticipatory socialization in a pluralistic environment. By the time they are age-eligible to serve, a majority (approximately two-thirds) of U.S. Mormon males, for a variety of reasons, do not fulfill missionary assignments. According to Thomas, Olsen, and Weed's church-sponsored survey, those who definitely "indicated that they were not going on a mission had also made that decision relatively early. This decision, too, grows from a general lifestyle that makes the possibility of a mission very unlikely. Many of these young men come from families that were not active in the church or had a group of close friends for as long as they could remember, most of whom did not consider going on missions" (1989, 10–11).

Even if persistent church efforts in the future do not significantly increase the proportion of LDS youths who accept missionary assignments, the failure would only be a relative one. The consistent ability to channel at least one-third of all age-eligible young men (and no doubt at least the same proportion of young women were they to be encouraged to the same degree as the young men) into a two-year, unpaid service entailing considerable work, personal sacrifice, and curtailment of individual freedom must be considered a remarkable institutional achievement.

LDS Missionary Service and the Rite of Passage Model

According to a widely used anthropological formulation, cultural rites of passage universally reveal a ritual pattern of three sequential stages, featuring separation, transition, and incorporation. In this sequence novices first are physically and/or symbolically separated from their previous statuses in the community; second, pass through an intensive transitional stage (often characterized by a certain amount of hardship, deprivation, and self-mortification) in which esoteric vocabularies, mythologies, attitudes, and behaviors appropriate to the new status must be learned and an acceptable level of skill mastery demonstrated; and, third, return to ordinary society and are incorporated back into the community as a new class of persons with expanded rights and responsibilities to exercise (Van Gennep 1960).

The general pattern does appear to correspond to basic elements of the Mormon missionary experience, both in the training phase and in the mission field itself. Technically, however, we should describe the acceptance and performance of the missionary role as a turning point status in a culturally defined career sequence for Mormon males while limiting the term *rites of passage* to ceremonial occasions that formally symbolize significant status shifts in the sequence. By "turning point status" we mean a phase of development to which the community has attached so much importance that personal career choices at that point are often expected to lead in one decisive direction or another. We would hypothesize that culturally defined turning point statuses often create the necessary conditions for self-fulfilling prophecies to occur, especially when some degree of stigma is associated with unconventional choices in the process of social development.[7] Thus, for many young men who do not accept missionary assignments, their failure to do so may be perceived by family or members of the local congregation as foreshadowing a loss of faith. For some young men, such as our older brother Don, it may indeed come to signify the extent of their alienation and rebellion against the admonitions of parents and/or Mormon officials and an outright withdrawal from active involvement in the religious life of the Mormon community. We should point out, however, that missionary service is not a necessary prerequisite for continued lay activity in the LDS Church; many Mormon males who do not fulfill missions go on to participate and advance in church offices. Precise statistical information on these alternative commitment patterns, unfortunately, is not available.

We should also point out that several LDS general authorities have repudiated the idea, as popularly understood, that missions function as rites of passage for Mormon youths.[8] Their concern, as church overseers, seems to be one of maintaining primary focus on the proselyting and conversion functions of missionary work rather than personal development as such. They want to reinforce the concept of a mission as a high and holy calling that demands exceptional spiritual qualifications to fulfill, not as a place to send one's children to shape up or iron out their personal problems. They emphasize that it is the duty of every LDS young man to be worthy to serve a mission before receiving a call and, likewise, that the duty of every parent is to ensure proper spiritual preparation of children for eventual missionary service. Church officials certainly would like to counter the inference that any young man can serve a mission or that prospective missionaries are not screened carefully for their worthiness to serve.[9] In short, it is the responsibility of church leaders to reiterate the religious ideals of the church to members who vary considerably in the realization of these ideals. To say that not all are qualified to receive missionary assignments does not invalidate, of course, the proposition that the experience and new status of those who do serve will be shaped by a sequence of passage rites. A key function of these rites, like that of church functionaries' public rhetoric, is to idealize the importance of the new role responsibilities being assumed by the novice missionary.

There are a cluster of authorizing rites performed for prospective missionaries that dramatize their passage into the LDS missionary role. These typically include ordination to the Melchizedek priesthood (for males); bestowal of a patriarchal blessing (if one has not already been received by the novice at an earlier age), in which one's future callings in life, including missionary service and temple marriage, are usually foretold and elaborated; formal interviews by the local bishop and stake president to determine a candidate's worthiness to serve; being set apart as a missionary by a candidate's stake president or some other high-ranking ecclesiastical authority; participation at a farewell testimonial sponsored by the local congregation in which novice missionaries typically confess their faith and their determination to succeed in the calling to preach the gospel; and initiation into LDS temple worship, in which one receives the temple endowment (promises of divine empowerment and ultimate exaltation in God's kingdom) in a covenantal ceremony to obey the law of consecration and serve the church. This series of ceremonial rites of passage functions, in an escalating pattern, to commit novices to a missionary status from which it becomes increasingly difficult to withdraw or abandon should they begin to doubt their decision to serve.

The formal process of becoming a Mormon missionary typically is initiated by the local ward bishop, who regularly interviews the males of his congregation around their nineteenth birthdays and may also interview unmarried women after the age of twenty-one. The bishop inquires as to the candidate's willingness to perform full-time missionary service and urges the acceptance of a call to do so. If a young man or woman is agreeable, worthiness to serve must be ascertained through what may prove to be grueling personal interviews conducted by the ward bishop and the stake president. Bishops and stake presidents are instructed to probe a candidate's moral character, especially with regard to sexual chastity, abstinence from alcohol and drugs, and loyalty to the authority of church leaders.

Assuming that a candidate does not confess to any serious transgressions, disqualifying habits, or fundamental disbeliefs and thereby fail the worthiness interview (those who do are urged to repent and may be given a probationary period in which to demonstrate good-faith efforts to reform), forms are filled out and sent to headquarters in Salt Lake City, where the Church Missionary Committee meets weekly to process applications and make assignments to specific areas of service according to the needs of the missionary system worldwide. Once assignments have been made and issued in the form of an official letter from church headquarters, with the signature of the church president affixed, candidates are formally set apart and given a blessing in a simple ceremony, by the laying on of hands, to be missionaries of the Church of Jesus Christ of Latter-day Saints. Before 1970 this was always done in Salt Lake City by general authorities of the LDS Church (members of the Council of Twelve Apostles or First Council of Seventy).[10] Because of the vastly increased number of missionaries constantly being processed through the system, however, the rite is now performed locally by the candidates' stake presidents. After being set apart, male missionaries must address each other by the title of "elder" (the basic office of the Melchizedek priesthood), and female missionaries are to be called "sister" or "lady missionaries" (a term used widely among missionaries when we served in the 1960s but which has subsequently lost favor among more recent missionary cohorts). These titles symbolically dramatize novice missionaries' separation of identity from their previous secular statuses and their passage into a sacralized interlude of religious training and consecrated service to the church.

Arguably, it is the missionary farewell service that has the greatest emotional impact on a novice's emerging missionary identity. The other ritual occasions associated with passage into the missionary role, including the temple endowment ceremony, are much less public in nature; typically they are occasions at which only a few other people are present to witness the symbolization of the religious commitments a novice has made. In contrast, it is at the farewell testimonial where novices are presented publicly to the local religious community—the relatives, peers, and ward members who have been most influential in shaping their course of action up to this point. It is these people whose esteem and good will the fledgling missionaries most want to have and maintain. These are the people before whom novices make a public commitment, demonstrating requisite faith and conviction through use of religious rhetoric common to the Latter-day Saint tradition. Having witnessed a novice speak and testify in accepting missionary obligations, members of the local Mormon community may now regard and treat him or her as a true adherent of the faith—someone from whom continued adherence may be expected in the future. If one's resolve to pursue the missionary course faithfully to its conclusion eventually begins to unravel, it is the idealized expectations of these people in particular that one must anticipate disappointing.

Before accepting missionary calls in the spring of 1964, the two of us had just completed six months of army basic training in California and Oklahoma as members of the Utah National Guard. Before that we had finished our freshman year of college at the University of Utah in Salt Lake City. A U.S. president had just been assassinated, the civil rights movement was about to fracture into militant fragments, student activism was beginning to surface on college campuses, and the U.S. government was preparing to commit its military might to a fatal escalation of the war in Vietnam. And in these turbulent times we were getting ready to preach our inherited faith to unknown souls in a foreign land.

We are fifth-generation Mormons, and our parents had always encouraged us and our brother Don (who was two years older) to serve missions for the LDS Church. Both parents had fulfilled proselyting missions in their own youths and were life-long active members of the church, faithfully having served in an uninterrupted series of lay callings subsequent to their missions. Don's interests while growing up, however, coincided very little with ours. We were mad about sports, whereas Don cultivated a serious interest in art; in later years he taught art at the University of Utah and contributed to the development of modern art in his native state (Poore 1996). Predictably, over the years the two of us formed a close alliance in sibling rivalries against our older brother. We also had a younger sister, Susan, (twelve years our junior) whom we favored with solicitous affection. In adolescence Don gravitated toward friends who had little or no interest in the youth activities of the LDS Church; for the most part, the two of us retained a circle of friends who—although occasionally remiss in their observance of religious norms— came from families active in local Mormon congregations in Salt Lake City. Our parents were deeply disappointed when Don rejected the proposal of a mission call but were thrilled when the two of us agreed to missionary assignments in Mexico. At the time, we were twenty years old.

The following chapter illustrates the importance attached to missionary farewell services by LDS communities and is based on edited excerpts of an audio tape transcription of our farewell in May 1964.

Notes

1. Although the LDS Church does not publish or provide precise figures on the distribution of missionaries based on gender, according to missionary department personnel, single sister missionaries now constitute about 20 percent of the total missionary force. It is likely, therefore, that somewhere between nine thousand and ten thousand young women serve full-time proselyting missions for the LDS Church.

2. A collection of articles exploring the relationship between religious observance and family life, including LDS families, can be found in Thomas (1988). For additional research measuring the strength of family influence on Mormon religiosity, see Cornwall (1987, 1989). The secondary influence of peers, relative to parental influence on religious choices made by LDS youth, is documented by Duke (1992).

3. As recently as January 1994, LDS bishops and stake presidents were instructed in a statement from church headquarters that "a young woman should not be recommended for a mission if it would interfere with a specific marriage proposal. . . . Though capable and effective, young women do not have the same responsibility to serve full-time missions as do young men who hold the priesthood" (*BYU Daily Universe*, September 28, 1994, 3). Embry quotes Apostle Thomas S. Monson as saying that missionary work for young women is "optional"; if they wish to serve, "we are happy to have them," but "we do not wish to create a program that would prevent them from finding—or place hardships in their way toward finding—a proper companion in marriage, because that is their foremost responsibility" (1997, 4).

4. The concept of anticipatory socialization is developed in Merton (1968, 319–25). A study done by the LDS missionary department, "Characteristics of Successful Missionaries," confirms that not only is willingness to accept a missionary calling a function of parental example and socialization but also, once in the field, that the best predictor of missionary success is the kind and amount of religious preparation experienced by Mormon youths while growing up (Hart 1995, 3).

5. For an analysis of the origin and application of the law of consecration by Mormons in the nineteenth century, see Arrington (1958).

6. Unlike Mormon males, young women must wait until they are twenty-one before they can receive a call to serve a full-time mission, a rule that suppresses rather than stimulates female missionary enlistments. To our knowledge the official rationale for this gender discrepancy in age eligibility has not been stated publicly. We have been told informally in interviews with church officials that young women are called at a later age than young men in order to maximize their opportunities for marriage. One latent consequence of these gender-based age rules is the creation of a larger pool of marriage-eligible young LDS women available for Mormon males when the latter return home from their missions while simultaneously encouraging a traditional Mormon courtship pattern in which returned male missionaries marry somewhat younger females. In addition, waiting until they reach the age of twenty-one before calling single women to missionary service maintains an imbalanced sex ratio of younger males to older females in the field. These age discrepancies are believed by LDS officials to reduce the likelihood of distracting mission field romances between sister missionaries and their male counterparts.

7. For discussions of the concepts of self-fulfilling prophecies and stigma, see Merton (1968) and Goffman (1963).

8. Thus, for example, Apostle Gordon B. Hinkley (subsequently President Hinkley) emphasized in a mission presidents' training seminar that missionary work is not a "course in personal development, a rite of passage, a finishing school for young men and women. A missionary is called to serve, to fulfill the divinely given mandate to spread the word of God and build his kingdom on earth. Of course there will be personal benefits. These will come in proportion to the degree of selflessness evidenced in service" (*The Ensign*, September 1990, 74).

9. According to a report published in the *Salt Lake Tribune* (July 3, 1993: D-1), "Missions may no longer be automatic for eligible youth of the Church of Jesus Christ

of Latter-day Saints. A March 1993 policy statement sent to LDS priesthood leaders codifies strict behavioral standards for missionary candidates. . . . Any exceptions to these guidelines must be submitted to the First Presidency. These guidelines are not new, the church says, but based on long-established principles. 'Full-time missionary service is not a right, but a privilege,' says the document's cover letter. 'Missionary service is for the benefit of the Lord and his church to fulfill his purposes. Its objective is not primarily the personal development of an individual missionary.' . . . Ken Gardner, a former mission president in New England, says mission presidents will welcome these standards. 'It will have a great impact on the few missionaries who wait until getting into the mission field to clear up problems,' he says. 'This will not keep any young people from service. Just making sure they invest enough time in preparation. . . . The responsibility is now back on parents to make sure that their kids are ready and worthy.'"

10. For descriptions of earlier patterns of LDS missionary preparation in this century, see Snow (1928) and Cowan (1984).

1

~

Farewell

Salt Lake City, May 17, 1964

It had already been a long meeting. Too long, really: three preliminary speakers, two musical numbers, and the usual congregational hymns and passing of the sacramental emblems of bread and water to an overflow crowd of ward members and visitors. The Liberty Ward/Liberty Park Ward Chapel, constructed in 1908 and situated fifteen blocks from Temple Square in Salt Lake City, had recently been renovated but still lacked air-conditioning. Windows had been opened in hope of catching an occasional breeze, and the rhythmic motion of hand-held fans was increasing as many of the congregants attempted to circulate the still air. Increasing also was the scattered wailing of infants and the fidgeting of young children who had already passed the limits of their endurance.

In a quavering but earnest and resolute voice, Marjorie Coombs Shepherd was now addressing the congregation: "This is certainly a thrilling sight, to look down at all the faces of our dear friends and family. And it's also a thrilling occasion for us, as you can well imagine. It's something that we've looked forward to for a long time. I guess I've looked forward to it ever since I came home from my own mission and anticipated the time that I would have sons to send into the mission field. Today we deeply appreciate your presence here and your words of encouragement to us."

Marjorie was forty-eight, a mother four times over, and devout in her LDS faith. During the Great Depression she had left her home in Salt Lake City to serve an eighteen-month proselyting mission for the LDS Church in the economically devastated regions of North Carolina, Kentucky, and Tennessee. It was there that she met "Shep"—her husband to be, a returned Mormon missionary who was touring the area where he himself had labored for the LDS Church several years previously. At the podium this day, in the Mormon ward where she had raised her children, Marjorie expressed elation and relief. At last two of her children had decided to accept their religious duty to serve God in the mission field. There had been some doubts—her eldest son Don had refused the call and married out of the church—but now the family's missionary tradition would be sustained. It was these related themes of religious heritage and her family's moral duty to live up to that heritage by faithfully serving the church that dominated the remainder of her remarks.

"As we were singing the opening song," Marjorie continued, "'Shall the Youth of Zion Falter,' and the verse that says 'true to the faith that our parents have cherished, true to the truth for which martyrs have perished,' I couldn't help but think in my mind of *our* parentage and the heritage which we have. Our boys have a wonderful heritage. When I think back, on both sides of my family—my mother's and my father's, and Shep's mother's and father's families, back to great-grandparents and, in two cases, great-great-grandparents of the boys who joined the church and gave up everything they had to accept the gospel—it makes me grateful that we have that heritage. I can't remember who it was, but I recall hearing someone say that the pioneers came out here willingly because they were forced to [laughter]. And in a way that's true. They *were* forced out of their homes. They didn't have anywhere else to go. They were driven. In some cases their homes were burned. Some of them even gave their lives. And yet, they had their free agency; they didn't have to do this. But I'm thankful that our grandparents and great-grandparents had the courage and the faith that the Lord promised to those who were willing to give up everything, that they might have eternal life. I'm thankful too that I haven't been put to that kind of a test. I don't know whether I would have the faith to carry me through or not. But I'm thankful for what has been handed down to me, and I hope that my children will feel this gratitude and appreciation for what is their heritage."

Reaching the conclusion of her brief comments, Marjorie reasserted the firmness of her convictions and offered words of admonition and blessing to her sons: "In closing I would just like to bear my testimony to you brothers and sisters, and especially to my family and children. Even though we may look back with pride upon the heritage we have, we can't sit back and rest on the laurels of our forefathers. Each and every single one of us has an obligation and responsibility to carry on. I am thankful for this opportunity which our boys have. I know that if they are prayerful and if they work hard and strive to learn the Spanish language, if they will have love in their hearts for the people with whom they come in contact, if they will overlook their differences and faults and see only the good and be willing to accept them as they are, I know that the Lord will bless them."

As Marjorie took her seat, the congregation readied itself to hear what Alvin Shepherd would have to say concerning his sons' appointments to serve the LDS Church for two years in Mexico. Alvin (Shep) was an expansive, gregarious man who enjoyed being with people and loved to reminisce with old friends. If not formally eloquent in his speech, he was nonetheless a self-confident speaker who seldom prepared or used notes. Although popular with his associates, Shep had often struggled financially, moving from one sales job to another as he attempted to overcome old business debts and support his family. But today was a day to savor, a day to share with friends and loved ones.

"Brothers and sisters, I'm so happy tonight to be here with you," Shep began. "You know, all of us at some time or other have our problems and discouragements. Sometimes we wonder about the struggles we have to make. As I have sat here tonight and as I have seen the faces of you grand people who have come to be with us, to help us rejoice in the occasion of our boys going into the mission field, I thought that all the problems that you have and I have—all seem insignificant and so far away when we have the spirit of our Heavenly Father to be with us, when we have our friends and our relatives and those who are close, whom we love, with us on an occasion of this type."

It was also a day for Shep to reflect on his experience, to identify himself with his sons and connect their approaching experience with his own. It was a time to reaffirm kinship links and acknowledge the sustaining reciprocity of the local religious community of which he was a part. "I must mention one or two names tonight. Sitting in the back of the hall there's a man who came in just as the service was starting with his wife: Brother and Sister Kjar. Brother Joseph Kjar was my bishop when I was called over thirty years ago to go into the Southern States Mission. My mother was his ward clerk. A short few months after my father was killed, Bishop Kjar saw fit to call me into the mission field. And now it's been just a few short months since my mother passed away, and Bishop McLean has seen fit to call our two boys into the mission field.

"I was reading my missionary diary not so long ago, and every once in awhile I would find a reference to the feeling of the closeness of my father, when I was depressed or sorrowful in my mission. I'm sure as our boys go into the mission field that there's no one who ever lived who wanted to see them go on a mission more than my mother and their grandmother. And I'm certain her influence will be with them, and also their grandfather's.

"We have most of the high council and their wives here tonight, the stake clerks, former stake presidents, and the current stake presidency of the Liberty Stake. These brethren on the stand are men that I have learned to love and to appreciate. They have supported me and I hope I have supported them. And so I am grateful my brothers and sisters for the friends that are here. Others have called, unable to be here. We're grateful for the relatives that are here."

Shep paused as he surveyed the congregation. There was an unusually large number of young people in attendance—schoolmates and friends of the twins. These associations now became the theme of the remainder of Shep's extemporaneous discourse. "Our lives are full. But the thing that's been great, brothers and sisters, is our children. All through their lives they've had lots of friends, and it's been such a pleasure as they've grown up to have their friends in our home, to get acquainted with them. I look around now and see many of them that Gary and Gordon have grown up with. It makes you happy and thrilled to know that these boys and girls—young men and women now—have played such a part in our sons' lives and that they have played a part in their friends'.

"I think of Chuck over there, Chuck Radlow, who's going to Stanford University on one of the finest scholarships to be given; a brilliant, outstanding young man. Chuck and Gary, of course, served together in the student body presidency at South High two years ago. Nothing would keep Chuck from being here tonight, from being on the program to play a piano solo. He came up from school, made a special trip. I understand he's got to hurry. He's got a tough exam tomorrow morning. I don't know how clear his mind is going to be for that exam.

"And then I think of David Lingwall over there. David comes in and out of our home—doesn't have a lot to say at times. But I was thrilled tonight with the clarinet solo that he played. I think many of us were waiting to see what he was going to play [laughter]. But once we got him going, he did an excellent job. We love you, David. I hope the boys are an inspiration to you.

"Then these other two young men sitting here have been in our home a lot. Mike Mitchell came into the church about a year ago. Before that he wasn't a member. But didn't he give a sweet prayer to open this meeting? Mike was an outstanding athlete at South High—captain of the football team his senior year. He played softball with our boys; went to the All Church Tournament for the McKinley Ward and was honored as the outstanding player of the church, before he was even a member. And the thrill that came to us when Mike came over one day and said 'Gordon, I want to be baptized now. I'm going to join the church. Would you baptize me?' You know brothers and sisters, it's marvelous to live in a home and have the young people come into your home and see these things happen.

"Lorin Larsen there, he's going to give the closing prayer. He's grown a little taller than the rest of them [Lorin stood more than six feet five inches tall]. When he served in the army national guard he chose, and I think they encouraged him, to join the MPs [military police]. When he stands up you'll see why [laughter]. Lorin has got his mission call. He'll be going next month to the Eastern States New York Mission and will have a grand time serving at the World's Fair."

Then, after reiterating his personal convictions and gratitude, Shep concluded by invoking the blessings of God for the congregation and for his children: "May the Lord bless you all. May he bless our two boys, and may he bless Donald and Susan. Touch their hearts. Bless them with a desire of service and love and understanding."

Gordon was nervous. Over the years he had become almost phobic about public speaking. Ever since turning twelve years of age he had stubbornly refused to accept any church speaking assignments, even after Bishop McLean had become quite insistent in his requests. Mormon youths are supposed to be exposed to regular opportunities for public speaking so that when the time comes for them to render missionary service (or accept other adult religious duties) they will be prepared and more effective in their performance. But this time Gordon was prepared. That is, he had spent a considerable amount of time thinking about and rehearsing what he should say on the occasion of his missionary farewell. There was, however, the distinct possibility that once he faced an audience he would blank out and have nothing to communicate except stammered emotions. This was precisely what Gordon feared most. Unlike his father, he had no trust in his ability for extemporaneous expression.

Alvin Shepherd squeezed Gordon's arm, whispered a word of encouragement, and suddenly Gordon found himself moving toward the pulpit as though in a trance. It was now his turn to say something. He stared at the microphone for several uncertain seconds and then began in an awkward cadence: "Our newly remodeled chapel is certainly beautiful. But I don't know about this stand—the way it seems to serve you right up into the jaws of the audience [laughter]. I think you can tell how calm I am [laughter]. I must have cut myself about fourteen times while shaving today" [more laughter as the congregation took cognizance of the tape on Gordon's Adam's apple].

Inane comments, perhaps, but the laughter was bracing. The generous receptiveness of the congregation encouraged Gordon to believe that he was going to be all right, and that he could handle this speechifying business as long as he had sufficient time to prepare his thoughts. He proceeded to express a litany of appreciation and gratitude to those who had meant the most to him while growing up, beginning with his parents. A strong sense of duty (one shared with Gary) toward fulfilling parental aspirations was clearly evident in his brief tribute: "I think I'd be very ungrateful if I didn't express a number of thank-yous. I'd like to thank my parents for everything that they've done. They're strong people. They're strong in the church. Their faith is strong. They've laid whatever foundations we possess; they've set an example, and they've set a standard. Now it's true, we've not always risen to that standard. In fact, many times we've fallen way short. But my mother and father have done everything in their power to raise us in a manner which the Lord has commanded. They will be found blameless before him."

Gordon then spoke of his brother Gary, relating a single anecdote from their recent national guard experience to which he attached religious significance. He told of how the sight on Gary's M-14 rifle had been bent the day they were supposed to qualify in marksmanship at the firing range at Fort Ord, California, affecting his ability to shoot accurately. A minimum score was required in order to graduate from basic training. Anyone scoring less than the minimum would be held back (at least that was the threat made by training officers) and would have to repeat the course while his comrades moved on to more advanced training assignments in other parts of the country. Fearful of separation and feeling completely helpless, Gordon crouched behind a convenient sand dune and prayed for divine assistance to help Gary through the test: "the first time," Gordon admitted, "that I have prayed earnestly for help in many years." At the end of the day, Gary's score on the rifle range was the exact score needed to pass. "Most important," Gordon concluded as he reflected on the experience, "it was together in basic training that Gary and I further strengthened our brotherhood and mutually confirmed our desires to serve missions for the church.

"I've got another brother and a little sister," Gordon continued. "Don, maybe you're not aware of the admiration and respect that I have for you and your artistic talent. I know that we had many a battle royal in our younger years but I'd like you to know that, in between brawls [laughter], Gary and I never passed up the opportunity to drag our friends downstairs to show off your art work. And Sue, I probably won't even recognize you when I get back, but I want you to know that you've been a wonderful little sister."

Having acknowledged indebtedness to family first, Gordon went on to single out his closest boyhood friends for appreciation—particularly Lorin, Mike, Dave, and Chuck—as well as several adult neighbors and local church leaders who had played influential roles in both his and Gary's formative years. All were being recognized as part of the intimate social network that had helped to shape and channel the course that had brought both Gary and Gordon, within the structure of Mormon society, to this religious turning point in their lives. "I would like to thank all those who have influenced me," Gordon summarized, "who have taught me, who have set an example for me, who have stood out high in their character and accomplishments. In expressing thanks tonight I think there is just one whom I could thank and it would be sufficient for all. And that, of course, is the Lord. Perhaps going on a mission is a good way to do this. Perhaps it's a good way to pay back a portion—a small portion—of the many things he has given to me."

For Gordon, this was the first time that he had made such public confessions. It seemed to him that the occasion demanded it, that if he was going to accept a mission call he should do so with serious intent and commit himself to work hard to overcome his fears, his pride, and other perceived weaknesses; he should commence now to speak as a willing and dedicated representative of his church, even though he realized that his religious faith and understanding were still far from being mature. He had given careful thought to what he was going to say next—it was to be a declaration of a new attitude and of his determination to succeed in performing the missionary role that he and Gary were about to assume.

"It seems to me that today is a pretty important occasion. In fact, I'd like to go so far as to say that you here are witnessing a great event. Now it's not a great event because the Shepherd brothers are going on missions—it's not a great event because we're being shipped out of the country for two years [laughter]. And it's certainly not a great event on the basis of today's proceedings alone. But it is a great event because two young men have been called by God to preach his gospel. And that because of this, no matter how poor or mediocre we may prove to be as missionaries, there will be somebody who will recognize the truth and be brought into the church. And is this not a great event? Is it not a great event when the membership of God's church is increased? That because of it there will be others who will be able to participate in the greatest work in the world today, that of building up the Kingdom of God on the earth. Are these not all great events? Is this not cause for celebration? I think it is. And I think we've been shouldered with heavy responsibilities. I'm particularly apprehensive about the responsibility that's been given to me. I know that the only way that I will be able to carry out this responsibility is through constant prayer and by remaining close to the Lord; that if I do this I will be blessed, I will be strengthened, I will be given guidance, and I will be able to do the work that is necessary."

Like Gordon, Gary was not especially fond of public speaking. Still, as student body president of his high school, he had gained significant experience and a measure of self-confidence in addressing large gatherings. Striding toward the pulpit, Gary eyed the big clock on the wall. The meeting had already run ten minutes overtime, and another ward was waiting outside to occupy the chapel for its own Sunday services. As the final speaker, he was going to have to hurry: "Time is very short. As a matter of fact it's gone, and so I'm afraid I'm going to have to save my sermons for the Mexican people [laughter]. But there are a few things that I'd still like to say."

The things that Gary had to say were remarkably similar in both their form and content to the remarks just concluded by Gordon. There were the same kinds of acknowledgments and tributes to the same individuals, particularly to his parents and twin brother. There was the same underlying confessional tone in reference to perceived shortcomings and follies of the past supplemented with a determined resolve for atonement through committed effort and reliance on God's help. These are attitudes typical of those who submit to the demands of a call to discipline themselves in the service of what they believe is a transcendent cause.

"I would like to let you know that it's a real pleasure to be standing where I am this afternoon," Gary said. "It's a dream of my parents come true and a hope of mine fulfilled, that both Gordon and I might be found worthy and willing to serve missions for the church. And it's a pleasure too because of you people who are here this afternoon. A good friend of mine once asked me when it was that I was the happiest in life. I thought that was a good question, but I didn't have a good answer. I think I do now. I enjoy myself most when I am in the company of my good friends and with people whom I love and respect. And so you can see, I'm very happy this afternoon. Thanks to Mike Mitchell, a very close friend. Mike's been almost like a brother to Gordon. Thanks too to Lorin and Dave and Chuck, because they've been our brothers too.

"I remember back at conference time, in general priesthood meeting, I think it was President David O. McKay who said that one of the greatest blessings that could come to a father or a mother would be to have a son or a daughter sincerely say that they had been born of good parents. My brothers and sisters I say to you that I have been born of good parents whose greatest concern has always been for their children. For this I am very grateful, and of them I am very proud. I just hope that we can live up to the high hopes they have for us and that some of the disappointments along the way to this afternoon can be made up.

"People often ask me, do I like being a twin? Well, I don't know what I would ever have done without my twin brother. So many times Gordon and I are almost the same person in thought and feeling. We've been constant companions for each other all through our lives. Gordon's a challenge to live up to because he's a better and stronger me in so many ways. Gordon is a strong person. He has a strong character, strong convictions, and he stands up for the things that he believes are right. And the things that Gordon stands for are good; they're going to pay off in the mission field. Who could ask for a better friend than my twin brother?

"Also today I'm grateful for my older brother Don. I'm proud of the many successes in art and at the university that he's achieved. And of course our little sister, Susan, who so eagerly observes and wants to follow all that we do; we all love her very much too."

Seated also in the chapel but unmentioned in either Gary's or Gordon's tributary comments were three young women, each to be significant in the months ahead. There was Beckie Jones, who was introduced to Gordon through Mike Mitchell's fiancée and subsequently had written faithfully to him during his six-month stint in army basic training. And there were Natalie Fletcher and Kathy Dempsey, both of whom were romantically involved with Gary. Kathy and Gary had dated steadily in high school and then broke up during their freshman year at the University of Utah. Gary started dating Natalie the summer before military basic training, and their relationship had quickly escalated. Now, in the few weeks between army and mission, Kathy was pressing to rekindle the embers of their former romance, leaving Natalie to wonder about the security of her own. Before the brothers' missionary adventures in Mexico were to end, Beckie would be serving an LDS mission in New Zealand, Natalie would be doing the same in Austria, and Kathy would be married. And in four years Gordon would marry Beckie following her return from New Zealand.

Gary concluded, as did Gordon before him, with a declaration of his resolve to commit himself to the missionary cause of the LDS Church and a confession of his dependency on the grace of God to see him through the tests to come: "I'm happy with my call to serve in the Mexican Mission. I'm happy for the chance I have to take part in the great work of the church and also for the opportunity I have of strengthening my own beliefs and increasing my own testimony of the truthfulness of the gospel. For I shall have a stronger testimony than I have now, and my faith in Jesus Christ as the savior of this world, the son of the living God, and in the divine mission of Joseph Smith, shall grow, and it shall become strong. This has been promised to me in my patriarchal blessing. I've also been promised that through diligence and through conscientious effort I will be blessed with wisdom and understanding, and that through prayer I shall have the spirit of the Lord to be with me in all things. It is my hope and prayer this afternoon that I may live in accordance with these blessings and that some day I might be worthy to receive them, that Gordon and I might both serve honorable missions, and that we might return home again having done the best work of which we were capable."

The meeting had been a long and taxing one. Many of the speakers' remarks had been repetitious in both form and substance. Nonetheless, it may be presumed that most of the congregation left that day feeling that the religious expectations of Mormon society had been satisfied. The idealization of certain core LDS religious values had occurred. A suitable amount of sincerity and seriousness had been displayed by the fledgling missionaries, demonstrating the kind of character transformation expected of Mormon youths as they cross the threshold into adulthood. The values of family, kin, and community bonds had been rhetorically reiterated. And, in fact, the local religious community itself—in the process of assembling for and witnessing this farewell event—had been reaffirmed in its collective commitment to the missionary cause of the LDS Church.

A significant ritual occasion in their passage had been completed. The next day, Gary and Gordon would begin their formal education as Mormon missionaries.

PART TWO

∾

Trainees

Introduction:
LDS Missionary Training

Following the ceremonial rites of passage, the second phase of missionary initiation in the LDS Church revolves around an intensive period of formal religious preparation and training at a church missionary training center (MTC). Instituted in 1961, the oldest, and by far the largest, MTC is situated in Provo, Utah, adjacent to the campus of Brigham Young University. Beginning with centers in São Paulo, Brazil, and Mexico City in 1977 and 1978, respectively, missionary training centers subsequently have been established in major LDS recruiting areas throughout the world wherever sufficiently large local missionary forces can be maintained. In addition to Brazil and Mexico, Mormon MTCs are also located in Buenos Aires, Argentina; Santiago, Chile; Bogotá, Colombia; London, England; Guatemala City, Guatemala; Tokyo, Japan; Seoul, Korea; Temple View, New Zealand; Lima, Peru; Manila, the Philippines; Apia, Samoa; and Nuku'ulofa, Tonga (Avant 1994, 11).

Access to temples and temple worship has been linked institutionally to missionary training as a fundamental aspect of missionaries' spiritual preparation.[1] Thus, training centers have been established only in cities where LDS temples are also located (Cowan 1992, 914). The missionary department's long-term goal is to organize MTCs in every country where membership numbers and levels of lay activity warrant the construction of a temple. According to Charles Didier, an LDS general authority, "The best preparation is always in your own country. Not only does the church avoid the cost of transporting missionaries somewhere else for training, but also the local aspect is much more effective. We'd like to have one in every country" (Wells 1990, 6).

The Provo Missionary Training Center

In March 1994, Mormon officials dedicated a two-hundred-thousand-square-foot expansion (a five-story classroom, four-story residence hall, and multipurpose building with a two-thousand-seat auditorium) to the MTC complex of sixteen classroom, dormitory, and administration buildings that had existed since 1976 on twenty-six acres between the Brigham Young University campus and the Provo Temple. The Provo MTC has the capacity to house and train up to 4,200 novice missionaries simultaneously (Avant 1994). President Gordon B. Hinkley has said that as the number of missionaries called to service continues to increase, "the new [Provo] center would probably not be expanded further. A similar complex would be added somewhere else" (*Church News,* November 2, 1991, 3).

Each week, between five hundred and seven hundred new missionaries arrive at the Provo MTC.[2] Those assigned to English-speaking missions go through a two-week course of proselyting instruction and personal skills training, while those assigned to foreign-language missions must spend eight weeks in language training while going through the same proselyting program as their English-speaking counterparts. More than forty languages, including Finnish, Estonian, Mandarin, Tagalog, and Laotian, to mention only a few, are taught at the Provo MTC, a number that increases as new countries are opened up to missionary work. More than a third of nearly nine hundred part-time instructors teach Spanish, the most frequently taught language. The instructional staff consists of Brigham Young University students who must be returned missionaries proficient in the language they teach.[3] Missionary instructors at the MTC are screened, tested, trained, and closely supervised and evaluated by the MTC's full-time administrative staff.

In addition to young single males and females, retired couples also enter the MTC for proselyting instruction and language training. The demand for experienced church workers is great (*The Ensign,* May 1992, 24, 42, 45, February 1996, 7–12). Mormon leaders are attempting a substantial increase in the number of older couples who volunteer by stressing that those in good health and who are no longer obligated to care for children at home and have the necessary financial means are under the same religious mandate to render missionary service as the young men of the church (*Church News,* March 28, 1987; *The Ensign,* August 1981). Since the 1990s the number of senior couples laboring as full-time proselyting missionaries has ranged between 1,600 and 1,700, or about 7 percent of the total LDS missionary force worldwide (*Church News,* August 5, 1995, 3). Their greatest contribution lies in their work with members in new congregational units, which often grow so rapidly that experienced local leaders are lacking and member retention becomes a serious problem. Other couples are assigned to be temple workers or staff LDS visitors' centers and tourist attractions.[4]

Historical Background of MTC Training

Some have argued that LDS missionary training has its origins in the "School of the Prophets," which Joseph Smith organized in 1833 in Kirtland, Ohio (Cowan 1984; Jensen 1988). The School of the Prophets' curriculum, however, focused primarily on Mormonism's emerging prophetic theology rather than on missionary training as such. Apart from on-the-job training in the field, there was little standardized preparation of Mormon missionaries throughout the nineteenth century. In 1925, prompted by concern for the spiritual welfare of newly called missionaries who came to Salt Lake to "wander around" before being set apart and receiving the temple endowment, the "First Presidency approved a Church Mission Home and Preparatory Training School. A Salt Lake City home was purchased, remodeled, and furnished to accommodate up to ninety-nine missionaries. . . . The week long program for departing missionaries emphasized gospel topics, church procedures, personal health, and proper manners" (Cowan 1984, 5, 1992, 913). Later, adjacent properties were purchased, and the mission home's facilities were expanded to accommodate larger cohorts of missionaries.

The LDS language training program for missionaries was instituted in 1961 and originally provided instruction only in Spanish:

> For several years prior to 1960, church and BYU officials considered the advisability of offering language instruction to missionaries. The occasion to launch this program came when missionaries assigned to Mexico and Argentina experienced lengthy delays in obtaining visas. On December 4, 1961, the Missionary Language Institute (MLI) opened with a class of 29 elders in temporary quarters in a Provo hotel and various BYU buildings. . . . In 1963 church leaders gave its director the authority and stature of a mission president, and the MLI became known as the Language Training Mission (LTM). (Cowan 1992, 913)

At the time of our preparation for missionary work in 1964, missionaries assigned to Spanish-speaking countries first spent the traditional orientation week at the Salt Lake City mission home and then went to Provo for three months of intensive language training.[5] By the time we arrived at the LTM, its operations had been moved to Knight Mangum Hall, originally a women's dormitory on the Brigham Young University campus.

As the number of languages and missionaries to be taught rapidly increased during the 1960s and early 1970s, available on-campus facilities for the LTM clearly were no longer adequate.[6] In 1976 a $26 million, self-contained complex for language and missionary training was dedicated, and in 1978 church officials decided to eliminate the old Salt Lake City mission home and send all newly called missionaries, including those with assignments in English-speaking missions, to Provo for orientation and training. At that point the LTM changed its overwhelming emphasis on language instruction to increasing emphasis on proselyting skills; consequently, its name was also changed to the Missionary Training Center (Cowan 1984, 108–11).

Dominant trends in Mormon proselyting programs since World War II, both in missionary preparation and in the field, include increasing reliance on uniformity of the proselyting message and how missionaries are to deliver it, goal-setting and outcome measurement by objective criteria, standardized and programmatic training, systematic supervision of missionary performance, and cost-benefit accountability. These are all characteristics of the modern, bureaucratic ethos of corporate rationality and illustrate the American business approach to missions. In particular, the missionary department's growing administrative control over LDS missionary work after World War II accelerated the standardization of programs (Jensen 1988, 31).[7]

Even though church leaders had always urged lay members to support the missionary effort actively, "proselyting continued to be a slow process during the 1950s. Missionaries spent several months instructing converts prior to baptism, making sure that they fully understood every aspect of church doctrine and procedure before asking them to become church members. Mission presidents could see that their elders, left to their own teaching approaches, hoping for spiritual guidance but often faltering in presenting the gospel in a convincing way to non-Mormons, needed help" (Irving 1976, 22–23). A trend thus developed toward the use of standard, systematic lesson outlines and visual aids in LDS missions throughout the world.

In 1953 *The Systematic Program for Teaching the Gospel* became the first set of missionary lessons published by the church to be used in all LDS missions. Before then, a number of ad hoc plans had been developed as proselyting aids and used in different missions of the church with varying degrees of success. And, as Jay Jensen has observed, "Having a systematic plan to present the message of the church gave rise to a systematic plan for training" (1988, 29). The First Presidency called a conference for all LDS mission presidents throughout the world in Salt Lake City in 1961. As a result, "missionary work would never be the same, especially in mission field training" (Jensen 1988, 31). At the conference, a churchwide program for systematically involving the laity to implement the slogan "Every Member a Missionary" was unveiled, and a new missionary plan was presented: "A Uniform System for Teaching Investigators."

Reflecting a rational, sales-oriented approach, the "Uniform System" consisted of six missionary lessons to be memorized and used verbatim by all LDS missionaries worldwide in teaching potential converts (commonly referred to as investigators) about the basic tenets of Mormonism. "Because of their design, the lessons were called discussions. . . . Visuals in the form of cutouts that attached to a flannel board helped missionaries to follow the correct sequence for each discussion." The key to proselyting success was presumed to be a standard message presented in a simple but systematic way. In addition, the daily activities of all missionaries were henceforth to be regulated by a standard schedule: "When to arise, when to study both as individuals and as companions, what to study, when and how to proselyte, and when to retire" (Jensen 1988, 32–33).

That particular system was still in use at the time of our induction into missionary training in 1964. Although considerably more institutional attention is now given to shaping missionary attributes and interpersonal communication skills, we concentrated almost all of our time and energy on learning the language and memorizing the six investigator lessons. Fortunately, we came to excel at memorization, a talent not shared equally among missionaries in our training cohort.

The missionary department's unstinting efforts to refine proselyting strategies and training procedures have centered on the goal of preparing more individual missionaries "to have great converting power" beyond their native talents (Jensen 1988, 4). Over the years, the department has evaluated the teaching characteristics of those missionaries most successful at winning converts; the research indicates that the way in which proselyting materials are presented to investigators, not just the standardized content of the missionary message itself, correlates with increases in convert baptisms.[8] Church researchers inferred that certain communication skills, transcending rote presentation of the investigator lessons, were important factors in the conversion process. They called such communication skills the "commitment pattern," simplified for pedagogical purposes into a four-step formula (prepare, invite, follow-up, and resolve concerns) that missionaries could be taught to use when guiding listeners through the stages of investigation, conversion, baptism, and becoming faithful lay members of the church. Thus, emphasis in training eventually shifted from sheer memorization of lesson plans to training missionaries on how to implement the commitment pattern more effectively. Whether programmatic attempts to refine individual missionaries' communications skills lead, on average, to significant increases in proselyting productivity has not been demonstrated. Thus, "since 1970, the only factor that seems to have accounted for an increase in convert baptisms is an increase in the number of full-time missionaries." Undaunted, however, missionary department executives continue to operate "on the assumption that missionary training can make a difference to increase converts" (Jensen 1988, 1).

As a result of missionary department research on missionary training and the conversion process, a second world mission presidents' conference was convened in Salt Lake City in June 1985, and yet another new set of missionary discussions was adopted: "The Uniform System for Teaching the Gospel." This system, taught and used throughout the world by LDS missionaries, departs from the aggressive salesmanship of earlier plans in favor of a more human relations-oriented form of persuasion. Standard investigator lessons still are learned but need not be memorized word for word; missionaries are permitted to use their own phrasing in explaining religious precepts and encouraged to "teach by the spirit" in their testimonies and responses to investigator questions.[9] They have greater flexibility in presenting the content of their message while systematically incorporating the commitment pattern in all of their discussions with investigators. Also introduced for universal use at the 1985 conference was a new training manual, *The Missionary Guide.* According to Jensen, "Missionary Department leaders have taken the position that all training materials must be built around the commitment pattern. The *Missionary Guide* has become the training manual for all missionaries in the church. . . . The discussions and the *Missionary Guide* have been implemented in all MTCs as the two principal tools to help missionaries learn and use the commitment pattern" (1988, 43).

The Missionary Training Organization and Regimen

Every week, hundreds of newly called missionaries arrive at the Provo MTC at scheduled intervals throughout the day for orientation and induction into missionary training. The orientation session constitutes one additional rite of passage ceremony for the novices, who may be accompanied by parents or other family members and are initially gathered in an auditorium to be greeted by a member of the MTC mission presidency. Following a congregational hymn, prayer, and introductory remarks, novices and their families are shown a short film that is designed to be an inspirational sketch of the MTC experience, alleviate apprehension, and, simultaneously, reinforce the importance of missionary norms of conduct associated with their new religious identities. Novice missionaries are reminded that the MTC is no ordinary school but a sacred place, detached from the mundane concerns of the profane world—a place where their diligent obedience will put them in constant contact with the spirit of God.

Following the film, the presiding member of the mission presidency reviews the schedule of events that will follow (registration, payment of fees for room and board, purchase of books and supplies at the MTC bookstore, issuance of missionary name tags, companion assignments and district formation meeting, and introductions to classroom instructors and district branch presidents who will function as the missionary trainees' academic advisors and ecclesiastical authorities respectively) and summarizes specific MTC rules. At the conclusion of the orientation session, brief—often tearful—family farewells are allowed as novice missionaries are separated from their parents and other well-wishers. As they leave the auditorium through a separate door, the newly inducted missionaries are greeted conspicuously by the mission presidency's representative as "elder" or "sister," the new religious statuses that have been conferred upon them. This ritualized orientation was not part of our induction experience in 1964. At that time, those leaving the Salt Lake City mission home either departed directly to their fields of labor or were bussed, as we were, to Provo in the evening and began language classes the following day, with little ceremony involved.

The organizational complexity of the Provo MTC has increased greatly since its original inceptions as the Language Training Institute and Language Training Mission. When we entered the LTM, all aspects of the program were administered by a mission presidency consisting of the president and his two counselors. From 1961 to 1970 the president of the LTM was Ernest Wilkins, an innovative language educator chosen from the Brigham Young University faculty by ecclesiastical authorities in Salt Lake City to institute the church's language training program. Wilkins's counselors (Lewis Bastion and Ben Martinez) were recently returned missionaries at Brigham Young University who had outstanding mission records and language abilities in Spanish.[10] Both became zealous and effective role models for missionary trainees, who were organized into zones (according to language being learned, either Spanish or Portuguese at the time) and, within zones, smaller cohort units—"districts"—of ten to twelve missionaries. A missionary from each district was selected to serve as a district leader or supervising elder (the designation commonly used at the time). Each district was assigned a language instructor (who then like now had to be a returned missionary and Brigham Young University student who had appropriate foreign language experience) who advised and supervised the group's activities. In most cases, the language instructors also became admired role models for the fledgling missionaries under their tutelage. (The role model functions of the teaching staff appear to be as important now as they were in the 1960s.) Finally, in keeping with one of the earliest Mormon missionary practices, each missionary was assigned a companion with whom to work and study.

Today, the administrative structure of the MTC features three related but distinct organizational lines of authority: the ecclesiastical organization, the missionary training organization, and the support/administrative services organization.[11] The mission president and his two counselors preside over the ecclesiastical organization. Under their supervision is a set of district presidents and, in turn, under them function approximately fifty branch presidents who preside directly over the spiritual welfare of a number of missionary cohort districts. All of those who minister in MTC ecclesiastical positions, including the MTC president, are lay volunteers who accept temporary assignments to serve. Few, if any, are trained linguists. Some happen to be professional educators but, if so, only coincidentally; principally they are men drawn from the local Mormon community who have extensive lay experience in Melchizedek priesthood callings. Branch presidents conduct weekly Sunday services for their MTC districts and are supposed to interview and counsel their missionary charges on a weekly basis.

Missionary training itself is now overseen by the MTC's administrative director, associate directors, and directors of language training (appointed to supervise instruction in different language categories, including English) rather than the mission presidency. In contrast to MTC ecclesiastical authorities, missionary training administrators are a professional staff whose programs and training policies are commonly shaped by recommendations developed through the MTC's own in-house research evaluation unit. Many of those who currently hold professional staff positions have, in addition to their church-related experience, academic credentials in education, administration, or the social sciences. Linguists from the Brigham Young University faculty may be consulted on training methods but have no direct control over the language training curriculum at the Provo MTC.

Finally, the Provo MTC's dramatically increased size and its attempts to minimize novices' contact with the outside world have created the need for a large support and administrative services staff that provides such things as house-cleaning and building maintenance; proselyting and materials development; a book store, barber shop and beauty salon, and mail room; personnel and teacher applicant offices; food, media, travel, clinical, and medical services; and MTC security.

Missionary trainees spend from ten to twelve hours a day in the classroom with their district cohort. They also are expected to spend time outside of class in companion or personal study. Studies include LDS scriptures, languages, and proselyting techniques. Those assigned to English-speaking missions can begin to familiarize themselves immediately with the investigator discussions and designated communication skills associated with the commitment pattern. Missionaries going to foreign-language countries must first begin learning the rudiments of that language. "The intensive methodology used in foreign language instruction is based in part on a program developed by the U.S. Army: Trainees learn by listening and repeating" (Cowan 1992, 914). The emphasis in this approach is to develop conversational ability through verbal drills rather than literary or writing skills. It may be claimed that "in eight weeks, missionaries are reasonably adept in conversation and can teach gospel lessons in a foreign language" (Cowan 1992, 914), but surely that is a generalization based on idealized program goals. Although they are provided a good foundation in language development, most Mormon missionaries discover upon arriving at their destinations that they require several months of additional practice and exposure to native usage before they become reasonably fluent in the language.

Still, the degree of language acquisition routinely achieved on a large scale at the MTC must be regarded as a remarkable institutional accomplishment. After all, language programs at the MTC must be designed to accommodate the limitations of teaching staff as well as missionary trainees. The instructional staff is made up of part-time, nonprofessional teachers who, because of their student status at Brigham Young University, have a relatively high rate of turnover. They are well motivated, however, and willing to implement the regimented MTC program. And, because they are missionary veterans who are close in age to most of their students, they are often more effective counselors than their superiors in either the ecclesiastical or training hierarchies. At the same time, missionary trainees are not an elite group of hand-picked language students. Most of them are, however, like their instructors, highly motivated. Whatever variation or refinement of language method is employed, its ultimate effectiveness in the relatively short period the MTC instructional agenda allots seems to depend chiefly on missionaries' willingness to devote long, intensive hours to study and practice.

The MTC's curriculum does not emphasize critical thinking, a major difference between the ideals of secular education and most forms of religious education. Religious education typically concerns itself with indoctrination of a particular faith and its successful propagation rather than with detached discussion; it is far more likely to emphasize the memorization and recitation of sacred texts than to encourage their critical analysis or creative interpretation (Moran 1983; Taylor 1984). The only reading church authorities authorize for missionaries, both in the MTC and in the field, is *The Missionary Guide,* investigator discussions, official church magazines (*The New Era* and *The Ensign*), and the "standard works" (canonical scriptures) of the LDS Church: the Bible, Book of Mormon, Doctrine and Covenants, and Pearl of Great Price. As modeled by ecclesiastical leaders, the correct way for missionary trainees to read the scriptures is with awe and faith in search of personal inspiration and passages that buttress LDS theology rather than as historical-cultural documents. Questions typically are resolved by appeals to authority—either one's immediate superior in the ecclesiastical hierarchy or to apologetic books or addresses by LDS general authorities.

MTC rules impose significant restrictions. Missionaries may not receive any visitors unless there is an emergency, nor are they to make personal telephone calls. Missionaries are expected to write faith-promoting letters home once a week but are cautioned against writing more often than weekly; they are discouraged especially from writing frequent letters to girlfriends or boyfriends. Missionaries are to stay with their assigned companions at all times and are confined to MTC premises. They are not permitted to see movies or television, listen to popular music, or read literature extraneous to the MTC curriculum. Mission leaders justify such restrictions as safeguards against the disrupting intrusions of the outside world, which they believe can impair the necessary spiritual development of missionary trainees.

Other MTC norms that contribute to obedience and organizational control include constant supervision and surveillance of missionary performance through the companion system, weekly interviews with instructors and ecclesiastical authorities, and daily self-evaluations; minimization of personal discretion through the complete scheduling of daily activities and restrictive dress and grooming codes (dark business suits, conservative ties, and white shirts for elders, and conservative dresses and suits for sisters); institutionally organized occasions for systematic verbalization of personal conviction and commitment through frequent daily prayers (both privately and in groups) and testimony sessions in classes and district meetings; and regular exposure to Mormonism's most sacred religious symbols and authority figures through weekly attendance at MTC devotionals, where LDS general authorities are featured regularly as inspirational speakers. Of particular importance are regular visits to the Provo Temple to renew one's religious covenants.

Participation in the temple ritual, formulated by Joseph Smith and elaborated by Brigham Young in the nineteenth century, can be bewildering for initiates and stimulate disquieting reservations in some cases rather than the intended experience of sacred confirmation and spiritual enlightenment.[12] The LDS temple ceremony involves the symbolic enactment of creation, fall, and redemption—as foundational Mormon doctrines—punctuated by a series of vows that commit participants to obedience, sacrifice, chastity, and a willingness to consecrate their personal resources to the church in exchange for God's blessings (Talmage 1962, 99–100). Novice participants, although escorted and receiving assistance, proceed through the same ceremony as experienced participants.[13]

Thus, temple worship becomes an important adult experience for novice missionaries. Because Mormonism is not a very liturgical religion in its public worship or lay auxiliary programs, most LDS youths are not prepared by their previous church roles to participate in highly ritualized events that require ceremonial attire, ritual recitations, and formal vows of silence about the substance of the experience. Repeated visits to the temple tend to dispel discomfort with the ceremony, but lingering questions may persist for some individuals. That was true for both of us in our limited exposure to the temple. Because there was no Provo Temple at the time of our missionary training, our temple experience included only two sessions in Salt Lake City and a single excursion to the Manti Temple (a pioneer edifice located about an hour's drive from the Brigham Young University campus) when we were at the LTM. In any event, induction into LDS missionary training is designed to give concrete meaning to the notion of being set apart, of assuming a new status in a more sacred realm that must be largely disassociated from previous social identities. It is this sense of separation that the temple ritual dramatically reinforces as novice missionaries pursue their training.

Criticism and Defense of Missionary Training

The MTC has become an increasingly cloistered environment. It has acquired many of the specific characteristics of monastic life and therefore the general characteristics of what Erving Goffman called a total institution: "A total institution may be defined as a place of residence and work where a large number of like-situated individuals, cut off from the wider society for an appreciable period of time, together lead an enclosed, formally administered round of life" (1961, xiii). Unlike correctional, custodial, or military training institutions, monasteries and convents consist of religious communicants who have withdrawn from the world to abide in the contemplative life and to single-mindedly serve God rather than secular interests (Leclercq 1961). What is similar to this in the LDS Missionary Training Center is the residential segregation of religious cohorts from the outside world in conjunction with the systematic organizational regimentation of individuals who have religious callings to subordinate themselves to the realization of what they believe is a higher spiritual cause. It is commitment to a higher cause that justifies ascetic discipline and personal deprivations (Kanter 1972, 115; Shibutani 1986, 460–64). Like the "new order" Franciscans, Dominicans, and Jesuits in their day, Mormon missionaries do not absorb themselves purely in contemplation and self-abnegation but emerge from their cloistered preparation to exercise an active ministry of preaching and conversion.[14]

Such a regimented system may seem disturbing to many Americans, especially in recent times when public hysteria over the perceived menace of "cults" has become widespread (Anthony 1990; Bromley and Shupe 1981, 1987; Lewis, ed. 1994; Richardson, Best, and Bromley, eds. 1991; Sherwood 1991). Cults are popularly viewed as diabolical groups that entrap and brainwash otherwise normal individuals into committing morally repugnant acts. The LDS Church itself has been branded occasionally as a cult in this pejorative sense (Decker and Hunt 1984; Mackey 1985). Beyond such fantastical charges, more responsible critics argue that the LTM in particular creates a totalitarian environment of relentless conformity and "thought control" that impedes the development of personal autonomy (Berleffi 1987; Groesbeck 1986; Miller 1986; Woodward 1981). Dominant American values of individualism and democratic decision making (influenced historically by the Protestant Reformation, including repudiation of monastic orders and ecclesiastical absolutism) often appear to be violated when voluntary religious groups sponsor such rigid training regimens. In contrast, however, military organizations, under the authority of democratically elected civilian leaders, are granted legitimacy in both their goals of collective obedience and the authoritarian, sometimes brutal, methods they employ in recruit training.

Like other evangelical leaders historically, LDS authorities often incorporate military metaphors in their rhetoric (Tanner 1982). To them, charges of "brainwashing" seem both preposterous and irrelevant. It is the religious crusade itself—realization of God's plan to build his kingdom on earth—that matters above all else. Church leaders idealize and defend unhesitating involvement and devotion to the LDS missionary cause as a transformative test, a commandment of God. They emphasize that there will be determined adversaries and great struggles to endure but that ultimately the faithful will prevail in carrying out God's work on earth. Analogous to the kinds of justifications often offered for military life, LDS officials extol missionary training as an ennobling experience that mitigates the moral corruption of purely self-interested activity, an experience that etches on youthful minds the social values of duty, unity, courage, and discipline in pursuit of a transcendent cause. We also find military metaphors to be useful in conceptualizing certain aspects of Mormon missionary life and will continue to use them occasionally at different points in our analysis.

The majority of Mormon missionaries are quite young, of course. Their training is intensive but relatively brief, and their motives for serving missions are not entirely uniform in focus or strength. Thus, we should not be surprised to observe a considerable range of reaction on the part of individual missionaries to the rigors of MTC training and, later on, to the mission field experience itself. The missionary department has not released, and will not do so, completion rates at the MTC. It is well known that many missionaries struggle through their training and that some become profoundly discouraged and even alienated by the relentless pressure of the MTC program (Bergera 1988; Berleffi 1987). A certain percentage of the trainees drop out, but, based on anecdotal reports, at least 95 percent or more of a missionary cohort typically manages to complete the training program and proceed to their assigned fields of missionary labor (Bergera 1988). If this estimate is more or less accurate, it is a remarkable statistic. Compared to other demanding voluntary organizations such as graduate school, the Peace Corps, Protestant seminaries, Catholic religious orders, or special military schools, the MTC attrition rate is very low.

The stereotype of youthful rebellion against adult standards and authority must be balanced by recognition that most adolescents—when involved in collective causes or group activities in which they believe—are zealous, conforming, and susceptible to authoritarian direction (Bronfenbrenner 1970; Shepherd 1976). Assuming an elemental faith in their religion and voluntary acceptance of their calling, the youthfulness and enthusiastic naiveté of most LDS missionaries are of great advantage to the training agenda of the MTC. For the most part, these young people in their late teens and early twenties are far more willing to submit to authoritarian controls and personal demands than older adults would be. (Both in the MTC and in the mission field, retired couples who serve LDS missions are, in fact, much less regulated than their youthful counterparts.) The mission experience is inserted into the lives of young Mormons as they begin to contemplate their transition to adulthood, and most are eager to acquire the attendant responsibilities and respect that their Mormon background has led them to anticipate. For many, their faith may be imperfect, but they want to believe; their knowledge may be meager, but they want to augment it. They still may be somewhat immature, but the majority are willing to submit to organizational discipline.

∽

When we entered the Language Training Mission, the program was divided into two phases, Level One and Level Two. Level One was an intensive, crash-study course of grammar, vocabulary, and pronunciation in the assigned language. Emphasis was placed on oral drills and repetition of memorized language dialogues that had religious application (the basic language-learning method still used at the MTC). After five weeks of language immersion, we were advanced to Level Two, where we began memorization of the six-lesson "Uniform Plan for Teaching Investigators" (which we simply called "the Plan"). These lessons were sequentially designed to prepare investigators to accept baptism in the LDS Church. The goal of Level Two was for missionaries to memorize all six lessons, word-perfect in the appropriate mission language, before their departure to the mission field. Now, missionaries familiarize themselves with the basic contents and organizational structure of two investigator lessons at the MTC and, subsequently, are expected to learn the remainder under the tutelage of their initial "trainer" companion in the field.

At the LTM, we were given daily quizzes, and comprehensive tests were administered and scored every week for letter grades. MTC instructors no longer grade pupils in that way. Missionaries are required now to make daily self-evaluation ratings and hold weekly goal-setting interviews with their students individually. For us, performance in memorization and tests became a major preoccupation; for many missionaries in our training cohort, it was a source of considerable anxiety. The sustaining belief was that if we applied ourselves with humility and diligence the gift of tongues would eventually be bestowed and our capacity for learning a language would be accelerated greatly. Many in our cohort, however, experienced difficulty, especially those without previous language training. Some were unable to keep pace and eventually were transferred to English-speaking missions. The practice of washing out floundering students and reassigning them to other missions has been discontinued. Now, virtually all those who begin language training complete the course, even if their performance is poor.

At first we felt overwhelmed and anxious about our ability to perform adequately in the LTM program. In spite of the formal structure of adult supervision, we never sought reassurances or personal guidance from either our instructors or LTM officials. To one another, however, we did confess our doubts and self-criticisms and turned to fasting and prayer in our attempts to secure greater spirituality, theological conviction, and supernatural aid. But from the outset we were also motivated to apply ourselves to the limits of our abilities and to improve and succeed as missionaries. We committed ourselves unreservedly to the study of Spanish, especially to the extensive tasks of memorization that were so strongly emphasized. In contrast to what often had been a lackadaisical approach to learning in high school and our freshman year of college, we quickly adopted a devout work ethic and systematic study habits that we were to carry into the mission field.

Our youthful moralism and tendencies toward self-righteousness were immediately apparent as we routinely indulged in disdainful criticism of many in our missionary cohort, particularly when we thought they were being pretentious, insincere, or insufficiently dedicated to their studies. This too was a practice we carried over into the mission field. Making moralistic judgments of others' performance can, of course, be taken as an indicator of the extent to which individuals personally identify with institutional values and standards. Identification with institutional ideals, however, is seldom if ever complete; it is always part of an ongoing and uneven process of self-definition in which contradictions and strains typically emerge to cast doubts on one's own moral consistency.

Although conforming and willing to make rapid adjustments to the rigorous requirements of the LTM, we also nurtured an individualistic orientation toward our development and maintained a corresponding ambivalence toward organizational authority. We tended to persist in personalizing authority as something based on individual merit rather then inhering, without question, in an institutionally designated status. On the one hand we were deeply impressed by the projected missionary examples set by the LTM presidency and the apparent moral character of many of the language staff instructors, which stimulated our aspirations for status advancement in the missionary system. On the other hand, we keenly resented being closely supervised and, on occasion, would express open defiance toward the hierarchical authority invested in missionary peers if they lacked our respect and attempted to impose regulatory controls over us. In spite of our religious training, the undomesticated strains of individualism in our characters allowed us to rationalize the infraction of certain mission rules, such as entertaining visitors and abandoning our assigned companions to spend more time with one another.

We not only admired and were influenced by standard missionary role models but were also attracted to more unconventional LDS peers such as Chuck Radlow and Steve London, whose inquisitive intelligence and ironic sense of humor we valued. Radlow was an old friend from childhood days, and London was in our missionary training cohort. Into our chronicle of events we have injected occasional letters received from both Radlow and London. Their letters highlight the sometimes intense struggles of religious faith that some Mormon youths experience as they confront the missionary expectations of their culture. Both young men were introspective and given to critical questioning. London accepted his mission call but wrestled with his religious doubts and sense of alienation from the missionary system throughout his assignment. In contrast, Radlow was more deeply religious and heretical in his thinking. During the time recorded in this volume, he was never able to overcome his acute ambivalence toward institutional religion, and he remained uncommitted, never accepting a mission call and gradually losing his Mormon faith. We, however, were much more conventional in our willingness to suspend lingering doubts and skepticism as we ambitiously pursued full integration into the missionary system. A strong sense of family duty, to our parents and to one another, was the overriding factor in our motivation to become successful missionaries.

For us, the larger reality was our willing submission to the demands and sacrificial expectations of missionary life. We were regularly reminded by the LTM presidency and instructional staff that even though we were on a college campus studying a foreign language we were to regard ourselves as missionaries, separated by our sacred callings and obligations from worldly concerns and subject to all the restrictions and discipline of the missionary organization. And so, while others of our generation were being drawn into the growing maelstrom of social conflicts of the 1960s we immersed ourselves in the relatively insulated world of Mormon missionary life. Events occurring in the larger society, especially civil rights struggles and the Vietnam War, were on the periphery of our awareness, but our perception of the world was quickly dominated by—and became narrowly focused on—events occurring within the plausibility structure of the mission organization.

NOTES

1. Temples are not to be confused with LDS chapels, which are the centers of local ward activities and weekly religious services. Temples are set apart for the Latter-day Saints' most important religious rituals, including member endowments, marriage, and baptism for the dead. For authorized descriptions of the LDS temple and its ritual functions, see Talmage (1962), and Packer (1980). As of 1995 there were more than twenty-two thousand LDS wards and branches worldwide and forty-six temples in operation, with twelve additional temples in various stages of planning or construction (*The Ensign*, May 1996, 21; *Church Almanac, 1997–98*).

2. MTC statistics, unless otherwise cited, were obtained through conversations with MTC administrative staff.

3. A 1993 campus survey indicated that more than fourteen thousand of Brigham Young University's thirty-one thousand students had served LDS missions. This provides a sizable and field-experienced teaching pool from which the MTC annually is able to draw its instructional staff (Walsh 1993, 1).

4. One other small but important category of missionary training consists of several hundred sister missionaries who are called annually to proselyte in developing countries and are given "additional assignments" in welfare and health services (*Church News*, March 21, 1981). In addition to standard missionary preparation, welfare service missionaries are trained to teach new members basic principles of sanitation and self-reliance. Health missionaries (who have educational and occupational backgrounds in medically related fields) do the same and are equipped to provide basic health care services to both members and missionaries.

5. Based on the belief that ever more efficient training methods would allow the church to cut training costs, the training period for all languages eventually was reduced to eight weeks (Jensen 1988, 36).

6. By then, temporary language facilities were also established at LDS Church colleges in Ricks, Idaho, and Laie, Hawaii (Walgren 1975).

7. In addition to training missionaries to present doctrinal lessons to people who express an interest in Mormonism, the LDS Church also expends substantial resources in public relations and advertising campaigns through television commercials, satellite broadcasts, concert tours by the Mormon Tabernacle Choir and various Brigham Young University performing groups, pageants, exhibitions, and visitors' centers. All function to create a more favorable public image, which in turn helps blunt sectarian opposition to the church and facilitates more effective missionary efforts. In recent years LDS missionary officials have been training a selected number of newly called missionaries for telemarketing shifts of several weeks' duration at the Provo MTC before to their departure to field assignments.

8. For references to these unpublished studies, see Taylor (1986) and Jensen (1988).

9. One of the chapters of *The Missionary Guide* is entitled "Help Others Feel and Recognize the Spirit" and concludes that the "principles presented in this lesson will enable you to help others feel and recognize the spirit of the Lord in their lives. The people you teach will eventually feel the spirit as they sincerely pray to know the truth and listen to your message and humble testimony. When you sense that others are feeling the spirit, tell them what they are feeling and help them understand it" (1988, 84).

10. Both Bastian and Martinez served later as mission presidents in Mexico in the 1970s, with Bastian headquartered in Torreón and Martinez in Mérida. Bastian also served as the first president of the Mexico City MTC in 1978.

11. Our description of MTC organizational structure is based on interviews with MTC administrators and instructional staff.

12. For contemporary articles on the LDS temple experience, see Buerger (1987), Hicks (1982), Leone (1978), and Packer (1980).

13. Worthy church members are encouraged to return regularly to act as proxies for deceased ancestors in temple ceremonies. It is the performance of proxy temple ordinances, including baptism for the dead, that stimulates intensive Mormon genealogical activity.

14. For a historical account of Christian monastic orders, see Knowles (1966).

2

✧

Missionaries in the Service of God:
The Salt Lake City Mission Home

Salt Lake City, May 18, 1964 (Gordon)

First day in the Salt Lake Mission Home. Mom and Dad dropped Gary and me off this morning, but we'll see them again before leaving for the Language Training Mission in Provo. It turns out that President and Sister Brown, who supervise the mission home, are old friends of the family from Cowley, Wyoming. Mom and Dad introduced us when we arrived and, subsequently, Sister Brown called on me to open our initial missionary meeting with prayer. I was startled silly. There must be over two hundred missionaries here in our group. After I prayed and sat down, Sister Brown got up and gave a little lecture on the proper format for public prayer, which apparently I failed to follow. At any rate, I'm glad Gary and I will go through our preparation together before parting company in Mexico.

May 18 (Gary)

It's been a full day, as every day must be from now on. Our time has been spent receiving instructions from general authorities and other men of high calling. It's also been a tiring day and I will be glad to crawl into bed in a minute. Gordon was called upon to open our classes with prayer this morning and came through with a really fine effort.

It may take some time to get used to the various companions we will be assigned. Elder Jerry Walker is certainly no Gordon, but I've always been able to get along with people. I must work hard, struggle against laziness, and make a sincere effort to become closer to God.

May 20 (Gordon)

This afternoon I was set apart as a missionary by Marion D. Hanks of the First Council of Seventy. Gary, Mom, and Beckie were able to witness the ordinance. Gary was set apart by Milton R. Hunter, also of the First Council of Seventy. I was given a great blessing and admonished to be a gentleman to all I meet as I represent the church and perform the duties of my calling.

The time here at the mission home has been filled with talks given by general authorities of the church. In our spare time we study the first lesson of the missionary plan, which we're supposed to have memorized by the time we leave here at the end of the week.

My first companion is Elder Giles from Detroit, Michigan, for whom I've developed an immediate liking. Gary's companion, Elder Walker, is a little less likable on first impression, but time and greater familiarity should take care of that. Anyway, trailing around twenty-four hours a day with assigned companions has not yet been annoying at all, but wearing a suit and tie every day is going to take some getting used to. I'm starting to get the usual rash around my neck.

May 20 (Gary)

Today I was set apart as a missionary in the service of God by Milton R. Hunter. Mother was present and took a few brief notes on what was said. In general I felt that much of this blessing followed along the lines of my patriarchal blessing. Gordon received a tremendous blessing at the hands of Marion D. Hanks, full of insight and understanding. Gordon is applying himself here, is taking the work seriously, and works hard—much more than I. I know my commitment needs strengthening. When we finally part company in Mexico, I can see that I will miss Gordon's personal integrity and subtle example in matters of character that he has always set for me.

May 23 (Gordon)

So far this companion business has worked well, mainly because I have a good companion. Elder Giles is humble and sincere in his motives to serve a worthy mission (unlike a few of the pompous phonies I've seen here, some of whom seem mostly interested in their appearance and try to talk like general authorities). Since he's not going to Mexico, however, I'll lose Giles as a companion when we leave for language training in Provo. One guy in our group—Elder Mandrake—actually preens and rehearses his lines in front of a mirror to get his artificial smile just right as he delivers the missionary door approach.

Gary and I have both been placed in an accelerated group for learning the missionary discussions. We've completely memorized the first lesson and have moved on to the second. The only discouraging thing about this is that we'll have to learn them all over again in Spanish. According to our instructor, learning the lessons in English will make it easier for us to learn them in a foreign language when the time comes.

In addition to learning the missionary lesson plan, every day we receive instruction from prominent church leaders. We have been strongly admonished to confess any sexual misbehaviors that were not fully reported to our ward bishops and stake presidents before being set apart as missionaries. If not, we are told we will become guilt-stricken and ineffective in our work. Apparently several elders have been sneaking over to the church office building to make confessions. As for me, I don't intend to make mountains out of molehills. My own unconfessed adventures seem relatively tame to me and I don't feel particularly guilty about not telling. I have vowed in private and in good faith to commit myself to the work and, as far as I'm concerned, that's the end of it. Gary feels the same way.

Another activity of this week has been several trips to the Salt Lake Temple with all the other missionaries. Frankly, I'm glad Gary and I went previously with Mom and Dad for our temple endowments. For many of the missionaries going through for the first time it can be a confusing experience. There's a lot about the temple ritual I don't yet understand. At one of the temple sessions missionaries were allowed to congregate in the great assembly hall on the upper floor of the temple for the purpose of a question and answer period with Apostle Harold B. Lee, which was helpful and reassuring.

May 24 (Gary)

We spent much of yesterday afternoon in the temple and I still haven't got the hang of it yet. Then this evening we walked over to the Assembly Hall on Temple Square and took seats in the choir section above the speakers' rostrum. Apparently it is a tradition for each cohort of new missionaries to experience giving their testimonies to an audience of family, friends, and well-wishers from the same place where many of the leaders of the church have stood since the days of Brigham Young. Time did not permit each of the two hundred or so missionaries to speak, so those most anxious to do so began filtering down through the seats to form a loose line behind the podium. I felt that I should join the flow to the front as a sign of my commitment, but I held back until it was clear that there were already more waiting than could be accommodated. My reluctance was partly based on the usual fear of facing an audience without being prepared, and partly because when I spotted some missionaries like Elder Steve London (he's one of our roommates), piously making their way forward, it made me feel a little cynical about the sincerity of many of the testimonies being offered, including my own. I really don't know Elder London that well yet, but my initial impression is not very favorable. London wears his hair long in a kind of Beatles' cut and is constantly flipping his foremop out of his eyes. His manner and speech seem haughty and put-on, and he's been playing hooky from study sessions at the mission home. He's in the Mexican group and will be going with us to study Spanish at the Language Training Mission. He's also been assigned to the Veracruz Mission, same as Gord, so I guess we can expect to see more of Elder London in the days ahead.

3

☙

"The Rumors Were All True":
The Language Training Mission, Level One

Provo Utah, May 25, 1964 (Gordon)

We left Salt Lake last night by bus for a three-month stay at the Language Training Mission in Provo where we will study Spanish before going on to Mexico. Mom and Dad, a lot of friends, and a flock of relatives were all at the bus station to see us off. Lorin Larsen will be going into the mission home in a couple of weeks himself prior to departing for New York. It doesn't look like Dave Lingwall's plans will include a mission. Mike Mitchell still plans on getting married at the end of the summer, and both Natalie Fletcher and Kathy Dempsey appear to have hopes for Gary. Beckie slipped me a bulky letter before we left. She's a strong girl with a lot of good qualities and I hope she'll want to keep writing to me.

We were greeted on the BYU campus by a group of missionaries who have been here in the language program for awhile. In some ways it's been sort of like our experience at the reception center in army basic training last fall at Fort Ord (rules, regulations, restrictions, and every minute of the day planned and scheduled), but without all the screaming and intimidation by drill sergeants. Instead, a real effort to make us feel at ease—while emphasizing the importance of our work and the need for self-discipline—has been made. It was after midnight before we got to bed. My new companion is Elder Davidson, a shy, quiet kid from Arizona. My other roommates are Elders Brent Booth (who looks like a solid guy) and Steve London (whom I already met in Salt Lake and whose vanity might take a little getting used to).

May 27 (Gary)

It would be so easy to go crazy here. The rumors were all true—the Language Training Mission is the basic training of the mission field. We are really being pushed hard. It's a little discouraging to look ahead to all that we must learn, so we're just taking on one day at a time and doing our best. But this is what I wanted and needed. I may be confused and frustrated, but I'm also keeping awake all day and I'm constantly working and using my time to accomplish objectives. Muy bien, no? I still have the same companion. It turns out that Elder Walker is actually a pretty good guy; just a little homesick. I wrote several short letters tonight during a portion of study time, which violates an expectation that letters are only supposed to be written on Saturday afternoon. But I'm inclined to write when I feel the need, as long as my work doesn't suffer in the long run.

May 27 (Gordon)

We've only been here for two days but they've really been pouring on the work. It's hard to believe that I'll ever be able to carry on a genuine conversation in Spanish about the gospel (or anything else, for that matter) before we leave for Mexico. Best to concentrate on daily objectives, I guess, rather than worry too much about final outcomes.

May 28 (Gordon)

We had our first Spanish test today. My performance was both good and bad, with high marks on the written and oral questions and low marks in pronunciation and dictation. I've decided to fast from Friday night through Sunday. For those of us without previous language training it's a real struggle. Maybe the fast will help. I know I'm not satisfied with my performance so far. I wish now that I had studied some foreign language in school.

May 31 (Gary)

The work around here hasn't become easier and they say it gets much harder. I'm curious to see how I'll work under constant pressure. Pretty well, I have a hunch. Gordon and I both did fairly well on our first week's Spanish test yesterday, but we worked for it. We had yesterday (Saturday) afternoon and evening off, so I did my washing and ironing. I should have studied last night, but Elder Walker was really discouraged—he said he wanted to forget it all for a while and go to a show. [This was permitted at the time. Missionaries are no longer allowed to see movies.] So we did, and while we were walking into town, Beckie Jones and her mother drove by. They screeched to a stop and I talked to Beckie for a few minutes. She said she hoped to meet Gordon tomorrow afternoon on campus, which is really fracturing the law. As a matter of fact, the law around here is pretty puritanical, a copy of which follows below.

Language Training Mission Regulations

1. *SPEAKING YOUR MISSION LANGUAGE.* During the three months you are in the Language Training Mission you will be expected to make English inoperative and to practice your mission language at all times. 2. *DEPORTMENT.* You are under mission regulations and your deportment in every aspect should be that of a missionary who has been set apart. You should avoid assiduously all pranks, practical jokes, loud laughter, and improper manners. 3. *CLOTHING.* As Elders and Lady Missionaries, you should dress in accordance with the position you now hold. When leaving quarters, Elders should always wear a coat, tie, and suit. Lady Missionaries need not wear heels but they should always wear hose. 4. *COMPANIONS.* You must *always* stay with your companion. Pray with your companion and learn to love him or her and to work as a team. 5. *CORRESPONDENCE.* Write to parents once a week. Write to girlfriends (or boyfriends) only occasionally. 6. *TELEPHONE CALLS.* Calls to or from relatives should be limited to emergency cases only. 7. *TRAVEL.* Do not ask permission to leave Provo unless it is an emergency case involving members of your immediate family. Missionaries must have permission from the President of the Language Training Mission to operate a motor vehicle. 8. *VISITORS AT THE LANGUAGE TRAINING MISSION.* Members of your family and your friends should realize that you are on a mission and should not visit you. You should not accept invitations to dinner with parents or friends. 9. *GIRLFRIENDS OR BOYFRIENDS.* In no case should they come to your quarters or should you go to theirs. Do not plan to meet with them on campus, at church, downtown, or any other place. You should avoid excessive letter writing or any communication which would tend to distract you from your primary objective. 10. *RECORDS AND REPORTS.* Keep a daily record of the way in which you spend your time. Hand the report to the supervising elder of your district each Saturday morning. Keep an accurate account daily of the money you spend and report it at the end of each month to the mission president. On the reverse side of the weekly report write a brief letter to the president telling him about your accomplishments, problems, or anything that is in your heart. 11. *EXERCISES.* Unless you are ill or have an excuse from your doctor you should report for exercises in the gym three times a week.

May 31 (Gordon)

My thirty-six-hour fast might have done me some good. Language lessons seem to make a little more sense and I think I've made some progress. Our district held a testimony meeting this afternoon and I was the first to admit that my convictions are not as strong as they should be, but that in the meantime I'm determined to work as hard as I can to strengthen them. Others followed with similar admissions. Elder Mandrake said he was shocked to hear such confessions and expounded on the strength of his own beliefs, saying that he was more positive and sure in his testimony of the church than he was that the light would come on if he turned the switch, which he then proceeded to do with a dramatic flourish. Still, one of the best meetings I've attended. Afterward, I discovered that Beckie had been waiting outside Knight Mangum Hall for three hours to see me. We walked around campus and talked for awhile. It was a major violation of mission rules that didn't really sink in until after Beckie had gone. I felt a little uneasy about it but I have not been at all distracted from my commitment and language studies. There are some missionaries here who are really homesick and pining away over their girlfriends, and it makes it difficult for them to concentrate on their work. This has simply not been a problem for Gary and me. In fact I've never been so single-mindedly focused in my whole life.

June 3 (Gary)

The work continues hard, although for some reason tonight I have a few spare minutes to do some writing. Gordon and I are both shedding the precious little extra bulk we acquired in army basic training—I've lost ten pounds, and Gordon has somehow, somewhere lost close to twenty pounds. We eat most of our meals, and the food is fine, so "Ich weiss nicht," I mean "yo no se" [I don't know].

Gordon and I are in rooms next to each other, but so far we haven't been able to get together too often outside of class. Our personal schedules are filled. No previous friends are down here with us. Keeping occupied keeps one contented. Sometimes. Sometimes it can drive one crazy. I'm not crazy yet, and I feel like I'm making some headway with the work, but I'm just getting my toes wet. Meanwhile it doesn't look like my companion, Elder Walker, will last here much longer. He tries hard, but he's learned practically zero and he's flunked every test flat. He's a good guy and could do a good job in an English-speaking mission. If Gordon and I were teamed up as companions I know we'd be learning a lot faster. Companions have to work together on the language, and it's a lot harder to dig it up for yourself when your companion is so slow. Still, we're not hurting yet.

June 3 (Gordon)

I'm doing much better now with the Spanish dialogues that we have to memorize every couple of days. I'm the only one in our class so far who has maintained an A average in memorization. I'm a little slower in understanding and speaking, unfortunately—that's the part that really counts. Beckie came by again last night, parking in the lot across the street from Knight Mangum Hall. I went out and said hello, but she didn't stay long.

June 7 (Gordon)

We had our second test yesterday. My grades were about the same as they were for the first exam. I see signs of improvement but there is still a long way to go. Last night Gary and I stayed up until 1:00 A.M. gabbing with Elder London about the church and speculating about what the future holds in store for us in Mexico. A friendship is beginning to develop with London, who is both the smartest and laziest missionary in our group. Our struggles to get him out of bed in the morning in time for class have been monumental. He never seems to study much but picks up the language faster than anyone else.

June 7 (Gary)

I was assigned to give our district priesthood meeting lesson this morning and did a botchy job. I really admire a person who can express himself well and, at the same time, make his remarks meaningful and interesting. I'm extremely impressed with the quality leadership and excellent teachers here in the Language Mission. I have seldom seen sharper men. Their level of speaking and teaching ability is something I want to set as a goal for myself to take potshots at.

Elder Walker flunked his tests again yesterday, so he needed some cheering up last night in the form of another show. We saw *The Wheeler Dealers* and *Murder at the Gallop*. Lee Remick rates ten on the Richter Scale.

Just finished writing a letter to Natalie in which I casually suggested that she and Beckie come down to Provo to watch the Fourth of July parade, and that Gordon and I would try to accidentally bump into them.

June 8 (Gordon)

Study demands and pressure to keep up have been increasing, if that's possible. I can't let myself slip and fall behind. Gary and I have been getting up before 5:00 A.M. to put in a little extra study. We figure that if we used to get up that early to deliver the *Salt Lake Tribune* when we were kids, we ought to be able to do at least the same now in order to learn Spanish.

Down in the laundry room yesterday Gary discovered that another missionary had swiped his best shirt and was ironing it for himself. When Gary confronted him, the jerk's unbelievable response was that someone had swiped *his* shirt, so he felt entitled to take this one! I had previously wondered why it was thought necessary to have keys for dressing room lockers in the Salt Lake Temple. Hard to believe there are still dishonest people like that in a place like this.

June 13 (Gordon)

Survived a pretty pressurized week. Every week seems to get tougher but apparently we're gaining a greater capacity to handle it since we seem to stay about even, with our heads barely above water. My marks in memorization are still the highest in the class but it's been a real struggle to keep up. Test again tomorrow. It's easier to feel like a student here than a missionary. We get spiritually revitalized every Sunday, though, in priesthood, sacrament meeting [the Mormons' principal Sunday worship service], and fireside gatherings. President Wilkins is top-notch. Two very good counselors also: Martinez and Bastion, both former missionaries to Central America. In contrast to the pep squad atmosphere and slogans which we were peppered with by some of the staff at the Salt Lake mission home, these men are dignified and urbane, yet completely serious about missionary work, and are inspiring teachers.

June 13 (Gary)

Even though I kind of blew the exam this morning, I was feeling good about things and at peace with myself ten minutes later. I think one of the hardest things for a missionary at this place is to retain a spiritual feeling and be aware of the ultimate reason for being here. So much emphasis is placed on learning the language that it's easy to assume the attitude of a full-time Spanish student going to school. Each missionary must be responsible for generating and maintaining his own spiritual strength and incorporate it into his studies. If I can only remember to do this, I know my work will be easier. No, yo no hablo en el Español todavía. Pero, solo hace tres semanas que estóy aquí. Yo puedo leér y esribír Español. Grande cosa. [No. I don't speak in Spanish yet. But I've only been here three weeks. I can read and write Spanish. Big deal.]

Anyway, our classes are mostly verbal exchanges and oral repetitions with the teacher more or less conducting the music. In this way we cover fifty to sixty pages in our grammar book each week. Every day we are given a one-page dialogue to memorize and present in class the next day for a grade. We also have prayers, scriptures, etc. to give in Spanish during all of our classes and meetings throughout the week. We get an hour off from class work for gym every day, and more time off from 9:00–10:00 P.M. (This last time period is actually used for district meeting and memorization work.) Tests are finished Saturday morning by 10:00 A.M. and then the rest of the day is free for washing, ironing, writing letters, studying, and general goofing-off. Sundays are pretty well shot-up with meetings, except in the afternoon, which is supposed to be used for studying the scriptures.

Elder Walker has been reassigned to the Australian Mission and is leaving tomorrow. I don't know if I'll get a new companion or not. Several other elders who weren't cutting the language got axed too, and there are more who are hanging on by their cracking fingernails, Gordon's companion, Elder Davidson, included.

I wrote a letter to Don [Gary's and Gordon's older brother] today. First one I ever have, I'm sorry to say. I let him know how we feel about him, and recognized that we haven't always been very good brothers. I hope he will want to write back. I was also glad to get a letter from Chuck today, addressed to both me and Gordon, in which he expressed his usual mixture of hot and cold feelings about his own missionary aspirations and ended by suggesting the possibility of a rendezvous in the near future. This, I think, we can manage to do.

LETTER FROM CHUCK RADLOW

Dear Gary and Gordon:

I guess the Mormonizing machine has been cheerfully grinding away all barriers of sin, niggling doubt, desires to run to some obscure, hidden corner of the universe and hide, and all other obstacles inimical to the faith, the word, and spreading of the good news. I also presume that you are learning Español and finding the memorization of a hundred different conjugations a trifle tiring and perhaps a bit provoking. I sort of picture you moving about at the sound of a bell through the world of the cloistered monastery with habit, rosary, and sullen humility combining to form the perfect monks and disciples of our Lord.

There is an entire section of the Stanford library devoted to Mormonism on the bottom level of the stacks. I spend some of my time there deepening my knowledge of the word. Two weeks ago I unfortunately picked up a book on Mormonism written with more than a definite ANTI tone. This relic of the past contained, among other interesting ridicules, an account of the temple ceremony gathered from several apostates who supposedly told all. One hour later, after reading every detail in disbelief, I left the library to run into my priesthood advisor and have quite a long discussion about the whole thing. Seriously, if that account is based in any kind of truth, I'm afraid I'm going to have to muster a great deal of faith to be able to enter the temple myself. I couldn't help feeling that it was all some kind of nonsense, unnecessary, unwarranted, offensive to the modern mind, etc. Yet I almost felt as if I was committing some morbid sin by plodding through the gory details and then feeling so repulsed by it all. I've begun to feel that it is an impossibility with any kind of intellectual honesty to swallow any beliefs whole under the sanctified word of faith. Perhaps I will only be able to piece together fragments of understanding in this life. If God wants my love and belief I surely hope he wants a belief based on conviction and knowledge which must be worked for, not secured by rattling an unconvincing testimony. I fear I'm condemned to an eternal quest of this sort and sometimes it comes pretty slowly.

Burnett [a mutual high school friend] is off on his mission for Britain in two weeks. That guy is so afraid of his own inadequacy I really feel sorry for him. I hope he can adjust to it and turn a feigned pride into a dynamic humility. Sometimes we isolate ourselves from the real world of sin and corruption in a safe subterfuge of sanctity, condemning weakness and hating evil. I fear this state of pride, of superiority. The real world is in your Mexico with hunger and fear and desperate decadence.

I have heard that Natalie Fletcher is head over heels in love with you, Gary. I suppose this devotion should sustain you for awhile anyway.

The summer is going to be sort of strange without you guys around. At times, I feel like a deserter or a coward and other times I think that it is taking a lot more courage to stay away from the missionary leap. I'm losing all faith in fate and destiny. We are the sole molders of our life and attitude. I used to blindly hope that somehow the world machine would take care of me, form me, mold me, send me out in a preordained direction with no particular problems. I now revolt against this notion, against a prescribed set of acts, and find more and more that we are the masters of our fate if we wish to be—and we must be. I feel that this is what God wants. He stands as assurance, as a coach on the sidelines, but we play the game and call the moves. President Kennedy was right: "God's work on earth must surely be our own." Humility is an elusive quality, but I shall reserve my cogitations on that subject for a later time.

Is it possible to arrange a meeting on the sly in the near future? Are there any ways of temporary escape? I'd like to talk with you again before you go. Perhaps one small sin won't send you careening to hell. It's a thought anyway. If not, I'll just keep on scribbling away.

Hope the brainwashing proceeds well.

Your bud, Chuck

June 18 (Gordon)

I made a spectacle of myself yesterday by dropping my food tray in the cafeteria—crashing silverware and broken glass, a big mess all over the floor. The whole cafeteria erupted into uncharitable schoolboy applause for my clumsiness. I went purple with embarrassment at the juvenile response of my fellow missionaries, some of whom do not seem at all ready to go into the world as representatives of the church.

Elder Davidson and I get along well enough, but we're not particularly close as companions. Davidson is doing poorly in Spanish and he's not working as hard as he could to improve, either. I should try to help him more than I do, but find myself selfishly more concerned with getting my own assignments done. Gary's willingness to sacrifice his personal study time to help his struggling companions is nothing short of saintly. Test scores for last week were consistent with previous performances; I'm still flunking dictation, although I'm doing okay to very good in everything else.

June 20 (Gordon)

Beckie came by today but I didn't get a chance to see her. She brought me some new towels and had one of the missionaries in our zone (who reported that when she approached him he thought he was having a vision and had seen an angel) deliver them to me.

The time is really passing by swiftly. It seems like Saturday (test day, laundry day, letter-writing day) rolls around before you can mumble "hasta luego." We are still being plastered to the wall with new parts of Spanish grammar every day, plus a new page of dialogue to memorize. I guess the theory is that it will all sink in sooner or later. Right now it's a rush just to get down the bare bones of Spanish grammar and vocabulary before we start memorizing the six missionary discussions two weeks from now. Sunday is the best day of the week here. We get to sleep in till 7:15 A.M., then Sunday school at 8:00 A.M. The classes are excellent (conducted in English) and are presented by returned missionaries who also teach the Spanish classes. Priesthood meeting is at 10:00 A.M. and we split up with our own district, with one of our district members being assigned to give the lesson. The afternoon is ours to study, read, etc. Then sacrament meeting at 6:00 P.M. conducted entirely in Spanish, followed by a fireside at 8:00 P.M. in English. Next week I'm supposed to give a talk in Spanish—that will be a trial I do not relish thinking about.

June 20 (Gary)

I never know what day it is except for weekends. Gordon and I have just about learned to doggy-paddle. But we won't be breaking any world records for awhile yet. I've plotted with Chuck, via the mail, to have him drive down here tomorrow morning and go to priesthood meeting with me. I don't think anyone would object in this case, but I doubt that any of the instructors will notice anyway. If someone accidentally calls on Chuck to offer a prayer or something in Spanish, he should be able to handle himself. [Chuck had taken several years of Spanish in high school.]

June 21 (Gary)

I feel good right now before going to bed because it's been a good day. Gradually, I'm catching a greater glimpse of my real role here. And, at the same time, I'm slowly learning a little Spanish to boot. Chuck made it for his visit this morning. I found him wandering around in the rain about 7:45 A.M. I guess this is a lot of the reason why it's been a good day. Chuck attended priesthood and Sunday school meetings here with me, and then we spent about three hours talking. No one much noticed him, and we had an interesting discussion about various and sundry topics before he had to leave to attend Sam Burnett's missionary farewell. Tonight at the fireside the speaker happened to be the former president of Stanford University's LDS Institute of Religion and Chuck's old ward teaching companion. In his talk he told us about his brash, intellectual young sophomore companion who had the audacity to question the plan of salvation, saying it should have been done some other way (this during a visit at the home of some wayward member). All this was highly amusing to hear. Too bad Chuck couldn't have stayed.

Arthur Shepherd, the celebrated composer [founder and first conductor of the Salt Lake City Symphony Orchestra], was a direct relative of ours. Music supposedly runs in the family. I guess it ran the other way when it came upon Gordon and me. Actually, though, I was assigned to lead the music last week for our zone meeting. A very bad scene indeed. Not only that, I also had to offer a closing prayer in Spanish, and next week Gordon and I both have talks to give (in Spanish of course). Boy, I haven't even got time to write a talk in English, let alone learn to give one in Spanish. No new companion yet. I sort of make a threesome with the other two elders in the room. But one of them is having a pretty bad time with the language and may not last. Gordon's companion might not either.

June 27 (Gary)

I still have control over every faculty but a couple of times during the last few days the thought "how nice it would be to go crazy" did cross my mind. It's been grueling but here it is Saturday again, and I can relax a minute. Every night this week I have gone to bed about 11:30 P.M. and every morning I have gotten up at 5:00 A.M. I've been trying to help one of my roommates, who's having a tough time, so my study time has been his, and I've had to do my own work whenever I can squeeze it in. My new companion's name is Elder Ernie Atkins. He's from Bountiful, Utah and a great guy. He's the friendly, cheerful type and has a sincere, simple faith. But he doesn't know how to go about studying and learning effectively. He's had a talk with President Wilkins every week, and every week President Wilkins suggests that he transfer his mission. But Elder Atkins badly wants to remain here and keeps asking for another chance. I don't think it's any use, though. He's hopelessly lost and just beating his brains out. Looks like I'm going to lose him too—a perfect score so far with companions down the tube.

At present time I'm living in a private home just off campus with the rest of my district. We just moved this morning. One hundred new missionaries arrived last week, and another batch is due tonight. There isn't room for everyone at Knight Mangum Hall, so we got the boot. This will only be for about a week, however, then our entire zone will move permanently to Helaman Hall. I blew my talk at morning devotional (in Spanish), of course, but I'll grow from it. Gordon gave his Friday and did a fair job. By the way, we weren't special or anything—everybody has to speak when their turn comes.

I have continued to suggest to Natalie that she and Beckie come to Provo on Saturday for the Fourth of July celebrations. I'm still in the dark about the Language Mission's plans for the occasion. We will have the day off, as usual, but it's possible that they might have some sort of compulsory shindig organized for the missionaries to attend. In any event, I suggested that Natalie call Mom and make arrangements to meet the folks at the parade, and I do believe that Gordon and I will be able to slip away from campus and meet all of them downtown.

June 28 (Gordon)

Our district has decided to go on another thirty-six-hour fast to try and improve our performance in learning Spanish. Frankly, I'm a little worried about my weight loss. Coming out of army basic training three months ago I was at the peak of health. Since then I've lost fifteen to twenty pounds.

Tests again. My consistently poor marks in dictation indicate that, while I've become a whiz in memorization, I still can't understand spoken Spanish for beans. Friday I gave what was supposed to be a two-to-three minute talk in Spanish at our morning devotional (it was more like forty-five seconds). Gary gave a slightly longer talk Saturday. I can write down and memorize words, but find myself at a complete loss if I'm supposed to speak spontaneously. Gary and I get some relief from the pressure-cooker atmosphere most afternoons during our gym period by shooting baskets or throwing a football around at the George Albert Smith fieldhouse. We're supposed to speak Spanish all the time but usually take advantage of our time together to have a decent conversation in English.

Elder Booth has been made supervising elder of our district. I was angered by Elder Bronson (who unbelievably has been promoted to zone leader) for first announcing that I had been called as supervisor. Then, after I expressed surprise and was congratulated by Gary, he informed us with a stupid grin that he was merely joking "to see how you would react." Am I just a poor sport or is this sort of behavior as asinine and uncalled for as I think it is? Bronson's a pain. But Booth is a good man.

Our ranks are being thinned out, as some in the district who haven't been able to hack the language training here are reassigned to English-speaking missions. Gary's first companion (Elder Walker) is long gone and his new companion, Elder Atkins, will probably follow shortly. Elder Patterson, affectionately known as Elder "Otra Vez," has been sent to Alaska. Elder Patterson got his nickname from classroom performances. Every time our teacher would ask him a question in Spanish, Patterson would glance nervously around the room and respond, "Otra vez?" (Again?), apparently the only Spanish phrase he knew.

June 29 (Gordon)

Grades for last week show significant improvements in pronunciation, grammar usage, and even dictation (finally). My marks in dialogue memorization have never faltered. At our Sunday devotional President Wilkins told us about a critical letter he received from a missionary who went through the Language Training Mission and is now in the field. The missionary complained that he had not been taught enough common vocabulary words, that when he arrived at his destination he didn't know the names of everyday household appliances, etc. President Wilkins' response was that these are things we must learn for ourselves. We have minds and curiosity. We have dictionaries. They will teach us here the rudiments of Spanish grammar and a basic vocabulary, especially as applied to the gospel of Jesus Christ. We will learn as much or as little as we ourselves are willing to work for. We will not be spoon-fed everything we need to know.

4

༔

Impossible as It Seemed:
The Language Training Mission, Level Two

Provo Utah, July 3, 1964 (Gordon)

Wednesday we started work at "second level" which means, among other things, that we will begin to memorize, in Spanish, the six missionary lessons used to teach investigators. All six lessons are supposed to be learned word-perfect by the time we leave for Mexico. We were promised an unforgettable experience by President Wilkins, which I suppose means we can expect to work harder than ever. Gary and I have made plans to celebrate the Fourth of July tomorrow by meeting with the folks at Beckie's parents' house, who live here in Provo. Most of the other missionaries will be attending a variety of holiday activities planned by the mission staff, but I doubt that our absence will be much noticed. Sunday I'm supposed to give the priesthood lesson to our district (in English, fortunately).

July 5 (Gordon)

Yesterday Gary and I met Mom and Dad downtown at the parade and then spent the afternoon with them at the Jones'. Beckie's mother tried to rattle me by posing as an investigator with a lot of pointed questions about the church, but I quickly got her to change the subject by rattling off some memorized lines in Spanish. It was great to see everybody, especially Beckie, and get a break from the grueling routine of our studies.

We are now meeting evenings in the cafeteria of Knight Mangum Hall with the *"Escuchantes"* [listeners]—native speakers of Spanish who play the role of investigators and listen to those portions of the missionary discussions that we are supposed to have memorized so far. It's a nerve-wracking but valuable learning experience for us; for the *Escuchantes* it must be sheer torture to hear us butcher the language night after night.

July 5 (Gary)

Yesterday our Fourth of July scheme came off perfectly. Gordon and I managed to detach ourselves from some rather vague, mission-sponsored holiday activities and met Natalie, Beckie, Mom, Dad, and Beckie's parents at the parade. Beckie's parents then invited us all over to their house for a backyard picnic. Seeing Natalie and the folks again almost made the last six weeks vanish as though we had never been away. I wonder if it will seem like that two years from now? Anyway, I'm happy about the way things turned out. It was another violation of the rules, but a real relaxer for Gordon and me.

Crowding in the Language Mission is increasing; another hundred *nuevos* [newcomers] pulled in tonight and none of the present troops will be leaving for awhile. The lunch line today backed up out of the cafeteria, up past the mail boxes, and down a classroom hallway. It took over half an hour to serve everyone. While we were waiting for our food, I read a *Life, Look, Post, Time,* and *Sports Illustrated* that were located on the foyer magazine shelf—had to catch up on some Gentilish-type literature. I read that they're trying to introduce transparent blouses, dresses, etc. in the U.S. And here I am going to Mexico. Rats.

It's 5:00 p.m. so I figure Lorin Larsen is sitting in a trance on the stand in his ward for his missionary farewell about this time—the end of his world draweth nigh. Even though we like them, our personal worlds are usually pretty selfish. Leland will soon find a new life in the mission field from which to grow and gain experience.

July 7 (Gary)

Very little time for writing these days. Received an upbeat letter from Chuck.

LETTER FROM CHUCK RADLOW

Dear Gary:

Summer school is in full gear but I am unfortunately not. The lectures are outstanding, the texts are well chosen, BUT I have little motivation to study for study's sake. Perhaps I'll simply audit the whole thing. Classes are abnormal psychology and inter-American (Latin American) relations. If I ever decide to head off on a quest for the Holy Grail by accepting a mission call, I figure number two here will be quite helpful.

I am constantly reimpressed with man's essential goodness, his innate striving for the better, for love, warmth, concern, and mercy. So many "hardened" men of the world have concealed within, ready to sneak out in unexpected and subtle ways, a wealth of precious, indefinable love—coming so quickly and often so shyly that we miss it. Gary, you found it long ago. It's always been the greatest of your attributes—the ability to see beyond the stone brain into a human heart. It is what made you a great friend and student body president at South High, and will make you a great missionary.

The gospel becomes more beautiful, dynamic, and inspiring to me everyday. God is there, hears, cares, loves, answers, and rejoices at our progress. I have been impressed over and over again in my summer reading (which is actually moving along quite well!) with the depth of application of Mormon philosophy and theology. I guess it sounds pretty phony, but it's quite important to me to see this life from many angles. Sometimes I wish I had two or three separate brains so I could think all I wanted to at once. Put a good word in for me with the boys at the head office and I'll do the same for you. I promise I won't be so lax with the scrawlings next time. Write soon—I'm really anxious to know how you're doing.

Your bud, Chuck

July 11 (Gary)

How come this week went so slow? It must have been last July fourth that Gordon and I met with Natalie and Beckie for the afternoon. Time is supposed to whiz during a mission. But the days have been long and hot and sticky and pounding. Well, we now know the first lesson by heart. Fifteen pages. Forty-seven to go. I don't like to think about trying to remember all six lessons in a few weeks from now. The first lesson alone takes at least forty-five minutes to present. The whole works will take over three hours. I can't imagine myself rattling off Spanish for three solid hours when, in reality, I don't know zilch about the language. But we are getting a few smarts as the days go by, and we're working hard.

It's kind of pathetic the way Gordon and I treat our companions. We just go ahead and plan things together, as we always have, and if that's convenient for our companions, fine—if not, even more fine—then we can be alone from them. Gordon thinks my new companion (and zone leader), Elder Devin Bronson, is a snook. He really isn't, but he has made a few ill-advised attempts to boss me around a bit. It's not an enviable situation, but an inevitable one. Gordon and I just happen to have been a good team all our lives.

July 11 (Gordon)

We finished memorizing the first lesson this week, fifteen pages' worth. Gary and I were the only ones in our class to get A's for memorization. The rest of our Spanish development is another story but, on the whole, I think we're doing all right. I'm not sleeping well, though—keep dreaming in muddled Spanish. I wake up around 4:00 every morning in a semiconscious state repeating phrases we've memorized from the Plan. Our district has moved across campus to take up residence in Helaman Hall, but we still attend all classes and meetings at Knight Mangum. Our rooms are much smaller than the old ones, which makes it hard to study. Early every morning I leave my companion snoring in the room and walk over to the patio outside the Cannon Cafeteria to review the discussions an hour before breakfast. Tomorrow I have to give a talk (in Spanish) in Sunday school. It's going to be sweaty; I haven't had time to work on it yet. President Wilkins will be there to listen—yikes.

July 18 (Gary)

I'm on a bus headed for the Manti Temple, which is about an hour and a half drive from Provo. I had planned to write my weekly journal entry on the way. That's why my writing looks like I've broken five or six of my fingers. It's an old, hot, sticky, bumpy baby of a bus. Anyway, I think I'm going to be sick over the peanut butter sandwiches provided in our sack lunch, so I'll try again later.

July 18 (Gordon)

Back from an all day excursion to the pioneer-constructed Manti Temple. I tried to write some letters on the way, but a rickety bus and maniac driver discouraged me. Gary attempted to do the same, but dozed off, muttering in his sleep. Had a good visit with Elder London, who enjoys speculating on theological topics. The temple ceremony seemed a little less confusing this time, although I'm still uncomfortable with it.

July 19 (Gary)

I managed to keep from becoming sick on the bus yesterday but I fell into a miserable, stuporous, head-jerking, jaw-aching, Spanish nightmare-filled, fitful doze. But the Manti Temple was beautiful, rising up on well-kept grounds in the middle of nowhere. Uncle Bob's Garden Room mural is beautiful, and it was exciting to have his art serve as a backdrop for some of our activities. [Robert L. Shepherd was Alvin Shepherd's brother and a well-known Utah artist.] The temple ceremony itself, however, still seems strange and I am not yet able to generate much genuine enthusiasm for participating in it, especially after having heard Chuck's horrified account of an old temple exposé that he discovered and read in the Stanford Library.

July 20 (Gary)

Here it is Monday morning and I have just a few seconds to scrawl a couple of more sentences before class. Elder London came by my room last night to talk over a few problems just as I had begun writing in my journal, and he stayed until after midnight. His pre-mission sexual worries make mine seem pretty squeaky clean in comparison. An intriguing discussion. Elder London is very open and very reflective.

We're experiencing a big trauma in our district, which actually has become a more or less permanent feature of our group. Seems we have one or two goof-offs; the district, as a whole, isn't doing as well as it's supposed to and an objective observer might detect the existence of some poor attitudes. London has been singled out for his lax study habits, even though it's obvious he has a gift for language. London typically begins a review session in class knowing virtually nothing of the page we're supposed to have memorized. He will read the page carefully, listen to his partner (me) recite the material, then take a stab at reciting himself, resulting in numerous errors. But *then,* on his second recitation attempt, he passes off the entire page, word-pefect, with no need of prompting. Incredible. Anyway, I don't feel like Gordon and I are contributing to the larger problem—who knows?—but we get our work done the best we can. The whole district will be undergoing companion switches today.

We are also slated to finish the second lesson today. Only four more weeks, for sure now. For some reason, Gordon and I both got word yesterday that our visas have come in. Every group out of here to Mexico so far has had to wait at least one to three extra weeks for their visas, and a lot of visas never did show up—the affected missionaries just transferred somewhere else. So— we'll be pounding on Brother Gomez's door sooner than we had counted on [Gomez was a mythical Mexican investigator referred to in the Missionary Plan]. Meanwhile, we got a letter from Lorin last week in New York. He says he's stationed in the richest county in the country, and the people aren't too interested in listening to Mormon missionaries from Utah. According to him, they've had only one baptism in that area in two years.

July 26 (Gordon)

Time is starting to get short. In just three weeks we will finish learning the sixth lesson. Monday we start work on the fourth. Up to this point we have memorized almost forty pages of the Plan. We are able to memorize faster now, and our grades seem to be picking up, so there's no reason to complain. Others are still having a hard time—Elder Mandrake, for one. The disintegration of Elder Mandrake's cocky self-esteem and holier-than-thou attitude has been remarkable. He's had to struggle with the language and, with mounting frustration, has had great difficulty in memorizing the discussions. He can't figure out what Gary's and my "trick" is for memorizing. Neither can I. Just pounding perseverance and repetition.

This weekend we've been having a mission conference—a lot of good talks on missionary work, with emphasis placed on teaching through the spirit of the Holy Ghost rather than table-pounding argument or logical, intellectual proofs. President Wilkins' remarks were especially penetrating. There are three essential ingredients, he said, that contribute to our happiness in this life: To love, to be loved, and to be actively engaged with those whom we love in a good cause. He was absolutely right. That is what I seek, what we all seek.

Last night we were diverted with a little entertainment provided by us missionaries plus a professional singing trio of former BYU students. Their part of the program was great but ours was a bomb—a crude two-minute skit that centered around Elder Hondo's belching ability.

July 26 (Gary)

I'm using some of my good study time to read an interesting book entitled *The Fate of the Persecutors of Joseph Smith*. It's easy enough to think of Joseph Smith as a martyr, dying a noble death. But sometimes it's hard to remember that Joseph Smith was a real man and easier to think of him as somebody like Uncle Sam or Santa Claus, just a symbol. But he must have suffered terror and pain, as a man now would, and when bullets ripped his body his blood freely flowed. It wasn't a pleasant way to die. We "know" all of these things, of course, but we aren't really aware. History tends to gloss over; what we come to think of as reality is not really a very good remembrance.

Both Gordon and I are satisfied with the "great companion trade." My new companion is none other than Elder Steven London. Gordon and I have both completely reversed our initial negative reaction to Steve and have already established a good friendship. Steve's from Ogden, is sharp-witted, very intelligent, and highly interesting. He's also lazy and lacks motivation. But he's honest with himself about his weak spots and has a desire to search for and know truth. I don't like to preach to people, especially when I'm living with them, so I hope I can just be a helpful example and meanwhile enjoy the personal association.

August 1 (Gordon)

I was called out of the audience of our morning devotional yesterday to give my testimony in Spanish. Ran out of memorized phrases to reiterate after twenty or thirty seconds and then stammered quite a bit. Who knows what I said? Gary and I are scheming to leave our companions and sneak off campus tonight to see an American Legion baseball game at Timp Park.

August 2 (Gary)

If I overlook the fact that I average about five hours of sleep a night since Elder London and I have been companions (due to some fascinating late-night discussions we've had), Elder London has made this place a lot more enjoyable for me. Right now he's lounging around on my bed, playing his guitar and singing blasphemous ditties.

Last night Gordon and I walked down to Timp ball park in Provo to watch the American Legion tournament for a change of pace. Brought back a flood of old memories. When we were younger Gord and I used to spend hours playing ball together in this same ball park while Mom and Dad visited with friends who live in Provo. Quickly comes the day when our lives will branch for the first time, and we're both drawing a little closer before we leave.

Every time I walk past the stream that runs through the older end of campus, I have to struggle against an impulse to take a running dive. I hope I have a decent dream tonight. I'm still being tormented by babbling incantations in Spanish.

August 2 (Gordon)

Forgot to mention that I was assigned to work with Elder Hondo several weeks ago, and that Gary and Elder London are now partners. The truth is, of course, that Gary and I have functioned pretty much as a team ever since we've been here, even though we've never been formally assigned together as companions. We've also become fast friends with London who is more than willing to indulge our appetites for good conversation. Hondo's a fun character who could not be accused of being overly pious. I wonder about his commitment to missionary work, however, especially in Mexico. He's from Los Angeles and doesn't seem to like Mexicans much—calls them spics and beaners. How to preach the gospel of Jesus Christ and build the church among people that one despises?

My progress with the language seems to have accelerated considerably. Gary and I both continue to excel in memorization of the discussions. Last week I scored 100 percent on presentation of the fourth lesson and Gary's score was 98 percent—the two highest marks in the class. We need to be aware of cockiness, however, since our ability with conversational Spanish is still a disgrace.

Beckie and Natalie drove by last Sunday and happened to see Gary and Elder London standing in front of the window of their dormitory room. We all went down and talked for about two hours instead of studying our scriptures. Actually, Gary and I had already memorized all of ours. London, as usual, had not.

Friday I traveled to Salt Lake with Elders Booth, Hondo, and Powell to get our visas. Gar should be getting his next week. While I was in Salt Lake I stopped by the house to pick up my passport; visited with Mom and talked to Dad on the phone. I've never seen the place look better. Didn't get back to the BYU campus until 7:00 P.M., just in time to present the fourth discussion to the *Escuchantes*. We also had to get our shots the other day at the BYU Student Health Center. I wasn't too keen about lowering my pants for a shot in the fanny administered by a blushing young (and pretty) student nurse. If all goes well we should be leaving for Mexico in about three weeks.

August 3 (Gordon)

Beckie was here last night. She looks better all the time—tan and healthy in contrast to the likes of us, who are pale and underweight as a result of our monklike existence. Early in our stay here Gary and I both decided to forego the noon meal in order to use the time for study. Though we no longer feel the need to do this, I've never been able to regain the lost weight. Elder Hondo seems quite taken with Beckie. Wants to write her a letter.

I think the Lord has helped us a great deal and things have been much easier for us this past month. As a result, maybe we've been slacking off a little, shaving too many corners off the mission rules.

August 7 (Gary)

Received something of a fire and brimstone letter from Chuck.

LETTER FROM CHUCK RADLOW

Dear Elder of Israel:

   Look buddy, when I'm working on humility I'll thank you to cut the flattery, which has always been my mighty downfall into the depths of carnal pride (oh save me from my glorious self!) and self-adoration. Seriously, though, the kind words in your last letter were appreciated and actually needed at the time to restore some waning faith in my self.

Sam Burnett has been off on his quest for the Holy Grail [left on his mission] for several weeks now and true to form has failed to communicate with anyone save his parents here in the Happy Valley. Several of his old flames are really hurt, but Sam's sincerity and desire to serve God sometimes blind him to the fact that loving God is senseless unless it is expressed in action through love for his creations—our brothers and sisters. Sam has always been a sort of Don Quixote—wanted to be so noble, but fighting windmills instead of realities. A mission can turn into the nonsense of a crusade or it can get to the core of the human predicament, open the self to a new awareness of the purpose of the eternal struggle and just possibly catch a ray of what real joy is. A mission can be the thing to do, a cultural phenomenon, a parent-satisfier, an escape from seemingly unfaceable problems, a misty illusion of nobility and charity, or what it was to Paul: "WHAT MUST BE DONE." "Woe unto me if I preach not the gospel." Yes and woe unto Gary Shepherd and Chuck Radlow and Elder London. Woe unto us all if we fail to stop dawdling around in life, being blown about by every fancy and whim and "wind of doctrine" that happens to whip by. Woe unto us if we don't turn feigned pride and ego defenses into a dynamic, humble partnership with God. Gad, how did I get so carried away—I'm afraid it's par for the course. Part of this was precipitated by hearing of one Elder London, who evidently has something in his cranial cavity besides scar tissue, is among the most blessed and fortunate people in the world to be on a mission, and yet has a "lousy attitude." Good attitudes are found when on one's knees. Perhaps Brother London needs to do some crying unto the Lord. It changed one Chuck Radlow's life a lonely night in March and it would probably do Elder London a world of good.

I'd like to visit you at the "Y" again before you go! When's a good time for sneaking in? Let me know and I'll make a quick appearance. I really miss you Gar. You're the best bud I have and are responsible in more ways than you know for what successes have come my way in the last few years. Probably won't see you for four or five years after you leave, so let's brave the wrath of the Almighty and your mission president and get together.

Your bud, Chuck

August 9 (Gordon)

Two weeks from today I'll be in some church in the jungles of southeast Mexico. A returned missionary told us that the temperature will be about 99 degrees and the humidity just as high. Went to town yesterday to do a little shopping. Gary and I were looking for some light plastic raincoats. London was with us and, with his usual irreverent humor, referred to our purchases as "holy ghost coats" because of their plastic transparency. Mike Mitchell and Karen Moon dropped by unexpectedly today (Sunday). I haven't talked to Mike since leaving Salt Lake in May. Chuck Radlow was also here visiting with Gary all day yesterday, following our weekly exams. It appears that we haven't had much success in complying with the rule that discourages visitors. Right or wrong, seeing Mike and Chuck was stimulating and boosted our morale.

August 9 (Gary)

I made it into Salt Lake last Monday. My visa came in right after Gordon's, so I drove five other missionaries from my district in a mission vehicle to Salt Lake to sign our papers. After we finished monkeying around town we went to the house for a few minutes and visited with Mom and Dad. Chuck came over and I talked with him for a while too. We dropped by Natalie's on the way back out to Provo, but no one was home. Salt Lake looked pretty good to me after a summer of exile.

Looks like we'll be leaving for Mexico Wednesday the nineteenth of August at approximately 8:30 A.M. I've got a hunch that Mom is trying to drum up a clamoring crowd to bid us goodbye at the airport. Maybe the early hour will be inconvenient for some of them, and maybe I anticipate too much anyway. Actually, I guess I'm hoping for a large turnout, not so much for ego boosting but because a greater number and more confusion might soften some of the tension and awkwardness that is sure to occur between Natalie and myself now that Kathy is likely to be there too. Kathy's letters to me this summer have increasingly implied a serious desire to reestablish our old relationship, and I have not particularly discouraged the possibility.

It's hard to realize that so many of my friends will be gone from my life when I return two years from now, as indeed many no doubt already are without my even being fully aware of it yet. But progress in life is growth, and many things must be painfully torn from baby hands only to be replaced in reconciliation with something better. Better, that is, if we accept change with the determination to build new dreams into reality. Well, so much for philosophy. Chuck came down again Saturday afternoon for a few hours. We had some good talks and I'm satisfied that we have a friendship that continues to gain strength. Chuck impressed Elder London mightily. He philosophized, lectured, sermonized, and played the piano for us. (By the way, Elder London is leaving with Gordon for southern Mexico and we'll all be at the airport together.)

The other day I had my glasses in my shirt pocket, leaned over, and—splat: a crack perfectly down the center of both lenses. I gave a talk this morning in Sunday school and had to hold the Book of Mormon right up to my nose so I could read a scripture. Prior to that I amused everyone when I arrived at the stand and sat down in a chair that was right on the edge of the platform, and the whole works tumbled over backwards about three feet down. President Martinez helped untangle me and asked if I was hurt. I said no, just embarrassed; he said not to be embarrassed; I said what do you mean, don't be embarrassed?! Then I jumped up on the stand and gave a great talk.

Our Spanish comprehension is growing rapidly. We followed the whole show in sacrament meeting tonight, catching the meaning of practically all of the addresses given. Naturally we're a little apprehensive with the thought of finding ourselves in Mexico in a few short days, but our desire to serve with diligence in the Lord's work is also growing.

August 16 (Gordon)

Busy weekend. I'm afraid we continued to break a fair fraction of the mission rules, particularly with respect to visitors. Mom, Dad, and sister Susan were here Saturday with travelers checks for us to take to Mexico. We had lunch and conversation at the new Wilkinson Center cafeteria. Chuck was also here again. This time he spent the night in a sleeping bag on the floor. He attended our district party in the evening and priesthood meeting the next morning. About the time Chuck was leaving, Mike Mitchell arrived, and Gar slipped over to the Wilkinson Center with Elder London to visit with Kathy Dempsey and her parents. Mike and I had a lengthy conversation in which he expressed his concerns about his forthcoming marriage to Karen Moon and anxiety about going through the temple. Can't say that I blame him. Karen's parents don't seem too keen about the match (I'm confident that will change once they get to know Mike better and find out what a good guy he really is), and the temple can be a confusing experience, especially for a recent convert to the church like Mike. I hope and pray things will work out for them. Finally, I expect Beckie and Natalie to come by any minute to top off the weekend. P.S. They did.

August 17 (Gordon)

In anticipation of our departure for Mexico in two days, a number of missionaries from several different districts assembled this morning for a short prayer meeting. Gary was asked to offer the prayer and everyone there was moved by his words of humility and strength. When we arrived at the Language Training Mission we were assured by the mission presidency that, if we applied ourselves and followed the program, we would successfully memorize all six missionary lessons in our mission language by the time we were ready to depart for the mission field. As impossible as that seemed, Gary and I took them at their word. At the end of the course we now find ourselves among a small handful of missionaries who can actually repeat all six lessons of the Plan and do it word-perfect. This has produced a genuine sense of accomplishment and has bolstered my self-confidence. But I also realize that it will take months of additional effort in Mexico before I really learn the language to the point where I can become an effective missionary.

August 18 (Gary)

It was not my intention to write regularly in this journal during our stay at the Language Training Mission. I have, in fact, only written sporadically (mostly on weekends) and so far have only accumulated a set of odd comments and observations. I expect to do better once I'm actually in Mexico—that will be tomorrow and the butterflies are mounting in droves.

It's incredible how swiftly the time here at Provo has passed. The work has been demanding and challenging. But through intense study a good foundation has been laid in Spanish. And, no doubt as important, I have found personal growth and new strength and an inkling of what lies ahead in the next two years. My thoughts of the future are mixed with reflections on the events of the last three months. Gordon plays a prominent part in the majority of images that keep swirling through my brain. We've shared both the hard work and increasingly fun times here, as in all other times of our lives. Others—old and new—are also on my mind. Elder Jerry Walker was my first companion—a pretty good guy, but he had an extremely difficult time with the language and, after a few weeks, was transferred to Australia. Next was Elder Ernie Atkins: good-natured, strong, simple faith, but he also had problems with the language and was finally sent to New Zealand. Elder Devin Bronson was my third companion, but he and I didn't have much in common. He was relatively fluent in Spanish from previous school studies and, apparently because of this, was appointed zone leader during the latter portion of the summer. I saw little other merit in his abilities and resented what I perceived to be his false piety and attempts to exercise unwarranted control over me. Luckily, our whole district soon underwent a companion change, and I was assigned to be with Elder Steven London for the remainder of our time as students of Español. Elder London has an amazing mind, great potential. We've gotten along very well. However, Steve has shown almost no motivation and extended himself very little. I'm hoping that Steve will find what he is honestly seeking for in the mission field.

Contrary to mission rules we did have visitors on occasions. Mom and Dad came several times, as did a number of friends. Chuck even stayed over one night, sleeping in our room at Helaman Hall. Chuck's last visit was just earlier this evening as I was packing. We talked of things that bound us closer in friendship and the part we have played in each other's lives. He gave me a small, philosophical book entitled *The Prophet* as a gift, and we knelt together in companionship and prayer before he left, asking the Lord to bless us both. I've also had several visits from Natalie and one from Kathy and her parents just two days ago. I know Natalie feels strongly about me at the present time, as does Kathy. There is a problem here now but perhaps not in two years. Both are exceptional. I have loved Kathy once, but I am not now in love with Natalie. Time will no doubt tell, but in the meantime the airport promises to be agony tomorrow. My thoughts lead me to this, an unpleasant enough ending, but there's nothing to do but try for a decent night's sleep and face the music tomorrow.

PART THREE

Apprenticeship

Introduction:
The LDS Mission Field Organization

In Mormon missionary parlance the term *field* not only refers to geographical areas where missions are established and missionaries actively proselytize but also "connotes the existence of boundaries or divisions that separate each mission. In the early history of the LDS Church, a mission field encompassed large geographical areas, such as the European continent" (Jensen 1988, 20). At one time, the Mexican Mission encompassed not only the entire Republic of Mexico but also Central America and portions of the southwestern United States. The LDS conversion rate accelerated worldwide after World War II, however, and "combined with the great distances that mission presidents had to travel to meet with missionaries and members, it appeared that greater progress could be possible in smaller mission fields" (Irving 1976, 22). Thus, one of the most visible structural trends in Mormon missions since World War II has been the constant subdivision of mission field administrative units, resulting in ever shorter areas of control and closer, more systematic supervision of missionaries in the field.

By the time we entered Mexico as Mormon missionaries in 1964, the LDS Church had divided the Republic into four mission field areas, with headquarters in Monterréy and Hermosillo as well as in Mexico City and Veracruz, where the two of us were sent. Since 1964, the number of Mexican missions has grown to eighteen. Mexico City alone is divided into three separate missions, and additional mission headquarters have been established in the cities of Chihuahua, Culiacan, Guadalajara, Mérida, Oaxaca, Puebla, Querétaro, Tampico, Torreón, Tijuana, and Tuxtla Gutiérrez (*Deseret News Church Almanac, 1997–1998*).

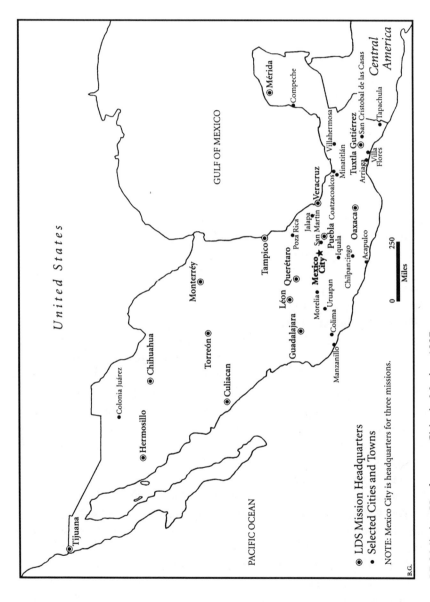

LDS Mission Headquarter Cities in Mexico, 1997

⊚ LDS Mission Headquarters
• Selected Cities and Towns

NOTE: Mexico City is headquarters for three missions.

Mormon Growth and Conversion Appeals in Mexico

In 1964 the LDS Church in Mexico had approximately forty thousand members (Irving 1976, 39). By 1996 there were approximately 735,000 Mexican Mormons, the majority of whom had been converted since the 1980s.[1] Most significantly, in 1964 there were only two LDS stakes (the ecclesiastical equivalent of a diocese) in all of Mexico: one Mexican stake organized in Mexico City in 1961 and the other organized in Colónia Juárez in northern Mexico by early Mormon settlers in 1895. Almost all congregational units in Mexico in 1964 were branches (fledgling congregations insufficiently staffed by lay members to implement the complete institutional program of the LDS Church) organized in districts under the supervision of non-Mexican mission presidents. By 1994, three decades after we entered Mexico as young missionaries, there were twenty-eight stakes in Mexico City alone (more than any other city in the world outside of Salt Lake City and Provo, Utah) and 125 stakes throughout the Republic—all staffed by Mexicans. Under the administrative jurisdiction of Mexican stakes there were, by 1994, 780 wards (the equivalent of a parish) and 603 branches.[2]

What is Mormonism's appeal in the religious economy of modern Mexico? Mexico is a large country of diversified resources and, for several generations, has struggled to modernize its industrial base to keep pace with explosive population growth and a chronically underemployed labor force (Fox 1993; Levy 1987; Marquez 1994; Riding 1985). In sharp contrast to the construction of magnificent public facilities and the accumulation of fabulous personal fortunes, widespread poverty and illiteracy continue to be major problems. With a population approaching twenty million, Mexico City has become a magnet that draws migrants from all over the Republic who are searching for jobs and opportunities. At the same time, much of the Mexican populace is strongly nationalistic (Mabry 1982). Mexico has been politically stabilized since the 1920s by consolidation of the revolution through single-party rule. The uncontested power of the Institutional Revolutionary Party (PRI) is beginning to crack, however, as a result of increasing debt, official corruption, and insurgent peasant uprisings, among other contemporary problems for which the government is held responsible (Collier and Quaratiello 1994; *The Economist,* October 28, 1995; Gentleman, ed. 1989; Middlebrook 1995).

Culturally, Mexico has been unified by the glorification of its Indian heritage and assimilation of indigenous culture in the institutions and traditions of the Catholic Church. Mexico is still overwhelmingly Catholic, but systematic government secularization of public institutions since the revolution of 1910–20 has led to a loosening of absolute Catholic domination. As Knowlton observes, "The configuration of Latin American society itself is being transformed. Religious pluralism is now the norm, although many still resist the idea" (1996, 159). Protestant sects, particularly evangelical and pentecostal groups, are beginning to spread throughout Latin America, including Mexico (Cook 1994; Dow 1993, 1997; Martin 1990; Stephen and Dow 1990; Stoll 1990). As in many other Latin American countries, personal devotion to Catholicism in Mexico now tends to be much greater for women than it is for men, many of whom only pay lip service to the religious authority of the church and refuse to abide by its rules.[3]

Mormonism has become an important part of the religious movements that now represent a major challenge to traditional Catholic hegemony. While in Mexico, we struggled to win Catholic converts and often found ourselves in direct competition with Protestant clergy and other lay evangelists in Mexico's expanding religious economy. Our mission leaders encouraged us to concentrate on converting Mexican men and not just their wives or children. This we tried to do, with some success. But often we were frustrated in our attempts and, in many cases, came to view recalcitrant adult males as the primary obstacle to our proselyting efforts.

F. LaMond Tullis, a political scientist at Brigham Young University, has written (1987) that the earliest Mormon converts in Mexico were drawn primarily from the rural poor and, subsequently, the urban lower class. More and more converts, however, now come from the emerging Mexican middle class in metropolitan centers.[4] Many are still relatively poor, but their children are encouraged to rise socially and economically. Tullis reports that the LDS Church has acquired a positive image and government support in Mexico due to the reputation of its schools and its progressive social ethic. Mormonism—with its emphasis on sober striving, performance of civic duty, and providential guidance—appears to resonate with many Mexicans' upwardly mobile social aspirations during a period of national growth, stress, and uncertainty. Perhaps most important, the Book of Mormon's ideology concerning the chosen status and divinely appointed destiny of Native Americans dovetails with Mexican nationalism and has become an exceptionally important pillar of the Mormon faith in Mexico.[5] In addition, those for whom passive member commitments fail to satisfy a longing for stronger community attachments find Mormonism to be an active religion that entrusts them with significant lay responsibilities. Extensive lay participation in the LDS Church provides a clear-cut social identity and purpose in an often impersonal and rapidly changing world; it stimulates the belief that ordinary people can contribute personally to a great cause for which they will be blessed both in this life and in the life to come.

Mormon Missions in Mexico

In the latter quarter of the nineteenth century, Mormon authorities began searching for potential areas of colonization outside the borders of the United States in order to escape legal prosecution from the antipolygamy crusade then being directed against the LDS Church by its political and religious enemies. "By 1885, The U.S. persecution of the church for polygamy resulted in many church leaders in the United States going into foreign countries to find homes for their multiple families, and some of them founded Colónia Juárez in the state of Chihuahua, Mexico. Later, colonies were founded at Díaz, Dublán, and also in Pacheco, Oaxaca, Morelos, and San José, Sonora" (Rubalcava 1992, 899–900). Although plural marriage was illegal in Mexico, the law was not enforced, and there was no interference in the marital relationships of Mormon colonists until the LDS Church itself put an end to the practice following U.S. congressional hearings in 1906 (Van Wagoner 1989, 177).

In many ways, the small network of colonies in northern Mexico formed the basis for later Mormon missionary efforts throughout the Republic during the twentieth century. Anglo Mormon colonists, many of whom became naturalized Mexican citizens, supplied Mexico with missionaries and mission leadership for several generations.[6] Thus, for example, all our mission presidents in Veracruz and Mexico City were Anglo colonists, and many of the most successful missionaries in both places were third-generation Mormon colony youths.

Revolution and counter-revolution in Mexico during the first two decades of the twentieth century severely inhibited Mormon missionary activity.[7] Several branches were established in and around the rural environs of Mexico City, but unstable political conditions made systematic proselyting difficult and retarded church growth. Furthermore, "the revolution of 1910 called into question the legal titles to land or other property given by the Díaz regime. This question became particularly complicated because of the anti-clerical provisions of the constitution of 1917 . . . [which] refused to recognize any church legally; accordingly, without such recognition, a church could not hold property in Mexico." In fact, a clause of the new constitution "confiscated all church property and made it the property of the federal government" (Johnson 1977, 78). These acts, intended to undermine the power of the Spanish-dominated clergy of the Catholic Church, made it much less easy for any religion to function freely in Mexico.

Difficulties for Mormon missionary activity mounted in 1926 when the government prohibited foreign clergy from entering Mexico to engage in any religious work. Thus, staffing and day-to-day administration of the LDS Mexican Mission was placed temporarily in the hands of a small nucleus of Mexican converts. Indirectly, however, mission affairs were regulated under the authority of an Anglo mission president residing in El Paso, Texas (and later in Los Angeles, California), who reported directly to church headquarters in Salt Lake City. This administrative hiatus contributed to the growth of a nativistic movement of Mexican converts, who eventually posed a serious challenge to the ecclesiastical authority of the LDS Church in Mexico.

In 1934 a small number of Anglo missionaries, born in the Chihuahua Mormon colonies and possessing Mexican citizenship, were sent to introduce the Mutual Improvement Association (MIA)—an LDS youth organization— to Mexican branches of the church in Mexico. As a result, in later years U.S. Mormon missionaries were able to enter Mexico as instructors of language, sports, and other cultural activities under the auspices of the MIA rather than as religious preachers or clergy. Through this legal subterfuge (apparently supported over the years by sympathetic government officials), Mormon missionary work was slowly reinstituted in Mexico. In 1936 Spanish-speaking Mormons living in the southwestern United States were partitioned into the Spanish-American Mission, and headquarters of the Mexican Mission were reestablished in Mexico City. By then, however, a growing faction of Mexican members had petitioned LDS authorities in a series of conventions to appoint a Mexican mission president—*Mexicano de sangre y raza* (Mexican by blood and race), not just birth—to preside in Mexico (Lozano 1983, 64–84).

At their third convention in 1936 the dissidents broke ranks with church leaders in Salt Lake City and declared the formation of an all-Mexican mission presidency for the governance of church affairs in the Republic. Salt Lake authorities responded to the schism with firmness and a certain amount of patience. They had no intention of allowing local leaders to circumvent the centralized governing procedures of the church, but they also wanted to minimize the institutional damage caused by the breach. Unrepentant leaders of the "Third Convention" were quickly excommunicated while simultaneously being invited to return to the good graces of the church. For more than a decade, effective missionary work in Mexico was severely hampered as World War II intervened and Mexican members were confused by conflicting claims of ecclesiastical legitimacy.

After the war, LDS authorities made a concerted effort to restore religious unity among the faithful. In 1946 a majority of Mexican *Convencionistas* were reconciled to Mormonism's hierarchical authority through the negotiation efforts of mission leaders and an important symbolic visit by church president George Albert Smith (Irving 1976, 17). The official membership and priesthood offices of many excommunicants were restored, and several small but modern chapels were slated for construction in Mexico City, Puebla, Pachuca, and Cuautla (Lozano 1983, 96). This initiated the modern LDS church building program in Mexico that has resulted in the construction of hundreds of Mormon chapels throughout the country, particularly since the 1970s. Before then, religious services had been held in private homes, storefronts, rented halls (still the norm in smaller towns during our missionary tours), and a few adobe meeting houses of local construction. Missionary work again began to expand, local church units were reinvigorated, and, presumably, an important lesson had been absorbed: It was in the church's ultimate interest to cultivate and develop local church leaders in foreign countries rather than risk nationalistic schisms in reaction to paternalistic rule from afar.

As the LDS Church reemphasized its commitment to missionary work in Mexico, the government agreed to a quota system that allowed up to 350 North American missionaries, in the guise of cultural specialists, to hold visas in Mexico at any one time. The quota system not only made Mormon missionary work possible, but it also created constant bureaucratic delays and legal challenges by local Mexican authorities and clerics who opposed Mormon proselyting. In addition, the quota remained constant although the demand for more missionaries continued to increase at a rapid rate. The apparent solution to government restrictions on missionary visas was to increase drastically the number of Mexican missionaries. That was accomplished through the development of stake organizations (beginning in 1961) staffed by Mexican leaders, seminary and institute programs for Mexican youths, and, eventually, the construction of an LDS temple (dedicated in 1983) in Mexico City, with adjacent facilities for a missionary training center. In 1992 the Mexican government adopted a new constitution that nullified many of the country's formerly anticlerical statutes. The following year— 114 years after arriving in Mexico—the LDS Church was formally registered as a legally recognized religious organization with the right to own property in the Republic of Mexico (Hart 1993b, 3). By then, church growth had been so great that Mexico was virtually self-sufficient in supplying its own missionary force.

The LDS Mission Field Organization

Following their initial preparation at an MTC, new Mormon missionaries may be compared to fresh combat replacement troops who must adapt to field conditions and continue to make learning adjustments if they are to function effectively. In the field, missionaries are exposed to certain risks and genuine challenges, as well as to disappointments and frustrations that compete with the faith-promoting experiences they have been encouraged to anticipate. The inevitable idealization of missionary service that occurs in the process of LDS religious socialization often is contradicted by the reality of various field deprivations and unanticipated difficulties and by human imperfection and recalcitrance, including the missionaries' own. Reaction to such discrepancies was a theme that quickly emerged in our correspondence and journal narratives. Most Mormon missionaries appear to succeed in making the accommodations necessary for sustaining an effective level of performance, but some become disillusioned and demoralized. The majority, however, complete their assignments; only a few ask to be sent home.[8]

Apart from having to confront actual investigators in unfamiliar and occasionally exotic places, perhaps the biggest institutional transition that novice Mormon missionaries experience is that they have greater daily autonomy in the field than in the closed world of the MTC. Even in the field, however, Mormon missionaries are restricted to their mission boundaries and are monitored in most of their activities through a network of supervisors, weekly reports, conferences, and regular interviews with mission leaders.

The Companion System

The most basic level of missionary monitoring is achieved through continuation of the companion system first encountered in the MTC.[9] In principle, Mormon missionary companions are never to part company except for officially sanctioned reasons. (In our missionary experience that was a rule, like many others, which occasionally we and other missionaries violated, usually for practical reasons.) A missionary who deviates too blatantly from proselyting norms cannot realistically expect to avoid detection—and possibly being informed on to mission leaders by a more orthodox and concerned companion. One significant departure from the MTC system is that the status and authority of companions in the mission field are not typically equal. One missionary of the pair normally is designated as senior companion and the other as junior. This disparity in status is a source of both efficiency and potential friction.

New missionaries automatically enter the field as junior companions and are placed under the tutelage of a senior or "trainer" companion. Under the direction of the senior companion, missionaries conduct daily lesson plan and scripture classes, kneel together in prayer every morning and evening, and testify to one another of their religious convictions before leaving their quarters to proselyte. Like combat veterans, senior companions are supposed to be mature, experienced missionaries who can function as role models for their neophyte partners, an aspect of the companion system that represents an essential extension of missionary socialization. It is an especially important aspect of missionary practice in a foreign land where, in addition to proselyting techniques, the workings of a new culture and language must be assimilated before one can become an effective missionary. In addition to helping junior companions make these adjustments, the senior companion is ultimately responsible for planning the pair's daily activities and making final decisions about the teaching and preparation of investigators for baptism.

Predictably, the companion system produces a wide range of interpersonal relationships. For some companions, there is immediate compatibility; for others, rapport is never fully achieved. Personality differences often emerge, and major conflicts, not to mention petty annoyances, are common (Adams and Clopton 1990). Some seniors may prove to be exceptionally good agents of missionary socialization and become patient teachers, sensitive to their juniors' learning pains. But other senior companions may be less sterling exemplars who are relatively indifferent to their companions' adjustment problems; a few may be dictatorial and insensitive, stifling rather than encouraging their juniors' development. At the same time, junior companions are not universally satisfied with their roles, particularly as time passes in their apprenticeship. At first dependent on their seniors, they may become increasingly anxious to test their wings and play a larger part in the missionary enterprise. Some come to idolize their senior companions and try to emulate their ways. Others become resentful. Many work hard at overcoming initial deficiencies and set goals for themselves, but some may show little self-initiative and become millstones to their seniors' missionary efforts. Some juniors are stoic about their subordinate status and simply bide their time until they themselves are elevated to the rank of senior companion; others may constantly gripe and complain. Companion relations, in both their positive and negative variations, are a major theme of our mission field writings.

Companion Reassignments and Transfers

Companion switches and transfers to different localities within the mission are common features of Mormon missionary life. As in military organizations, such changes are necessitated by constant turnover in the missionary force. But they also stimulate a revitalizing circulation of personnel that alleviates potential boredom, complacency, and companion conflicts. (At the same time, of course, transfers also may break up effective companion teams, create new companion strains, and renew adjustment problems.) From a developmental point of view, such changes multiply a greater diversity of experience and provide individual missionaries with new challenges. From an organizational point of view, constant circulation of personnel helps weld the mission into a small, gemeinschaft society in which most missionaries get to know each other on the basis of direct, personal relationships. Reputations are established, missionary myths and folklore are perpetuated, and powerful informal controls are developed within a network of individuals who are increasingly familiar with one another. Frequent circulation of personnel also creates incentives for advancements, fuels ambition, and forms the basis for the mission field's mobility and promotion structure.

Missionwide Publications and the Reporting System

Many LDS missions publish monthly bulletins or newsletters that contain statistical summaries of the local missionary effort, editorials written by the mission president and other missionary leaders, announcements of new procedures and teaching programs, and news of transfers, companion changes, promotions, and missionary arrivals and departures. The larger the geographical boundaries of a particular mission, the more likely that such publications will be vital sources of information to missionaries and reinforce individual commitment to mission ideals and objectives. That was definitely true for us and most of our companions in Mexico. We eagerly awaited the latest issue of our missions' monthly periodicals: *El Clarín* in Gary's mission and *El Faro* in Gordon's.

In both of our missions, field missionaries as well as mission leaders carefully scrutinized and compared statistical documentation of individual and district performances. Performance indicators such as the average number of hours worked per week or the number of investigators being taught could enhance or tarnish one's reputation as a dedicated missionary. When high-effort statistics converged with high-success statistics (i.e., number of convert baptisms per month), one's achievements were duly celebrated at mission conferences or in the pages of the mission periodical. Such recognition, even though disclaimed by some religious leaders as a valid motive for missionary performance, was, in our experience, of substantial importance in the mission reward system. We quickly learned the importance of statistical measures as a way of evaluating and motivating our performances.

Our daily activities in the field were structured by a set of specific goal expectations and quantified work quotas. These included a certain number of hours (seventy) to be spent every week in effective proselyting work, the number of visits to be made and lessons to be given to investigators, and the number of weekly study classes with one's companion, as well as time spent in personal study. Each missionary filled out weekly written reports to document the extent to which mission work goals were being met or surpassed. With every report, missionaries were to include a brief letter to the mission president, indicating the missionary's state of enthusiasm, companion relations, and the progress (or lack thereof) of his or her efforts. Any baptisms that were achieved were to be included, along with the converts' names, ages, sexes, and other personal information. Reports were passed every week from missionary companions to district supervisors and zone leaders responsible for compiling statistical summaries; then they were forwarded to the mission president and published in the mission periodical. Although quota norms may vary, standardized reporting procedures continue to be followed in LDS missions.

Mission Conferences and the Mission President

Regular gatherings with other missionaries are an important source of mission field motivation and regulation. Weekly missionary meetings typically are conducted throughout the missions of the LDS Church in which companion pairs assigned to a local district come together to instruct and encourage one another. Larger zone and missionwide conferences are also celebrated periodically with the mission president and, occasionally, with a visiting general authority from church headquarters. Not only can the larger conferences boost esprit de corps by temporarily reuniting old missionary companions, but they can also reinforce missionaries' conceptions of their work through an institutional display of authority and unity. The plausibility structure of the mission organization, and hence the plausibility of one's missionary role, is reaffirmed at missionary conferences. Speeches are given, exhortations are made, and all the missionaries assembled testify to one another of their convictions and renewed desires to serve God.

Conferences also provide occasions for mission presidents (and general authorities when present) to conduct searching personal interviews to assure the ongoing worthiness of each missionary, to detect and resolve personal problems, to admonish better efforts when necessary, and to act as an authoritative and (hopefully) compassionate counselor in whom missionaries may confide their deepest concerns. Mission presidents are now supposed to schedule personal interviews with each missionary every six weeks. During our time in Mexico, interviews were conducted much less frequently, on average, because of larger mission areas and greater administrative demands on the president to oversee the ecclesiastical affairs of local branch and district organizations.

Mission presidents are full-time volunteers (men with extensive ecclesi-astical experience in Mormon bishoprics, stake presidencies, or other respon-sible lay positions in the LDS Church) who consent to leave their homes and occupations when called upon and take their families with them to preside over missionary work in an assigned area for three-year periods.[10] The mis-sion president often assumes the status of a revered father figure in the eyes of the young missionary charges under his authority. The mission president's wife is to support him as a companion and become a role model for sister missionaries. Although the church provides housing, a car, and a monthly stipend for living expenses, a mission president's calling "is not a remuner-ative position, but interrupts professional employment; whatever financial losses accrue are part of the expected sacrifice" (Day 1992, 914). Counselors in the mission presidency are typically local church members who reside in the mission area and serve as part-time volunteers.

The Mexico and Veracruz Missions, 1964–66

In 1964 the president of the Mexican Mission (Gary's mission area, with headquarters in Mexico City) was Leroy Hatch. The following year, Hatch was released from his assignment and replaced by Jasper McClellan. The president of the Southeast Mexican Mission (Gordon's mission area, with headquarters in Veracruz) was Seville Hatch, Leroy Hatch's brother. All three men were natives of Colónia Juárez and second-generation descendants of the original Mormon colonists in northern Mexico. Although Anglo, both Hatches were Mexican citizens, which gave them a legal status that non-Mexican clergy lacked. As a young man, Leroy Hatch had served a Mexican mission in the early 1930s, just before the Third Convention rebellion, and is credited with helping introduce the MIA program in Mexico. He went on to obtain his medical degree from the University of Mexico and practiced medicine in Colónia Juárez. Seville Hatch was a successful fruit farmer who had served as a bishop, stake president's counselor, and member of the Juárez Stake's high council. McClellan left the colonies to live and work in Salt Lake City, but at the time of his mission appointment he was supervisor of the church building department in Mexico City and a member of the Mexico City Stake's high council.[11]

Administrative Structure

In regions where Mormon membership is sparse and lacking in men who have been ordained to officiate in the Melchizedek priesthood, a mission president may be designated as the ranking ecclesiastical authority over members as well as missionaries. This was typically the case in most of Mexico from the earliest days of Mormon proselyting in the Republic into the 1960s. Where local priesthood leadership was lacking, the mission president often delegated proselyting missionaries to act as branch presidents or serve in other branch or district offices. That pattern was still common at the time of our missionary service, especially in the smaller towns. But "in 1961 several policy changes went into effect that revolutionized the church program in Latin America. Church leaders felt that the missionaries were spending far too much time with administrative duties in the branches and districts and instructed mission leaders that the elders should confine their efforts to proselyting and leave local administrative positions to native members" (Irving 1976, 23). By 1994, fewer than 5 percent of local Mexican congregations were under the jurisdiction of mission organizations.[12]

As membership rates rapidly began to escalate during the 1960s, Mexicans assumed local leadership positions in increasing numbers, as did Mexican youths who accepted missionary assignments. In 1964 only fifteen Mexican missionaries (eight of whom were sisters) worked in the Veracruz Mission, and twenty-three (fourteen of whom were sisters) were assigned to the larger mission in Mexico City. Local missionaries were a distinct minority (fewer than 20 percent) of the total LDS missionary force in Mexico in 1964; by the 1990s their number had grown to at least 90 percent of those serving (Wells 1990, 6).

Each of our respective mission organizations was divided geographically into zones, and the zones were further subdivided into districts (still the basic LDS mission field organizational units). The mission president appointed a missionary to preside over each district as supervising elder (or district leader). In turn, districts were supervised by a select number of seasoned missionaries, referred to as "traveling elders" when we first arrived in the mission field but by 1965 called "zone leaders." Finally, the mission president chose at least one missionary to serve as his assistant. (Formerly, a missionary assistant to the president might occupy the position of second counselor in the mission presidency, a practice that was discontinued in our missions in 1965. Now, the mission president always designates two missionaries as companions to serve as his assistants at mission headquarters but never as members of the mission presidency.) The principal duties of district and zone leaders were to motivate and work with the missionaries under their jurisdiction and make periodic reports to the mission president on the progress and problems of missionary work in their areas.

The daily affairs of the mission were monitored and administered from a central office (mission home) situated nearby or adjacent to the living quarters of the mission president. The office was staffed by a small number of missionaries appointed by the president: a financial clerk to keep careful records of mission expenditures, allocate funds, and help manage the mission budget; a statistical secretary to process the records of new members and prepare monthly reports for the missionary department in Salt Lake City; and the mission president's personal secretary to handle all of his correspondence with church headquarters, local ecclesiastical leaders, government officials, and missionaries' parents. Now, the mission office staff also typically includes a supply manager and a vehicle coordinator.

We had only marginal contact with sister missionaries, who made up about 15 percent of the force in Gary's mission and, over time, between 12 percent and zero percent in Gordon's. After 1964, no new sister missionaries were assigned for several years to the Veracruz Mission. Sister missionaries (especially Anglos) rotated in and out of secretarial positions in the mission office, but so did male missionaries. In our experience, staff secretarial assignments were not stereotyped as women's work, and most sister missionaries spent the majority of their time proselyting in the field.[13]

Proselyting Techniques

Our chief methods for attracting investigators were through referrals from members (providing contacts with relatives, friends, or neighbors) and especially, in our Mexican experience, through tracting: going door to door, leaving pamphlets and a brief introductory message for all those willing to listen. The aim of tracting was to make return appointments in order to commence the lesson sequence outlined in the recently instituted "Uniform System for Teaching Investigators." Tracting has declined over the years because research has demonstrated the much greater effectiveness of conversion through existing social networks rather than random searching.[14] In both *The Missionary Guide* (1988) and *Mission President's Handbook* (1990) tracting was ranked only fourteenth on a list of sixteen recommended proselyting methods, most of which involved different strategies for working through member contacts. For us, however, tireless tracting was emphasized as essential to missionary labor, a way to demonstrate our faith, and a means of discharging our responsibility to testify about the restored gospel. Typically, there would be a division of labor among companions when teaching discussions to investigators, with one missionary teaching part of a lesson and his or her companion teaching the remainder. Senior companions were supposed to stay alert to their junior's presentations and be prepared to intervene if any perceived confusion or problems arose during the discussion.

The first investigator lesson in the "Uniform System" emphasized Mormons' beliefs concerning the organization of the primitive Christian Church, its eventual demise through spiritual corruption and apostasy, its latter-day restoration by Mormonism's prophet-founder Joseph Smith, and the principle of modern revelation. The second lesson featured the role of the Book of Mormon (which the LDS Church accepts as a scriptural complement to the Bible) in the restoration of the true church. The third lesson focused on the Mormons' health code requirements, summarized in the Word of Wisdom, a revelation announced by Joseph Smith. The fourth lesson introduced the LDS conception of the plan of salvation and emphasized the atoning mission of Jesus Christ. Lesson five was an elaboration of lesson four, concentrating on the purpose of earthly life and humanity's divine potential as the literal offspring of God. Finally, lesson six provided a review of topics previously discussed and included a set of requirements that new members would be expected to obey: premarital chastity, marital fidelity, observance of the Word of Wisdom, and faithful payment of a 10 percent tithe to the church. Every lesson, including the first, emphasized the need for investigators to make a commitment to be baptized by a specified date at the conclusion of their investigation of Mormonism.[15] For Mexican Catholics, this meant giving up their devotion to the Virgin Mary (adored as *La Virgen de Guadalupe*) and the saints.[16] It also meant a transference of religious allegiance from the pope in Rome to the Mormon prophet in Salt Lake City and to the lay priesthood leadership of a local LDS branch or ward. And, for many investigators, it meant sudden abstinence from drinking, smoking, and extramarital affairs.

As missionaries, we assumed that if investigators completed the lesson sequence of the "Uniform System" they would, and should, be baptized into the church, even if we had only been contacting them for a few weeks. For many, conversion occurred in a relatively short time. Naively, we were occasionally puzzled by people who demurred and refused to convert even after finishing all six lessons. In other cases we were sometimes skeptical of the depth of understanding or sincerity of commitment but would usually baptize people anyway if they professed conversion. This was justified on the grounds that they were being given an opportunity to know the truth and could be joined in further fellowship and taught by other members who were stronger in the faith.

The Conversion Process

Although Mormons believe that conversion occurs through a process of spiritual communication that requires divine inspiration and a subjective personal witness, modern Mormonism is not particularly emotional or expressive. It is, rather, a programmatic, action-oriented religion that emphasizes the rational exposition of its beliefs, the development of a systematic understanding of its doctrines by lay members, and the practical application of knowledge in religious enterprises as well as in worldly pursuits.[17] Mormon missionaries have always been urged to "teach by the spirit," particularly since the missionary department modified its emphasis on memorized lessons in 1985. At the same time, unrestrained charismatic or pentecostal preaching by missionaries is contrary to modern LDS proselyting strategies and, if practiced by individual missionaries, undoubtedly would be responded to by contemporary LDS authorities with alarm and official reproach. Although significantly more charismatic in the nineteenth century, the Mormon missionary approach has always been predicated on a belief in the need for, and efficacy of, rational argument within the framework of commonsense literalism (Hughes and Allen 1988; Underwood 1994). Thus, although it has implemented a series of teaching revisions since the 1970s, the LDS Church remains committed to a standardized conversion program through a series of doctrinal lessons. In the process of teaching these lessons, missionaries give testimonies and offer prayers that frequently convey emotional sentiments, but even they have a rational character. Testimonies reinforce points argued in the lessons, and missionary prayers typically contain supplications for spiritual enlightenment and understanding on behalf of their investigators so their ability to gain religious knowledge and make correct decisions might be increased.

Our identities and religious commitments as Mormon missionaries in Mexico were, in part, formed and reinforced in response to adversarial relations with other religions. In the process of teaching doctrinal lessons to our investigators, we anticipated and prepared for scriptural debates with religious antagonists. Such argumentative encounters, which required skill in using biblical proof texts, were a fairly common occurrence in our Mexican missionary experience, especially with Protestant competitors. Among missionary peers, knowledge of the scriptures and debating ability constituted a significant aspect of our reputations.[18]

Regrettably, our missionary journals and correspondence do not offer much insight into the process of religious conversion. For the most part, we matter-of-factly reported the progress of investigators going through the lesson sequence but said little that might help outside observers comprehend specific patterns in religious motives and aspirations or what factors were associated with investigators' susceptibility to religious conversion. In retrospect, we surmise that many were seekers predisposed to a religious conception of life but whose experiences with more familiar church institutions in

Mexico had, for a variety of reasons, left them questioning and dissatisfied. We appealed to and taught many who were socially marginal in various ways, with relatively weak commitments to established community networks, or perhaps they were simply interested in things American.[19] Some immediately appeared to find whatever they sought in religion and eagerly became active, devout participants in the lay structure of the LDS Church. Others, to our dismay, seemed more dependent on their personal relationships with us than on their commitment to the doctrines or member obligations of the Mormon religion. In many cases, newly baptized members would become inactive once the missionaries who taught them were transferred to new assignments. The LDS Church has struggled for years, with some recent success, to establish effective fellowship and leadership programs that integrate converts into active roles in local branch or ward organizations (*The Ensign*, February 1989, 27–31; *Church News,* October 21, 1995, 5).

Upon arriving in Mexico, we experienced comparable patterns of missionary adjustment in a foreign culture. Although we took pains to mask it, we initially were bewildered and homesick. We knew next to nothing about Mexico—neither its history nor its culture.[20] We occasionally got our hands on news magazines such as *Time* or *Newsweek,* and even more rarely we were able to watch news reports on Mexican television (few of our investigators or church members had televisions). Weekly letters from home and less regular correspondence with friends in the United States helped keep us in touch with the outside world, but to a surprising degree we were isolated from the daily flow of contemporary events. Our struggle to master the Spanish language was compounded at first by health problems that taxed our physical strength and reduced our effectiveness. Like most missionaries in our cohort, we suffered periodically from bouts of diarrhea (which we casually referred to as "the trots," "runs," or "Moctezuma's revenge") and associated symptoms of nausea and fever.[21] But once we adjusted to Mexican food and missionary living conditions, we maintained reasonably good health. Both of us expressed initial dismay at what appeared to be the slovenly domestic habits of many of the Anglo missionaries we encountered. We continued to lack confidence in our language abilities, however, for as long as we occupied subordinate positions as junior companions.

We both were assigned to work with a wide range of senior companions. We greatly admired and respected some, whereas others became the objects of our moral scorn because of what we perceived as a lack of serious devotion to their assignments. Our personal preoccupation with resisting demoralization was often expressed in self-reproaches concerning our lack of spirituality or incipient laziness (typically equated in our thinking). As junior companions we both defined constant study of the language and scriptures as a measure of moral commitment. For us, our studies became a way to maintain self-respect while remaining subordinate to senior companions whom occasionally we did not respect. In reality, most of our missionary companions were relatively average youths, laboring in difficult and demanding conditions, whom we were prone to judge through the moralistic prism of our religious zeal. We persistently prodded some to abide by mission standards, tract more diligently, or avoid romantic attractions to member girls, which no doubt exacerbated tension. But even in these cases we did not defy the ultimate authority of the senior companion to set the pace of our proselyting efforts.

After more than three generations of religious struggle, Mexico rapidly was becoming one of the LDS Church's premier proselyting areas. Although related to companion compatibility and mutual effort as a team, our success in attracting converts was primarily a function of location. Thus, when paired with motivated companions in Mexico City, Gary enjoyed a good deal of success. In contrast, Gordon spent much of his time during this period working in smaller towns, where people were more closely attached to their traditions and kinship groups and the Catholic Church was better able to mobilize anti-Mormon resistance campaigns. As a result, even when matched with highly motivated companions, Gordon's success at attracting converts generally was much less than that which Gary and his companions achieved in Mexico City, where many inhabitants were uprooted from traditional ways of Mexican life. Consequently, more individuals in the capitol city were open to investigating new meanings, new forms of faith, and a new system of religious authority.

We have used missionary transfers as an organizing device for arranging our material in the remaining chapters of this volume. We will follow one of our stories until the time of a transfer, switch to the other's account until a transfer or companion change occurs for him, too, and then return to the other's story in his new situation. We decided to intersperse the letters we received from one another within the context of the journal narratives as a way of summarizing portions of our experience. They were often written with a more evaluative slant than found in the journals, are sources of occasional humor, and often add information not contained in the journal accounts. Our letters served as outlets for frustration and criticism of missionary companions and also for self-criticism and mutual bolstering. Through our correspondence, we

attempted to maintain links to our civilian identities by exchanging information about the activities of boyhood friends, occasional sports and world news,
and concern about the well-being of our family and its finances (which were
often precarious). We regularly wrote about our correspondence with girlfriends, ostensibly waiting for us back home, and speculated about the prospects for marriage, higher education, and occupational careers after our missionary service. Most of all, however, our correspondence reinforced a mutual
commitment to stringent standards of dedication and achievement. It would
be difficult to overestimate how much these letters buoyed our morale as well
as helped us keep our critical faculties sharper than they might have been otherwise.

Notes

1. This figure was obtained from an article on worldwide LDS membership growth
and published in the *Church News,* March 2, 1996, 3.

2. Beyond general membership figures occasionally published in such official LDS
Church periodicals as *The Ensign* and *Church News,* statistical, country-by-country
breakdowns for particular member categories (age and gender, for example) or organizational units (stakes, wards, or branches) are difficult for non-church-sponsored
researchers to obtain. LDS officials are highly sensitive to the potential uses to which
membership data might be put when released outside of formal channels of control.
Requests for membership information must go through an official approval process
and are frequently denied. The most recent statistical data on Mexican stakes, wards,
and branches that we were able to obtain came from the 1994 "Church Directory and
Membership Statistical Reports," which are compiled annually for internal administrative use but not for public consumption. The occasional statistical generalizations we make throughout this volume about Mormon membership growth in the
towns and cities where we labored as missionaries during the 1960s are all based on
this 1994 report.

3. Women in the United States also appear to take religion more seriously than
do men. According to Gallup surveys, they are significantly more likely than their
male counterparts to report that religion is very important in their lives, belong to a
church or synagogue, and attend religious services (*The Gallup Report: Religion in
America* 1987). At the same time, Stark and Bainbridge (1985, 413–17) report that
many new religious movements appeal disproportionately to women but that the
most successful (including Mormonism) are more likely to recruit both men and
women in approximately equal numbers. In a personal communication to Lavina
Fielding Anderson in 1996, Don Lefevre, an LDS Church spokesperson, noted that
females constitute nearly 53 percent of the LDS membership. He was, however, unwilling to offer statistics on the activity rates in the church of Mormon men compared to Mormon women.

4. Knowlton reports that throughout Latin America "Mormonism is strongly concentrated in Latin America's cities. It is not a rural religion, with a few exceptions. Its efforts to move into rural areas and work with rural populations, particularly the indigenous ones of Mexico, Central America, and the Andes, have been relatively unsuccessful. In part this is because the social structure of the church, with its emphasis on residence-based congregations, is designed more for towns and cities than for rural life. Not only is Mormonism biased in favor of cities and urban skills, it arrived in Latin America at a time of unprecedented urban growth. Since World War II Latin America has shifted from predominantly rural to predominantly urban in the distribution of its population. The urban growth has been phenomenal and has meant the problems of urban planning and human need have overwhelmed the cities of the region. Mormonism and many other new religions have found fertile soil here for growth" (1996, 169–70).

5. For additional information on Mormonism in Mexico and Latin America, see Brown (1978); Grover (1977); and Tullis (1980). For an analysis of the role of the Book of Mormon in appealing to the national ethnic identity of Mormon converts in Guatemala, see Murphy (1996).

6. "LDS Leadership and the Mormon Colonies," written by E. Hugh Memmott in 1991 for Brigham Young University religion professor Bruce Van Orden, reports that eighty-five mission president assignments were given in the twentieth century to natives of the Mormon colonies in northern Mexico.

7. For accounts of Mormon life in Mexico during the revolution, see Beecher (1975); Thomas (1980); and Young (1968).

8. The LDS Church does not release missionary attrition figures. Based on our missionary experience and conversations with mission presidents, returned Mormon missionaries, LDS evaluation researchers, and missionary department officials, we conclude that the drop-out rate for Mormon missionaries in the field is remarkably low (under 5 percent). Although the standard two-year missionary term of service for Mormons is not directly comparable to traditionally longer missionary terms among Protestant missionaries, Wilson and Siewert observe that Protestant attrition in the field due to retirement "is minor compared to resignations. . . . It is generally thought that up to half of all new missionaries do not last beyond their first term. . . . The drop-out rate of missionaries whose formal education ended with college was 33.3 percent . . . for those with graduate education it was 14.7 percent" (1987, 63).

9. For an analysis of the missionary companionship as an important socializing agency for Mormon youths, see Parry (1994).

10. Before assuming their duties in the field, mission presidents and their wives attend a three-day training seminar at the Provo MTC and, once in the field, attend periodic leadership training seminars conducted by general authorities who preside in area presidencies worldwide. Mission presidents are accountable to LDS headquarters through standardized monthly reports that include mission expenditures and proselyting productivity. In turn, the missionary department sends a monthly world report to each mission president, indicating his mission's baptismal success compared to every other LDS mission in the world.

11. Biographical information on the Hatches and McClellan was obtained from *The Improvement Era,* April 1962, March 1964, and August 1965.

12. This figure was calculated from the 1994 "Church Directory and Membership Statistical Report."

13. In her study of sister missionaries, Jessie Embry concludes that until the 1960s, office responsibilities were often stereotypically given to women missionaries (1997, 113, 117) and cites oral interviews with women who served LDS missions during the 1940s and 1950s and spent most of their time on secretarial tasks in mission offices rather than proselyting in the field. Mission presidents now widely share the perception that sister missionaries often work more effectively with investigators than male missionaries (Embry 1997, 125).

14. In discussions of LDS missionary efforts in Europe and Australia, Decoo (1996) and Newton (1996) enumerate problems connected to the more traditional LDS missionary method of tracting. Based on research sponsored by the LDS missionary department, *The Ensign* published several articles in the 1970s (see, for example, the June 1974 issue) detailing the relative effectiveness of conversion through member references. Summaries of additional studies on members contacting friends or nonmember parents and relatives for missionaries have also appeared (*The Ensign,* August 1990, October 1990, June 1995). For published scholarly research on conversion through existing social networks, see Lofland and Stark (1965); Rambo (1982, 1993); and Stark and Bainbridge (1981).

15. Although the format of missionary lessons for investigators has undergone extensive revisions since the 1960s, emphasis on these same substantive topics and basic Mormon doctrines has remained constant. The lesson plan in use since 1986 also features six separate lessons, but earlier and more continued emphasis is placed on the central role of Jesus Christ in Mormon theology. Distinctive Mormon teachings, such as the apostasy and subsequent restoration of the true church of Jesus Christ through the prophetic agency of Joseph Smith, are emphasized in later lessons rather than at the outset of the lesson sequence. There is greater stress on the family as the basic unit of the church but continuing emphasis on the Book of Mormon as an inspired scriptural record and on the doctrines of baptism for the dead and eternal progression, as well as on such membership requirements as regular attendance at meetings, compliance with the Word of Wisdom, marital and premarital chastity, and payment of a 10 percent tithe.

16. Household displays of sacred objects such as crucifixes and statuary are, of course, commonplace in Catholic cultures. But in Mexico, devotion to the Virgin of Guadalupe is particularly intense, and her standardized image is ubiquitous throughout the country, even in otherwise highly secularized settings. Outside of their own temples, Mormons share a traditional Protestant aversion to concrete forms of symbolism and iconography. Resolute removal of pictures and statues of the Virgin of Guadalupe and the saints from their customary places in investigators' homes was, to us as Mormon missionaries, the most visible expression of conversion sincerity and commitment to the new religious perspective we had taught. Our naiveté concerning the depth of many Mexicans' cultural attachment to these symbols generat-

ed much mutual bemusement and frustration, as our diary accounts amply reveal. For an analysis of the Virgin's great appeal at all levels of Mexican life, see Wolfe's classic essay "The Virgin of Guadalupe: A Mexican National Symbol" (1958).

17. For an exposition of the rational, pragmatic character of Mormon theology, see McMurrin (1965).

18. Programmatic efforts have been made to soften the LDS missionary approach by emphasizing the family and spiritual benefits of Mormonism rather than scriptural argumentation. But church authorities and mission leaders still expect missionaries to have a thorough knowledge of the scriptures. Although our course of religious study in the field was primarily self-motivated, current missionaries are directed to spend time daily strengthening their knowledge of LDS doctrine through a formal course of scriptural study outlined in *The Missionary Guide.*

19. For sources summarizing research on the role that different types of marginality (often characteristic of immigrants, migrants, single people, the young, and those with modest or uncertain occupations) play in susceptibility to religious conversion, see Bromley and Shupe (1979); Rambo (1993); and Snow, Zurcher, and Ekland-Olson (1980). Both the recruiting benefits and liabilities of Mormon missionaries' connection with American culture are reviewed by Mauss (1996).

20. Some attempts were made at the LTM to provide us with instruction on Mexican culture, and, subsequently, cultural manuals for different countries have been prepared for student missionaries at the Provo MTC, but the limited training period—which emphasizes accelerated language learning, doctrinal study, and the acquisition of missionary skills—leaves little time to learn much about the customs and history of the country to which one has been assigned.

21. Much like their counterparts in Protestant mission agencies, Mormon officials for years took a fatalistic attitude toward missionaries' health in foreign environments. Following studies done in the early 1980s that documented the extent to which Mormon missionaries suffered from gastrointestinal diseases in developing nations (Briem 1984), the LDS Church has taken steps to develop a missionary health-care program. The program is overseen by a medical advisory committee that consists of credentialed physicians and health-care specialists. Missionaries are now introduced to a health maintenance program at the MTC and receive gamma globulin shots on a regular basis in all developing countries. As a result, the incidence of hepatitis among Mormon missionaries (a common occurrence when we were in Mexico) has been virtually eliminated. In addition, health-care specialists (doctors and nurses) are being called to serve missions in areas where local facilities are often lacking. These specialists are not licensed to practice medicine in foreign countries, but they can supervise the health care of missionaries and consult with local medical providers. The medical advisory committee's goal is to have a health-care specialist assigned to Mormon missions in every developing nation.

5

∿

"Like a Strange Little Kid":
Gary's Story as Junior Companion in Nueva Santa María

Gary's first assignment in Mexico City illustrates the abrupt transition and corresponding adjustment problems that novice Mormon missionaries experience as they move from their training phase to actual fieldwork in a foreign environment. Divorced from previous social networks of family and friends that sustain one's sense of self in civilian life, novice missionaries immediately become dependent on the senior companions to whom they are assigned for guidance. Gary's first senior companion, whose language and missionary skills were highly impressive, was lost as a tutor after only a week when he fell ill with hepatitis. Shortly thereafter, Gary himself experienced more mundane health problems (nausea and diarrhea) that complicated his struggle to adjust to a demanding new way of life. Health, diet, and physical fitness emerged immediately as major adjustment concerns. Gary's subsequent senior companion proved to be an effective proselytor, but a period of mutual accommodation was required in order for them to work together harmoniously. (Another missionary pair who shared the apartment with Gary and his companion were simultaneously a source of additional camaraderie and exasperation, the latter because of their sloppy domestic habits.) Undoubtedly the single biggest adjustment problem was becoming proficient in conversational Spanish, a struggle that produced substantial frustration and feelings of inadequacy and self-doubt. In spite of these and other initial problems, Gary and his companion worked hard and began to realize considerable success in their proselyting efforts.

In the meantime, Gordon was assigned to San Martín, a small market town in the Southeast Mexican Mission, where he went through a similar pattern of early adjustment: moral indignation in response to the perceived spiritual laxity of some veteran missionaries, health problems, companion switches, and especially his struggle to gain greater language competence. All of Gordon's three senior companions during this brief period were skilled missionaries (two were Mexicans) whose examples of dedication were to stand Gordon in good stead in the months ahead. A striking contrast to Gary's situation was the fact that San Martín had been newly opened to LDS proselyting. Missionaries there had to help nurture a fledgling branch of the church, a responsibility that occupied a good deal of their time.

∾

Mexico City, August 20, 1964

The send-off scene at the Salt Lake Airport was harried and frustrating. Our missionary cavalcade from Provo didn't arrive with all that much time to spare. Most of the missionaries in our group had their own circle of family and friends on hand to say goodbye in a general hubbub of confusion. Hurried hugs for Mom, Dad, and Susan. It then seemed like Kathy and Natalie appeared out of the throng simultaneously. Natalie was visibly stricken by Kathy's near presence. I gave Kathy a quick squeeze and she pressed a dollar bill into my hand for luck. We walked briefly together down the concourse, then I mumbled that I needed to see Natalie, who was walking on ahead. I caught up with her, put my arm through hers, and chatted mindlessly as we completed trekking to the departure gate. Goodbye with a modest kiss and not much further said. I wish Natalie's tears were only for farewell, but I fear they were more for a sudden sense of betrayal.

Our flight took us first to Los Angeles, then we jetted directly into Mexico City, arriving there at about 4:30 P.M. With a large, painful lump in my throat, and fighting off sudden, surprising chills in my heart and welling tears, I shook hands goodbye with Gordon for the first time in our lives. It's not likely that we'll see each other again during this mission. And yet, though separated, I know we will go about our work as missionaries and not be hindered by our mutual loss.

Gordon's group (Steve London and Brent Booth) remained at the airport for a plane to Veracruz. My group (Patrick Powell, Devin Bronson, and Steven Hondo) was met on the other side of customs by two missionaries from the Mexico City mission home, who loaded us into a Volkswagen van. Practically my first view of Mexico on leaving the airport was of two little boys pissing at each other on a traffic island in the middle of the boulevard.

After spending a welcome night's rest in the beautifully modern mission home, the other new missionaries and I sat at breakfast with President Hatch, various mission officials, and Apostle Marion G. Romney and his wife (who were coincidentally visiting). Brother Romney flashed a humor that kept the table smiling. After short interviews with President Hatch and Brother Romney, I was delivered to the District of Madero, in the Colónia Nueva Santa María, here in the City. My first senior companion is Elder Gary Pullins, who is also supervising elder. First impression: Pullins is intense, takes the initiative, self-confident, possesses seemingly perfect Spanish, movie star handsome, and is evidently a baseball player of some renown. [He would become head baseball coach at Brigham Young University.] There are two other missionaries who share the apartment with us: Elders Ron Crompton (short, mild-mannered, only a few months left of his mission) and Dennis Colvin (tall, skinny, and good-natured; Colvin was just a month and a half ahead of our cohort at the LTM). I must say that I'm a bit taken back with the horrendous mess all over the place in our apartment. But whatever, I think I've got a good man as a companion, and I'll do my best to get along and measure up.

August 21

This afternoon Elder Pullins and I made visits with some of his investigators who are scheduled to be baptized soon. The homes, at first impression, are quite shabby and run down, but you quickly forget to notice. I offered a prayer in Spanish at one home but otherwise didn't take much part in the discussions. My companion seems to have nearly perfect command of the language and delivers his message smoothly and effectively. My own ability with Spanish is painfully poor at the moment. I know I will have to work with more concentration than I ever have. Hope I will prove strong enough to do what needs to be done.

August 22

Elder Pullins has been somewhat sick since I arrived here. We spent most of the morning riding a bus to see a doctor in some distant part of the city. This afternoon we again visited with my companion's investigators who are ready for baptism. So far I've genuinely enjoyed the people. The little kids seem to be especially attracted to me (maybe my lack of speaking ability makes me seem more childish and sympathetic). Of the investigators we visited, five were in fact baptized this evening. They were all females, ranging from about ten to twenty years of age. I baptized all five in a little font situated in the courtyard of the local chapel and confirmed one of them in English. This is the first time I have ever officially exercised my priesthood in conducting an ordinance.

We do all of our traveling by bus or cab. Elder Pullins put me in charge of getting two neighboring families to the chapel tonight, while he took care of another family. I was barely able to communicate and had no idea where the chapel was, but we took a cab and managed to arrive in time for the services. It looks like we'll be eating most of our meals in restaurants or street cafes. It's relatively cheap and more efficient than having to shop, prepare meals, etc. I'm not especially crazy about the food yet but I don't feel like I'm starving. Wonder why? I haven't really eaten much since I've been here.

August 23

Not much action today—just short stops with previous investigators to encourage their attendance at meetings, etc. I still don't have much confidence in my ability to speak, but I'm understanding more each day. Elder Pullins insists on the two of us speaking Spanish together most of the time, which is no doubt the proper thing to do, but I feel like a strange little kid around him and don't really understand what we're doing half of the time. I'll have to start talking more. I have a genuine desire to work, but it's frustrating not being able to communicate freely. I greatly look forward to the time when I will have conquered the language barrier. I also get the feeling that I've lost some weight—the food and I still don't agree too well. I realize the many problems that beset me now are to be expected and highlight the adjustment that I must make. Tomorrow we begin our first real tracting. Naturally I'm a little nervous but also looking forward to it.

August 24

We did do some tracting this morning, although I was a mere ornament. Elder Pullins did all of the talking, taking a few minutes at each door to explain who we were and then attempting to arrange for our return at a later time to present our investigator lessons. We made several good contacts for future visits. Elder Pullins remains sick, however. We traveled a goodly distance outside of our area to see the doctor (who is evidently a church member) again this afternoon, and he gave my companion some pills.

August 25

Elder Pullins felt increasingly sick this afternoon and we stayed in the apartment. I studied and wrote a few letters while he tried to sleep. In the evening I had to visit our families alone and explain that my companion was sick and that we wouldn't be able to visit them as scheduled. My Spanish was bad but they understood what I was trying to tell them.

August 26

Elder Pullins saw President Hatch, who is a doctor, this morning. Looks like he has hepatitis and so is going to stay awhile at the mission home to recuperate. Meanwhile, I teamed up with Elder Colvin—one of our apartment mates—for some afternoon tracting. He's been in the field for about a month and a half, so his Spanish is better than mine, but he's far from being fluent. We did manage to get into some homes and made several appointments for return visits. This evening we even presented the first lesson to a younger couple who seemed quite interested. I started out and did fairly well for about four pages' worth of the lesson plan but then hit a mental block and lost my place. Elder Colvin took over but didn't finish the lesson because he allowed himself to get sidetracked with other questions and it became quite late. The couple remained interested—or maybe amused—and we set a date for another visit.

Got a letter from Gord. Wonderful to hear from him. I miss Gord more than I know. His introduction to the Southeast Mexican Mission was a little bumpy, and apparently he's as frustrated as I with the language barrier, but he still sounded cheerful and optimistic. I know I have a long way to travel before I reach the spiritual level I must obtain in this mission. But with growth in language, growth will come in other things too.

LETTER FROM GORDON

Gar: If you're still in Mexico City, we're less than a hundred miles apart. I've been assigned to work in a town called San Martín, which is located on the other side of Popocatépetl, the famous volcano mountain south of the capital. I'll try to give you a quick summary of what's happened to me since we parted company at the Mexico City Airport. Once in the air again I kept looking out the window at the darkness and lights from cities and towns below, wondering what these places held in store for us in the months to come. Upon stepping off the plane in Veracruz we were greeted by a stifling blast of tropical air and the blaring sounds of a marimba band. For a crazy moment I thought the band was in celebration of our arrival, but it turned out that there was some celebrity on the plane. In reality, *nobody* was there to greet us. London, Booth, and I were all disconcerted but nobody said much as we retrieved our luggage. We stood around for about twenty minutes before a sloppily dressed missionary, who said he was the mission secretary, finally showed up. No explanation for his lateness. It was well after midnight when we were dropped off at the missionaries' place in Veracruz, where we were given a mattress to sleep on the floor. The house was a mess and London was disgusted by the shabby conditions. I'm afraid he didn't endear himself to many of the missionaries here (three pairs plus mission office staff) by going into the bathroom with a bucket and brush to scrub the mold off the walls. (Veracruz is a giant greenhouse—I've never experienced such suffocating humidity.) Burned up by what he called "the pestilence" of the missionaries' living conditions, London wanted me to join him in making our feeling known. But I didn't see the wisdom in that. The Veracruz missionaries had just fired their maid (who was supposed to cook and clean for them) and have not yet found a replacement. They were out of food and had nothing to offer us but a couple of smelly hard-boiled eggs and black beans, which looked like they had been fermenting in the bottom of a dirty kettle for longer than I want to know about.

I have to admit that my first impression of the Southeast Mexican Mission was a little under expectations. President Hatch was out of town presiding at a mission conference somewhere, so I don't know when I'll meet him. Some of the mission office staff seemed to lack spirituality and ambition. For example, Elder Stevenson, who picked us up at the airport, is apparently a goof-off who is spending the last days of his mission in the office to curtail the damage he might otherwise do in the field. He practically says so himself. So, my introduction to the mission field was a little surprising, but I'm determined to make the best of things. I know we've got a lot to learn before we start passing judgment.

Two days after landing in Mexico I was assigned to San Martín Texmelucan, a town of about ten thousand people. I traveled by bus to get here from Veracruz. I was nervous, to say the least, but I did manage to get off at San Martín, rather than at some other stop along the road. I had the missionaries' address in San Martín but not the foggiest idea how to find it. I felt like a man from Mars, wandering around San Martín for over an hour—in and out of the market place area (crowded, noisy, smelly, chaotic) and past several big (and grotesque looking) Catholic cathedrals. Some of the natives stared, most ignored me, and I talked to nobody. I was making my second trip across the central plaza when I bumped into my new senior companion and his junior as they were emerging from a little store. They were as surprised to see me as I was glad to see them. Apparently they never got the telegram telling them I was coming. In any event, my new companion looks like a good one. His name is Bill Martineau. He's from the Mormon colonies in northern Mexico and has known President

Hatch all his life. Martineau didn't have to attend the Language Training Mission because he learned Spanish as a second language growing up in the colonies. He's a hard worker, a good teacher, and the members of the branch here have a lot of respect for him.

San Martín has a relatively new and struggling branch of the church with less than fifty members. In fact the town was just opened to missionary work this year. Elder Martineau is only the second missionary to take charge here as senior companion and branch president. He baptized several large convert families just before I arrived, but those may have been nuggets of gold in an otherwise barren field. According to Martineau, we're really going to have to dig hard to uncover any new prospective investigators. This part of the country is especially known for its strict Catholic observance and intolerance of other religions. Here in San Martín the Catholic Church began waging a propaganda campaign against *"los predicadores Mormones"* [the Mormon preachers] as soon as the missionaries started tracting six months ago. Little signs have been posted on doors and in public places all over town with the following message: "En esta casa somos CATOLICOS y no acceptamos la visita de los PREDICADORES MORMONES. Evítemos la pena de despedirles si nos visitan. Grácias." [In this house we are Catholics and we do not accept visits from Mormon preachers. Spare us the trouble of dismissing you if you should try to visit. Thank you.]

Gar, I don't know about you, but for me it's been like starting from scratch with the language. I can barely understand a word of native Spanish (so fast, so difficult to follow), and of course I walk around with my beak buttoned all day. It's one thing to have all the lessons memorized and quite another to communicate spontaneously with people. I've got to come out of my shell. I ended up trying to present the Joseph Smith story at the second house (a pathetic shack) that we visited my first day tracting. Butchery. I suspect Elder Martineau underestimates my mental ability but I wouldn't blame him if he did. I'm supposed to speak a couple of words at sacrament service tonight, so naturally I'm going to let this suffice for now and get on with the preparation of my talk. If you haven't already written, do so.

Your brother, Gord

August 27

It looks like Elder Pullins is going to stay at the mission home for several weeks, but no one seems to know yet what they're going to do with me. This afternoon Elder Colvin and I went out tracting for awhile with his regular companion, Elder Crompton. Later, Elder Crompton accompanied me to one of our investigator families—the Brillones, who are supposed to be baptized Saturday—to present a slide show ("What Is a Mormon?"). This presentation is an impressive and powerful missionary tool. Also, a letter came from home today. Sounds like everything is all right. I worry about Dad's work and the family finances. I pray things will work out so that Gordon and I won't be a bigger hardship than can be borne.

August 28

Spent the morning cleaning up the mess in the apartment, then studied and read while Elders Crompton and Colvin went out tracting. Elder McKechnie, second counselor to the president, came by in the afternoon and we tracted together for a few hours. Didn't meet much success. Elder McKechnie is a tall, rawboned, rural-looking sort of guy, soft-spoken and low-keyed. I like him a lot. After returning to the apartment I went right back out again with Elder Crompton. We presented two first lessons and then a sixth. I did poorly through nervousness and lack of self-assurance. Once again I realize how much I lack in my calling right now. I must become more humble, more serious about the responsibility I have taken upon myself, more sincere in my desire to accomplish the spreading of the gospel, while being less concerned with my personal interests. I know I need the spirit of truth, and I seem to lack it now.

Apparently I'll be getting a new companion next Monday. Elder Pullins might be in the mission home recovering from hepatitis for several more weeks. I didn't get very close to him in the few days we were together, but I respect his worth as an effective missionary. Meanwhile, we have baptisms scheduled for tomorrow: one family of three (the Brillones) for sure, possibly more. I'm not quite sure what needs to be done, but I'll be getting competent help from the mission office staff.

August 29

I visited our families in the morning to be sure they were ready for baptism in the afternoon. They all said they were not and wanted to wait longer. However, Elder Pullins slipped out of the mission home for a few hours, and he and Elder McKechnie visited the families again. In the end, six of our investigators were convinced that they were ready for baptism as scheduled. We held services in the evening at the chapel and I baptized all six, including brother and sister Ulloa, their daughter, and sister Brillones and her son and daughter. Afterward, I came home alone, bought some cookies and a soda pop at a corner store, did a little reading and then, being nothing but tired, flopped into bed and immediately fell into a deep sleep.

August 30

This morning was stake conference. We (Crompton, Colvin, and myself) rounded up all of our investigators and took them in cabs to the chapel. From there we had arranged for a bus from the Mormon school at El Arbolío to transport us all to the new stake center [dedicated in 1961 as the first native stake in Mexico] which is in the middle of the City. Carl Buener of the Church Building Committee and Apostle Boyd K. Packer of the Council of the Twelve Apostles were the visiting authorities. Approximately two thousand people attended both sessions. In the morning brother Packer read a speech in Spanish that he had prepared for him. I didn't feel it went over too well; certainly most of the spirit of his address was lost. However, in the afternoon he spoke by an interpreter and his remarks were most impressive to everyone. The dedicatory prayer he offered for the stake center was inspired and everyone present was deeply touched.

I met my new companion, Elder Kenneth Wilkes, at the conference, and he moved into the apartment this evening: short, fifties'-style brush-top with side-wings, and energetic. He seems like a pretty good guy, not quite as assured or as smooth as Elder Pullins, but he's supposed to be a hard worker and I think we'll get along fine. Although we still have a few families left from Elder Pullins' regime, we'll pretty well be starting from scratch tomorrow.

August 31

This afternoon we visited all of our old families and after that we began tracting. Didn't meet too much success. I started to feel sick after awhile—chills, fever, headache. We kept at it until 8:30 P.M. and by this time I was really feeling lousy. When we got back to the apartment I had the "runs" and was in and out of the bathroom every few minutes all night, with vomiting included. According to Elder Crompton this is the normal reaction experienced by most missionaries to the changes of food, etc. after about two weeks in the mission—it usually lasts a day or so. Hope so. I'm feeling disanimated [mission slang for feeling discouraged or lacking in spirit], to say the least.

September 1

Just as rotten this morning. Don't know how many times I was up during the night. Had a little study class with Elder Wilkes this morning, but then went back to bed. Later today Elder Crompton brought me some ginger ale and soda crackers to settle my stomach. I feel much better now. Still a little weak and still have the runs, but the sick feeling is practically gone.

September 2

Had a good night's rest and woke up this morning hungry, but feeling fine and ready to go. Still have the runs but I expect to be over that in a few days. Bought a section of cantaloupe and a glass of juice at a fruit stand for break-fast—good, but not very filling. Elder Wilkes and I then made some return visits from previous tracting finds. I gave half of the first lesson in one home. My pronunciation is lousy and I'm going to have to start concentrating on it more. Returned to the apartment about 1:30 P.M. and joined the other two elders in making tacos. They tasted pretty good, and by now I was starving—gobbled down ten to fifteen of them. We went out to give another first lesson in the afternoon to three teenagers. They seemed more amused about the whole thing than genuinely interested. My Spanish remained crummy. Easy to get along with Elder Wilkes so far. He's an effective missionary, and I think we'll make a good team if I can ever learn to talk right.

September 3

A totally miserable day. I felt a little sick again this morning and the diarrhea started to get worse. Went out to work with Elder Colvin this morning be-cause Crompton and Wilkes were at the mission home attending a supervis-ing elders' meeting. Afterward, I again felt practically on the verge of starv-ing to death, so we bought a couple of cans of chicken noodle soup and some crackers for lunch. Tasted great but didn't go very far. I'm starting to become somewhat concerned about nourishment. When not feeling sick I've almost always been hungry. We don't eat regularly—we skip meals, eat snacks, and the things we do eat are not going to keep me in good health very long. I still don't care much for the native food, but we've got to get organized and start eating better.

Letters today from Chuck and Kathy. It was a real pleasure to hear from both of them—Chuck reasserting his friendship and Kathy determined to be patient for two years. The unfolding of this story—Kathy and Natalie—will be most interesting.

LETTER FROM CHUCK RADLOW

Dear Gary,

I have never felt so close to my Father in Heaven as I did the night be-fore you left for Mexico and we knelt down to pray together. I don't know if you felt the same way I did, but I'll never forget it. You're right, our friendship was certainly strengthened that night, and I'm glad I enraged my parents by making that final trip to the Language Training Mission. I can tell from the tone of your letter that you have the right missionary spirit. I envy you more and more every day. Natalie had some interesting comments on the scene at the airport. I'll bet that was quite a trying experience for all of you. I'm certainly glad I wasn't there to see you squirm.

I know how very busy and anxiously engaged in a good cause you are, Gary, but please find the time to at least drop me a card every once in a while. As Alyosha Karamazov said, the remembrance of the good times of childhood are often enough to keep us on the right path in the years that follow. I want you to know that you are my example in innumerable ways and that I too don't want to lose track of you. You're doing the Lord's work and there is nothing greater or more important than that. I don't want you to rest until I'm on a mission myself, and I know there are going to be times when I need prodding. So even if it is only a post card, keep in touch with your old buddy Chuck. I've learned to love you like my own brother, Gary. And just as you feel part of you is gone with your separation from Gordon, I want you to know that I have felt your loss too. I pray for you always.

Tú hermano [your brother], Chuck

September 4

Put in a long day tracting but didn't make much apparent headway. I still have the runs and it really hampers my effectiveness and enthusiasm. We ate a little better today but still not well enough.

September 5

Tracted all morning without much success. My spirit and enthusiasm are still not where I want them. I feel run-down and weak. Still have the runs. Hope my physical problems will clear up soon. I need to be happy and energetic to do this work right. My Spanish isn't improving much either and I'm starting to slip into daydreaming. I do have the desire to perform this work with all my heart, and I only hope that I'll have the grit to overcome small problems and get on with it.

September 6

Fast and testimony meeting at church this morning. Took some of our investigators. Listening closely to the services is a good way to improve my Spanish, but I could barely keep my eyes open. I've been tired and drowsy all day. Hope I can start off tomorrow with a little more energy. At least my plumbing seems to be plugging up a little now.

September 11

This past week has seen busy days. We don't get in until late each night and I haven't had time to do much writing. We continue to concentrate our tracting in the huge Unidad Nonoalco, a complex of apartments constructed by the government, and we have high hopes for several families we've found there. We're going to visit a Protestant family of twelve members tonight—the Setinas—and they have thus far seemed quite interested to hear our message. They accepted the first lesson very well, and I think we're going to baptize them. Tomorrow we are going to baptize a mother, her daughter, and the daughter's little boy. A good feeling came over me the other day when we were giving them the fourth lesson, and I was able to do a much better job than usual. I know this is the spirit I must have to overcome my own selfish wants and really get involved. Also tomorrow we're baptizing part of the Miranda family—the mother and her young son and daughter. The mother has been ready since I've been here, just afraid to take the final step until now.

September 12

We baptized five people today: Hermana Miranda, her son and daughter, and also Hermana Robledo and her oldest daughter. We're expecting another baptism tomorrow and by the end of the month we hope to total between fifteen and twenty. So we're baptizing people, yes. But I don't feel as though I've had all that much to do with it yet. It's more like Mexico City is ripe and ready, and I just happen to be here. I admit I've still been homesick, and my mind wanders back to carefree days too often. I know deep down I have the grit to get the job done; I just hope I haven't become too lazy and spoiled to try. Tonight there was a fiesta at the ward and we brought our favorite family as guests—the Setinas. They are maintaining an intense level of interest and we have high hopes for them. We've only given them two lessons, and yet it seems as though we've all been good friends for a long time.

Received another letter from Gord today. Some sort of foul-up. He just received my second letter a few days ago and never did get my first. He's been having the same problems as I: sick with the food, trouble with the language, a hard time really getting down to brass tacks, etc. I know he'll pull through—it's me I worry about.

LETTER FROM GORDON

Gar: Just got your letter dated September 13 today, but I never received any earlier ones. I hope the unreliability of the Mexican mail doesn't plague us throughout our missions. [Mail service was to become, in fact, a persistent object of complaint.] Anyway, it was more than good to finally hear from you. I've been getting steadily dejected as all hell. Until yesterday I hadn't heard from a soul, with the exception of one letter from home. Also, I wouldn't be surprised if I'm down to my old twelve-year-old fighting weight of about ninety-five pounds. So far I've enjoyed various minor afflictions, including a good case of the trots, a heavy chest cold, laryngitis, a migraine earache, occasional dizziness, and daily nausea. I put in one good day puking every time I drank so much as a glass of water. I'm coming out of it though. Today I got hold of a decent loaf of bread and ate the whole thing. I feel a lot better. Also, I finally got some mail from everybody, including you, Mom and Dad, Beckie, and Mike Mitchell (a wedding announcement). So, in short, I really am feeling much better.

My first companion, Bill Martineau, was promoted to supervising elder and transferred to Oaxaca. My new companion is a native Mexican (José Louís Lara) with two weeks left in his mission to complete. He doesn't speak any more English than I speak Spanish. It's hard to say whether this will help me or not. It's a struggle to communicate effectively right now. I wish there was less of a language barrier between us so I could learn more from him without feeling so helpless. In the long run I should benefit. Elder Lara's a vigorous specimen, no doubt about that. We're out of the house by 7:30 or 8:00 in the morning to visit and encourage new members by teaching them supplemental lessons and some of the standard church hymns. (He coaches them on lyrics and I'm supposed to make sure the melody is right. Ha!) We return to the house around 9:00 for breakfast (I still haven't adjusted to the food yet and have almost no appetite), then it's back out to tract and do missionary work the rest of the day, often till late at night with only a brief break for a bite to eat in the afternoon and a snack at night. Our method for having *clases de compañero* [companion study classes] is for me to recite scriptures and portions of The Plan while we're out speed-marching down the street to tract or to make a visit. I'm feeling pretty beat. My health has improved somewhat this past week but I still feel nauseated most of the time. Still I have to admire Elder Lara's dedication and determination to maximize our efforts, especially with the new members who depend on our help. Every morning from the shower I'm treated to a lusty rendition of Mexico's national poem, or whatever it is, especially the line "México! México! Creo en tí!" [Mexico! Mexico! I believe in thee!], which Elder Lara shouts at the top of his lungs. I assume Elder Lara will quickly become a leader in the church when his mission ends and he returns home to Mexico City.

Gar, this is really going to be a test for us, especially these first few months while we're struggling with the language. Our mettle is going to get a scraping right down to the core and we'll get a chance to see what we're made of. If we let them, these could be two miserable years. I don't know how you've been doing but I'm ashamed of my own puny efforts to progress and of my longings for things that I've agreed to sacrifice for the Lord's work. I know a lot of this is natural, all part of the adjustment process and so on, but it's still a question of what we're really made of at the bone. I'm anxious to find out.

The Lord bless you. Write every chance you get, Gord

September 16

We've been getting home so late every night that I've just flopped into bed without writing. The Setina family came to both services last Sunday and seemed to enjoy them. That same night we dropped by their apartment and they invited us to have tamales and hot chocolate with them. When we finally left they came with us to show us a faster way home. We had a crucial third lesson with them on Monday night. We were concerned about Hermano Setina's possible reaction, because he smokes quite a bit, but he didn't bat an eye when we explained the Word of Wisdom—just turned over all his cigarettes to us. After the lesson we enjoyed a good dinner with them and basked in their remarkable friendliness. I now feel sure they're going to be baptized.

Today is Mexico's Independence Day, and all of the missionaries are taking the day off, since few people are likely to be at home. This morning we arose early and joined another dozen or so missionaries in playing basketball at a nearby gym. Never played worse in my life. This afternoon we're going to a bullfight, followed by a movie in the evening. Elder Wilkes has been rubbing me a little the wrong way the last few days, and no doubt he has similar feelings about me. Hope I can be grown up enough to get along and overlook petty differences.

September 19

The bullfights on Independence Day depressed me. The great "El Cordobéz" was the featured matador, and I could appreciate his skill and courage, but the ritual killing and howling crowd did not appeal. But the movie in the evening did: *The Great Escape*, a WWII prisoner-of-war yarn. Movies are very inexpensive here, very popular, and shown in quite elaborate, modern theaters.

Elder Colvin and I tracted together all Thursday morning. I'm improving slowly, but I am improving. Of course I know that the biggest obstacle is my own lack of real effort to speak Spanish on a regular basis. Thursday night Elder Wilkes and I presented the "Qué es un Mormón" slide show to the Setina family. Hermano Setina is having a tough time giving up his smokes, but he's practically cut them down to nothing. We're counting on him giving them up completely before the twenty-sixth of this month.

Finally had a little tiff with Elder Wilkes yesterday. He felt that I've been eating more of the food we jointly purchase, so he shouldn't have to pay as much. I hate to squabble over bowls of cornflakes, but it ticked me off and I consider him something of a tightwad. But of course I've always been free and maybe too careless with my own money. I'll probably be nursing nickels myself in two years' time. Anyway, we cleared the air a bit and got on pretty well this morning. I'll do my best to keep inconsequential trivialities from messing us up. But the main thing, I think, is to overcome my own pride and shortcomings. Stop daydreaming too and start learning Spanish, huh?!

September 23

We keep getting in late at night (midnight or after) and I'm usually a little too tired to do much writing in this journal. We've been tracting a lot this week but haven't had much success. The Setina family has now had five lessons and their baptism date is the twenty-sixth. Hermano Setina is still having a rough go with his smokes, but he's only taking a few puffs a day now and we're hoping he'll make it by Saturday. We have dinner every time we visit with them. Elder Wilkes and I are getting along much better now, but I'm not fond of trotting around on someone else's leash. Already I'm more than looking forward to the time when I'll be senior and can run my own show.

P.S. Letter from Gordon arrived with today's mail. He's been transferred, has a new companion, and sounds upbeat and content. His apparent good spirits are a boost to my own.

LETTER FROM GORDON

Gar: If you didn't notice by my return address, I'm now in Puebla, one of Mexico's biggest cities about twenty-five miles south of San Martín. Elder Lara finished his mission and subsequently I was pulled out of San Martín. My new companion is another native Mexican (Cipriano Orozco) but he's completely different from the fiery Elder Lara. Mainly, he speaks English. Plus, he's genuinely a darn good guy, easy-going, extremely considerate to his moldy green companion and we've been getting along great. I benefited from Elder Lara's example of dedication and hard work but it's hard to say how much, if any, I progressed with the language or in missionary skills during our short time together. I hate to admit it but I'm secretly glad that my new companion speaks good English. My spirits have really picked up. I must confess that working in Puebla has been a vacation compared to San Martín. The initial pangs of homesickness and frustration that I suffered, along with bouts of poor health, have begun to subside. (Unfortunately, though, my hair is starting to thin out on top. At first I thought it was just the lousy haircut I got last week, but I'm beginning to realize now that I'm losing my hair. All I can say is that I hope you're doing the same.)

All of this is only a temporary situation, however, until the mission home can send a new replacement elder, then it's back to the little town of San Martín for me. You may as well continue writing to San Martín because we go up there three times a week to check on our investigators and direct the Sunday services. Don't know how long I'll be in Puebla—might be only for a week or two. The cost of living is greater here than in San Martín and I'm going to have to pinch pennies to make it through the month. We pay the maid more here but my diet will be much improved, I think. We get pancakes and even Kellogg's cornflakes with real bottled, pasteurized milk instead of the warm, watered-down stuff that's ladled out of cans by street vendors in San Martín and is unfit to drink. Elder Orozco says (with a shudder) that working in small towns like San Martín reminds him of Huixtla, Chiapas, a hamlet in the jungle near Guatemala, where he spent several difficult months early in his mission battling tropical heat, leeches, mold growing everywhere, and hostile, indifferent people. After a taste of city life I can understand Orozco's preference for Puebla, but there is a real spirit of unity and optimistic struggle among the members in San Martín that is very appealing. Well, we gotta leave now for a visit. Here's my picture, taken the day after I landed in Veracruz. Send yours. No dunks [baptisms] yet—expecting, though.

Your brother, Gord

September 27

Yesterday we baptized the Setina family (with the exception of Eduardo, the oldest boy), bringing to a close the brightest experience (so far) of my mission.

All of the family have looked forward to their baptisms since we set the date, and I feel they took the step realizing its importance. Man, the water was cold, though. The smallest boy started to cry when he came into the font, because he wasn't expecting the shock, but we eventually got them all in and out.

Friday we bumped into a missionary who had just been excommunicated several days ago for getting sexually involved with a member girl. He's from Salt Lake City, went to Highland High School. He's found a job here and is going to stay in Mexico. I can't imagine anyone in his position not looking ahead far enough to see the tragedy that would surely be inevitable.

Have decided that I had better start doing some exercises: push-ups, sit-ups, etc. when I first get up in the morning and am waiting for the heater to perk the water. Note on laundry doings: most of it gets done in the bathroom sink with hand soap and a toothbrush for shirt cuffs and collars.

September 29

Could be we've got another top-flight family on the line by the name of Cerón. We tracted them out yesterday and tonight presented the first lesson to them. It's a family of seven and the older boy and girl are especially sharp. The father is an orthodox Protestant but seems willing to listen. The mother is a salty old battle-ax who claims she couldn't care less about anything to do with religion. But I liked her right off the bat anyway. Even if we don't wind up baptizing her she says she won't interfere with anyone else's decision in the family. She didn't show much interest yesterday, but the older girl insisted on inviting us in to talk and afterward invited us back to present lessons. Have a good feeling about them.

At least my pronunciation seems to be improving (my opinion). My conversational ability is another tale, but there is progress there too. I know I do best when situations make demands and I feel spiritually on track.

October 3

Have been having some minor battles around the apartment. Elder Wilkes is a hard worker, but he does enjoy a practical joke, and Elder Crompton is probably even more inclined towards horseplay. This morning Wilkes threw a firecracker into the bathroom while Crompton was sitting on the pot and slammed the door shut again. There was a muffled explosion, an outraged yell, a brief interlude of silence, then Elder Crompton emerged with a steaming blob of plaster on his head that had been dislodged from the ceiling. To get even, Crompton fired miniature stick rockets at us from the window as Wilkes and I were leaving to tract. Unfortunately, the spark exhaust melted several big holes in Elder Colvin's polyester shirt as he stood by observing. I have to shake my head a little at this kind of stuff. But actually I'm more annoyed by Crompton and Colvin's slovenliness than anything else. Wilkes and I always clean up and wash our dishes, then the other two come along and leave a big fat mess. They never buy any groceries either, and they're always getting into our food. Consequently, Wilkes locked up all the dishes and food in our suitcases. Resorting to this sort of behavior is ridiculous, but still nobody has been too mad at anybody yet—both Elders Crompton and Colvin are too good-natured.

I've been feeling much better physically since I started exercising after getting up in the morning. Also, we're eating a heck of a lot better now compared to those first frantic weeks of starvation. For breakfast we either make pancakes, French toast, hot cereal, or have fruit and *pan dulce* [sweet rolls]. We make sandwiches for lunch, and usually eat a cheap, 4–6 peso [less than 50 cent] dinner, which is actually fairly good, at little sidewalk restaurants called *comidas corrida* [quick meals].

We're giving the third lesson tonight to the Ceróns, our Protestant family of seven. They accepted the second lesson quite well and our hopes are still up (the mother won't be there, though). Afterward, we had a visit with an old lady, but her son put in an unexpected appearance and Elder Wilkes got into a real argument. Wilkes boxed his ears back, but of course it didn't do us any good. I can't get over how much better the missionaries express themselves in Spanish when talking religion than in their own mother tongue.

Another welcome letter from Gord—forebodings of problems with yet another new companion, just as he's beginning to draw a bead on what this missionary business is all about.

LETTER FROM GORDON

Gar: I'm waiting for my fourth companion in six weeks—a mission record I'll bet. They sent a nine-month junior to take my place in Puebla as companion to Elder Orozco, but nobody has shown up to take charge of me yet. So the three of us have been tracting together and we're all in San Martín right now to conduct Sunday services. It's hard to believe, but I'm actually anxious to leave Puebla, get back to work in San Martín, and start fanning the coals of our previous proselyting efforts. Since dividing our time between Puebla and San Martín we've lost most of our investigators.

You know, the first couple of weeks I was here I think I was perfectly miserable and didn't really know it—just kind of sensed it. Puebla was a vacation. Spent most of our days on buses traveling to reference visits through members. It was a good break but I hope I didn't get used to loafing too much. By the way, I don't know if I mentioned before that I got in on some baptisms recently: five of Elder Orozco's investigators in Puebla and one from San Martín. The family from Puebla was from a poor area of town but very hospitable—kind of peculiar, though: the old man looks like Genghis Khan and his wife looks exactly like Yogi Berra. But the funny thing is that all the kids are quite handsome. Anyway, a really wonderful family. Elder Orozco kindly allowed me to do the baptizing, even though I contributed very little to the actual teaching of these people.

FLASH: We interrupt this letter for some deep meditation—Gar, you've gotta mention me in your prayers tonight. My new companion, Elder Gerald Splinders, just arrived on our doorstep and Orozco is getting ready to return to Puebla. Splinders used to work in Veracruz and, frankly, he was one of my first bad impressions of the mission. I don't think his Spanish is very good, he doesn't know all of the lessons, and from what I have gathered of his reputation, he's a slacker. I hope I'm wrong about all this. I often get in trouble making snap judgments, but after having had three good companions, it might be a long couple of months ahead here for me in San Martín. Gar, when you write, add your accomplishments, success, progress, and points of pride. Word from you lifts me as no other can. Make me work hard to keep up with you, because when I hear of your good deeds it makes me feel proud, and I want to run a little harder so that I can hit the tape at the finish line, right at your side.

Your brother, Gord

October 14

Little bit lazy about writing lately. Haven't been around the apartment much the last week, though. Right now, things look very bright for the month. We have all kinds of good investigators and a lot of them have just dropped in our laps. This afternoon we baptize an old widow. Saturday we hope to have five or six more, including the three Cerón kids—they're really sharp. The mother would never listen to us, and now the father doesn't think he's ready yet, but he will be. I'll have to keep a better record of the people we're teaching and how they progress.

It appears that the Mexican Mission is on top of the missionary heap worldwide. Our mission has a goal of 3,500 baptisms by the end of the year and it looks like we'll make it. The District of Madero led the mission in baptisms in September. We haven't been working any harder for our success—to the contrary. The Lord has blessed us, though we haven't been particularly worthy.

Bad news from Kathy. The doctor thinks she has rheumatic fever. I've anxiously been waiting for word about the final diagnosis. I pray she might draw on her inner strength to battle off discouragement. Natalie writes that she's been completely content and happy at home, and this has in fact been my prayer for her. We might be moving to a better apartment in the Unidad Nonoalco next week. Hope so. We have bedbugs in the bed and blood on the sheets.

October 17

This afternoon we're baptizing three *hermanas* [sisters]. One of the girls—a teenager from northern Mexico who has had previous contact with missionaries—came to us about a week ago asking for baptism. We've been giving her lessons along with the Hernandez girl, whom we are also baptizing today. We expect to baptize the Hernandez boy next Saturday. The Ceróns caved in on us unexpectedly last night. The kids say they want to wait and investigate more. I hope they'll eventually come around, but right now it doesn't look too good. The rest of our visits seem to be going well. It's amazing how many people we've found this month to teach. I don't think we've been able to tract for over a week. We still have a handful of reference visits we haven't yet had time to check out.

The Yankees lost the World Series to the Saint Louis Cardinals. We saw scraps of most of the games at members' and investigators' homes, including a dramatic ninth-inning home run by Mickey Mantle to salvage one of the Yanks' wins. The U.S. seems to be cleaning house in the Rome Olympics. Khrushchev is out on his nose. China exploded an A-bomb. Continued atrocities against Negroes and civil rights workers in the American south. More trouble in Vietnam. Things are starting to look a little shaky around the old globe.

October 19

Since district meeting this morning we have been in the apartment cleaning up the mess and getting some washing done. My patience is wearing thin with Elders Crompton and Colvin. Whenever they're around the place is a pigpen. When I buy food and leave it out, Elder Crompton eats it. Trying to be a nice guy is fine, but I just keep getting run over. At least Elder Wilkes and I are getting along better all the time. Wilkes is certain that Crompton and Colvin somehow planted bedbugs in our bed awhile back—we discovered a whole nest of them in our box springs. Changed mattresses with them while they were gone. I've been in misery from bites for a long time.

October 25

After a mixed week of wasting time and running around like madmen, we still have only four baptisms in the pot in October. However, we're baptizing three today after church (the Córdabas family), and next week could tell a big story. The Ceróns seem gone for good, which is too bad because the two kids are about as sharp as I've seen.

October 27

Lost the Córdabas on Sunday. They came to the chapel with their baptismal clothes, but their parents and other relatives have been giving them such a hard time that they finally decided to wait. Señor Córdabas will be leaving the city for two months to work, so although we may have planted seeds we won't pick any apples. We also made a visit with Mrs. Cerón yesterday and got a look-see under her tough old exterior. Turns out that her husband is the snake in the grass. He's had children by ten different women and has been a real cad in all. His wife has good reason to be bitter. But he keeps attending church services and showing interest. So we're going to keep working with the family and see if we can't do some good. We have a special tape on chastity that we've arranged with Mrs. Cerón to present to the family some night this week. Elder Wilkes and I are getting along better every day. He has a wry humor that I wouldn't expect to see much of in somebody from Idaho (pardon the derogation).

October 28

Came back to the apartment this afternoon and found a little note in the door from Elder McKechnie advising me of my first mission transfer. So long District of Madero, Elder Wilkes, fifteen baptisms (maybe), and more than likely the Big City too. I was somewhat surprised to find that my immediate reaction was disappointment. Not too long ago I would have been excited about the change. Two factors have made things different. One, that I was starting to get more into the swing of things, feeling at home here, with growing confidence in myself as an effective missionary. Two, Elder Wilkes and I were showing definite signs of hitting it off very well together. Any personality problems we had to begin with have been resolved, and we were both growing in respect towards each other for the things we were, overlooking the things we weren't. There's no doubt that Elder Wilkes is an extremely effective missionary, and I gained some valuable points from observing his presentations. I don't mind leaving behind the baptisms we have planned for Friday and Saturday, just so long as they do get splashed. I don't feel that my first two months have seen enough personal growth. Nevertheless, the Lord has still blessed my companions and me in bringing a number of people to a knowledge of the gospel. That counts. Well, another beginning, and I usually don't much like them. Who knows where I'm going? Find out tomorrow morning at the mission home.

6

～

"My Job's to Keep Him on the Stick": Gordon's Story as Junior Companion in San Martín, Puebla

After a series of companion changes during his first six weeks in the field, Gordon remained in San Martín with his fourth senior companion for the next three and a half months. This was a continued period of personal struggle and adjustment for Gordon, particularly in relationship to his new senior companion, whose slack work habits and missionary attitudes contrasted sharply with those of Gordon's previous senior companions and with his intense ambition to be a successful missionary. Although Gordon gradually developed some tolerance for his companion, he also cultivated a self-righteous sense of moral superiority, which was channeled into a self-directed program of study and scripture memorization. Like Gary, Gordon remained frustrated and self-conscious about his deficiencies in conversational Spanish, but he also began to develop his capacity to give prepared addresses—regularly assigned Sunday talks in the San Martín Branch. At the same time, he increasingly became sensitized to the significance of peer-based reputations through participating in missionary conferences, district holiday outings, and periodic working visits from supervising elders. Gordon also developed a fond attachment for the Mexican members in San Martín, which was reciprocated and strengthened, in part, as a result of the members' disapproval of and conflicts with his companion, who assumed the role of branch president. Missionary work proved difficult in San Martín, where the local Catholic Church was strong, and only a few converts were recruited during Gordon's stay.

Through his letters to Gordon, Gary revealed a parallel pattern of experience, particularly in regard to his relationship with a new senior companion after being transferred from Nueva Santa María to the Roma District in

Mexico City. Like Gordon, Gary became disgusted with his new senior companion because of his apparent indifference and lack of missionary zeal. He, too, became preoccupied with the problem of maintaining his standards of dedication and missionary morale. His efforts at personal development through daily study led him to begin reading extensively in LDS church history, which became a life-long interest. Gary was inclined to attribute a drastic decline in recruiting success during this period to his senior companion's lack of diligent effort. His letters also show, in several ethnocentric accounts, a growing contempt (shared by his missionary peers) for the teachings and practices of Mexican Catholicism.

San Martín, October 4, 1964

My new companion arrived today during Sunday services. I've been consigned to remain in San Martín with Elder Gerald Splinders. This could take some real getting used to. With Elders Martineau, Lara, and Orozco I was fortunate to be assigned as a junior companion to three of the best in the mission. Splinders, on the other hand, was probably the most disagreeable example of the several missionaries I was unimpressed with when I first arrived in Veracruz. Hope my first impression was wrong. I'd like to get started off on the right foot with Elder Splinders and revive the missionary effort here in San Martín, which has floundered after a two-week lapse without full-time missionaries stationed in town.

October 5

We visited a good member family, the Osnayas, after church last night. In fact, they invite us to their home regularly for evening meals. They've been members of the church for years (converted in Mexico City) and formed the nucleus for the branch here when the missionaries first came to San Martín last year. The Osnayas own land in the foothills outside of San Martín where they cultivate roses for sale to floral shops in Puebla and Mexico City. At the moment, Hermano Osnaya and his adult son Dionísio are the only active priesthood holders in San Martín besides me and Elder Splinders. Hermano Osnaya can't understand why I don't speak more when we visit, because the previous junior companion here apparently babbled all the time. He calls me "El Silento" [the Silent One] and says I'll never learn Spanish if I don't talk more. He's right. I can't help speculating about what my progress would be if I were in an English-speaking country where I could immediately assert myself with some degree of confidence and contribute significantly to the work. Here I'm like a child. I sometimes wonder if I'll ever learn Spanish well enough to function adequately, let alone fully achieve my potential as a missionary. In any event, Splinders didn't hit it off very well with Hermano Osnaya, whose support we depend on a lot here in San Martín. Our prospects will be less than promising if we don't maintain good relations with branch leaders.

October 10

After his first frustrating week here I conclude that Splinders is incompetent and doesn't have a grain of common good judgment. He becomes belligerent and takes a defeatist attitude as soon as things go wrong. He terrifies little kids when he picks them up and tries to sit them on his lap. (He means well, I guess, but his brusqueness starts them bawling.) He writes down names without addresses and streets without numbers, crosses them off our list when he can't remember, and we end up losing potential investigators. Worst of all, his tactlessness is often offending to the branch members. It's now late in the afternoon and he's been sitting on the can in the bathroom for the past half hour while we should be out working.

At least I received a letter from Gary today which, as always, is uplifting to my spirit. As my companion and I walk home at night I frequently gaze at the pale peak of Popocatépetl in the distance and silently call out Gary's name, wondering what he is doing, what he is thinking, and wondering if he can sense my spirit as I imagine the City of Mexico glittering in the moonlight on the other side of the mountains. It is a source of comfort and strength (but also of yearning—yearning for what?) to know that he is nearby.

LETTER FROM GARY

Gord: I have a hunch you've got things a lot tougher than I do. The Big City makes things much easier. For instance, everybody is baptizing like mad down here, including us last month (our district led the mission, and, if I'm not mistaken, our mission led the church). I received a letter from our cousin Steve Burton, and he said that my companion and I accounted for more baptisms my first month than he did during his whole mission to Missouri and the Midwest. It almost seems too simple, as though we really haven't had anything to do with it. Come to think of it, I guess we haven't. October could be even better; we have a heck of a lot of promising investigators. Still, I know doggone well that I'm not in tune yet, and I'm not making a big enough effort to get there. Well, how are things working out by now with your new companion? Is he a loser as feared? If he is, I know you're not going to let him pull you down. We're going to have to learn to do a little roaring at people when necessary.

Have you been doing any exercise? If not, I recommend that you start. I haven't felt physically finer in a long time, and I feel guilty if I let a day go by without doing any push-ups or sit-ups. Not only that, but we are finally eating pretty well and I'm not a bad cook: French toast or banana pancakes in the morning with hot *atole* [a thick, corn-based drink]. We even make our own syrup. Your success and welfare are always my top concern.

Your brother, Gar

October 17

Last night we had a mortifying religious debate with the *Testigos* [Jehovah's Witnesses], a colossal three-hour waste of time during which we got our ears soundly boxed with the scriptures. Elder Splinders fumed and flustered and I contributed absolutely nothing besides my presence. The mortifying thing about it was that we were at the home of the Vargases, a recent convert family formerly associated with the *Testigos* who invited us over to defend their decision to convert to Mormonism. Elder Splinders ended up retreating to the kitchen, and since our unwelcome visitors could see that I was verbally handicapped, they finally left. I could understand almost everything that was said though. I'm becoming more and more confident in my Spanish ability, even though my performance last night would hardly indicate it. Fortunately, the Vargas family's faith remained unshaken. They have a lot of kids who care little for scriptural arguments but are very attached to the missionaries and other branch members.

Also, my appetite has returned. After weeks of periodic nausea and diarrhea, I'm actually starting to like the food, especially the *frijoles negros* [black beans] we get with practically every meal, including breakfast. A letter from Gary has started me doing exercises in the morning—push-ups, sit-ups, etc., and I'm beginning to feel much better. Maybe with my physical strength on the rebound I can also develop greater patience for Elder Splinders and his bumbling ways. Contributing to my improved spirits is the fact that we've finally found a promising investigator family to pin our hopes on: Alfonso Velazquez, a self-employed tailor, and his wife Delfina, whose door we accidentally knocked on while searching for an inactive member family. Instead of turning us away, Alfonso invited us in, listened with great interest to what we had to say, and wants to hear more.

October 18

Supervisor Elder Muir and his junior companion were here to work with us today. Did a lot of tracting but, as usual, not many return visits turned up. Muir is short and red-headed—calls himself "Elder Pelorojo" [Elder Redhead]—and a little cocky, but can back it up with real ability. (It's not uncommon for missionaries to use Spanish names here or be given nick-names. In fact, I'm becoming known to the members in San Martín as "El-der *Pastor*," Spanish for Shepherd.) Elder Muir informed me that I'm to be one of the speakers at the forthcoming conference in Puebla. Apostle Rom-ney will be in attendance, of all people. The talk must be in Spanish, so I'm going to be getting up extra early every morning to prepare. I don't want to make a fool of myself if I can help it. Actually, I've got plenty of time to study. Elder Splinders is not one to overwork. We practice giving the les-sons much more frequently to one another in our *clases de compañero* than we do to real live investigators. This is supposedly for my benefit, but it doesn't do me a whole lot of good since I already know the lessons by heart, much better than Splinders. According to Muir, Splinders became discour-aged early in his mission when he was made a senior companion too soon, before he had matured or learned the language well enough to take the responsibility. He asked to be sent home but instead was made a junior companion again. Now, with over a year in the mission, he is being given a second chance to prove himself. Muir says my job's to help keep him on the stick.

October 25

We just returned from our three-day missionary conference in Puebla, pre-sided over by Apostle Romney. At 5:00 A.M., the morning of conference, I went up on the roof of the Puebla elders' big house to put the finishing touch-es on my talk. Elder Cory was startled an hour later when he came up to take pictures of the sun rising over Popocatépetl and found me rehearsing—he evidently thought I was crazy. I'm glad I was well prepared, though. Did a fairly decent job of presenting the talk at conference later in the day. I got some nice compliments, including some from President Hatch (who I met for the first time) and his second counselor, Elder Whetten—another out-standing missionary from the Mormon colonies who took me under his wing in Veracruz for a few days when I first arrived in the mission before sending me off to San Martín. [In 1996 Elder Robert Whetten was called to serve as president of the Paraguay Asuncíon Mission.] President Hatch is very infor-mal and easy-going—all the missionaries like him. I also had an interview with Apostle Romney (as did everyone else) in which I confessed that my companionship with Elder Splinders was not the greatest, and that in my opinion our missionary work was suffering. He simply told me to be patient and do my best. Good advice, which I try to follow, but unfortunately I'm not always able to conceal my impatience. Splinders probably thinks I'm self-righteous. He says I'm too strict, too serious. Ha! He should have worked with Elder Lara. I really don't think that I'm all that puritanical. I just want to feel at the end of each day that we've been making an honest effort to accomplish the work to which we've been called and committed ourselves to perform.

I'm reading as much as I can in Spanish, most of it out loud to improve pronunciation and fluency. I've begun committing to memory scriptures from the Bible, Book of Mormon, and Doctrine and Covenants. Every day I memorize a scriptural passage and then rehearse the ones I've already learned so as not to forget any of them. This may or may not help me become a better missionary, but at least it's helping me to expand my vocabulary.

Our investigator, Alfonso the tailor, continues to progress well. He and his wife have had three lessons and are ready for the fourth tomorrow. They say that so far they accept all of our teaching and hope to be baptized soon.

October 28

Somebody tossed a couple of rocks through our window last night. Some friendly neighbor kids no doubt. We still get our share of funny looks in the neighborhood.

October 31

Last night we attended a little fiesta to celebrate the birthday of one of Martineau's converts. The chilied tamales served at the party were almost more than I could tolerate. This morning my companion was sick and I didn't feel so hot either. Elder Splinders spent the day in bed and I read in Spanish and studied the scriptures. In the afternoon and evening I went out with José Luís Vargas, a thirteen-year-old member boy who idolizes the missionaries (even though he observed our scripture fiasco with the *Testigos* at his home two weeks ago), and presented the fifth lesson to our one serious investigator family—Alfonso and Delfina. José Luís is a good kid. He and his family (nine brothers and sisters!) were baptized by Martineau just before I arrived in San Martín, and he now wants to serve a mission himself when he's old enough. From Alfonso's we walked all over town checking some tracting visits that Splinders and I made previously in the week. I was forced to speak more Spanish today than ever before (I got José Luís to critique my pronunciation in between visits) and did all right. I see glimmers of hope.

November 4

We're not doing much. Elder Splinders hates tracting, but that's the only way we'll ever find new investigators to teach. Conference admonitions and resolutions to work more effectively have already faded. We spend hours every week patronizing the little *tienda* [store] down the street where we stop for *refrescos* [soda pop] so Splinders can chit-chat with the chubby proprietress, who he thinks is cute. Splinders justifies the visits as a way of talking to people about the church, but we're just wasting time. On the bright side, we gave the tailor and his wife Delfina the sixth lesson (which Elder Splinders has never learned, so I ended up giving it myself, with Splinders occasionally interrupting to comment), and they're scheduled to be baptized next week.

Gary writes that he has been reassigned to a new senior companion (who doesn't sound much better than mine), but is still in Mexico City. As for me, I don't expect any changes for some time to come.

LETTER FROM GARY

Gord: My first change came when I was least expecting it. Elder Wilkes and I were fast becoming friends after a slow start. Not only that, but we had worked like madmen all month, had five baptisms in the water and twelve more set up for the last two days in October. Elder Wilkes baptized them yesterday and my replacement got the credit. They got baptized, that's the important thing.

My new location is still in the City and includes portions of both the richest and poorest sections of town. The apartment is a palace compared to the old place: seat on the toilet (and it flushes), my very own private bed (without bed bugs), a kitchen bigger than the size of a closet, and containers to put garbage in rather than tossing it behind the pot or piling it up in the corners.

On the other hand, the spirit of the Lord is a notch or nine lower around here. My new companion is porculent Mike Smelt from Ogden, Utah. He likes to live comfortably and he hates old women and little kids—especially if they're Mexican. He doesn't believe in working too hard, and his Spanish wouldn't win any awards. The other two elders who live here—Ray Throgg and Tim Bayer—lend their unspiritual spirit to the atmosphere. The prevailing attitude seems to be that this is just a two-year obligation and not a very pleasant one at that. Of course, I've been in trouble before with snap judgments. And actually, at a pre-missionary level, they're all pretty good guys. The other two, especially, are funnier than

heck. We joined with them the other night at the movies to see, of all
things, *Tom Jones*. It made me feel like Joe College back home with his
roommates, and it drained the good feeling I had derived earlier in the day
when we baptized four people Elder Smelt had been teaching prior to my
arrival. So, maintaining the right spirit around here is going to be a bit of
a battle.

Nevertheless, in spite of these concerns I am also feeling a strange
sense of happiness. I've noticed, for instance, a sudden jump in my Spanish and in my confidence to use it. A long way to go, naturally, but a big
improvement. And I know I'm going to play a much bigger personal part
in the proselyting efforts than before. If I can only humble myself more
and study more, I feel sure the Lord will bless me here. In like vein, given
the companion you're saddled to now, I imagine there is some good
growth in you. Responsibility always adds stature, they say. And how did
your conference talk go? I've escaped any such duties so far, but not for
much longer, I have a hunch.

Kathy's case of rheumatic fever isn't thought to be severe, but it's bad
enough and she'll be confined to bed for quite awhile. I know it's going to
be discouraging for her. Her letters continue to indicate she's convinced
herself to stick it out for me. And Natalie? I like her a lot, and her letters
tell me she's thinking the same as Kathy. She and Beckie have apparently
become the best of buddies; I don't know how the heck things are going to
wind up. Write sooner than I did. We've got a lot of prayers going for us.
Kathy says we're both mentioned in their family prayers. I add mine for
you to the pile.

Your brother, Gar

November 10

Our baptisms fell through. Alfonso and Delfina aren't married. Apparently
people here have a more relaxed attitude about marriage formalities than in
the U.S. and common-law marriages are in fact quite common. We'll have
to get them legally married before they can be baptized. The marriage license
is 60 pesos [about $5], and that represents a small obstacle. Splinders and I
have offered to pay the fee.

It's getting cold, especially at night. I've had to put out another 60 pesos
for a wool jacket to keep from freezing.

November 14

In another week I will have been in Mexico for three months. I'm becoming
quite fond of San Martín, especially of the branch members who are warm-

hearted and generous with their meager means. I'm also more or less resigned to my companion. We're getting along fairly well, but I must be careful not to allow his lack of ambition to become an excuse for weakening my own standards. I've also got to keep my sarcasm under better control. I'm sure Splinders is not overly fond of me either. The other day, partly in jest but partly in seriousness, he wondered out loud as to when I would be transferred out of here. But I suppose I should take heart—Gary reports in a letter today what seem to be even worse companion problems.

Alfonso and Delfina demonstrated their seriousness about the church by going through a civil marriage ceremony. Their baptism is scheduled again for next week in Puebla. Alfonso is delighted, and even Delfina, who has always been less receptive, is happy with the steps they've taken.

LETTER FROM GARY

Getting pretty fast in the letter department, but I've got the time. Initial negative impressions about my new place are unfortunately turning out to be all too true. There is definitely a loss of purpose among the elders of this apartment, my companion being the worst offender. He's lazy and he's sloppy. He doesn't exactly brim with love for Mexicans. He gripes constantly. We have done a fair amount of tracting, but when my companion gives a door approach, he practically puts the "no" into people's answers. The other night we were right in the middle of giving a first lesson to a large family when Elder Smelt suddenly packed up his flannel board and we left. I got a bit hot with him for it. According to him, these people weren't ready yet to understand our message. As far as I was concerned, I didn't think he should pass that kind of judgment. I saw no reason why we couldn't at least have finished out the lesson. He said he didn't like struggling through a lesson when he didn't feel it would do any good. I told him I didn't think we could be all that fussy at the moment, etc.

With all the extra time available from the slackening of effective missionary work, I'm able to put in some good study hours, both with the language and the gospel. I figure I will have finished reading in Spanish all the Standard Works, including the Bible, in about five months. Also, I'm always first one up in the morning (around 5:30 A.M.), and while I'm waiting for the water to heat up, I knock out fifty sit-ups and fifty push-ups. I've even got the other elders in the apartment making sporadic attempts to exercise. My companion especially needs it. Unlike previous senior companions, Elder Smelt is a serious eater, and we never miss a meal. Groceries are cheap, and we dine mostly in the apartment. I'm gaining a little weight myself, which is fine as long as it fills out the right places and doesn't go to my gut. Speaking of food and fitness concerns, I had become worried about a persistent pink coloring of my urine a few days ago. But President Hatch, who is a doctor, diagnosed the problem as the result of eating cookies containing cheap food coloring—a comical ending to what I feared might be the onset of some unspeakable Mexican bladder disease.

In hopes of better days, your brother, Gar

November 21

Life with Elder Splinders has had its ups and downs, but last night we were rewarded with our first baptisms together in San Martín: Alfonso Velazquez and his wife Delfina. Our accidental meeting of these people shows that the Lord guides us even if we're not always worthy to have his spirit. I wish the happiness of the occasion could linger. Elder Splinders and various members of the San Martín Branch (especially Hermano Osnaya) are at odds and the trouble is brewing worse all the time. Splinders takes some pride in calling himself *"Elder Terremoto"*—Spanish for earthquake, but the members are not amused. I'm partially sympathetic and partially disgusted with him. I've gotten to know Elder Splinders well enough to understand some of the problems he experienced growing up that now affect his behavior, but at the same time he has to learn to take responsibility for the consequences of his actions.

November 28

We moved from our former domicile (which also served as the branch *capilla* [chapel]) to a new residence right in the middle of the town marketplace. This, in fact, is the area of town where I wandered around lost after first arriving in San Martín. Kind of an unsightly neighborhood. Our new *capilla* is right next door to a pulque [a drink made from the fermented juice of the maguey plant] and tequila cantina. And on market days there's not a square inch of space for either cars or foot traffic. We practically have to flail our way through the throng around our doorway with the flannel board in order to make it into the house. Some of the members were not too thrilled with Elder Splinders' selection, but he was oblivious to their complaints. But allowing for this, and the usual gruesome Mexican paint job (my bedroom is painted with dark blue and red walls—wonder what that will do for my dreams at night?), plus one or two other minor inconveniences, it's kind of a slick old mansion that's a lot bigger than our previous place.

Thursday we went to Puebla for Thanksgiving dinner with the other missionaries in the district (sixteen altogether) and then finished off the day by going to see a movie. The lady missionaries (one pair) cooked a turkey—

burned it to a crisp (I didn't know you could do that with a turkey)—but they were good-humored about it and we had a good time. Good to see some missionary faces other than my companion on occasion.

November 29

Yesterday I tried an experiment with my companion. I was curious as to what might happen one day if I failed to prompt or nudge Elder Splinders. So I didn't say anything, made no suggestions concerning the day's activities, and passively followed Elder Splinders' lead. As a result we had no *clase de compañero*, didn't leave the house until 10:00 A.M., and didn't make any visits or go tracting. Instead we wandered down by the river to see if there were any good spots to baptize (in case we ever do any more) and then ended up going downtown to blab with the red-headed girl who works at the Singer Sewing Machine shop. We returned to the house around noon and didn't go out again until 6:45 P.M. to give a lesson at Alfonso's. I think Elder Splinders simply decided that the month was already shot, so it couldn't do much more harm to take the day off.

LETTER FROM GARY

Gord: Belated Thanksgiving greetings to you. The English-speaking branch put on a turkey dinner with all the trimmings for 25 pesos [$2]. First gringo food I've eaten in over three months. Stuffed myself.

On the missionary front, things are getting worse. We haven't gotten past a second lesson with any family since my first week here. We usually put in a respectable amount of tracting time every day, but we might as well be trying to sell Christmas cards in July, given the lack of spirit and enthusiasm that accompany us. Naturally, I blame my companion for most of our poor showing. In my estimation, he's a lousy missionary all the way, and I haven't got an ounce of respect for him. At the same time, I don't do much to help the situation, just sit and shake my head in disgust. I tell myself: "Bide your time, you'll eventually be a senior and then it's your show." But meanwhile precious time floats down the drain.

Yesterday was my companion's birthday. Of course we took the day off. Among other entertainments, we visited the famous Basílica de Guadalupe, built to honor the supposed appearance of the Virgin Mary to Júan Diego (an Indian convert to Catholicism) in 1531. The huge, ornate structure tilts noticeably and is slowly sinking into the swamp upon which it was constructed. We witnessed devout penitents crawling for miles to the entrance on bloodied knees. It all seemed more of a carnival sideshow than something holy. We were greeted by a blaring drum and bugle corps marching down an isle as we entered the building. Balloons festooned the chandeliers, scores of people walked around the interior or stood talking while a priest chanted to mostly empty pews down in the front. A young boy even wandered through with his bicycle in tow.

Although we're not accomplishing much, the days seem to be swiftly slipping by in a routine of going-through-the-motions of missionary activity. I'm beginning to catch myself in lazy moments. I suppose that becoming indifferent is a gradual, barely detectable process, like acquiring a pot gut. My intention is to avoid both. Your letters always cement this resolve and buoy my spirits. Your companion problems sound at least as bad as my own, yet you continue to hang in there in a way that I need to keep emulating.

Your brother, Gar

December 3

The weather has been overcast and cold, with the exception of any snow, roughly comparable to what I would expect in Salt Lake City at this time of year. The old house where we live is frigid—no central heat, no fire place, and hot water must be heated in the morning with a tiny wood-burning stove. My one blanket is not enough to keep me from shivering through the night. With Christmas expenses coming up this month for Mom and Dad, I'm not sure I can afford to buy additional blankets. I've been piling my raincoat and wool jacket on top of the covers for extra warmth, and have even tried sleeping with clothes on in a losing effort to keep from freezing. This is not the tropical climate I expected to find in southern Mexico. Splinders' apparent reaction to the cold is to go into hibernation. He sleeps in till 8:00 A.M. or after, and we seldom go through the motions of a *clase de compañero* anymore. But I still rise before 6:00 A.M. and study on my own.

I've been keeping up pretty steadily with my study of the scriptures. So far I've got fifty-three committed to memory and approximately another fifty or so according to subject and location. I've read *Jesus the Christ* and the *Articles of Faith* by Talmage in English, have gotten through about half of *A Marvelous Work and Wonder* by Richards in Spanish [all LDS doctrinal books], and I'm also re-reading the Book of Mormon in Spanish. Also, one of Gary's past letters got me doing push-ups and sit-ups and now I do fifty every night before I go to bed. And my speaking ability in Spanish? Our maid just returned from a trip to Mexico City where she ran into Gary at one of the chapels there. She was confounded at first and thought Gary was me: "Son ustedes, iquales, iguales!" [You are identical, identical!] She praised Gary's

Spanish and admonished me to improve mine: "Hay qué mejorar, hermano!" [You need to improve, brother!] Actually, I am slowly improving, thank goodness.

December 9

All of a sudden we've got three more baptisms planned for next week. We've been making bus trips out to San Matías, a rural village outside of San Martín, to teach three sisters who have some kind of kin connection with the Osnayas. One of the sisters just married a member of the church from Mexico City who is anxious for her to join also. In fact, we were invited to the wedding party in San Matías, which was attended by most of the village. I struggled to choke down some of the hottest tortas and tamales I've ever tasted and then washed them down with *jamaica* water (a kind of sour punch made from flower petals). Many of the villagers prefer pulque or beer. Elder Splinders could barely hide his disgust. He says he hates drunks and refused to talk with any of the men who had been drinking, leaving me to apologize for his curtness.

LETTER FROM GARY

Gord: I'll start on this right now while I've got *bastante* [enough] time. Arrrg, it ticks me off. Not only your letter lost, but I haven't heard from home since before Thanksgiving, and a letter from Chuck wandered around for two weeks before finally arriving. I'm getting peeved by the day. I sent your Christmas card early because I thought you might have been moved further than across the street, and I anticipated forwarding delays.

During my first two months in the District of Nueva Santa María, Wilkes and I averaged seventy-five to eighty working hours a week. Now, Elder Smelt and I are skimming fifty hours, and a lot of that is spent on trolleys. However, a couple of weeks ago the mission home surprised everyone and made my companion supervising elder. The idea is that added responsibility also adds incentive. Happily, in this case, it has—a little. We're putting in more effective time and finding better visits. But we're still below par and no real breakthroughs are in sight. The days drift by with a kind of grudging effort being made on our part. We trudge through the vast labyrinth of dank tenement dwellings that boarder the heart of the old business district. This is probably not a safe place for two gringos in suits to be wandering around, although we seem to be largely ignored. Every once in awhile we pop out from the gloom of side streets to find

ourselves on a main thoroughfare, whose modern buildings and fashion-
able store display windows seem totally incongruous with the crumbling,
impoverished regions from which we have just emerged.

Yesterday, we had a completely different kind of experience. Natalie
had sent me the address of her uncle, who has been living in Mexico City
for some time now as a Ford Motor Company executive, so we decided to
look him up. Found his residence on the penthouse floor of a very ritzy
apartment in a very exclusive neighborhood. I don't think I've ever
stepped foot into a more impressive habitation—it only took up the whole
eleventh floor of the building. Señor Fletcher was just getting ready to
leave for a big business banquet and was dressed in a tuxedo. He resem-
bled Natalie's father in appearance and seemed a bit nervous. After I introduced us we sat down for a brief chat. He told us that in his youth he
fulfilled a Mormon mission to France but had since turned "black sheep."
He said that although he smokes and likes to "take a little nip once in
awhile" with his friends he is still dedicated to the principles and philosophy of Mormonism.

Señor Fletcher likened his work here in Mexico to a sort of mission, in
that he can instill ideals of honesty, fair dealing, and industry in the men
who work under him. He then asked me what I thought of Mexicans. I
told him we worked with them every day and learned to get along. His response to this was: "Frankly, I think they're the most immoral bastards
that I've ever met." After my companion agreed with him, I invited Señor
Fletcher to attend church, but I kind of doubt he'll ever come around to
visit us. He was evidently in a hurry to make his dinner date, so we left,
but it was certainly an interesting twenty minutes.

With regard to personal development issues: I've had more time for
studying, but I'm afraid I haven't been as consistent as you. I memorize a
scripture almost every day, but I don't remember them very long. I look
up twenty to thirty words a day in my Spanish dictionary and memorize
them while riding the trolleys. I feel like the language is improving, but
I'm still jerky from lack of spontaneous speaking outside of canned presentations during tracting and the *pláticas* [investigator lessons]. I've
upped my push-ups to sixty, also sixty sit-ups and fifty deep knee bends. It
wouldn't be hard to go to pot quickly. But I remain in good health so far;
haven't even had the runs since my first two weeks.

By the way, ran into another old gal a few Sundays back who knows
you from Puebla [Gordon's maid in San Martín]. She said your Spanish
was improving leaps and bounds. Also heard some kind words about both
of us from Elder London in a long-awaited letter that arrived a few weeks

back. I'm sending it along, imagining that you'll find it interesting reading. As you will see, London hasn't changed much, according to himself. He wants to accomplish good things but somehow the old ignition spark must have gotten doused in younger years.

Well, I feel like I've been getting a little mud spattered on my own nice clean shirt. I figured I'd been dumped into a more or less spiritual cesspool when I first transferred here, but I also figured I could keep from skidding in myself. Sort of slippery, though. But I'm still determined to work as hard as I can and I know you are too. That helps more than anything else. The truth is, I've always had to reach beyond my limits to keep up with you. Hang on for awhile and it won't be long before the Shepherds get a chance to really prove their mettle.

Your brother, Gar

LETTER TO GARY FROM STEVE LONDON

Dear Gary,

Well, it was mighty good to hear from you. Though I've never doubted your inevitable success there, I too have thought and wondered many times just how it was all going for you in the city Mexico and, notwithstanding this tardy reply, would like to exchange frequent letters. You taught me some things about the value of friends, even, at times, as motivators, and I consider myself blessed to know you.

As you might suspect, I'm still drifting around, even here. Crossing lots of imaginary lines in airplanes didn't result in any magical changes. But in the past three months I've been able to catch glimpses of testimony, achievement and proficiency, happiness, and success, which are at once inspiring and consoling. Perhaps it's just the effects of time, but I like to think that maybe a growing sincerity of desire (and hence of purpose) are contributors. It's a long way out of the doldrums yet, but every time I get right thoroughly bogged down, a little blessing comes along in the form of a letter from an old companion or something, and once more the Lord has kicked me in the butt.

At any rate, I'm glad to be here. It scares me to think that without this mission I might never wake up, albeit that awakening is little more than a sure promise for the future. I've even at times been able to find myself grateful for the things that always deserved that feeling. But I'm still piddling around with the lesson plan. In the very best London tradition I haven't studied or learned a bit of it. How are your presentations? My companion is another story. We haven't furthered the Lord's work an inch in three months. Not one single baptism (with all the overtones of ineffectiveness and lack of honest effort which that implies). Right now I'm thinking I'd like a new partner and try it again. But then I imagine that having companion changes, like crossing borders, won't work any peculiar miracles.

The travelers [zone leaders] were here not long ago. I asked about Gordon, and they had nothing but good things to say. Evidently his first companion was Martineau, then the Great José Luís Lara, and now that dip from St. George, Utah who, judging from a short brush I had with him in Veracruz over the pestilence which he didn't seem to mind in his house, is thoroughly out of it. I was glad to hear that Gord was sticking him out, but then I've never doubted *his* sense of direction either.

Lots of things deserve a bit of worry. How easy to slip into the well-worn ruts of mediocrity. Or better said, how difficult to escape them. Too many missionaries here are phonies. And who do they kid? I don't want to be a phony. Too many aren't quite as good as they think they are. I want to know myself. Too many seem not to know that they're not all there is to be. I wonder what great things I'm missing from lack of awareness. Complacency, feigned satisfaction—that can't be happiness. There must be happiness. I've learned something of what you taught me about wringing a little left-handed pleasure out of the painful or difficult. Hell, that's what it's all about. In the *Prophet,* that Chuck had you give me, Kahlil Gibran pins this down with a fine statement on joy: That when you have it, a little look into your heart will reveal it's only that which has given you pain which is the source of your joy.

If I have my way, Gary, throughout this mission and much more so afterward, I'd like to be among the company of your friends. It goes without saying that good friends are priceless. You're one I'd like to have as very best. Hope to hear from you soon. Now that contact is established, we might be able to try some of the stuff of men—if young at that.

Until then, Steve

December 13

Last night we baptized two of the three sisters who live in San Matías. Our attempts to get them to Puebla for the baptismal service scheduled at 7:00 P.M. turned into a minor fiasco. The girls were late to begin with and then the rickety old bus that (sometimes) passes through the village didn't show up until 6:45. By the time we got to Puebla it was past 8:00. We then discovered that the Puebla members were putting on a drama festival in the chapel. The Puebla elders had taken off on a *día de campo* [excursion or field day] and had not previously said a word to us about the mix-up in the chapel. We improvised by holding the opening services in the lady missionaries' apartment next door, repaired across the street to the baptistery room in the chapel where we performed the baptisms to a background of irreverent murmurings and scattered applause from the drama festival, and then returned to the LM's apartment for the confirmations. I directed the services, gave a talk, confirmed the girls, and did a pretty good job of botching all three assignments. Somewhere in all the confusion I lost my composure and my Spanish was comparable to that of Elder "Otra Vez" Patterson, who was re-routed from our LTM cohort and sent to English-speaking Alaska. There are times when my Spanish shows greater signs of regression than progression and it's kind of mortifying. I've now participated in eight baptisms since I've been in Mexico. San Martín's not an easy town, but doggone it we should do better than that. I wouldn't feel badly about it if all efforts had been made, but they haven't.

December 15

Our work hasn't picked up much but at least Elder Splinders and I have been getting along much better and that makes things a little easier to take. Splinders is a farm boy, was forced on a mission by his grandma, received regular lashings from his old man, has never dated any girls (but likes chubby ones), got disanimated when they tried to make him a senior companion too soon (and was almost sent home by his own request), is crude and rude and most of the branch members in San Martín like him about as much as onions in your milk. He's impatient and unorganized and probably never will be a great missionary. On the other hand, even though he hasn't worked too hard, he's had a lot of baptisms with other companions, and he's not really a bad guy. Unfortunately he still has a knack for screwing things up. We've been without electricity for four days because Elder Splinders decided to fiddle around with the wires to the doorbell (without telling anybody) and apparently shorted out the circuit.

December 23

Elder Splinders and I purchased bags of oranges, peanuts, and candy at the market today to give the kids at the branch Christmas party, which the members have been planning for weeks. Splinders and I are not great friends but have learned to be more tolerant of one another. I even splurged and bought a thick wool sweater as a Christmas present for myself at the market to keep a little warmer when we're in the house, which has become cold as a tomb, especially at night and in the early-morning hours.

December 24

Christmas Eve, and while we're waiting for the branch members to arrive for the fiesta tonight, I've been writing a letter to Beckie. I can hear the bells ringing wildly from the big cathedral in the middle of town. For the first time, and in spite of our problems in San Martín, I'm beginning to fall in love with missionary work in Mexico.

December 25

It's 4:00 A.M. in the morning and it doesn't look like we'll be getting much sleep for awhile. Our branch Christmas party lasted until 1:00 A.M. and then Elder Splinders and I decided to stay up, since we're leaving soon for a district party in Puebla. The branch members really went all out for last night's Christmas celebration. They decorated the *capilla* and performed their version of the Christmas story, attired in costumes made by Alfonso, our recent convert, who is a tailor. There was enough food to feed the mobs of Moses. The main meal consisted of soup, tortillas and fish, and there was also a grisly salad made up of sliced beets, oranges, peanuts, bananas, lettuce, potatoes, and parsley sprigs.

Prior to the evening's festivities we did a little tracting and presented the first lesson to a strange man (to say the least) who was adorned with lipstick, eye-liner, face makeup, and had brightly painted fingernails. He was apparently more interested in us than in our message, but Elder Splinders seemed unfazed and scheduled a return visit.

A couple of days ago Elder Splinders got fired up and decided to get to work. I hope his spirits stay high. There's a lot of friction between him and the members right now. Elder "Terremoto" is viewed with disdain while Elder Pastor (which is what all the members call me) is viewed with sympathy as an innocent *nuevo* who speaks little Spanish but gets along well with the children.

December 27

Our Christmas party with the missionaries of the Puebla District turned into a fiasco with a near riot and food fight. There was the usual bad-mannered, elbow-poking, get-everything-as-fast-as-you-can-within-your-reach confusion at the dinner table. That was acceptable, but what followed got out of hand. We had a big piñata filled with candy and a large quantity of flour. After the piñata was finally broken, one of the Puebla missionaries impulsively smeared a handful of flour across a lady missionary's face (a very pretty, hot-tempered Mexican sister). She retaliated and before anyone stopped to think, a flour and food fight quickly raged throughout the whole house, eventually involving everybody except me. The flour was bad enough but when they started throwing pumpkin pies around, I went outside for a walk. (One of the Puebla elders made a move in my direction as I was going out the door, but he reconsidered when I advised him of the consequences if he got so much as a speck of food on me.) The Mexican LM really blew her stack and plastered one of the elders right in the face with a pie. He just stood there with pumpkin pie hanging from his glasses like a big piece of donkey dung. When things finally settled down, everyone got shamefaced and began accusing everyone else, down to the piñata makers, for starting the riot. Then we all trooped off to the bullfights (six bulls were cut to bloody ribbons and dragged out of the arena on their backs) and finally finished up the day by going to the *cine* to see *Lawrence of Arabia,* another bloody spectacle. I've never felt so alienated from the spirit of Christmas.

LETTER FROM GARY

Gord: This is sure a crummy time of year: Relatives descend, investigators depart to visit relatives, parties abound, and interest in listening to the *pláticas* of gringo missionaries wanes. Thus, visits fall to pieces, work is almost nonexistent, and insidious laziness lurks. Christmas cards and letters from friends rev up the old day-dreaming machine again. The mailman doesn't bother to come around but two or three days a week, and I'm stewing for foolishly sent packages from Chuck and the Dempsey household. We now have only one investigator family left to work with; we'll have to work like mad or January will flop too. While December has seen our missionary effectiveness diminish as the twenty-fifth grows bigger on the calendar, these same days have also seen me getting along better with Elder Smelt—at least urges to smash him in the back of the neck with the briefcase are becoming less frequent. No, we never could become close friends, but, as usual, I'm finding points to like in a person who at first did not much appeal.

Earlier this month was Guadalupe day, a big national holiday, as you know. So we went back up to the Basílica again (which I described to you in my last letter) to watch some of the Catholic abominations. Upwards of a million people were assembled on or near the premises. Some worshipers had begun crawling towards the cathedral on their knees from miles away; others crawled only the last hundred or so yards. Typical were two teenage girls who were being partially supported as they crawled holding onto a long pole carried in front of them by relatives. Their eyes were glazed, their knees were badly torn, and a woman kept passing smelling salts under their noses to keep them from fainting. All kinds of cheap tourist mementos were being sold in the cathedral plaza while various Indian groups performed ritual dances. My companion and I managed to push into the cathedral itself, but the press was so great we were lucky to escape out a side entrance with nothing worse than trampled-on shoes.

After the no-good mailman missed coming by the last few days, I did receive a bushel basket of cards and letters today. By the way, your clever Christmas card and photos arrived too. I notice that your hair is fleeing at about the same rate as mine. Unthinkable thing—the Shepherd twins return home bald.

I envy you right now, Gord. You're picking up invaluable experience out in that little town, not to mention the notice and respect of a lot of people in your mission. London has heard your name connected with good things by way of the traveling elders, conference talks, etc. The second counselor in our mission met the big shots from your way a few days ago and they also had some nice comments to make about you. Proud of you! Of the progress and reputation you are making.

Do you guys have to run the whole show on Sundays in San Martín or what? Here in the City there are wards and a stake, just like home. I have yet to give any talks or do anything more difficult than direct a baptismal service or offer a prayer. Days go by without me speaking any more Spanish than the tracting produces. Why, we haven't given a fifth or sixth lesson in almost two months, and only one fourth during the same time. I probably still can give them all word-perfect, though, and my pronunciation is improving because I read Spanish out loud a lot. But freelance conversation is still all shot. Always more than good to hear from you. Your last letter brought appreciative chuckles and a little more determination to try harder and do better.

Your brother, Gar

December 31

I'm twenty-one years old today. Who ever thought I'd live to be this old? I was surprised by the maid this morning who baked me a little birthday cake and wouldn't serve us our eggs for breakfast until I ate the whole thing. Tonight is the New Year's Eve party for the branch, but I'm not feeling too well (stomach-ache, headache, chills, etc.) and am going to lie down.

January 1, 1965

I got out of bed this morning at 7:00 feeling a little better, and found the house in a big mess from last night's party: Pepsi bottles, cornhusks, left-over tamales, and other debris scattered all over the place. Went back to bed. I got up a little later but Splinders didn't get out of bed until afternoon. I wonder what awaits us in the new year? We've beat on every door in town and I don't know where the next baptisms will come from because everybody here has told us no once already. Not quite, of course, and, too, we haven't exactly been Joseph Fielding Smith [a zealous Mormon apostle] or Alma the Younger [a Book of Mormon prophet] in our efforts. But it's unlikely that anyone will ever witness a day of Pentecost in San Martín.

January 5

It looks like this day is going to be completely shot. Elder Splinders is in bed with what he calls a cold but which sounds like little more than the sniffles. Actually, we've been getting along quite well lately. It's too bad his resolution to work harder collapsed. He was being pretty diligent for a couple of days. Meanwhile, the heels of my feet are callused and hurting so badly that I can't wear regular shoes. I've been tracting in tennis shoes for the past two days.

LETTER FROM GARY

Off to an inauspicious start on this New Year's day by sleeping in for the first time since I left home—didn't get up until 7:30 this morning. Tracting would prove fairly pointless, so I turn instead to letter writing. Yesterday we officially became adults. I feel more like fifteen than twenty-one, except that my hair is starting to flee, and my exercises every morning are done from fear of acquiring a pot gut. We're on missions preaching the gospel and baptizing families into the church, while most of our friends at home are going to school or getting married. I did nothing to celebrate the occasion of our birthday—how about you?

Last night we did spend New Year's Eve downtown at the huge Nacional Zócalo [National Plaza], so that my companion could take pictures of the lights. We passed through the great Cathedral of Mexico and again witnessed fantastic doings. Among the sights was an old priest collecting money from kneeling worshipers with one hand just as fast as he could wave his other hand in blessing. He was sort of like the old troll at the bridge, not letting people leave until they paid him their toll.

A missionwide conference was held at the mission home on Christmas Day, and a great many transfers/companion changes were effected. I was surprised (and admittedly disappointed) not to be among them. Tim Bayer, late of our apartment, was shipped elsewhere, however. We were fast becoming good friends, a friendship I would like to see continued at another time and place. Meanwhile, the conference itself was excellent, and I gained several kicks in the butt to apply myself harder and be more constantly aware of my responsibilities.

Whenever we get up to the mission home, I always browse the library. We have some fascinating holdings here, and I sneak out a book every chance I get. My readings so far have included: *Prophecy,* by Crowther; *Here Is Brigham,* by Young; *An American Prophet,* by Evans; *Mormonism and Masonry,* by Gavin; *The Restored Church,* by Barrett; and a start on the *Comprehensive History of the Church,* volume one, by Roberts. I've also read the Book of Mormon in Spanish and over half of the New Testament in Spanish. I've completed *Jesus the Christ,* started the *Articles of Faith,* and am well on my way in the Old Testament. I always carry a book with me and soak up a lot of reading on trolleys, buses, and at any other odd moment.

Well, much waits to be gained or lost in the year ahead. I'm still confident it will be gains. There's no real need to draw up a list of written resolutions. We know what has to be done. Of much greater worth will be those requirements for the year ahead that we can firmly etch into convictions and desires of the heart.

Your brother, Gar

January 6

Well, it looks like I've bruised my companion's feelings and disanimated him for the time-being. I lost my patience and told him that I was just as capable of getting us kicked out of a house as he and to stop butting in when I'm presenting my portion of the door approach or investigator lessons. He consequently clammed up completely and is punishing me with his silence. It's unfortunate, since we've been getting along so well lately. I just got fed up with being interrupted all the time by Splinders in ways that, in my opinion, did not help clarify or strengthen our presentations.

I've been in San Martín for almost five months and anticipate a transfer soon. As difficult as the work has been, I've come to like the place and have developed a real affection for the members, but I imagine a change in companion would do me some good. I feel healthier and stronger than I ever have since being in Mexico. I've upped my push-ups/sit-ups to seventy-five every night and have committed the same number of scriptures to memory as well.

January 14

Just got back from Puebla where I gave the lesson (on the concept of the restoration of the gospel) at our monthly district meeting. My companion's slothful work habits gave me plenty of extra time to prepare and Elder Purdy (the new zone leader) was generous in his compliments. I've got to watch my self-pride, though. So far the Lord's given me a big hand when I've needed it for special assignments, helping me through and making me look good. But I'm going to have to learn to draw more on an everyday strength and begin to meet the assignments of everyday, because I know I haven't done much yet in actual missionary work, contributing but a small bit to the preaching and teaching of the gospel.

I'm still expecting a transfer; according to Elder Purdy it could come any time. In the meantime, Gary writes that he has been moved from Mexico City all the way to Guadalajara.

LETTER FROM GARY

Gord: Just a quick note to let you know my new address. I moved Monday. Guadalajara is a ten-hour bus ride from the Big City. It's supposed to be one of the toughest places in the mission—like Puebla, a lot of Catholic fanatics. Glad for the change, though. I was stagnating fast where I was. Let's hope I haven't picked up any bad habits. Elder Smelt and I had finally learned to get along well enough together, but we certainly weren't producing much effective work.

My new companion, Victor Haney, has only been senior for a week or so and is a little shaky on the lessons, but he speaks excellent conversational Spanish, seems serious about the work, is a good guy, and I think we'll make a fair team. We have a big house to share with two other elders. The missionaries live upstairs and the branch holds services downstairs. Looks like I'll get my first taste of public speaking in Mexico. I expect I'll be here a while, and when I do leave, I expect to be a better missionary and speaking good Spanish. We've been on a pretty tight schedule here so far. Don't know when I'll be able to find enough time to write the letters I owe. We've got five lessons set up for tonight—that's more than Smelt and I gave during the whole of last month. Let me know, as soon as you can, what's been going on. I'll write a decent letter as soon as I hear from you.

Your brother, Gar

January 14

The new supervising elder (Elder Hidalgo) is here to work with us. Splinders gripes about supervisors and gets on edge when they visit but, frankly, I look forward to the break in monotony, the chance to see some fresh faces and catch up on a little mission gossip. Hidalgo's a native *Veracruzano* from Tierra Blanca (his father is president of the Veracruz District) and is supposedly a ladies' man—looks a lot like a young, dark Caesar Romero. His junior companion is Elder Hildenberg, who was in the cohort just behind us at the LTM and also projects a ladies' man image. Quite a *guapo* [handsome] pair. Anyway, my initial opinion of Hidalgo was not very high since he and Elder Zuñiga (another Mexican elder) were the ranking missionaries at the Christmas party last month and allowed things to get completely out of hand. But I've gotten to know him better and we've worked well together today. Hidalgo likes to have a little fun but he's also an intelligent, articulate missionary. Later: Passed by the post office this afternoon and found a telegram for me from mission headquarters. A transfer!

TELEGRAFOS NACIONALES

VENGA A LA CASA DE MISIÓN. LUGÁR NUEVO MINATITLÁN. [Come to the mission home. New place Minatitlán.] E. Seville Hatch.

Goodbye San Martín (I'll miss you). Goodbye Elder Splinders (I'll miss you a little less, but do wish you the best). We had our share of good times together.

7

∾

"How a Missionary Should Conduct Himself":
Gordon's Story as Junior Companion
in Minatitlán, Veracruz

Gordon's spirits were bolstered dramatically by his first mission transfer to Minatitlán, Veracruz, where he subsequently was paired with a series of skilled and highly motivated senior companions, all of whom were supervising elders who became important role models in Gordon's development as a missionary. It was in Minatitlán that Gordon began to recognize significant improvement in his language and teaching skills, but he was still plagued from time to time with self-doubts and questions concerning the sincerity of his religious convictions. Various material exigencies emerged in Minatitlán, especially as a result of a series of house burglaries that left Gordon and his companion almost destitute of adequate missionary attire. Low finances became a nagging concern, tropical heat took its toll, and the missionaries' living conditions were relatively primitive. In spite of these problems, Gordon felt uplifted and worked unstintingly with his companions to locate and recruit converts. Their efforts produced numerous promising candidates for baptism, but most eventually proved frustrating because of their male investigators' problems with drinking or recalcitrant refusal to comply with such LDS lay requirements as attending meetings or marrying their wives. (Common-law unions among investigators were a persistent obstacle to proselyting efforts in Mexico.)

Gordon and Gary began to realize that even though they were relatively inexperienced youths, their missionary status conferred upon them an adult religious authority that investigators and converts took seriously. Both brothers, along with their youthful companions, were often thrust into religiously important pastoral roles that required them to bless children and the sick or dying, conduct funerals, arrange marriage ceremonies, act as confidants and family counselors to Mexican adults overwhelmed with personal problems, as well as to teach, convert, and perform baptisms.

While Gordon labored in Minatitlán, Gary's initial optimistic hopes for a revitalization of his missionary fortunes in Guadalajara were dampened by yet another lethargic senior companion, whose constant fraternization with a member family and attraction to their eldest daughter became a major distraction from their missionary work. Flirtations with teenaged girls (both members and investigators) were occasionally problematic for many young male missionaries, whose sexual drives were expected to be rigidly sublimated to their proselyting efforts. Like Gordon, Gary experienced some religious dissonance during this period when he was confronted with discriminatory attitudes toward blacks, which was to become a significant concern for Gordon several months later in Veracruz, and his companions' beliefs concerning spirit possession. Mail delays and lost letters frustrated and angered both brothers, disrupted their mutually sustaining communication with one another, and periodically cut them off from the outside world.

Minatitlán, January 17, 1965

Friday I received my first geographical change in the mission. When the San Martín members learned that I was being transferred they seemed genuinely sorry to see me go and hurriedly organized a farewell party on my behalf. I've grown to care for these people a great deal and will miss them. Elder Booth is to be my replacement as junior companion to Elder Splinders. Maybe he'll work better with Splinders than I did, but I think the branch would be much better off if Splinders were transferred somewhere else as well.

I stayed in Puebla Friday night, then caught a morning bus for Veracruz. The abrupt descent from the mountainous, high-altitude country around Puebla to sea level in Veracruz was amazing. One moment I was traveling in country reminiscent of northern Utah-Idaho and in the next the bus was winding its way through the lush jungles around Orizaba, with what looked like banana trees and other tropical plants growing on either side of the road. Apparently this was the route Cortéz and his army took on their expedition of conquest from the coast of Veracruz to the Aztec capital near modern-day Mexico City.

I arrived at the mission office around 7:30 P.M. and talked briefly with Elder Muir (my first supervising elder in Puebla, who is now assistant to the president). I then hopped on another bus to Minatitlán, arriving here around 1:00 A.M. this morning. My new companion is Elder Robison, the supervising elder for the Coatzacoalcos-Villahermosa District. There's also another pair of missionaries here in Mina. Elder Robison seems to be a good guy and an excellent missionary. But since he's already spent six months in Minatitlán, he'll probably be transferred very shortly.

January 25

I've been in Minatitlán a week now and like it a lot. This is exactly the kind of tropical environment I pictured myself working in before I arrived in Mexico five months ago. It's a completely different place than San Martín: bright and colorful rather than drab; mud and moisture instead of dust. We're in the rainy season, which is supposed to be a relatively cool time of year, but the humidity is suffocating. I wonder what it will be like when it really gets warm in April and May?

The branch of the church here is well established and fairly large (about two hundred members), with good prospects for continued growth. [By 1994 there were nine wards and a stake center in Minatitlán, with more than five thousand members.] The oil industry in the region has made Minatitlán a kind of boom town in recent years. The branch and district presidents are both engineers, highly educated, who work at the big oil refinery on the Coatzacoalcos River. Unlike San Martín, all branch positions are staffed by native members. The church owns land in Mina but has not yet built a chapel here. Until it does, members are getting by with a big old house (formerly owned by a sea captain) as a place to hold church meetings. The yard is a jungle. Missionary quarters are upstairs and reasonably comfortable, but infested with insects. I just got through swatting the biggest spider I've ever seen over my bed, and moments later was joined in the shower by a giant cockroach, which I captured and flushed down the toilet. The brethren of this cockroach appear to have their nest in our refrigerator, of all places. Fortunately we don't keep much in there except a kettle of leftover frijoles. We have a huge colony of red ants in the backyard, which we steer clear of, and sometimes the mosquitoes get pretty fierce. I protect myself as best I can when we go to bed at night by sleeping with the sheet pulled over my face. One of the other missionaries here has been smart enough to purchase a Mayan hammock to which he can retire enclosed in a cocoon of mosquito netting.

Elder Robison is an excellent missionary—very methodical in his work. What a contrast to Elder Splinders. Instead of antagonizing people, he works at harmonizing with the branch leadership, and he's been very successful in obtaining investigator references through the members. [In 1996 Elder Lowell

Robison was called by the LDS Church to serve as president of the Monter-réy Mexican Mission.]

January 28

I'm not getting any mail. Nothing has been forwarded from San Martín. I'll have to write a nagging note to Elder Splinders to get him on the ball.

District conference will be held here next weekend with President Hatch in attendance. (This will be only my second meeting with the president since I arrived in Mexico.) Elder Robison expects to get his change then. In the meantime we're working quite well together. We take a bus that stops right in front of the house to our tracting area every morning. I'm going to have to concentrate on memorizing bus routes, streets, and homes of investiga-tors in order to show the new senior around when Robison leaves. The cost of living is high here, due mainly to the oil industry. People talk much more rapidly than in Puebla and San Martín, and are more difficult to understand, but my Spanish has improved and I do okay.

February 1

Conference was held over the weekend and, as expected, Elder Robison got his transfer. He left today to become the supervising elder of the Chiapas District in Tuxtla Gutiérrez. Elder Woodland, the other senior companion in Minatitlán, also got a surprise change to Campeche. That leaves me here alone with Elder Elison (who barely has two months in the mission), so it looks like I'll get a taste of what it's like to be senior for a day or two until our new companions show up. In fact, Elder Elison and I just finished pre-senting the fifth lesson to a family that apparently is not going to accept the gospel, but I was grateful at least to see how far my ability to speak Spanish has come. I'm far from having it perfected, of course, but I really am mak-ing progress. (Still no mail forwarded from San Martín *##@!!)

February 4

Three days of responsibility did me good. I managed some of the best inves-tigator lessons that I've ever given. Elder Elison seemed to assume that I knew what I was doing, so I acted like I did. My new senior companion arrived last night: David Rencher, who's from Saint Johns, Arizona. (Elder Calister ar-rived earlier in the day as Elder Elison's new senior companion.) Rencher has a reputation for being an outstanding missionary. I like him a lot already. He's completely unpretentious and serious about the work.

A letter—from Gary—at last. (Actually, *two* letters—Gary also forward-ed a second missive from Steve London.)

Gord: Haven't heard from you in a long time, so while waiting for whatever is blocking the mail on your end to dissolve, I thought I could at least try to catch you up on my latest round of adventures. Also, I'm passing along Elder London's most recent correspondence.

Guadalajara's reputation as a beautiful spot but tough missionary assignment seems mostly validated so far. We've been working recently, for instance, in a semi-impoverished suburban "colony" that has both my companion and me a little spooked. Several men approached us this morning in the street where we were tracting and said they wanted us to accompany them to their home for discussion. But they didn't sound or look sincere—more like hostile, and we put them off. Later this afternoon, another man passed by and told us to get out. Last night we were admitted into a squalid little adobe house by an old woman who was either drunk, crazy, or possessed. She raved and ranted, bowed down before a row of candles and images, and prayed and rambled incoherently. We finally got up to leave, but she clutched our hands with her incredibly dirty claws, refusing to let go and looking for all the world like a demon from hell. We had to force open her grip. My companion thought she had a devil; I doubt it.

We have generated some legitimate investigators, and even baptized three: a woman, her young son, and a young man in his twenties. The woman does have serious emotional and physical problems that are manifested in certain "attacks," or fits. Previous elders here apparently thought she too was possessed by an evil spirit, which they tried to cast out. My own immediate assumption was epilepsy (which now appears to be more likely, based on a recent doctor's examination). We have anointed and blessed her on several occasions, and I hope her new membership in the church will bring her the peace of mind and spirit she needs.

Two other sets of investigators wound up generating two kinds of failures. The first case, a professional mariachi and his wife staggered through all six lessons with only occasional signs of genuine conviction. When we went to pick them up on the day scheduled for baptism, they had skipped town. My companion thinks we should have prearranged an immediate baptism following completion of the sixth lesson. But I'm glad we didn't baptize them at all. Sometimes it takes more than just grinding through the lessons to achieve a sincere conversion.

The second case involved a couple where the husband was a retired U.S. Army sergeant, who didn't speak Spanish, and his Mexican wife, who didn't speak English. So we had to go through the lessons twice—once in English and once in Spanish. (It proved ridiculously hard to talk about the gospel in English.) Anyway, by the third lesson, we inadvertently discovered that the husband was part Negro. My first thought was: "That scotches him." But then I had to ask myself: "Why should it?" To write him off because he proved not to be serious would be one thing. But if he turned out to be sincere? You and I have always been opposed to race prejudice. But I guess I have also accepted, more or less, the church's policy of not ordaining Negro males to the priesthood without having thought about it very much. Anyway, I argued that we should continue teaching the couple to determine their true feelings, but Elder Haney was not enthusiastic. In the end I agreed to drop them, after a follow-up visit, on the grounds that in fact the man didn't seem to be taking us or the lessons very seriously.

Other areas of missionary activity: Our house doubles as the branch chapel, and around fifty adult members typically show up for most Sunday meetings. The branch leans heavily on the elders for help. [By 1994 the LDS Church in Guadalajara was divided into three stakes and twenty-two wards, all completely staffed by Mexican members.] Unlike you, I haven't previously had to speak in regular church meetings before this. I've now orated a couple of times, and maybe I don't sound so hot. I can't tell. But I do know what I'm saying, because I work on my talks for a couple of hours before meeting time. I have also contributed an uncertain hand to the branch musical offerings. This past Sunday, for instance, I volunteered to play a small lap organ (one finger, by ear, if you can believe it) while another missionary led song practice. This resulted in, without a doubt, the worst rendition of "An Angel from on High" that I have ever heard. At least my faulty playing was drowned out by the monotone chorus.

I've also had my first experience directing junior Sunday school. Child behavior doesn't change much between Mexico and Salt Lake (except that you and I were probably rowdier than the worst of them here). Reverence in all meetings is actually pretty bad. Women think nothing of breastfeeding their babies right in the middle of sacrament service.

I almost hesitate to comment much on my companion, Elder Haney, for fear of coming off as a chronic griper. But there has been slippage from my initial high hopes about our companionship. Elder Haney has been spiraling down into apathy for some time now. We are tracting less frequently and subsequently setting fewer return visits. At the same time, Elder Haney is increasingly squandering our time gabbing and goofing around with the female members of a member family (the Velazcos) who live near our house. I hope a recent, ill-conceived conversation on carnal matters has not added to this malaise in our missionary work. We were chatting on a variety of subjects while walking home the other night from a visit, when Elder Haney professed to be practically innocent of any basic sexual knowledge. I then proceeded, more or less, to discourse on the subject, and his complete entrancement egged me on. It was no doubt the wrong thing to be talking about under present circumstances, but I figured it was long past time for him to learn the common facts of life.

So maybe I'm part of the problem. But there are certainly other factors. Elder Haney is a friendly, outgoing person, but he lacks self-confidence in his role as senior (he doesn't know all the lessons, for one thing, and I have to take over most of the teaching when we get past the fourth lesson). He also seems to confuse socializing with members as the equivalent of effective missionary work. Maybe I'm not the best antidote for his problems, but his lack of constancy is beginning to tick me off. He's supposed to set the agenda, but I have an obligation to speak up when we get too far off track. I've delivered several little pep talks, in fact, with resulting promises from Haney to adhere to higher standards. But these resolutions tend to fade away in a day or so.

One area where Elder Haney is resolute and I am not is on the practice of fasting. He calls for us to fast fairly frequently when we encounter some problem with investigators or whatever. When these self-imposed fasts overlap with an official districtwide fast, it's just too many days to go without eating, and I oppose them. Fasting is supposed to have a salutary spiritual effect on our missionary efforts, but I must confess that I usually just wind up feeling drained and physically weakened.

I will end this long accounting on a positive note. Last Sunday, the four missionaries from our house were invited by a member family for dinner. Afterward all of the missionaries played marbles with several of the family's youngsters. It revived pleasant memories of younger days when marbles were the passion with us at Liberty Elementary School. I skunked them all.

Your brother, Gar

LETTER TO GARY FROM STEVE LONDON

Dear Gary,

There are the words of Thoreau: "[What] wealth it is to have friends we cannot think of without elevation." You are that kind of friend, Gar. Thanks for that and thanks for writing. It turns the mind up and away to higher things.

Witness from the return address that I too have moved. With the change came a supervising elder as my new companion. Happily, that didn't last long; though capable, he was a bit overbearing and given, at times, to belabor his companion's mistakes. They then sent a green senior to take his place, a rather singularly unimpressive fellow from Maine with whom I am now spreading The Word through these crooked and narrow little streets of Villahermosa. Once again I'm forced to state that one wouldn't often chose the company one's handed down here. Things are not really that bad; generally, we get along.

Thanks, Gar, for the journal entry enclosure in your letter. In it you penned an interesting closing reference to me: "what he's honestly seeking for." Well, since that August 18, I've come a long way. Unfortunately, *solamente* [only] as regards time. I'm commencing to seriously question the point of sincerity. In all honesty, the progress has been, at best, little. But I think I could tell you what I'm looking for, in part. It would be the Holy Ghost. I've caught a few scattered words from the general authorities on the subject. In our last missionary conference, Romney of the Twelve asked the elders that they examine their testimonies, asked that they see if their testimonies inspired them to diligence and excellence through a witness and vision of the work. He asked too if their testimonies generated all kinds of inappropriate thoughts, glances, etc., that were distasteful to them. Now those are good questions. After all, how can someone who "knows" that this church is true sit on his butt? But you see missionaries who know, "without a doubt," doing that all the time.

Well, of course the church is true. I tell people that I know that every day. You've just got to take a fast look around to see it. But getting your own witness is the trick. Apostle Henry D. Moyle said, a few years back in conference assembled, that when a man gets the testimony of the Spirit, he immediately sees himself in proper perspective with his fellow men and with God, and that he becomes responsive to the gospel plan. I've decided that although this church is one of eternal progression, or "becomings," in one Chuck Radlow's words, that the path is marked by certain "arrivings." This Holy Ghost business is one of them. The very next logical question is how to get the Ghost? I wish that I could here insert something new, something magical and irresistible, but I can't. I'm afraid it consists of "abiding counsels already given." For you to know just exactly what this means to me, read an article found in the youth section of the June '64 *Era* [an LDS periodical] entitled "Yearning Prayer."

As I think about you Gary, I can see that you are so very far down the right track. I'm reasonably sure that some others I know will not amount.

Of myself, there are serious wonderings. Why look further? When there is no response, what more will He give? Oh to feel spiritually and intellectually awake. Little change in the old kid, no?

Nothing but the very best reaches here about your brother, Gordon. You'd be quite surprised at where his name is had for good (conference talks, traveling elders' remarks, etc.). I have ummaterialized plans to write him. Chuck Radlow is the other of you extraordinary three: Otra vez, hay qué acercarme a ustedes tres. [Again, I need to get close to the three of you]. I've not yet written him either.

Tabasco, Villahermosa, is very green, very hot, very beautiful, and very much postcard archaeology. I like it, would like to see more of it. Don't love Mexicans yet, Spanish is crummy, pronunciation all shot, vocabulary intolerably small. And you, fine friend? Gary, I'd like nothing more than to meet you atop that refiner's fire mentioned in your letter and be mighty close all the way up. With that end, stay close, write always.

Your faithful and admiring friend, Steve

February 6

We had a little confrontation with a Baptist minister last night. I doubt that much good was done. Elder Rencher did most of the talking for our side and remained calm and patient. He did a good job of defending the church against the minister's verbal attacks, but the man simply did not want to listen to us.

The people we find tracting are often entertaining if not always interested in our message. Today, for example, we came across an old grizzled warrior from the days of the Mexican revolution. He didn't want to know about Joseph Smith but was more than willing to tell us about the good old days when he rode, as he claimed, with Pancho Villa. At the next house a lady was so displeased to see us that she unleashed her dogs. Fortunately they were muzzled and didn't do much more than scare the pants of us as they came bursting out of the house. At another place our attempts to present the first lesson were totally disrupted by baby pigs and a goat that kept wandering into the house and charging into our flannel board. We finally picked up and left midway through the lesson when a rooster came flying through the door and landed on Elder Rencher's back.

February 9

While out tracting today we were hailed by a young woman (Señora Esperón) on the street who said she knew we were Mormon missionaries and asked us to come by her home later to teach her and her husband about our religion. She's originally from Poza Rica and said her sister is a member of the church. When we stopped by in the evening to present the first lesson her husband was home from work, intoxicated with some of the local brew. She told us she's afraid he'll drink himself to death and is desperate to find a way to get him to stop. With exaggerated courtesy the husband insisted that we stay and make our presentation, which actually went over fairly well, given the circumstances. Both are young, handsome, intelligent people with a charming little son, two years of age. Hope we can do some good for them. We've been invited back for dinner tomorrow night.

February 11

Our return dinner engagement with the young Esperón couple was a big hit. We gave them the second lesson on the Book of Mormon, which they both accepted without batting an eye. The wife was anxious for us to continue teaching them, so we set another dinner appointment for next week and will present the third lesson on the Word of Wisdom. Not a hint of alcohol in the husband's demeanor tonight. His wife saw us to the door, squeezed our hands and thanked us. She said we had come in answer to her prayers.

Elder Rencher has an appetite for honest work—no padding of reports to impress the *jefes* [bosses/mission leaders] in Veracruz. We've been tracting and giving lessons eleven to thirteen solid hours a day. Tomorrow we're leaving to work with the elders in Coatzacoalcos, a port city located an hour or so from here up the coast. As supervising elder, Rencher wants to cluster the trips so that we visit the missionaries in one place, return home to Mina for a day to check up on our own investigators, leave again the following day for the next missionary visit, and so on. It will be tiring and expensive (the mission home pays for half our bus fares and meals on these trips), but if we concentrate on getting the traveling done with, instead of spreading it out over the month, we should have more time to effectively work with our own investigators in Mina.

I got some more forwarded mail (it's been delayed almost a month) and a new letter from Gary, who has just *learned* of my move to Mina. What has become of my letters to him?

LETTER FROM GARY

Gord: Got your little note of the 23rd yesterday. First inkling I've had of your new address (our mailman was sick and didn't feel like making his route for the last four days). Anyway, it's about time they moved you from San Martín. Naturally you'll tell me about the new place in your next letter. I'm just hoping that they landed you with a decent companion this time around. Speaking of companions, mine [Elder Haney] definitely won't be a candidate for assistant to the president, but we get along. I characterized him in more detail in my last letter, so I'll just reiterate here that he's a good guy, has a simple faith in the gospel, and wants to do well. But he doesn't know how to apply himself, wastes time, and lacks a lot of experience.

Another elder in our house has his wall strewn with all manner of trite slogans, so I extracted an observation from one of London's past letters and tacked it up along side: "How can a missionary, who knows this church is true without doubt, sit on his butt?" That bothered my companion for a little while. But he still gives a sincere testimony every morning before we leave the house and then we piddle away a lot of valuable hours the rest of the day. I don't know, I'm still looking for a stronger testimony than the one I have, but in the meantime, there's always self-respect. We've always worked pretty hard at that. I'm hoping that I won't lose some of the pride I've got, as long as I have to be subject to the impeding and disheartening whims of someone else. We've always been independent, disliked being told what to do, and felt rebellious toward assumed authority. Foolishness and folly, perhaps, but for me this has been the biggest personal stumbling block during my mission in achieving contentment with the work. I certainly haven't learned much humility in this respect, and I don't want to. Not that I've been a malcontent, but I know what I have to do, and I don't like other idiots botching it for me. So much for ranting. It will be a wait before seniorship beckons anyway. There's a long waiting line and no one is coming in or going out of the mission for awhile.

It's kind of hard to tell how my personal progress is coming from such close range, but wherever it is, I know it should be much better. Spanish still has a long way to go, but I can occasionally see faint flashes. What's with the seventy-five push-ups and sit-ups (Mom tells me)? I had to up my ante fifteen this morning to stay even. I think I weigh about 155 pounds, chest is filling out, gut reasonably hard, legs scrawny and in worthless condition.

Hey, how about that Old Testament? I'm almost sorry I started reading it. How did you like the time when Elijah curses the forty little children for making snide remarks, following which the bears come out of the woods and eat them all as punishment for being disrespectful to Elijah!

Natalie is now at the LTM in Provo to study German before she goes to Austria. Kathy had a relapse at the first of the month, but is improving again and is now starting to make long-range marriage plans. She'll go back to the University of Utah Library full time at $4,700 a year, with ideas of laying up some cash for the future. She also points out that spouses of full-time University of Utah employees are entitled to a 50 percent tuition reduction.

I'm afraid that my own plans and aspirations beyond the mission haven't crystallized much. Law is a long go, especially three years behind our graduating class, but it's worthy of careful consideration. Finances and marriage would have to be pondered in connection with seven more years of school. But whatever, I agree we ought to at least think we have some plans by the time we go home. Let's keep tossing ideas back and forth.

Hoping and praying that you are well, while I am stealing strength and support from you, as always, Gar

February 12

We had to defend ourselves against the attack of another Protestant minister today who has been observing us tract in the vicinity of his church. I should say Elder Rencher defended us again. This one had studied Mormonism, or so he claims, and is, in fact, somewhat familiar with our missionary program. He called into question the depth of our convictions and taunted us by saying that Mormon missionaries rely on memorized spiels without which our true shallowness in religion would be revealed. He said that serving a mission is simply a Mormon obligation and that unlike true ministers of the gospel our commitment to the Lord is merely for two years, after which we forget the Mexicans we've taught and eagerly return home to follow worldly occupations in the U.S. To his everlasting credit Elder Rencher rose to his feet and said, "What are you talking about? I intend to serve the Lord and his church all the days of my life, no matter where I might be, no matter what else I might do." He then proceeded to bear a strong, personal witness to the divinity of our calling and purpose in Mexico. But where was *my* voice? To my shame I said nothing. Was I afraid? Afraid of what? I don't know. I do know that Elder Rencher must be a little disappointed in my failure to support him better. It's apparent that I need to do some soul-searching and re-dedication to my missionary calling. I've worked hard at the task of becoming a decent missionary, but after today I realize that I still need much greater faith and conviction to do this work right.

February 13

Tonight we gave the Word of Wisdom lesson to the Esperón couple. The husband readily admitted that he had a drinking problem and wants to do something about it. We were encouraged to learn that he's not had a drink for several days, even though we said nothing about it last week. He consented to offer a prayer at the conclusion of our discussion and asked for God's help to strengthen his resolve.

February 14

Elder Rencher and I conducted a baptismal service at the *capilla* this morning after Sunday school. Our convert was a reference visit from one of the members. She accepted our message from the beginning and seems to have a strong testimony of its truthfulness. The services were greatly delayed, however. The motor to the water pump, which we depend on to fill the *pila* [baptismal font], broke down, and Elder Rencher and I ended up drawing buckets of water by hand from the well while everyone else stood around giving us advice. We were disappointed that the Esperóns didn't show up for church services today but were also glad that they and other investigators were not here to witness the fiasco of the pump.

February 16

We arrived home from San Andrés last night and discovered that the house had been burglarized. Our rooms were turned upside down, with our belongings scattered all over the place. A lot of valuable things were left untouched, but for some reason my shoes were taken (the good pair of Florsheims I've been saving) along with some other odds and ends from the other elders. The only other shoes I have left are just about shot.

Villahermosa, February 18

Elder Rencher and I are in Villahermosa, a picturesque city a hundred miles southeast of Minatitlán, working with Elders Thomas (who replaced me in Puebla as junior companion to Elder Orozco, but is now senior here), Naegle, Burch, and Chandler (Chandler has become so discouraged that he's requested President Hatch to send him home. Rencher's trying to persuade him to stick it out a little longer). Burch and I got caught in a downpour this afternoon while tracting and were thoroughly soaked. My shoes are completely ruined and look like Toltec artifacts. Unfortunately I'll have to get by with them for awhile longer until I can afford to buy a new pair next month. Maybe they'll look a little better once they've dried out.

To pass away the hours traveling on the bus between Mina and Villahermosa, Elder Rencher suggested we recite scriptures to each other from memory. When it was my turn it took well over an hour to give all the passages I have memorized in Spanish. Rencher said nothing when I finished but seemed surprised at what I knew. As for me, I wish I had much better language and teaching ability at this point in my mission. Memorizing is not enough.

I have come to admire Elder Rencher, who's not the kind of guy that you would assume to be a leader and outstanding missionary just by looking at him. But in fact he is. His well-deserved reputation in the mission is based on results, not on impressive appearance or manner. No one has worked harder or been more successful. Sent to open up Papantla, a small town north of Veracruz, Elder Rencher converted a locally prominent dentist and through him scores of people were subsequently baptized. Papantla became a missionary gold mine. Today, just a year or so later, Papantla boasts one of the most active, thriving branches in the mission. [Papantla subsequently has become a stake center, with seven wards.]

Just before leaving on our trip I got another letter from Gary, who's become pretty agitated with mail delays in Guadalajara. He says that Chuck Radlow is still planning on coming to Mexico for a visit next month. I wonder if Chuck will ever accept a call to serve a mission himself? Frankly, it's a little hard for me to picture Chuck, whose billowing philosophy on how to practice the Golden Rule often seems removed from the problems of real people living in places like Mexico, putting up with the daily grind of missionary life.

LETTER FROM GARY

Gord: I became a trifle pissed off yesterday. It was nice that I received five letters at once from various correspondents (including you), but no one has been receiving the letters I have been writing. I'm not sure why I've been dogged by messed-up mail wherever I've gone—while almost everyone else remains relatively unscathed—unless the old Bad Guy has merely stumbled onto a good way to bug me. If so, I congratulate him. To give you an idea: Our so-called mailman has missed making his rounds ten out of the last fifteen working days. Kathy hasn't heard from me in two weeks, although I've sent her four letters. I received a note of needles from Chuck saying that he had not heard from me since long before Christmas, and that he would appreciate a reply to the letter he last wrote (which accompanied a typewriter he also sent), so that he would at least know if his present had arrived (it never has), and what was I, an ingrate or something? The fact is, last time I heard word from him was in the middle of November, and in the meantime I have written him two subsequently lost letters accusing him of being a lazy lout and no good bum for not writing to me. By the way, Chuck is coming to Mexico about the twenty-fifth of March. As he put it, in his best Doctrine and Covenants imitation: "In other words, noodlehead, expect my bod to descend upon you and the other elders with lightening speed. Behold, I cometh whether wanted or not."

But anyway, so you're with a good guy now. That's great. Elder Haney and I are still getting along well enough, our work is starting to pick up (even though I have to keep pushing and prodding), and we may even baptize ten or so people in March. We have one real good family (the Torreses) who appear to be on the brink. They sit us down for a meal every time we visit. They've attended church meetings and have been impressed. The father is having a struggle with the Word of Wisdom, but shows signs of making progress. One problem: the two teenage daughters, I'm afraid, have taken more of an interest in us on a personal level than in our message. My companion gets a little giddy around girls after all those hermity years he spent growing up on the farm, and some minor flirting gets carried on. During the third lesson with them last night it became quite noticeable that neither one of them had anything on under their somewhat skimpy dresses, and throughout the discussion bare skin was observable in areas where it's not supposed to be observable. This did not enhance the spirit of the lesson.

Let me know as soon as this letter reaches you and give me a better idea of what's happening down your way. Your letters mean a great deal so keep punching them out when time permits.

Your brother, Gar

Minatitlán, February 22

I've come down with a cold. The day before yesterday my temperature suddenly shot up to 40-odd degrees centigrade, whatever that means, so I went to bed after lunch instead of going out to tract (first time I've done that since I was sick in San Martín). When I awoke an hour later the fever was gone, so we went back to work. I'm hoarse and congested but otherwise feel okay. Today I'm on my own. Elder Rencher left yesterday to attend a supervising elders' conference in Veracruz.

Later: Without a companion to work with I did very little today except study and keep a dinner appointment with the Esperóns, who continue to receive us warmly but have not yet attended church. For many Mexican Catholics our member requirements of active participation and regular attendance at church meetings run against their habits of passive religious involvement.

A few jump headfirst into church activity, but many others, like the Esperóns, are apprehensive and resistant, even when they accept our teachings as true.

February 25

In spite of a lingering cold, my health is generally good. But our diet sure has taken a nosedive. The maid gives us frijoles and tortillas for every meal and that seems to be the extent of her cooking skill. Elder Rencher complained and she said she needed more money. We're now in the market for a new maid. Tropical fruit grows in the yard. Papaya tastes like rotten cantaloupe. Mangos aren't bad (carrot-peach flavor), but are slimy and impossible to eat without making a mess of yourself. Our water pump is broken again and we're without any running water in the house. Until we get a new pump motor we've been showering in the morning by dousing ourselves with a bucket of cold water drawn from the well. We use the same method for flushing the toilet. I slipped and fell down the stairs yesterday while going for the bucket. Bruised my tailbone right smartly and I've been limping around ever since.

It looks like the mail situation will never be completely cleared up. I just got a Christmas card today from home, postmarked November twenty-fourth. At the same time I got a quicky response from Gary whose last letter arrived less than a week ago.

LETTER FROM GARY

Gord: I've got a new senior companion now. Elder Haney had been here for five months and finally moved on to new pastures a week ago. When his transfer telegram arrived he seemed pleased. But "Mom" Velazco, the member woman who lives a half block down the street from us, was not and carried on like she had just lost a son. All of the missionaries filed over to her house for hot chocolate and cookies to make her feel better (which we didn't do).

My new senior—Ray Throgg—is already known to me from sharing an apartment with him while Smelt and I were companions in Mexico City. So I also know I'll have to be contending with a more-or-less problem child. I like Throgg well enough on some levels—he'd be fun as a casual acquaintance—but we don't exactly see eye to eye on missionary attitudes. He's quite competent, but doesn't have much love for what he's doing. He's also the domineering, despot type. He played line in high school and outweighs me by a good fifty pounds (although a lot of his muscle has turned to flab). But if we continue to get along as well as we have during the first week, there shouldn't be any big problems, and although not everything will be accomplished that could, we should also savor some success.

Elder Haney and I almost got trapped by a couple of cuties a few nights ago, just before he left. Tracted-out two girls, and one of them (who looked about seventeen, said she was twenty-two) told us her husband would be back in the evening. So we returned later to talk to him, only of course he wasn't there. The girls had dinner all ready for us, suggested that it might be fun to go to a show, and informed us that they were planning a *día de campo* with us to some secluded spot they knew. Before beating a hasty retreat, we learned that we had stumbled into some big shot's virtual harem, one among many that he apparently has scattered around the city. The girls were getting a little tired of the game, and so decided to round up some fun on the side for themselves.

Sounds like you're suffering a few deprivations, but glad to hear that the important things are going well for you. My clothes have held up adequately so far, although my sewing kit has seen some use. When things calm down a little, I'll see if I can do some shopping for you. Way to be neglectful and get your stuff robbed. By the way, the weather here has been almost perfect—mid-September type. Once in awhile I envy your hardships, when life gets a little too fat around here.

Stay in there and I will too. Your brother, Gar

February 27

The house was broken into again last night while we were out making some visits. Same sorry story as before: our room was a total mess, with things scattered all over. This time Elder Rencher's typewriter was missing, along with some more clothing items and my little travel iron.

February 28

What a pathetic situation. Tonight we were victims of a third robbery in precisely the same mode as the others. I'm now missing most of my pants and shirts. Elder Rencher has lost everything but the clothes on his back. He was also pick-pocketed on the bus last night and is now flat broke. My own resources are low, but I'll share what I have with Elder Rencher (I loaned him 60 pesos [about $5] so he can buy a shirt tomorrow) and we'll try to make do as best we can. Meanwhile, something has got to be done about the break-ins. The new locks we got for the doors were obviously of no deterrence. We'll have to report our losses to the police tomorrow.

March 5

This past week has been an almost total loss. Our missionary efforts have been brought to a painful crawl while we've wasted a lot of time playing cops and robbers. Sunday evening, after the last robbery, we tried to set a trap for the burglars. Elder Rencher and I left as though we were going out to make a visit, but instead we circled around the back of the house. We picked up some sticks and snuck up the stairs to our rooms. The door was ajar—someone was in the house! With hearts pounding and more bluster than good sense we burst into the room to find Elders Calister and Elison poised with their own sticks, ready to give us a thrashing, since of course they thought *we* were the *ladrones* [robbers].

We spent most of the day Tuesday with the police, going all over town to check out some of their suspects. We ended up at the community fun spot, a strip of dance halls, bars, and bordellos on the outskirts of town. There we identified a young kid whom we had occasionally seen loitering around the house with a group of men. They arrested him on the spot, threw him in jail (a real pigpen), and subsequently arrested some other men whom we'd seen in the neighborhood. Since then we've made repeated trips into town to see what can be done. These men are being held by the police without any evidence and apparently they haven't even been questioned yet. They're probably innocent. When Elder Rencher urged the chief of police to set them free, the chief got peeved and told us to mind our own business, that he would take care of the police work in Minatitlán. It would be nice if he would.

Constant interruptions—all springing from the robberies—have practically put a halt to effective missionary work. But we've still got quite a few good investigators and there appears to be a big harvest awaiting us if we can just hitch up our suspenders and resist Satan's efforts to thwart our work. At the present time I'm getting by on three shirts (if you count the one the maid frayed to shreds in the wash), three pairs of socks, three pairs of sadly patched pants, and one pair of gnarled shoes. I wrote to Mom and Dad about the first robbery, but have told them nothing about the latest two. I don't want to be the cause of any additional financial burdens.

March 6

The extra locks we installed in the house are obviously not much of a deterrence to thieves. We can't let our missionary work go down the drain by not going out in the evening to make visits, so we've hired a security guard to watch the house at night. The mission home has agreed to pay the cost of his services.

Elder Rencher and I were appalled today by the ferocity of an eighty-year-old woman, the grandmother of a member family we were supposed to visit. Just before we arrived the family captured a small fox which had been raiding the chicken coop. The fox was strung up by the neck from a pole and was twisting desperately to free itself. We were handed a dull machete and encouraged to take some whacks. When Elder Rencher and I declined, the grandmother grabbed the weapon with both hands, gave a shriek, and rained blows on the fox until its skull splintered.

March 8

We went to the ocean near Coatzacoalcos yesterday afternoon and baptized a girl (Fidélia Gomez Martinez, age sixteen), whose parents are already members. It was a rainy, windy day, and the waves were coming in big and hard, creating explosions of foam as they pounded the beach. I changed into baptismal clothing behind a sand dune, and then we went out in the surf about forty yards and were almost bowled over by several big, salty swells. I tried to time the baptismal prayer so she would go under with an on-coming wave. Fidelia was apprehensive, and it took two attempts to get her completely submerged. Only my second baptism since coming to Minatitlán. We're working as hard as we know how but so far have little in the way of concrete results to show for our efforts.

The young Esperón couple we encountered last month has progressed nicely, however. They've received all but the last lesson. Most importantly, Señor Esperón has not been drinking since the first night we were there. Their baptisms will have to be delayed, however, because Señora Esperón is undergoing surgery tomorrow for what looks like appendicitis. The husband is tense and worried. We gave the *hermana* a blessing and I'm sure she'll be all right. We've also been working with another family that appears promising, the Ortegas (we call them the "Jungle Family" because of their residence in a densely forested area several miles outside of town), who have gone through the fourth lesson and have invited us several times to their home for dinner. Last time we went Hermana Ortega proudly served us liver and scrambled eggs. I gamely eat most everything our investigators feed us, but I have no tolerance for liver, no matter how it's cooked. The only way I could stomach a small portion was to accompany every bite of liver with a scorching little green pepper that completely annihilated my taste buds. Hermano Ortega is a puzzling man. His wife despairs of his cynicism, yet he somehow seems to be attracted to us and our message. He's intelligent and knowledgeable about world events but lives in near poverty and is often out of work. He has a wacky sense of humor (reminds me a little of Jonathan Winters) that makes it hard to know if he's really serious or not about his investigation of the church. But his wife certainly is sincere.

Gary writes that he has mailed me some clothing items which should arrive soon. His comments on self-respect express my feelings exactly.

LETTER FROM GARY

Gord: Your present worldly condition doesn't sound too hot. I've sent a shirt and a couple of pairs of socks to help out a little, hoping they'll arrive not too long after this letter. No remarks about the odd styling—it's the only button-down I could search out, and I figured that a missionary living in the jungle with that ridiculous Arrow shirt with the spastic collar as third best shouldn't be very fussy. Sorry the care package couldn't have been bigger; my own funds are anemic and can only stand so much blood loss at one time. Still, don't worry about the money. I've been saving a little here and there to take care of just such emergencies and, besides, we're both sponging our sheckles from the same source. Let me know as soon as the stuff arrives so I can be sure it's safe to send some more of whatever else you need.

I sympathize with your material miseries but I envy your spiritual and personal growth. Thanks for the admonitory comments in your last letter. I needed it. You're right about letting down. It's been a slow, practically unnoticeable process, but when I wake up and take stock I see how far I've slipped. It's not hard for most missionaries to allow sluggardly companions to leak out their own desire, but you and I have always been almost exclusively concerned in contending with ourselves. If we make every effort to maintain our own self-respect, then in spite of what others do, or fail to do, we can be happy and satisfied. That's the way it was in the Language Training Mission, and that's the way it should always be. I'm proud of your continued accomplishments. My own could stand a little buffing, but there's still a lot of polish left in the can. I think I've pushed the language breakthrough almost to the edge and in another month or so should see it rolling down the hill.

Anticipated personality clashes with my new companion [Elder Throgg] have so far failed to materialize in a serious way. Still, we couldn't be accused of over-zealousness in our efforts to spread around the Good Word. The most obvious hindrance to missionary enthusiasm has been a budding romance between my companion and a very sharp member girl—Neome Velazco, oldest daughter of "Mom" Velazco. Nothing bad has happened yet, but I fear more serious feelings are involved than in the usual hanky-panky flirting. As a result we're frittering away precious time while Throgg finds daily excuses to visit the girl, and our work is suffering. The number of romance problems that take place in the mission field is really an eye-opener. Just recently our mission secretary in Mexico City got engaged to a member girl and was sent home early in semi-disgrace.

How's your health? Mine's been great. Thanks for always reminding me who we are.

Your brother, Gar

March 18

We've accumulated a total of forty-five investigators but all of them seem to have problems and none are yet ready for baptism. We've discovered that three of the couples we're teaching, including the Ortegas, aren't married. Hermana Esperón is recuperating from her appendicitis operation and won't be fully recovered until the end of the month. In the meantime, I regret to say that her husband has started to drink again, which casts a pall over all of our previous efforts. I don't know exactly where we went wrong here or, if indeed, there is anything more we can do to help. We thought previously Esperón had turned the corner. We were surprised and saddened by his drinking relapse. With the *hermana*'s health problems, their situation does not look bright at the moment.

March 22

Intolerable, sweltering heat. Sweat dripping off my wrist and hand makes it almost impossible to write letters or in my journal without smearing the ink. By the time we leave in the morning to catch a bus to our tracting area our shirts are already soaking wet with perspiration and our shirts sticking to our backs.

Several of our unmarried couples already have draining financial debts which makes it all the more difficult for them to come up with the necessary cash for a civil service license. Justices of the peace here charge outrageous fees of 100 pesos [$8] for their services and that's beyond the daily means of many of our investigators. If we tried to pay for all the marriages of our unmarried investigators we'd quickly go broke ourselves. In fact, a number of our recent tracting contacts have been young unmarried women with children. It's often difficult to teach or talk to them because of their squirming babies who want to be breast fed during our presentation of the lessons. This afternoon we struggled to get through the first lesson with a topless young mother who shifted her hungry son from one breast to the other as we talked, dripping milk like a leaky spigot.

I'm afraid we've lost the Esperón family. Hermana Esperón has gone temporarily to stay with her sister in Poza Rica. Her husband now tries to avoid us and is drinking heavily again. Hermana Esperón is young, beautiful, and desperate. Her husband's a great guy when he's sober. The Jungle Family [the Ortegas] is still hanging on, but Hermano Ortega refuses to attend any church meetings and has done nothing to get a marriage license. He's going to have to take some initiative. We're not going to push anymore.

March 24

Yesterday we arrived home and found a surprise telegram for Elder Rencher. He's been made zone director of the Veracruz Zone and leaves tomorrow for Jalapa, Veracruz. The move was totally unexpected. We just finished an eighty-eight-hour week of solid work and were looking forward to the dividends of our efforts in the month to come. According to the telegram, my new companion will be David Smith, formerly supervising elder of the Puebla District. I already know him from my days in San Martín. He's a good guy and an outstanding missionary.

It goes without saying that I greatly respect and admire Elder Rencher and that I have benefited a great deal from our companionship. Before leaving he was generous enough to say that I was the best companion he's had. From Elder Rencher I've observed the power of humility when combined with diligence and purpose in action. He's shown me what missionary work should be like and how a missionary should conduct himself.

8

∾

"I'm a Damn Fool":
Gary's Story as Junior Companion in Guadalajara

During Gary's last three months in Guadalajara, conventional missionary work was almost completely eclipsed by his latest, and most obdurate, senior companion's budding romance with a young woman member and corresponding distaste for proselyting. Gary's relationship with his companion steadily deteriorated as he increasingly objected to his senior's lack of missionary commitment and struggled to resist a growing cynicism in his own outlook. Gary's frustration with his companion's approach to missionary work also was expressed in their lengthy, but ultimately failed, attempt to steer a large investigator family with several teenaged daughters through the standard lesson sequence. Much more so than in Mexico City, Gary was exposed in Guadalajara to participating in the religious and social activities of the local branch and to much closer involvement with the personal lives and problems of branch members. His stay in Guadalajara was highlighted by a short visit from Chuck Radlow (whose sudden appearance stimulated ambivalent reflections on the discrepancies between idealized conceptions of missionary life and Gary's frustrating subordinate status in Guadalajara), some limited opportunities to exercise his own approach to missionary work with a novice missionary during intermittent absences of his senior companion, and a somewhat strange (but humorous) encounter with what Gary and a temporary, novice companion initially assumed were supernatural forces opposing their missionary effort. But the leitmotif of Gary's account of his stay in Guadalajara was a growing sense of stagnation and oppression under a senior companion who had lost the desire to do missionary work.

In the meantime, Gordon's spirits remained high as his compatibility with companions continued in contrast to Gary's sinking relations. Gordon's letters in this chapter overlap somewhat with his earlier journal accounts in Minatitlán (in which, for example, the house robberies and tropical living conditions are reported). His response to Gary's thwarted and discouraging situation was to write encouraging, even admonitory, letters with references to his own struggles, faith-promoting experiences, and missionary growth.

Guadalajara, February 16, 1965

Elder Haney left for Mexico City tonight at 10:30. Spent most of the day getting him packed, visiting members and investigators to say goodbye, etc. In ways, I personally slumped a lot with Elder Haney. In other ways I progressed. Elder Haney needed pushing, and that's what I began to do, but not intelligently enough, I'm afraid.

I'll need my wits about me now more than ever. My new senior is none other than Elder Throgg—Tim Bayer's old companion from our days together last fall in the Roma District. Throgg's a person of ability but his seriousness about missionary work is not always evident, and there is a bit of a tyrant, if not a bully, underneath the surface of his caustic joking. I don't intend to get run over, but I do intend to do my best to make the time we spend together a success.

February 17

Spent part of the day introducing Elder Throgg to our investigators, and he seemed to make a good impression on most of them. However, I feel disaster is starting to hang over the Torres family. We were a half hour late to begin the lesson, waiting for everyone to show up. When we did get under way, some of the little kids were a bit of a nuisance, interrupting a few times. When Gloria's boyfriend arrived on the scene, Elder Throgg lost patience, made sudden excuses, and we left. Poor strategy, I'm afraid. All of them were stunned, embarrassed, and didn't know what to say. I only hope we won't lose them through Throgg's lack of good judgment.

February 18

We're getting marriage procedures under way for the Lunas and should have everything taken care of by next Monday. They attended sacrament meeting for the first time and were favorably impressed. They weren't exactly clad in costly apparel, but were scrubbed clean and obviously enjoyed the courtesy and friendliness of the members. We had set a second lesson up with Gloria Torres's boyfriend this evening, but he didn't show. Not a good sign after what happened last night. In addition, we again postponed our teaching visit with the Torres family. I'm becoming more worried. Four postponed fourth lessons now, counting two previous occasions with Elder Haney.

February 19

We're drawing closer to the brink of losing the Torres family—fifth time we've gone away without completing the fourth lesson. Tonight we only got as far as a simple review of religious authority when suddenly both Diana and Gloria raised their hackles and jumped to the defense of Catholicism, catching us completely off guard. Elder Throgg began reading scriptures to show where Catholicism is wrong, and they became more firmly entrenched in an "underdog" defense to fend off criticism. The frustrating thing is that they actually know the Catholic Church is in error, having beautifully accepted the first lesson on apostasy and restoration, and are looking for something better. But somehow we've made a wrong turn and are heading down a bad trail. Several factors enter in, I suppose: Mr. Torres's steadying influence is missed while he's gone on his business trip; it's been two weeks since they've really had a lesson; the intrusion of Gloria's boyfriend hasn't helped; and, finally, I think there is some hostility felt towards Elder Throgg as Elder Haney's replacement, particularly as Throgg tends to be brusque at times and quick to anger. Still, our flattened hopes were somewhat propped up again as we left, since the girls admitted that their surprise stand had mostly been a defensive reaction against what they had seen as unnecessary criticism. They said they are seriously trying to make a decision towards baptism.

February 20

Not a very fruitful day. An uncomfortably familiar tendency is beginning to emerge: we're starting to spend too much time dropping by the Velazcos' in lieu of actual missionary work. I did get a letter from Gordon today, whose account of jungle living makes our conditions here seem pretty soft by comparison.

LETTER FROM GORDON

Gar: My companions in Minatitlán and I are all a little vexed right now. Last night someone broke in, ransacked our house, strewed things all over and stole a number of clothing items which really impoverishes my wardrobe. As a matter of fact, all of my clothes are starting to go to pot. Two of my remaining pairs of pants have disintegrated in the rear end (I tried to patch them, but they make me look like I've got a big scar on my butt), and my remaining pair of shoes just split out along the sides. I'm looking less and less like a missionary and more and more like a beggarly peddler.

How's the weather in Guadalajara? Here, everything's a boiling sulk. Whenever you sit down after walking a bit the floodgates of perspiration are let loose, and in a couple of minutes you look like someone's washrag and smell twice as stale. You can't afford to cut yourself shaving or you develop a moldy scab that festers and grows all over your face. I've got several. We have all the inconveniences of a nice jungle town here: no hot water, battalions of mosquitoes, gargantuan leaping spiders in our bedroom, and hordes of militant fire ants in our back yard. It's not really all *that* bad; in fact, I like the place a lot.

Have you heard? Dave Lingwall's engaged to get married. I can't believe it either. By the way, what's the current status of Kathy's and your marital plans? (Good grief, I'm making it sound like you've already committed yourself.) As for me, I haven't heard from Beckie for over a month. I suspect that several letters were lost in the shift from San Martín, but I also detect a cooling trend in Beckie's and my relationship. I assume she's been dating other guys. Can't blame her if she is. We never made any promises to one another before I left for Mexico. With a year and a half yet to go before we finish our missions it's probably a bit early to get all heated up about future plans. Still, I'd like to leave the mission field with a clearer idea of what I want to pursue in life. Are you still playing around with the idea of a law career? Keep me posted on your thinking. Well, it's about time for us to go out and do battle with the infidels in this beastly heat. Let's see if we can't get our letters better coordinated.

Your brother, Gord

February 21

A pleasant Sunday, even though not much missionary work was accomplished. Labored this morning over my talk for sacrament meeting. After Sunday school (the Torres girls attended on their own), we had our usual Sunday dinner at the "Gringo's" pizza place. My talk on genealogy this evening was fair. The whole Torres family came, minus the mother. Diana and the third oldest girl stayed afterward for what turned out to be a good fireside at the Velazcos'. Some simple refreshments, songs, etc. followed the talks. Afterward, Diana invited us over to the Torreses' home for tamales, but Elder Throgg didn't want to go, so we made excuses. Again, I don't think we're being very smart in our handling of this situation.

February 22

We arranged for the Lunas to be married this morning. The proceedings took about ten minutes and didn't cost us anything. The whole family is set to be baptized tomorrow afternoon.

Went over to the Torreses' this evening for tamales and *atole,* but once again no lesson. Elder Throgg had previously accepted an invitation to eat at Miranda's with Elders Merkley and Winslow at 9:30 P.M., so we didn't have time to run through the long (and crucial) fourth lesson. I don't think Throgg is handling the Torres family very wisely. But we'll see what happens; they ought to be members by the end of the month. Tempers raised a few notches between my companion and Winslow (who is an easily provoked hothead) after we arrived home.

February 23

We baptized the Lunas this afternoon. They're good people. Unfortunately they've been receiving quite a bit of persecution from their neighbors. Hope it won't worsen. The *hermana*'s health isn't too hot, and they haven't the means to move elsewhere.

Neome Velazco had another rough spell at Mutual [Mutual Improvement Association, a week-night meeting for youths] tonight, caused, apparently, by Carlos after a shouting session. Carlos is a returned Mexican missionary but seems to be a complete ass. We'll have to have a little talk with him about cooling it. Anyway, Neome's attack was the same as on previous occasions: a dead faint in the chapel area; we carried her upstairs to a bed in our room; intense stomach pain/cramps after finally regaining consciousness. The regular doctor wasn't even home this time, so after the usual argument and confusion about what to do, Elder Throgg and I wrapped Neome in a blanket, packed her down to someone's car, and drove her over to the other side of the city to see a member doctor who belongs to the Unión Branch. The doctor gave her some shots, we waited for about a half hour until she calmed down, then took her home.

February 24

Another semi-meal at the Torreses' but still no fourth lesson. Diana had some visitors from their hometown, so we postponed again. Looks like we'll also have to postpone their baptismal date until next month. Meanwhile, neighbors are starting to give the Torres children a bad time. They won't play with the *"Mormones."*

February 25

An unfruitful day. Morning tracting brought no success. Afternoon was a waste. Spent some more time at the Velazcos'. Throgg, as Haney before him, likes it too well over there, particularly with Neome on hand. The Torreses are out for this month. Boyfriend Hugo was there again tonight, and after the usual snack, we only talked about the church in general terms. We'll give them all a review next time. But every day we put off on the lessons they become less serious about any sort of commitment to be baptized.

February 26

Received what amounted to a good kick in the pants from Gord in the form of an admonishing letter. I need it, too. He's a great source of strength for me and I can't be grateful enough for him.

LETTER FROM GORDON

Gar: I think I sense a little mold beginning to form on both of us. Let's shake it off. I know we've both got what it takes to make it to the top of our respective missions. We've been in the mission field a while. We know what there is to be achieved and we know what we're capable of. We know how far we can go if we want to. I hope these aren't just greedy ambitions. I know too that we have to place goals. I've achieved some success in the mission. I've felt proud of myself. But there has also been a constant battle to keep from slipping, and I feel as if my ideals and personal commitment may have slacked off a little bit of late.

When I was working with Elder Splinders in San Martín I had all the time I could want for personal study and, in general, I would say I made good use of that time. Naturally my well-formed study practices were altered once I transferred to Minatitlán and started working with ambitious companions. There just hasn't been as much time for self-indulgence and I've had to ditch a lot of it. I'm glad that through personal study I was able to develop a good scriptural foundation, though. My new companion, Elder Rencher, seemed a bit taken back when he discovered that my command of the scriptures was much greater than his own. We hadn't had a study class our first week together so we decided to have one on the bus while traveling to check on the elders in Villahermosa (Rencher is supervising elder here, in case you didn't get my other letter). So he asked me to give as many scriptures as I could by memory. I went on for over an hour, reciting scriptures in Spanish from memory. My companion sat there in silence, and at first I thought I might have alienated him. But instead, I believe I've gained his respect. Rencher's a dedicated missionary, a hard worker, and has a much stronger testimony than I.

Anyway, those scriptures were feeding me spiritually while I was learning them in San Martín. I realized that when I reviewed them this morning. When I finished, it felt good. And I remembered that this was the way I felt every morning after my own little class by myself in San Martín. It was really exhilarating to discover spiritual truths, see how they applied to life, and store them up in my own mind. Well, that's one facet of growth, I'm sure: a constant contact with that which edifies. I hope the realization of this need will help me keep on the ball, even though time and new levels of responsibility won't permit me to maintain certain self-absorbing practices of the past. School is over and it's time to get on the stick.

I will leave out repulsive details of jungle life, having the faith that you received my other letter that took care of all that. I finally heard from Beckie after two months of silence. The mail apparently played havoc with a couple of letters she wrote, so it looks like we're back on track again. Everybody around here has been dragging out scriptural prophecies of a third world war. That would sure spoil a few plans. And Vietnam? I shudder to think of us if we should ever get sucked into that mess.

Well Gar, when we parted company last August and I was choking down the old tennis ball in my throat at the Mexico City airport, I promised myself I'd do the best job I could at becoming a good missionary. I imagine you felt the same way. I've slipped occasionally, I know, but as long as I can keep reaching back and pulling myself up, I'll get the job done. Your fear was that you wouldn't make complete use of your potential, but I'm assured that you will. And this assurance keeps me going.

Your brother, Gord

February 27

The district missionary conference this morning at our house, with President Hatch in attendance from Mexico City, was good. The talent show in the evening was the usual chaos, starting an hour and a half late. So what, everybody enjoyed it. The great Benjamín Para, whom we all heard so much about at the Language Training Mission, was present as master of ceremonies. Para is short and powerfully built, with shoulders a yard wide. He's a native Mexican from a small town north of Mexico City and served such a successful mission here in the late 1950s and early 1960s that his deeds have already become legendary.

February 28

District conference continued in Unión today and was again very good. Neome Velazco talked with President Hatch afterward, and it looks like she's going to be a missionary pretty soon. She's wanted it badly and is ecstatic. I'm happy for her. Her physical and emotional problems will require a tight rein, but with her intelligence and energy she should make a fine missionary. Elder Throgg and I bought six pizzas for a little celebration party in the evening at the Velazcos'.

March 1

Día de campo with the Velazcos. Took a bus out in the weeds to some small resort area. It's a good thing for my companion that Neome will be leaving soon. They like each other a bit too much. Returned in the evening, cleaned up, and went to the movies—a couple of old losers. Not exactly my idea of a day of peace and relaxation.

March 2

Made brief visits with the Torreses and the Lunas, then returned home to sit in on the Relief Society [women's auxiliary organization] class at the house— two hours of pounding, but I guess that's the way they learn the gospel. Mutual this evening was dispiriting. The Torres girls came but giggled and goofed around all night. They show little respect for things of a serious nature and apparently have still not caught a glimpse of what the church is really all about.

March 5

Have neglected writing for a few days. Some worries afoot. My companion and Neome are falling in love. Neome's mission call was postponed by President Hatch—I had been assuming she would soon be gone and the problem would solve itself. Nothing bad has happened yet, but the situation is not good. Just as in the days of Elder Haney, we're over to the Velazcos' almost every spare moment, sometimes for hours. Neome has gone with us several times to check visits (ostensibly to gain missionary experience), and every day there are other excuses to be with her. I've been reluctant to say much up till now. On the surface, I've gotten along surprisingly well so far with Elder Throgg, but I can't keep quiet any longer. I wouldn't want to witness a tragedy, let alone be a passive contributor to it.

March 6

Spent all morning talking to my companion about Neome while we were in town cashing a check and shopping. We almost exclusively discussed Neome's apparent feelings for my companion and said practically nothing about his own feelings. The main thing is that the problem is now out in the open, and he's forced to stop drifting into dangerous rationalizations and take serious stock. Who knows what will happen next? But at least it's clear that they can't continue being around each other all the time. Either she must receive her mission call or Throgg will have to request a change.

March 8

Assistants to the president, Fergason and Bland, are visiting with us for a few days. Hope they'll lean a little on Elder Throgg. Throgg tells me he talked to Neome, but she denied anything more serious then friendship, leaving Throgg feeling foolish. He still won't admit his own involvement, but appears to be hooked fairly bad, and it's hurting him, our work, and starting to sap some of the starch out of me.

This morning we stayed home. My companion said he could feel the runs coming on as an after-effect of being sick the last two days. In the afternoon I mailed some shirts and socks to Gord, whose wardrobe has almost been wiped out by a series of house robberies. Then on to a little tracting and a stop at the Torreses'. Mr. Torres was supposed to be home but wasn't. I'm afraid we can about kiss them off. Saw a bottle of brandy on a counter in the house. Mrs. Torres told us it belonged to a relative. It's true they've fallen a long way, but we as missionaries must accept part of the blame for very poor handling. Back to the Velazcos' in the evening. It's almost like an addiction now. My companion has resolved to stay away during the day and only go over "nights when we're free." I have a hunch we're suddenly going to start finding that we have a lot of free evenings.

March 10

Elders Bland and Fergason worked all day with us. I went with Ferg in the morning, and we talked a little about Neome and Throgg. Fergason knows Throgg pretty well (they were in the same cohort together at the LTM), and he agrees there is reason for concern. He'll consult with President Hatch on his return to Mexico City.

March 11

Visited the Velazcos' *three* (!) different times during the day. We were about ready to eat this evening when old Hermana Beruben came limping over and wanted us to give some urgent counsel to her granddaughter, Cristina, who had just had a big emotional blow-up at home. A sad situation: the older brothers beat the girls, the girls are at each others' throats, the father's a tyrant. Throgg talked to Cristina for over a hour and got her more or less calmed down. Cris is a good girl, in fact remarkably good considering the circumstances. I credit my companion for counseling her in a very effective way. Who will counsel him?

March 13

Passed by the Velazcos' tonight, and they immediately clamored for us to eat and then visit the rest of the evening. But I'm about fed up and said I was going home. Had hoped that Throgg would make a stink about me leaving so we could clear the situation up a little, but he didn't—just stayed and I left. A dilemma for me, since I was the one leaving my companion. Further, I have chosen not to tell Elder Merkley, our supervising elder, about what's been going on with the Velazcos. I wound up waiting for my companion downstairs in the darkened *capilla* area of our house. Winslow came downstairs to fix a sandwich, so I ducked out the back and he shut the door, locking me out. Waited about an hour for Throgg to return and unlock the door for us both with his key. He was relieved to find that the other elders knew nothing of his remaining alone at the Velazcos', and we didn't try to resolve the larger issues. We've got to have a talk pretty quick.

March 14

Checked some visits before Sunday school. Met the Torres girls coming to church on our way home. My companion still won't set a new visit with them. Over to the Velazcos' after sacrament meeting to plan yet another outing for tomorrow, this time at least including all the missionaries.

March 15

The Unión elders and the Velazcos accompanied us on our outing to a miniature version of the Grand Canyon located not far from where I did my first tracting with Elder Haney. It was a long way down to the river bottom via a switch-back trail. Hermana Velazco only made it halfway down with the smallest girl and then holed up in a wayside resting place to wait out the day. The rest of us, upon reaching the canyon bottom, waded around in the river and tossed rocks in the water for a couple of hours. The climb back up was a killer. Elder Merkley and I left the others behind and eventually fell into a semi-competition to be first out. Merkley is a near-Olympic class wrestler who exercises faithfully to stay in shape. But I figured that those twenty-mile forced marches in army basic training had conditioned me to tolerate a fair amount of physical torture. Anyway, we climbed out in around an hour (Merkley surged ahead at the end), and the effort really exhausted both of us. I personally guzzled down eight soda pops at a nearby *tienda* and contemplated an alarming sunburn on arms, neck, and face while we waited for the rest of the group to surface. It took two hours more before Mom Velazco and her youngest kids straggled up, but I was almost surprised that she made it back at all—she must weigh close to three hundred pounds.

March 16

A bad day. Started off at 3:00 A.M. this morning when Elder Merkley's alarm went off early, but unfortunately no one noticed the actual time. We all got up, shaved, and dressed for district meeting—except my companion, who refused to budge from bed. Arrived at Unión about 3:30 A.M., and only after arousing the incredulous elders there did we discover our mistake. They naturally thought we were nuts. We returned home and then slept in until 7:45 A.M. Everyone was tired and sunburned from yesterday's exertions. We didn't do much all day in the way of work. We did manage to make it over to the Velazcos' a couple of times though, so Elder Throgg and I finally had a few words. It angered him to hear my remonstrances, but it cleared the air a little and let him know what I think about the hours we waste at the Velazcos'—especially connected with Neome—and was a relief of sorts. I don't know how this will affect our relationship, but I hope we'll not be seeing the Velazcos as often. As far as I'm concerned, Throgg has been shooting down the last part of his mission and I don't like to see it.

Elder Merkley was suddenly struck ill this afternoon with a very high temperature and severe headache. I paid out 100 pesos for medicine and doctor fees. The doctor is a member, but doesn't seem to know what he's doing, and Merkley looks pretty bad. Winslow will be giving him the medicine every few hours during the night, but if he's not better tomorrow, we will have to call President Hatch.

March 18

Merkley was in a bad way all day yesterday. The doctor came again with more medication, but he really didn't know what was wrong. We finally phoned President Hatch, and he was going to fly in to conduct a personal examination, but fortunately Merkley gradually started feeling a little better, so there wasn't any need. Maybe too much sun and soda pop from our day in the canyon?

Gar: Man, these have been hectic days. We've been ducking disaster ever since the robberies occurred. We've grappled with the blubbery and sweaty arm of Mexican justice, gotten into ridiculous scriptural tiffs with Protestant ministers, and must now flush our toilet with a bucket of water drawn from the well because our plumbing has broken down.

The police finally sent some detectives to investigate our robberies and we sicced them on a couple of raggardly loiterers whom we'd seen hanging around the house the night before the last break-in. We then spent the rest of the week trying to get them out of jail. Talk about an evil-smelling, dank, moldy hole—just a big cage with nothing more in it than the prisoners and a place to take a leak. It was pitiful. The authorities just threw those poor wretches in jail and left them there; never asked any question nor made any investigations. We went down town every day to find out what was being done, and finally asked that the prisoners be released, seeing that there wasn't a scrap of evidence against them. Well, they sat in there rattling their bars for over a week before they were finally liberated. In spite of these disruptions the missionary work here looks fairly promising. We've got quite a few investigators right now, but most of them are unmarried. That's getting to be a real problem. We're still hoping to have a respectable number of baptisms before the end of the month though.

Currently I'm in good physical shape, but the erosion rate along my hairline is alarming. As you mentioned in a previous letter: unthinkable that we might return home a couple of baldies. Push-ups are hard to keep doing in this hot weather. I go around all day feeling like somebody has taken a giant roll-on deodorant and smeared it over my entire body, leaving a sticky residue of stinging irritation.

Got your CARE package late this afternoon—came at a good time. I've been wearing my companion's socks and the same shirt for the past week. I think I'll be able to make it now, *poco a poco* [little by little], taking a little money out of savings every month for things I need. Hang on to your own money. We'll need to use whatever we can save for school when our missions end. Thanks again for the aid. It's good stuff.

Your brother, Gord

March 21

I directed the music in Sunday school today. I always do a terrible job, but the knuckleheaded branch second counselor can't seem to think of anyone else to call on. Had dinner at the Velazcos'—they've got serious financial problems. We were over there again after sacrament meeting, this time to use their shower (our pump is broken), but their electricity has been cut off, so we showered by candlelight.

March 22

Some days ago we came across a man who had already made extensive investigations of the church. We gave him a quick sixth discussion, and he agreed to be baptized right away because he'll be leaving town soon for an undetermined period of time. I went alone to pick him up this afternoon, but he had a change of heart and didn't want to go. I talked to him and his wife for about twenty minutes, but at this point I don't think it's up to us to force the final step. We may have scared him by rushing, but if he were really ready and convinced he would be more than willing. The wife wants her husband to be baptized, but she supported him and thought it would be better to wait. The news disanimated my companion when I returned empty-handed to the house, and he implied by his reaction that somehow it was my fault for not pressing harder.

Throgg wanted to see a show this evening and we didn't return until 11:00 P.M. A visitor was waiting outside the house when we walked up. It was *Chuck Radlow* (!) incongruously arrived from Stanford, USA, just as promised, only three days early. An odd feeling to see him again, 2,500 miles from home. Being confronted with an old friend in a new world now made familiar is almost more disorienting than one's own initial entry into that world. At any rate, as much as anything else, I've missed someone with whom I can authentically communicate in an intelligent conversation. We talked until 1:00 A.M. but didn't even dent the topic bag. Chuck will only be here for a few days, but I'm looking forward to what time we have.

March 26

The three days Chuck was here went swiftly by. Chuck worked with us the first day: tracting in the morning and afternoon, a couple of visits at night, a dinner-snack at the Velazcos'. His Spanish is about the equal of a new elder arriving in Mexico from the LTM. We went out to Tlaquepaque (the tourist/ mariachi village east of town) the next morning, and Chuck bought some trinkets for his mother. Talking occupied that afternoon and evening. Most of today was spent in town—arranging for Chuck's departure, more shopping, sightseeing, and talking. Chuck hasn't really changed all that much. A little taller, little skinnier, and—unfortunately like me—a little less hair. He talks a lot about loving one's fellow man, serving others, and sympathy for human problems. But I infer, from our lengthy conversations and close observation of his performance in a variety of social settings while he was here, that he still has some difficulty actualizing these kinds of noble sentiments when the old ego starts tugging. As always, Chuck puts his many talents to good use. He was irritating, amusing, and interesting. But perhaps I have been the one to change a bit since coming to Mexico, because I found myself feeling slightly disconnected from the close friendship ties Chuck and I have forged over the last few years. Maybe it was just the peculiar circumstances of our meeting. On the one hand I felt anxious about the distraction from our missionary work, this time due to *my* indulgence, not my senior companion's. But most of all I didn't like being stuck in the role of junior companion during Chuck's stay. I felt suppressed and thwarted, like I had to ask the teacher's permission to go to the bathroom. In moments of reflection like this I sometimes detect an infringing coldness where a spontaneous warmth used to reside, and I realize that I've been withdrawing into an adolescent mold of uncertainty and resentment. No need to over-analyze, just recognize what needs to be done and get on the ball again. But anyway, Chuck's visit was good in the end because his experiences and observations here should leave their mark. He'll take his memories home, sift them over some, blow them up a little, and ultimately be left with some important things to think about.

March 27

Elder Merkley received a telegram today calling him back to Mexico City. All four of us went over to the Velazcos' for dinner. Naturally Mom Velazco was for the moment grief-stricken, but Letícia kept herself under control (although she supposedly has a crush on Elder Merkley). Merkley's Spanish accent is hard to understand, and so some may superficially wonder about his teaching ability. But he's a top missionary where it counts. He works hard and is completely dedicated to his calling. I've seen my share of mediocrities in the mission field. A shame I haven't been able to see more missionaries of Elder Merkley's caliber.

March 28

Branch President Díaz's maid had previously expressed a desire to be baptized, so this morning I picked her up while Throgg went ahead to Unión to prepare the *pila*. But my companion had inexplicably left before we arrived, so I conducted the services by myself. Gave a crummy talk, did the baptizing, confirming, and offered a closing prayer. The lady missionaries were also at Unión with baptisms this morning and passed along a tale of being followed the other day by persons unknown. The church is supposedly under investigation in Mexico as an undesirable foreign religious organization. Elder Merkley's replacement as supervising elder hasn't arrived yet. Elder Winslow is ticked—he's put a year in now as junior and was expecting a promotion as senior this go-round. Can't blame him for being upset.

March 29

Joseph Clark will be the new supervising elder and Elder Winslow's companion. I've known him since I entered the mission. He's a good guy, easy to get along with. We also may have stumbled onto a good referral—the Durán family out in Tlaquepaque. Poor as rats, though. The husband only makes 10 pesos a day. Also, a talent night was held at Mutual this evening and some of the entertainment numbers weren't bad. The Torres girls (who keep coming to all of the meetings in spite of the distance imposed by Throgg) performed surprisingly well in a duet. Over to the Velazcos' for a little snack afterward. They're in serious trouble: broke and getting booted out of their house for nonpayment of rent. My companion is lending money to help out.

March 31

We made a few perfunctory visits in the morning. It's been a long time since we've done any real tracting. My companion is tired of it, and I doubt we'll be doing much door-pounding from now on—references and fiddling with members instead. Neome was sick again and we spent most of the afternoon with her at the Velazcos'. Between severe stomach pains she had spells when she couldn't breathe, choking and gasping for air. Fainted three times. We anointed her. The doctor arrived shortly afterward and administered shots. Her pain left quickly and she joined us downstairs for a late lunch. I'd hate to suffer the hell she must go through every few weeks.

April 1

Back to the Velazcos' after visits fell through. Neome was bad again, four days now. We stayed until 11:30 P.M. After we finally got to bed, América Velazco came over to the house about 1:00 A.M. and woke my companion. One of Neome's worst spells. My companion was there until 6:00 A.M. We're supposed to take Neome to a clinic today for "radiograms," whatever that means.

April 2

Wasted day. Over to see how Neome was doing—mostly better, but weak and in bed. We stayed all morning and also had lunch there. Rode around the afternoon on buses, wasting time and making sporadic visits with members. I seem to have lost weight lately—thinnest my arms and legs have been in years. Most of our meals are glorified snacks since Hermana Arrollo stopped cooking for us. I feel listless and tired, although I realize that most of this probably comes from our recent lack of effective missionary work.

April 3

No tracting. Made what are becoming our regular visits: members only, supposedly to "fellowship" and fish for references. But we're really just killing time. Chuck mailed a couple of books he felt would enlighten us: *The Future as History* and *The Other America,* both by Michael Harrington. Chuck thinks these are important contemporary works that we should read. They probably are, and spare time for such extra-curricular reading has once again become more frequent. Meanwhile, Chuck promises a longer letter with reflections on his Mexican excursion. Other mail included a letter from home. I hope Dad's reported new business venture works out better than previous tries. Otherwise, things could get even more sweaty, financially. I really ache for Mom and Dad and for any of the unpleasant days we helped contribute to their collection of worries. Gotta make it up.

April 4

Normal Sunday. No investigators at church services except the Torres girls. Diana talked to me and would like us to start teaching them again next week. Their father is out though. He never has come to church, and Diana says he's not really serious about joining.

April 5

Tracted a bit in the morning—first time for several weeks. Had an argument with an *evangélico* minister who handed us some literature on the bus, so my companion picked a fight for a little fun. Out of it. Then over to Tlaquepaque to be met with some bad news: the Durán family is being run out of their humble home for listening to us. Mr. Durán also got the boot from his 10 peso a day job. Their only income now is from the wife's sister, who works in the city in some sort of employment that involves handling acids for twelve hours a day, three days a week, for 30 pesos [$2.40] a week. Unbelievable. We are going to hire Mrs. Durán to work for us—cleaning the house and fixing the noon meal. That will give them a little income while looking for somewhere else to stay and Mr. Durán seeks another job.

April 8

President Hatch visited with us on Tuesday. He was here for Mutual and gave a masterful discourse on the proper relationship between branch members and missionaries. I'm sure he was particularly aiming at my companion and the Velazcos. For the past couple of weeks we've been spending the vast majority of our time at active members' homes. I haven't taken part with Elder Throgg in more than four lessons since he's been here. Our relationship has been just lukewarm since our first direct confrontation over wasting time at the Velazcos'.

Finally visited the Torreses again and talked to the old man awhile about the Book of Mormon. But that's all he's interested in—talking. Diana, however, told us she wants to be baptized. For conviction? I doubt it, but she's making friends in the branch and wants to go to the youth conference in Mexico City next month.

Winslow finally got his telegram to become a senior and will leave tomorrow night. He's a good enough guy when he's calm (which is not a predictable state for him), and we've usually hit it off pretty well. But I can't say I'm overly sorry to see him go. That will make one less test of patience.

April 9

A new elder arrived this morning as Winslow's replacement: Harry Christiansen. Short, terse, dedicated, and bound to be disappointed in a few days. He makes a good effort to speak the language whenever possible, though it's hard for him. I applaud his beginning attitude, and predict he'll make one of the better elders in the mission if he can withstand the unexpected start he'll receive from this household. What a comedown from the heights of idealism those first few days can be, and a slow, painful climb back up.

April 11

Ate dinner at the Aguilas' after Sunday school: beans, tortillas, eggs and hot sausage, and rice water. My companion gave his "Negro" talk at sacrament meeting (mostly speculations about Negroes being "fence-sitters," rather than valiant supporters of the Lord during the War in Heaven, and their subsequent punishment as dark-skinned, non-priesthood holders in this life, etc.). What is the point of all this? I find it offensive and inappropriate for a missionary talk. We were supposed to visit the Torreses' in the evening and talk to Diana but were detained by the Velazcos' and didn't make it. I continue feeling tired and listless—a combination of our lack of activity and improper diet no doubt.

April 12

We're in the middle of the hot season now, haven't worn suit coats for a month. I don't have any appetite, just thirsty all the time. Don't eat much, arms and legs keep getting skinnier. My companion is going to finish his mission in classic style: "riding his bags," as they say, all the way until time to go home. Trouble is, he still has months—not weeks—to go.

April 13

A little sick to my stomach in the afternoon. Threw up before Mutual, felt better. Kathy wrote and asked me to fast with her tomorrow. She keeps having relapses just when it looks like she's getting better. I was tired all day. Only real bright spot in the day was a letter from Gordon. Went to bed early.

LETTER FROM GORDON

Gar: Well, I've got another new companion, my seventh so far in as many months. Elder Rencher was promoted to zone leader of the Veracruz area, and my new companion is the old supervising elder of the Puebla District. He looks like another good one. Actually, I've had some of the best missionaries in the Veracruz Mission for companions. It's just that I got stuck with Elder Splinders for four months and split my time with most of the others for a couple of weeks each. Anyway, my new companion is Dave Smith, a fellow Salt Laker who attended East High and played football for them in '61. So we already have a few things in common and get along great. His Spanish is outstanding, his confidence infectious, and, like Rencher, he's more interested in results than making a name for himself.

We took a *día de campo* yesterday with the branch. Rented a bus and drove fifty miles to some lakes. The members went swimming, and I took advantage of the chance to take a nap for the first time in Lord knows how long. Later on, races and competitions were held. Elder Smith got running so hard in his heat of the hundred-meter dash that he lost his footing and did a belly slide in the dust. The same thing happened to the primary competition in my heat, and I breezed home an easy winner.

It won't be too long before they start making some new seniors around here, and I've got a feeling that I might be on the list. I snuck a look at my personal progress report and read some flattering comments by my last two supervising elders (actually my former companions, Elders Robison and Rencher). I'm not entirely living up to the compliments though. I should be able to speak fluent Spanish by now, but I don't know if I can or not because I rarely attempt to do so, except in the lessons with investigators. I don't exactly know what the problem is. For one thing, there are too many women running around in this hot weather with too little clothing (or underwear, for that matter). It's hard to keep the proper missionary spirit when you allow yourself lustful glances at some of your investigators. A ver si tengo la voluntad necesaria para resistir esta tentación [Let's see if I have the necessary will to resist this temptation.]

By the way, I was flabbergasted yesterday when we arrived home for lunch to find Dave Manookin—our old sports page photographer for the *South High Scribe*—waiting for us on the front porch. Manookin has been in the Veracruz Mission for over a year and at one time was junior companion to Elder Smith. He's had a lot of health problems, but is now on his way to Veracruz to become a new senior companion. First time I've laid eyes on Manookin since we graduated from high school and, of all places, we meet in Minatitlán, Mexico.

I've started a rather ambitious study project that I hope will be of help to me. I'm drawing up a detailed outline in Spanish of the *Articles of Faith* by James Talmage [a Mormon theologian], as a personal study guide. I need to put all the scriptures that I've learned into a larger perspective and understanding. More than anything, though, I need a better spirit. That's going to take some humbling and honest prayer. Letters from you are always a big help.

Your brother, Gord

April 14

Fasted until evening. Felt completely sapped and exhausted all day. Kathy asked for the fast to aid her in recovering her health and in making decisions concerning her work and immediate future. We left the house early this morning and actually put in a fair day's work until evening when we found ourselves at the Velazcos' again. They're going to be thrown out of their home any day, but have found a new, smaller place very close to the land where the new chapel will be built. All they lack now is money for the first two month's rent.

April 17

Apparently yesterday's effort was too taxing. Throgg decided we should take the afternoon off for horseback riding with the Miranda boys. I didn't have the least desire for words today and so said very few. I was glad at least to hear from Chuck. How far we've fallen short of Chuck's somewhat idealized reminiscences.

LETTER FROM CHUCK RADLOW

Dear Gary,

I have put off writing and just about everything else for the last two

weeks, for what reason I do not know, except that after my Mexican interlude I have lapsed into a period of lassitude which has to stop soon or find
me swallowed in the despair of sleeping more than waking. Actually, fraternity rush took up almost all of my time during the first week back at
school, and I suppose this last week has been some sort of reaction against
the humdrum of an endless series of mindless parties.

Muchísimas grácias for your hospitality and friendship while in Guadalajara. It was undoubtedly the finest vacation I've ever had. I have the
feeling that it has something to do with my present disgust for the halls of
learning. Sort of wish I was out there with you doing some really constructive work. It's kind of hard to make myself feel that all the abstraction
that has been going on in my life the last three years has much meaning
for the future. Anyway, the trip back to the States was a kind of hypnotic
trance. So many impressions run through my mind when I think of you
and your friends in Mexico. I hope the phrase doesn't sound trite, but my
testimony was really strengthened while I was with you. I think it was possible for me to see beyond the immediate problems you face in the mission to a vision, however dim, of the good that is being accomplished in
the long run.

I was so envious of the rich experiences you described to me of your
mission, and I don't suppose I'll ever forget some of the wonderful people
I met in our travels. My heart was full the evening I had to leave. Farewells
get more and more difficult for me, for those who mean so much become
more firmly embedded in my feelings of esteem, respect, and love. Guadalajara and Mexico and being called "Elder Radlow" are not very far away
at all: a couple of days, a handful of dollars. It seems so close.

But here I am back in the humdrum Aristotelian City of study and the
eight o'clock class, of pounding in the facts, of facing the words and words
and words. Well, for the time-being I guess I must be satisfied and do the
best I can. It's so hard sometimes to put it all into perspective and know
what is really worthwhile. Funny, I can still picture the ice-cream vendor
on the corner, and Letícia, and Hermana Velazco, and the elders, and the
chapel, and the visiting teachers. How warm and beautiful the memory.
How much I wish I could share it with you.

By now you have probably been transferred. If not, and you're still
with Elder Throgg, I hope he has gotten over his case of dawdling and settled down to business. I guess it's hard to "intensify the intensity" all the
time, but just the same.—As for myself and the brimstone path—never
fear, I really think I'm going to make it.

Your bud, Chuck

April 19

A completely fizzled day. Took off on a three-hour goose chase looking for a supposed gringo-style Dairy Queen in the weeds on the other side of town that Throgg had heard about. Walked in a giant circle for several miles, rode a bus all over, never did find it. Came home, made a pretext visit to the Gastelum's and ended up at the Velazcos'. Throgg is shameless about doing nothing. We're not even going through the motions any more. My companion is rapidly arriving at the point where missionary work becomes totally distasteful, so he schedules us to do as little of it as possible.

April 21

Natalie left today for Austria. Since being in the LTM to study German, Natalie's letters have become rather rare. Sounds like she has taken her preparation very seriously. Her thoughts (at least written ones to me) are entirely focused on the mission field.

My companion left with Elder Clark in the evening for Colima. Since Clark is supervising elder, it's time for his monthly visit with the elders there. Throgg wrangled a brief companion swap, no doubt for a change of scenery. Fine with me. He's the only scenery I want changed in my life right now.

April 22

Christiansen and I put in a hard day's work. Tracted until noon, not finding anything very special, but making several return visits, which we checked in the afternoon—none turned out. Gave a fifth lesson to a young investigator whom Clark and Christiansen have been teaching. He's going to be baptized this Saturday, so we'll have to give him the sixth lesson tomorrow. Also tomorrow we take the Venegases to be married so they can be baptized Saturday. Needless to say I enjoy setting my own work pace. We didn't waste much time. Elder Christiansen is a little over-zealous in dealing with people, and his limited Spanish is a handicap, but he will soon learn to apply himself more effectively without having to lose his enthusiasm.

April 23

A long, eventful day. Christiansen and I left the house at 7:30 A.M. and took care of the Venegases' marriage. Tracted until noon in Clark and Christiansen's area, then presented the sixth lesson to their youthful investigator. It turns out that he doesn't have his parents' written permission to baptize, but I told him to plan on tomorrow anyway, and that Elder Clark would have to talk to his family and get things straightened out. A sharp guy, really does want to become a member.

More tracting and checking on return visits. Kept tracting until 9:00 P.M. Despite Christiansen's extravagant hopes to the contrary, we found no really promising visits. (I hope I'm just being realistic and not catching some of Throgg's cynicism.)

Elder Christiansen and I were kneeling for prayer about midnight when we heard some banging noises in the room across the hall. Checked out the whole house and found nothing. Went to bed and I was just dropping off to sleep when I heard the noises again. Christiansen was snoring, but I was wide awake listening when suddenly the crashing slam of a door somewhere in the house shot me out of bed. I flipped on the light, grabbed Elder Throgg's machete, and we started searching again. Tiptoed downstairs in the dark and I knocked over the coat rack while fumbling for a light switch. I was a little startled—took a couple of swipes at it until Christiansen rushed into the kitchen and turned on the light. Again we found nothing after examining the entire house. All inside doors were open, however. Back to bed again, and this time when we heard the noises across the hall, we ignored them and went to sleep.

April 24

Clark and Throgg got back early this morning, apparently soon after Christiansen and I retired from spook hunting. Immediately back into the old swing of doing practically nothing. We did baptize the Venegases in the afternoon. Elder Clark also baptized his young investigator to whom I had given three lessons with Christiansen. Neome showed up at the service with one of her little brothers. They (Neome and Elder Throgg) are so obvious in their feelings they couldn't fool anyone anymore. My companion suddenly developed *ganas* [desire] for pizza and invited Neome and the kids to come with us. After eating we came home for the rest of the evening instead of going back out to work. Elder Clark was feeling sick, so I gladly substituted for him with Elder Christiansen to present a fourth lesson to one of their investigators. Slaughtered it. Christiansen carries his inexperienced zealousness to an extreme. Meanwhile, received a telegram from President Hatch in the afternoon informing us that he will be here Wednesday for a missionary meeting. My companion is sweating it, and in fact I can't think of any other reason for the president's coming. If Throgg is in trouble he has arrived at it with his eyes open to the consequences of his choices.

April 25

After sacrament meeting this afternoon, my companion and Neome got together outside while choir practice was proceeding inside. I stayed outside myself like some kind of dippy monitor for well over an hour until practice was done and everyone went home.

April 28

President Hatch and his wife both gave general talks at this morning's conference, and then President Hatch separately interviewed each missionary while the rest bore testimonies and practiced singing for the May district conference. My interview was brief. President Hatch indicated that he had ironed out a few things with Elder Throgg in relation to our work. Apparently so. After everyone left, Throgg said he wants to shoot for seventy-five hours next week and seventy hours each the two following weeks. The remainder of this week, however, looks like a last gasp of *flojeza* [laziness]: soccer game scheduled for us to see tomorrow, a show Friday. I hope my companion's sincere about wanting to shape up. What happens to the Velazco visiting will be the single biggest indicator of any changes in my companion's resolve to revitalize his missionary commitments.

April 29

Tracted in the afternoon for the first time in quite awhile. Had previously told one of the Gastelum kids we'd take him to the soccer game. But we stopped off at the Velazcos' en route and my companion said he didn't "feel well," so we wound up staying there and not going to the game. I had something to eat, and Neome tried to engage me in conversation, but she's always nervous and on edge whenever she has anything to say to me. I've never hidden my disappointment with her conduct. We left about 9:30 P.M. I'm sick of pretense and the Velazcos. I'll wait until next week's promise of work is supposed to go into effect. I'm a damn fool.

May 4

Got Throgg to agree to leave the house a half hour early in the mornings to improve our hours. After Mutual my companion told Neome and Mom Velazco, in front of me, that we will have to stop our constant visiting with them. But the words seemed to lack conviction and I guess I've lost my faith in what Throgg says.

May 6

Several letters today. Some bad news came from Mom: Don was divorced this past week. What a jolter. I feel especially bad, because I know doggone well that a portion of Don's present problems grew out of a suppressed and unhappy childhood, and that Gordon and I—however unwittingly and inevitably at the time—played major roles in that early beginning of unhappiness.

We were always the good kids who did everything right and soaked up most of the approval and attention. It seemed like Don's only way to carve out an identity for himself was to be a contrast to everything he thought we represented. But some potentially good news: Dad's latest business venture might just pan out, according to Mom. If even she has a few stars in her eyes, it must be a worthwhile project. I often worry about Mom and Dad's financial status as they begin approaching their older years. They deserve a chance to relax from constant money worries and debts and to enjoy life a little. I'm praying that this new job opportunity will provide the means for such security.

Gordon's and my missionary farewells were almost a year ago. It doesn't really leave us much time. I don't enjoy constant crabbing, and I don't think I've lost my enthusiasm and will to work. But here I sit, piddling away the precious days through subordination to an autocratic senior companion who was ready to go home months ago. Contrast this depressing state of affairs with the account I just received from Gordon. Currently, Gord and I seem poles apart in our missionary circumstances and companion relations.

LETTER FROM GORDON

Gar: Things have been going great here in Minatitlán. I don't imagine I'll get a transfer for another month or so and I hope I don't. Mina's a nice little town. If everything turns out right, we should get ten to twenty baptisms this month. What's the deal with you now? Is your romantically inclined companion still walking a shaky line, or has he been moved out of Guad? That's a pretty sad state of affairs to be mired in. I know you won't let his escapades get you down.

Last week we got some on-the-job-training on how to conduct a funeral. We had just returned to the house from a visit and found a note informing us that an old lady, whose son is a member, had passed away and that they wanted us to come over to her residence. All of her family and relatives were Catholic, but some of our branch officials took over and organized a hurried funeral service, calling on the missionaries for a prayer and extemporaneous talk. My companion Elder Smith was asked to pray and, of all people, they picked on the other junior companion, Elder Elison, who barely has five months in the mission, to be the principal speaker—he didn't even know the lady, my companion and I had been visiting her. I waged a tough struggle with my conscience for a couple of moments, then stepped over and offered to take the assignment. Elison thought about it for a second, then showed some guts by turning me down and struggled, with halting Spanish, through a tough ordeal of his own. I admired that. Elison is going to become one of the better missionaries around here.

The next day at the burial we were again asked to help out. Nobody with any religious authority was there, so we found ourselves in charge of the burial rite. Between the house and the *panteón* [cemetery] we tried to organize our thoughts. When we arrived, the four of us sang a hymn (we were the only ones there to represent the church). I offered an opening prayer, my companion directed and gave a fine, extemporaneous talk, and Elder Calister, the other senior companion, dedicated the grave. Although inexperienced at this sort of thing and not quite sure of what was expected, we managed, with the Lord's help, to do a credible job. As I reflect on this experience I'm amazed that we, who such a short time ago were all involved with the petty and self-centered concerns of adolescence, were able to successfully take charge of such a solemn occasion as a funeral. I was proud of the way my companions fulfilled their duties.

Hang in there Gar. A change of some sort for the better is bound to be in the offing for you soon.

Your brother, Gord

May 21

Yesterday, at long last, I received a transfer telegram and am now on a bus en route to Mexico City. I left off writing these past weeks because I was quite sure that Throgg had been browsing my diary, and I didn't want him to read the things I would have put down. The situation was worsening, especially with Neome, and I'm convinced serious problems will shortly erupt if Throgg is allowed to finish up in Guad. Elder Bronson was my replacement, and I told him to be watchful as long as Throgg is his companion. I thought Neome was going to turn cartwheels when she found out I was going.

Elder Throgg had an ingrown toenail removed a week or so ago and stayed around the house for a few days while Elder Christiansen and I made the visits and tracted. It was a good experience and a great relief for me. Elder Throgg and I wound up not giving a single lesson together in over two months. I either gave them alone or with Christiansen. It occurs to me now: Could Throgg have forgotten some of The Plan and avoided giving those lessons with me out of embarrassment and fear of losing authority? At any rate, work had slowed to a crawl again, and—understatement—I am relieved to finally be on my way. Only Mom Velazco and Letícia made it out to the station to see me off. Good of them to come. However, I'm probably viewed by the

Velazcos as a fanatical pain in the neck whose departure will ease a lot of tension.

As soon as Bronson showed up instead of a greenie [new, incoming missionary from the LTM], I figured I wasn't going to be made a new senior very fast. Who knows how long it will be now? Possibly three months more, since the current in-and-out flow of missionaries in the system seems to be pretty plugged-up, according to Bronson. But whatever, I can hack it as long as I get to work, wherever that might be. I've so far proved a poor prophet in some things, but I did have an inspiring dream last night that Gordon and I were working together as companions in Mexico City. If nothing else I know his example and influence will continue to lend me strength in the days ahead.

9

∞

"At Last! To Work Again!"
Gary's Story as Junior Companion
in Churubusco, Mexico City

After almost five depressing months in Guadalajara, Gary's transfer back to Mexico City led to a dramatic revival of his spirits and to almost instant and spectacular proselyting success in the Mexican capitol. Following a few days of initial uncertainty, Gary was teamed with his district's supervising elder, a missionary whom he had already come to respect through previous contact in Guadalajara and with whom he was to enjoy six weeks of uninterrupted rapport. They dedicated themselves to working long hours, pushing themselves to near exhaustion and in the process picking up so many promising investigator families that it was sometimes difficult to keep adequate track of them all. A hectic juggling of tracting efforts, lesson appointments, dinner invitations, and fellowshipping visits with recent converts and new investigators was necessary to monitor the progress of numerous prospective converts. Along the way, a number of investigators faltered, of course, but, for Gary, it was to be one of the most productive periods of his mission. Baptism rates soared in Mexico City, and the most motivated missionaries competed for peer recognition as preeminent proselytors. One sobering event that took Gary by surprise was the arrival of a lengthy, angry letter from Chuck Radlow, who unexpectedly announced his loss of faith in the LDS Church and repudiated the missionary enterprise. Chuck was to return, with considerable ambivalence, to the margins of the LDS fold a few months later, but his defection letter signaled an overt breach, never to be reconciled, in the religious ideals of his youth.

Gordon, transferred from Minatitlán at the same time Gary returned to Mexico City, also experienced substantial proselyting success with his new companion in his mission's headquarters city of Veracruz on the Gulf of

Mexico. (At the time, Veracruz was the most productive city for LDS recruitment and developing Mexican leadership in the southeastern part of the country. Consequently, missionaries in Veracruz were able to obtain more references from members rather than having to rely exclusively on tracting for prospective recruits.) Gordon's spirits suffered a mild decline, however, as he began to chafe in his role as junior companion and anticipate with some frustration his eventual promotion to senior. While he was a junior companion in Veracruz, he had to reconcile his missionary efforts to spread the gospel with the racially discriminatory practice of his church, which was offensive to both his and Gary's liberal racial attitudes. These complaints not withstanding, Gordon enjoyed the pleasant work conditions in Veracruz and was even able to indulge his love for playing baseball, an indulgence that tweaked Gary's envy in Mexico City.

Mexico City, May 21, 1965

Pulled into Mexico City about 6:30 this morning. Managed to make my way to the mission home, ate breakfast there, and received my new assignment: to the Churubusco District, here in the City. Robert Simms, who I barely know, will be my senior. I'm pleased that Lamoin Merkley is supervising elder; we share an apartment with him and his junior, Dewayne Altman. Elder Simms isn't very outgoing at first appearance—kind of a large, stoic person who doesn't have very much to say—but he's a hard worker and I don't foresee any problems with regard to doing our job. Elder Fergason did mention to me this morning at the mission home that they were thinking of moving Simms elsewhere before too long; also, that Throgg will be brought back to the City to finish up his mission out of temptation's way.

After I finished unpacking, Elder Simms and I gave a sixth lesson to a family of five members, which was fine until the husband balked at taking down his plaster Virgin from the wall. (We're supposed to baptize them Sunday!) We then went on to deliver a third lesson to a family by the name of Quebedo, and I kind of messed up the Word of Wisdom part—the man's a heavy smoker and wasn't very excited by the idea of giving it up. My legs ached all day from cramps sustained on the bus. Very grateful to slide into bed.

May 22

Tracted some long hours in the morning and found a few comebacks. When we came home for lunch, Elder Simms was told by Merkley that he is being moved out to Tulancingo. My new companion, when he gets here, will be Elder Goodmanson—another person about whom I barely know anything.

Went to show the film to the family we were supposed to baptize tomorrow, but the husband wouldn't come out, and instead we were told to go away by some guy who claimed to be a relative. We didn't much care for that and said we would wait to talk to the señor himself. Our stranger friend than informed us that he was the big shot in charge of immigration for the whole Republic of Mexico and backed up his claim by recounting to us the organization of the four Mexican missions, cited his familiarity with President Harold Brown [a Mormon colonist from Colónia Juárez who was Mexico City's first stake president] and our church lawyer, and finally produced a list of all missionaries who have left the country since December. He also informed us that several missionaries in the northern Mexico Mission have been expelled for proselytizing activities and hinted that we might end up in the same boat. We didn't stay to argue, and I doubt anything will come of it, although there has been a lot of trouble with passports lately. We stopped by to visit another member, and then I helped Elder Simms lug his bags to the bus station. Hardly got to know him, and I don't know our working area well at all.

May 23

My new companion didn't arrive today. He should be here tomorrow. I attended Sunday services in the morning and afternoon at the Ermita chapel. In between times I managed to locate four tract-out return visits that Simms and I made yesterday. X-ed them all for want of any further interest on their part. Elder Simms leaves us with several investigators receiving lessons, but from what I've seen none of them are particularly promising.

May 24

Elder Goodmanson remains delinquent. I stayed in the apartment and studied and read while awaiting his anticipated arrival. Later in the afternoon, Elder Haws and Elder Gerald Hatch (President Hatch's nephew, who transferred from Gordon's mission a couple of months ago) from the mission home stopped by to inquire about our run-in with the immigration official. I had to talk on the phone to the church lawyer (*Licensiado* Agricol Lozano), and I explained everything that had taken place. He asked for my passport number but didn't seem overly worried, even though our government friend has apparently been making some complaints. Immediately following this discussion another church official came directly to the apartment, and I went through the same story. Would be just dandy to get thrown out of Mexico and wind up in Texas or some other unappealing place in the States.

May 25

Another day gone by on my own. Went to the mission home early this morning with Merkley and Altman for Elder Clark's *relevo* [release from the mission field]. Good to see some of the guys I know again. Clark had just returned from Guad and said he had informed Elder Throgg that he would soon be transferred. I talked with President Hatch about the run-in with the immigration official, but he didn't seem overly concerned. I also took a book out of the mission home library: volume two of the *Comprehensive History of the Church* by B. H. Roberts, which I was reading at the first of the year before I left for Guad. Had to go out in the evening again for visits in spite of not having a companion. Only the Quebedos were home. The señor has a bad smoking problem, doesn't feel like he can give it up, and consequently doesn't want to involve himself further with insincere commitments. I talked to him and his wife for some time about the importance of the things they had been taught and the great need for them to pray, which they haven't been doing.

May 26

Great news today! After I checked out some visits in the morning I returned to the apartment to discover that I am now Elder Merkley's companion. Elder Goodmanson stumbled into the mission home from Colima this morning with hepatitis, so the decision was made to pair me with Merkley and have Elder Altman work with members until a new replacement elder can be sent. At last! To work again! Merkley will be my first good companion since those early days with Elder Wilkes. Merkley's a world-class wrestler [at the University of Central Washington before his missionary departure] with a real shot at the 1968 Olympics. He's a little over six feet tall, weighs about 190 pounds and stays in shape the best he can through intense calisthenics every day. He's a humble and dedicated missionary for whom I have the greatest respect. I have an immediate conviction that Merkley and I will achieve excellent results together.

May 27

Put in one of the longest days of my mission—a hopeful harbinger of what's to come. Left at 7:30 this morning. Traveled out to a distant colony, gave some lessons there, came back and gave the sixth lesson to three young people, who we'll baptize Sunday. Tracted in the afternoon and gave some more lessons in the evening, including one to a family of ten (the Guerros) who look very good. Over fourteen solid hours of genuine proselyting in all.

May 28

Merkley went to a supervising elders' conference this morning, so I tracted with Elder Altman. Kind of out of it. Altman does a lot of grumbling and smarts off to the people. But quickly back to the good stuff—Merkley and I tracted together in the afternoon and then delivered two excellent fourth lessons—one to a family of five (the Buenos), whom we're going to baptize Sunday (a widow and her children), and one to another family of five who seem pretty sure about baptism. As a matter of fact, with all the good investigators we have right now, June should be a highly successful month.

Forwarded letter arrived from Gord. He's just been changed too, and it looks like we also shared the same dream about working together as missionary companions.

LETTER FROM GORDON

Gar: I'm writing from Veracruz, my newest abode. My transfer was made on the spur of the moment and came as a complete surprise. Last Monday I was looking forward to working another month in Minatitlán (or so I had been informed by President Hatch himself at our conference over the weekend). The next day my companion (Elder Smith) was stricken with appendicitis and operated on. Wednesday I was on the phone with the Prez and he ordered me to abandon Mina and come to Veracruz as companion to the supervising elder here, Elder Burch, whose previous junior supposedly fell in love with one of the LMs [lady missionaries] and had to be moved out.

Tuesday I spent a restless night along side my companion's bunk in the clinic where the operation was performed. During his unconscious hours I sacked out on a fold-up cot that was about two feet wide and lost many pints of blood to mosquitoes while trying to prevent Elder Smith from strangling on his own tongue or falling on the floor from his equally narrow cot in the recovery room (which he very nearly did). Sometimes they do things a little funny around here. Anyway, I spent the next day introducing the other elders stationed in Minatitlán to our current investigators, said a quick goodbye to them and wondered how many would ever join the church. I then caught the last bus for Veracruz. It was about a five-hour trip and when I arrived it was after midnight. Not knowing the city or addresses of any of the missionaries, I simply had a taxi take me to the mission office. The doors were all locked, of course, so I boosted myself up a wall, shinnied up on the balcony of the mission office building and spent the rest of the night sprawled out on some lawn chairs. I had a crazy dream that you were transferred to the Veracruz mission and that we were working together as missionary companions.

I like Veracruz. It's a fairly large, modern city—lively, pretty—with a number of wealthy neighborhoods. Good missionary work too (Elder Burch has a number of baptisms already lined up for this month), and good living conditions. We live in El Edificio Galdi, a large apartment building in downtown Veracruz. The building has elevators and hot running water (no more drawing water from a well and heating it on the stove). Burch and I share the apartment with two other missionaries, Elders Rosenberg and Granger. Rosenberg is a weight-lifter and body-builder from Idaho, not overly spiritual but good company. Granger's a little strange and unpredictable—petulant, childish disposition in a man's body. Last night at the theater (we went to see a James Bond movie of all things) Rosenberg and Granger got into an argument which ended when Rosenberg invited Granger to step outside to settle it. Granger wisely declined and shut up for the rest of the evening. It was a bit tense there for a minute. I half expected to see someone's teeth on the ground. Apparently Rosenberg has about had it with Granger's antics.

Let me know if you've been transferred out of Guad. It's way past time for your mission leaders to assign you a decent companion. Good companions have sure made a difference for me up to this point.

Your brother, Gord

May 29

In our class this morning my companion and I agreed to shoot high. For once, setting *metas* [goals] seemed more than an obligatory ritual. I know we'll achieve them according to our sincere desires and efforts. Elder Merkley also made it clear that as far as he is concerned we will work together as co-equals, that he values my ideas and ability. This is really the only kind of relationship in which I work well. My estimate of Merkley's character goes up even higher. We tracted all morning and made three or four return visits—one with a family by the name of Rubio, where they all act a little odd but at least were very enthusiastic. Gave a combined fifth and sixth lesson to the Bueno widow and her four kids. We'll baptize them tomorrow. Then gave a second lesson to a young married couple from Yucatán, which went over very well. Finally, visited the Romero kids we've been teaching, in order to talk to their parents, but they weren't home. We're supposed to baptize them tomorrow, but difficulties might arise with the parents balking. We'll find out tomorrow.

May 30

Quite a day. Left early to talk to the Romero kids' mother and bring them to church. The mother wouldn't see us, but we were informed she didn't want them baptized yet. The oldest boy, however, is a nephew, and his own mother had no objections, so I baptized him after Sunday school. We then presented a first lesson to the kooky Rubio family that we found yesterday, and although they are rather strange, they accepted everything with unbounded enthusiasm. We next picked up the Bueno family for their baptismal service. My companion baptized this time, including the next oldest girl, who is somewhat mentally retarded, but we feel she is capable of grasping what's going on.

All the Churubusco missionaries had a confab with the bishopric and a member of the stake high council after sacrament meeting. According to them, a member of the local seventies quorum is supposed to be present at all baptisms and, whenever possible, is also supposed to attend one of the lessons we give to each good investigator family. I suppose these are good ideas to strengthen ties between the ward and new converts. But are there enough reliable and capable seventies in the ward to realistically match up with the far-ranging and constantly evolving work schedules of the missionaries?

May 31

After district meeting this morning Altman was informed that he will be moved elsewhere to be linked up to a new companion rather than stay here. So we will be left with his current visits to try and squeeze into our schedule. While Elder Merkley made one of our visits I went with Altman to brush up on all of his and to let them know of the change. Rejoined my companion at the apartment complex where we are teaching the large Guerro family and gave them the third lesson. The husband manifests high interest, but some of his kids at times seem disinterested. They're definitely good prospects, though, and I can see no reason why we shouldn't be able to baptize them. In fact, I can't believe how many good-quality investigators we have and are continuing to find. Unless things go all to pieces, June will be the best month of my mission.

June 2

Merkley and I keep having to separate in order to keep up with all of our appointments. I gave a fourth lesson by myself to the Quebedo family where the señor is still having a rough go with his smokes. All these extra visits are becoming complicated to handle, but no complaints. After those long months of inactive subordination in Guad, the constant effort and independence here are exhilarating.

June 3

Gave the fourth lesson and filled out baptismal papers for the Corona family—three people, all adults. Also had a sixth lesson with the Muñoz family, and although there were a few shaky moments on tithing, plus a few other problems, things seem to be ironed out now and they're scheduled for baptism this Sunday at 8:00 A.M. Finished the evening off with a late visit with the big Guerro family and they're looking increasingly better. For the first time the two teenaged girls became completely involved in the lesson, and they have all accepted their baptismal commitment for June 12. Great guns so far, but I'm just waiting for the Old Bad Guy to stick his foot in the door somewhere.

June 8

Almost a week gone by without my having time to jot down what's been going on. Busy?! I can't believe it. My missionary fortunes have experienced a drastic rebound. We've been putting in between eleven and fifteen hours of effective time a day and are being blessed beyond reason. We've seen a few fall. The young couple from Yucatán, for instance, have about fizzled. They were going great until the fourth lesson when the husband revealed a stone brain and fanatically insisted on clinging to his Virgin wall-hangings before we could even get the lesson underway. Most of our investigators are still hanging in there, however. The Corona family will be baptized tomorrow morning and the Muñoz family in the evening. Scheduled for this Saturday is the Guerro family, and they continue to progress and grow every time we see them. The señor of the Quebedo family is one of the sharpest guys I've seen during my mission, but he's been a heavy smoker and the habit is dying hard—I don't know here. We still have the Cervantes family, and although they lack only one more lesson, we haven't taught them for a week. At this point they look a little doubtful. The Rubio family has gotten kind of out of hand, thanks to the occasional lunacy of the *hermano*. Besides that, he's got all the vices bad.

June 9

Today was a day of baptismal services, ranging from our own (the Corona family) at 11:00 A.M., to the other elders' at 3:00 P.M., to ours again at 7:00 P.M. (the Muñoz family). Struggled through a spiritless lesson with the

Quebedo family in between services. The *hermano* is still smoking, although he's cutting down. Merkley and I were both tired after the lesson, and something was troubling my companion, so we decided not to become embroiled in another out-of-it discussion with the Rubios and broke our appointment with them.

June 10

The real work of the day didn't get started until after noon, but then it lasted until after 1:00 in the morning. Started off by going over to the other elders to pick up the projector and tape recorder, then delivered a first lesson to a young cop and his wife (the Armetas) that went over like a charm—except they don't really believe everything we told them. But they seemed sincere in wanting to do their part in finding out how true it all is. Back over to the Guerros' for the sixth lesson, which went over without a hitch. We'll baptize eight in the family, excluding only the oldest son, who hasn't heard all of the lessons yet and wasn't present tonight. The rest all seem to have accepted the gospel without reservation (Hermano Guerro being especially enthusiastic) and could be about the sharpest family I've had a hand in bringing into the church. After the lesson we ate a good enchilada dinner, then home, tired but happy and grateful for the blessings of a kind Father in Heaven. I know, and always have, that the Lord blesses us through our diligence and righteous efforts. And although we remain with many shortcomings—especially me, with some of my sorry past failings—we're doing our best and trusting to the guiding goodness of the Lord.

June 11

Spent most of the day tracting but didn't turn up much. We're both tired. Sitting in one house when it was my turn to present the tracting lesson, I had to give Elder Merkley a slight kick in the ankle to wake him up from dozing when it was time to leave. During the next presentation, while Merkley was talking, I lapsed into a bowed-head stupor from which I was aroused by Elder Merkley's complementary kick in the ankle at the moment when I was supposed to add my testimony to his.

The second lesson with the young cop and his wife (the Armetas) went over well, although I'm sure they still have doubts. The rest of our scheduled visits flopped. Returned home a little before 10:00 P.M., and although that's the earliest we've finished up in a long time, I was beat and fell asleep while my companion and I were kneeling for prayers. He finished exercising, took a shower, came back in the bedroom, and found me still on my knees against the bed in a dead slumber.

June 12

We baptized the Guerro family at 2:30 this afternoon. Quite a thrill. The *hermano* had tears in his eyes during the confirmation of his wife and children and after his own. They're some of the finest people I've known. Hermano Guerro is especially sincere in his feelings about the gospel, and they should all be tremendous additions to the ward.

Later we paid a short visit to Rubio without giving a lesson, although he's read deeply in the Libro de Mormon, the *folletos* [missionary pamphlets], and claims to be cutting down on his beer and cigarettes. He's strange, maybe a little off center.

We had another thrill in the evening after delivering a fifth lesson to the Quebedos. Hermano Quebedo has cut down his smokes to nothing, and his wife seems quite animated about baptism. Just before we ended the lesson, one of Hermano Quebedo's friends entered the house—an out-of-it *evangélico*—and immediately a bad spirit and tension prevailed. After the lesson my companion tried to give the guy a tract-out lesson, but kept being interrupted by the usual contentious comments. After a few unpleasant moments, Hermano Quebedo himself got ticked off and calmly, but witheringly, chopped our unwelcome intruder a couple of good verbal cuts, thus cementing much tighter our hopes for their eventual baptism next week.

June 14

President Hatch and his wife were at district meeting this morning, President Hatch giving his usual excellent talk. The district has possibilities of seventy-five baptisms for the month, about forty-five above its *meta,* but I imagine the actual number will turn out lower than the projection.

Wrapped up the sixth lesson with the Quebedo family in the evening. The father, mother, and two younger boys will be baptized tomorrow. The next oldest girl wants to wait a little longer. Dropped in on the Guerros and spent an enjoyable time chatting and discussing some gospel points, including genealogy work. A good spirit was present and I felt this was the way it should be—the gospel bringing a family together in love and unity.

June 15

Had an 8:00 A.M. first lesson scheduled with a family called Coranges, and wound up explaining tithing and other member obligations before we could even get the regular lesson underway. The man, his wife, and two teenaged daughters all sounded like they were thinking about joining up before they knew anything about us.

Performed a short but moving baptismal service for the Quebedo family this afternoon. I directed the meeting and gave a small talk. Hermano Quebedo couldn't suppress his spirit of fun and rose out of the water exclaiming, "*Sabroso!*" [delicious!]. He's one of the sharpest people it's been my pleasure to know, and, at the close of the service, he gave one of the best prayers I've heard offered by a new member.

June 17

We had a run-in with a Jehovah's Witness Wednesday at the Armetas' (the young cop and his wife) during the third lesson. Apparently the wife has been doing a little studying with them, and so our unwelcome friend came strolling in and tried to mess up the lesson. She didn't do a very good job, and by the time we left, she was in a bad light. Still, it's infuriating, and I'm afraid she's got a fair clutch on Hermana Armeta. We subsequently arrived a little early for a visit with the Cadena family and were treated to an excellent dinner of eggs, beans, hot buttered bread, chiles, hot chocolate, and rice pudding. The second lesson afterward went over fair, but they're still not too convinced and seem more interested in just being sociable.

Early this morning we traveled out to Santa Cruz for a first lesson with the Coranges family—the ones who were so interested in tithing at the tract-out stage. They accepted the lesson very well and keep talking like they expect to be members.

June 19

Paid a visit yesterday to the Guerro family after tracting, and, as always, enjoyed the love that continues to grow among us. A couple of punk *jóvenes* [youths] were directing a few derogatory remarks towards us outside the apartment, and Hermana Guerro really hit the roof—gave them a good roasting on our behalf. Other visits included the Armetas, the young cop, who still isn't convinced, less his wife. They haven't prayed, and I have my doubts about them. Ate a good dinner at the Cadenas' again, but by the time the husband arrived home, it was too late for a lesson. Showed films at the Quebedos', including a new one: "La Noche del Hogár" [Family Home Evening]. Wonderful people. Our *evangélico* friend was present, but he didn't have any comments to make and the time was enjoyably spent. We also gave a good second lesson to the Corangeses, and it looks like we might have five early baptisms in July.

Churubusco heads the mission this month with over fifty baptisms thus far. McRae and Powell are pressing Merkley and me for "honors," and unfortunately an undesirable spirit of competition and rivalry is being created. Another small sour note among all that's been good: my Spanish seems to be going to pot, pronunciation anyway. I miss the study program I've always followed—we rarely have time now. (This morning I did check out my third volume of the *Comprehensive History of the Church*. I've read two previous volumes in one month during spare moments, mostly on buses and trolleys.)

June 21

Woke up early this morning very sick. Vomiting, runs, and dry heaves at regular intervals. Drank some boiled rice water in the afternoon and began to feel better. Barely stirred from bed all day and logged a lot of sleep. Elder Merkley made a couple of visits alone in the evening. He says the third lesson with the Cadenas went over much better than anticipated.

June 22

Feeling better today. An early morning third lesson with the Corangeses was good. They look sure for next month. Then they invited us to stay for breakfast, and I almost got sick again on onion and cheese enchiladas. We went by the other elders' place at noon. Merkley and Carson became engaged in a friendly little wrestling match but ended up with Carson (how could he be so dumb?) getting ticked and going all out. Big mistake. Merkley almost flipped him through the window.

We baptized Delores Quebedo just before Mutual, our twenty-seventh baptism and last for the month. It looks like McRae and Powell will end up with twenty-six. We could probably have squeezed in a few more, but we didn't want to unnecessarily rush anyone just for competition's sake. Topped off a good day with a good-to-get letter from Gordon.

LETTER FROM GORDON

Gar: To coin one of Dad's phrases: I was thrilled to death to get your last letter! Your accomplishments and success and obvious high spirits sent my blood pounding and adrenalin spurting. I wish I could carry that same spirit and desire with me every time we go out to work in the morning. Unfortunately, I haven't always succeeded. I do believe, however, that a steady communication between the two of us is one of the best preventatives against hardening spiritual arteries and loss of desire.

I have another good and capable companion in Elder Burch. He's on the short side, lean and wiry, with an excellent ability to express himself in spoken Spanish. We're friends but not exceptionally close. He's one of those types who breaks into your half of the lesson to help out the investigators or clarify some point, which has the effect of (1) ticking me off and (2) leaving me unsure and shaky when the next pebble pops up in the lesson. I believe he's now interpreted my feelings about his interruptions and he doesn't do it any more, but I'm still a little sensitive, I guess. Ridiculous, of course. Come another month or so, and we'll probably both be senior companions. Elder Burch attributes his exceptionally fluent Spanish to working as a junior companion with a native Mexican elder for three or four months in the early part of his mission. I wonder how much better my own Spanish might be now if I had remained as Elder Lara's companion for a similar period of time. At some point language fluency becomes a matter of self-confidence and vice versa. At the moment I could use a little more of both. But it's also a matter of assuming greater responsibility in the work, which will come soon, I hope, when we're made senior companions.

Baptism-wise, the work here is the best I've enjoyed anywhere, with thirteen converts splashed to date and prospects for another dozen or so this month. Compared to the titanic efforts we made in Minatitlán with so few tangible results, it almost seems too easy. We're certainly not working as hard here, but I doubt that's the key to success. According to Burch, virtually all of his converts in Veracruz have come through reference visits given by the members. Veracruz has two thriving branches, with over four hundred members. There's talk about converting the Veracruz branches into a ward and eventually creating a stake here, which would be the first in the mission. At a recent district conference for members I listened to several riveting addresses by the native district presidency which I thought were comparable to any that we heard given by general authorities at the mission home in Salt Lake City. As we struggle with our investigator families, especially in the smaller towns, we often fail to appreciate the great strides forward the church is making here. With men of the caliber to lead that I've seen in Veracruz, the church in Mexico is bound to prosper. [Thirty years later, there were three LDS stakes in Veracruz and twenty-one wards.]

But there are some vexing problems too. For example, we're working with several promising families right now, but we'll either have to drop them or go through a painful experience and tell them that they can't hold the priesthood, because we've discovered that they have some degree of Negro blood. This seems to be the biggest problem for missionary work in Veracruz; a good proportion of the population has "the blood"—an odious phrase popular among missionaries in these parts. It makes Negro heritage sound like a disease, and I don't like it. We've already lost two investigator families because of the Negro doctrine. [Until 1978, when a formal policy reversal was announced, black males could not receive the LDS priesthood.] We've been advised by the church to drop investigators with any African ancestry and continue teaching them only if they request it. Figuring out who does and who does not have Negro ancestry around here is pretty much hit and miss speculation. I don't think we should have to make these kinds of judgments. We went through an awful attempt to explain why Negro males don't hold the priesthood to one family and they seemed understandably offended. Another mulatto family has been faithfully coming out to church and making inquiries about baptism. We'll have to sit down and have a talk with them too. It's a big mess.

On the light side, for the last couple of weeks we've been playing baseball every Tuesday morning instead of having our usual district class—real hardball, and we've picked up a few games with some local sandlot teams. (There are exactly nine elders here for a team, counting everyone in the mission office.) I've turned into a fielding phenomenon at third base, knocking down line shots and sucking up sizzlers all over the place, with only an occasional wild throw to first base. Yesterday we were challenged to a game by some Mexican teenagers and rallied to win 14-13. I managed to tag a round-house curve for a triple and knocked in a couple of runs for our side. Great fun. Next Tuesday I get my rotation on the pitcher's mound.

As I recall from past letters we agreed to bounce ideas back and forth about the future. Are you still tinkering with the idea of law as a career? I know we could do it. Also, just to keep in mind, I'd like to see the dream we shared about working together as missionary companions come to pass. How about a couple of days' worth of tracting in Mexico City, one year from this coming August, after my release in Veracruz?

Talk about an example. I know where my shortcomings begin. Those good reports you occasionally get about me make me feel like a faker. You, gentlemen, are leading the way. Fourteen baptisms already racked up this month with *thirty* on deck?! Good grief, how did it turn out? I'm proud of you.

Your brother, Gord

June 23

Took a long, mountain bus ride up to some little villages not far from Amecameca (where the first branch of the church in Mexico was organized during the last century) to visit the wife of a member (after all these years, he appears to be the only Mormon left in town). She's ready, and we'll baptize her in a week or so. Breathtaking scenery of a bluish-green hue, and amusing company on the rickety school-type bus. One pair of Indian women had a pig stuffed into a gunnysack. The pig managed to break free from the ladies' attempts to hold it down between them, but couldn't escape the bound bag, so we were treated to a squealing sack, assuming different shapes, as it squirted around in the aisle and between passengers' seats.

June 24

Enjoyed the usual early morning lesson with the Corangeses and breakfast afterward. They're excited about their coming baptisms. Hermano and Hermana Corange are cards, constantly taking cuts at each other. The rainy season is here in earnest and we stopped by the Corangeses' again in the afternoon, soaking wet from tracting, to pick up the raincoats we had inadvertently left there earlier. Both of us fell asleep during a momentary interlude while we were sitting on the couch talking. When we awoke about an hour later the *hermana* had quietly prepared dinner and insisted we stay to eat again.

June 27

Saturday morning after the supervisors' meeting our district played a basketball game against Roma. We eventually won, something like 100-96. I scored 20, hit about 10 for 15 from the field, but actually my play hovered between mediocre and spastic.

We gave a double lesson—fifth and sixth—to the Corangeses in the evening, because Sunday was the most convenient day for them to have their baptisms. It's remarkable how quickly they came around. They are a bit in love with us, too. We baptized them bright and early Sunday morning. Missed by one day getting thirty-three baptisms for this month's records (according to the way the mission home keeps track of these things), but now we already have six with which to begin July. One of the high council members spoke at sacrament meeting, a really out-of-it harangue. I just bowed my head and cringed. Glad no investigators showed up.

Family night Sunday evening with the Guerro family was a singular success. Had a program with everyone taking part. Showed our new filmstrip "La Noche del Hogár" and then ate a tasty array of refreshments. The Guerros continue to be very active in the ward and are wonderful people. Hermano Guerro is especially enthusiastic, studies the gospel industriously, and is even making tapes of church-sponsored, short-wave broadcasts from New York City. Thirteen-year-old Victor paid me a pleasing compliment and whispered in my ear how much he likes me. I could say the same about the whole bunch of them.

Elder Merkley and I are thinking about having a fast soon as an expression of thanks for the blessings we've enjoyed this past month. We've slowed down a bit the last several days, with fewer lessons and less tracting. But we'll bounce back and, as long as we merit the Lord's kindness, should be justified in every hope of continued success in July.

June 28

This morning was Elder Fergason's *relevo* (he's been assistant to the president the past five months) at the mission home. While at the *relevo* I heard some more good things about Gordon from a missionary who was passing through from the Veracruz Mission—popped my pride buttons and made me feel somewhat ashamed of my own weaknesses and meager efforts to apply myself with the kind of consistent determination that Gordon has always demonstrated. I don't know where I'd be without the occasional lift I get from him.

Had a unexpected surprise after the *relevo.* The BYU baseball team came down to Mexico City to play some exhibition games, and some of the players, including Clark Burt [a high school friend], have been staying at the mission home. Clark and I had a pretty good talk. He's lost a little bit of hair but has widened some in the shoulders and is looking real good. His own recently completed mission must have had a deep effect; said he wouldn't mind ending up as a seminary teacher. Apparently Clark still swings the same big bat—he mentioned that he'd cracked out a couple of homers in their game yesterday.

My companion bought a suit on the way back to the apartment. By the time we arrived home Merkley wasn't feeling well, so he napped for most of the afternoon. I engaged in some badly needed reading in Spanish and study of the gospel. Had a rather dead fifth lesson with the Cadenas in the evening with the usual meal afterward. Although no one's balking on their baptismal commitment yet, neither are any of them putting out much effort to study the *folletos* or read the Book of Mormon, and Hermana Cadena is still drinking her coffee.

July 1

A lot of tracting today—over eight hours' worth. We were a little worried about the Cadenas before we gave them the sixth lesson, but they came through like champs and have evidently been doing some serious thinking on their own. We'll baptize the father, mother, and youngest boy, Ramón.

Earlier in the day we zipped through a very good first lesson with an extremely friendly little guy and his wife. They had initially insisted that they didn't think they would be changing their religion very soon but we took them by storm, and they may change their minds faster than they counted on.

Unexpected and disheartening news from home. I was stunned to receive a lengthy letter from Chuck in which he eloquently proclaims his defection from the church. His reasons are many and his articulation of them impressive. But I believe that emotions and old insecurities override all, not to mention the apparent stupidity of Chuck's stake president. Chuck has been nursing a searing indignation ever since he flunked a mission interview over a common little sex problem, blown way out of proportion by his inquisitor. This reversal is seemingly too abrupt, too extreme, even for Chuck. I will have to let his letter percolate on the back burner of my mind for awhile before attempting a response.

LETTER FROM CHUCK RADLOW

Dear Gary,

I guess it's more than about time that I wrote to you. I made several false starts, but they all ended in abandonment. This summer has been extremely difficult for me in many ways. If there is anyone I can be completely candid with I guess it's you, so let me try to let you know what's been going on and how I feel at this point.

With everyone gone this summer—and I mean EVERY one—I have had too much time to think over things. I have been almost emotionally possessed with the problem of the church during the last year of high school and all of college. It has been a strictly emotional problem which has been abetted by the intellect. You know the story of my schizophrenia as well as I. Sounds almost like the Book of Mormon—"And thus we do see how quickly the children of men forget the Lord their God, how quick to do iniquity." That's me, a doubting Thomas, alternatively a rationalist and a mystic, the hopeful, the despairing, but above all stuck with the task of rationalizing a belief that regards itself as God's will, as THE way, the ONLY way, which pretends to make an organization of men into an expression of the Divine.

Every concerned Mormon faces the problems: the authoritarianism, the literalism, the sometimes overweening conservatism; and it is these that give rise to many paths. Some take on the banner of the quest for the Holy Grail and go out on a mission. Some accomplish much good. Some break up families, debauch themselves and destroy their faith. Some never

convert a soul, others manage one or two for two and a half years. Some
convert by the dozens, and in their wake I wonder how many homes were
split down the middle or how many lives were changed for the best. Many
of our old friends are returning from their missions. They have interesting
stories to tell, but one thing most of them have in common—no matter
the meagerness of their accomplishments, the work of the Mormonizing
machine has done its job and they are hooked for life. It's very difficult to
face the fact that two years and more may have been a waste, that it might
all be a joke, a mistake. And so the great cognitive dissonance rationalizer
takes over and minds are forever closed. This isn't the story of everyone. I
am convinced that much good is accomplished in some areas and missions. I am also convinced that a good portion of the missions of the
church are pure tragedies of really wasted years, accomplishing nothing
but making heartaches for oneself.

I was nearly on one of these missions myself last summer. And now
maybe you'd like to know the truth about why I never went. I've always
been pretty sensitive. I've seriously wanted to do the right thing. But in
this fight I have let my emotions take over my mind too often. You know
how I am at times like these—impulsive, quick, eager, sanguine, and often
completely irrational. And so I saw the great vision, as do so many Mormon youths who have fought with their doubts, and asked to go on a mission. Things were well on their way—physical exam, bishop's interview—
and then I went to see my stake president. His questions were worse than
obnoxious, they were diseased and ugly. And then he found out. I was
guilty of sexual sin. I abused myself. I wonder if you can begin to imagine
how much that little bit of stupid, damnable doctrine caused me to hate
myself and curse my body.

And so to repent and to fail and then to beg for a chance and cry and
want to do right. I keep picturing myself begging the stake president to let
me go while I told the rest of the world it was for other reasons that I
stayed home. But a month and a half wasn't enough repentance time, and
besides, he told me, how could I be trusted. Damn. Damn a filthy, perni-
cious, impossible doctrine. To hell with that bunch of stupidity. I can exercise the little bit of love that's in my heart without the approval of President Taggeson or a ridiculous, outmoded moral code. That's easy to say
now. But then I was an evil black sinner, possessed by the darkest demons,
untrustworthy of the Lord's work.

And so I wrapped myself in a cloak of purity and tried to be godly. I
tried to follow all the rules of the Mormon blessing machine—put in a
good act and out comes a blessing. No more perfect legalism ever devised.

I closed up my mind and tried to stuff every problem into an inflexible mold. Doubts struck, but I overcame them quite neatly—until this summer. Gary, I'm afraid I'm through deluding myself. I'm beginning to learn to live with me, and the church is becoming a smaller and smaller part of that entity.

Suddenly I found myself again asking the eternal questions: just why do you think you have an option on God's word, and what about God? What, where, and so what? If we can't really know anything about God then why batter one's head against the wall searching for the impossible? And so I slowly drained myself in an attempt to re-achieve stability and came out with precisely nothing. I have never wanted so very much to cease existing in a world where the best is but a calculated guess, where we can't stop killing each other and hating each other, where there is an over-abundance of I-it relationships and so few instances of real love. Every rationalization seemed to disintegrate in my hands. I came to hate this church, with its cocky, know-it-all sureness, and then to reciprocally hate myself because I was a hypocrite. I became disgusted with the hundred irrelevancies pounded at me every Sunday. What care I if there are three degrees of glory (some people have even got fancy charts showing who's going where), or that Joseph Smith had a revelation commanding the brethren to build him a house, or tithing is somehow like down-payment on a palatial estate in the Celestial Kingdom.

How much longer is God going to let his church treat the Negro or anyone with darker skin as something less than human? What is the church saying? What are the prophet and the apostles NOT saying? If God was concerned enough to fill the Doctrine and Covenants with page after page of utter banalities and personal rebukes and petty nonsense, just why, just how much longer can he wait around to do something positive for his black people? The fine brethren thought it was just dandy to come out in the nation's papers against repeal of 14B of Taft-Hartley [prohibiting compulsory unionism] and sign their names to it. Now just where were they during the civil rights legislation?

Oh, but plant the seed in your heart my son, and when it starts to swell and it breaks your soul and consigns you to everlasting hell because you can't muster the strength to close your mind, you'll know. Know what?

I am getting fed up with the continued denouncements directed at those terrible, atheistic professors at our colleges and universities. I am enraged and saddened by accusations on the church editorial page directed at the worse than poisonous liberal, the modern Mormon who parades as a good guy, but who is subverting our youth into believing that the scriptures might actually mean to love God and not fear him, that the scriptures themselves might be liable to different interpretations.

I've tried, Gary. I've tried and I can't believe it any longer. I can't have faith in what appears to me to be becoming a growing vision of the totalitarian state, where appeal to authority supersedes appeals to one's heart, mind, and integrity. How can I really convey to you the extent of what's been going on in me for the last five years. I've wanted to kill myself so much this summer that I've spent hours thinking over the possible methods. Now isn't that dandy? What an ass I am. Well, I'm coming out of it again. Schizophrenia has not triumphed yet. But I'm facing the world much more cautiously, much more tentatively, with as few expectations as possible. I guess I've been burned too many times to come charging out on my steed in search of the Holy Grail anymore. No, my ambitions are much more humble this time. If there is a God up there or out there or around the corner, I haven't seen him or heard him or felt him. If he's a he and a great, perfect person out there on Kolob, I can't begin to imagine what I have to do with him or he with me, or how I can ever unravel what is an expression of his will and what is a projection of my own. I see no reason to postulate an extra-worldly meaning to this life. Look, Gary, we are here, right here and now, and we do the best we can. We're different, but we're all in the same silly game together. You are doing what you must, and I will do what I must. If I believe in anything, I guess I believe in the faint possibility of love. I can't explain it, but it's all I have left—the kind word, a bit of understanding, a helping hand when it's most needed—not theologies, and cosmologies, and genealogies of the dead and gone, but a hopelessly confused world of three billion living souls who can know what a bit of peace is and what happiness is when somebody cares. The Mormons try it every once in a while, and they probably do as good a job at institutionalizing the procedure as anyone.

But it isn't the only way or even the best way for everyone. Its exclusiveness, its dogmatism, and its very real, overweening pride have all but killed it for me. The empty meetings that perpetuate one another on their own stagnancy, the endless theological debates, the stiff-neckedness, the growing legalism in theory and practice, the hidden ritual, the growing compartmentalization, the almost hysterical defensiveness are becoming too much. Open myself to the blind indifference of Camus' universe? Perhaps, but not quite. To begin one's life on a basis of skepticism. To live each day open and ready, unafraid to change, allowing the old to be replaced by the inevitable. To love my neighbor with as much as there is in me. To use organizations only as long as they are means and never ends in themselves. To be compassionate and try to understand what drives us all to commit the senseless egotisms we are caught in. To let my life be the expression of my religion and let God or love or whatever is the meaning of it all be expressed in that life. This is what I am about. A bit calmer. A bit older.

I've learned to love you, Gary, and if there is anyone on a mission or a true believer that I can respect it's you. I respect you for your courage and your integrity, for your ability to love and make it work. I even respect you for your mission, for I believe you've made the best of it and done a great deal of good. I hope you will be able to understand how I feel—kind of like Atticus Finch in *To Kill a Mockingbird,* or the painter and her grandfather in *Night of the Iguana*—resigned but still rebellious, a cynic but still full of hope. I can't go on subjecting myself to the pain of trying to resolve the irresolvable. I will accept what I can and grow as my life proceeds, but I'm through trying to make the entire world conform to the mold of my childhood. Perhaps I'm reaching Sartre's Age of Reason, or perhaps I have substituted a delusion for a delusion. I'm not ready to throw the baby out with the bath, but the lines are being drawn. I'm afraid thoughts of a mission or the temple or confessions of faith are out of the question for a long time to come. Maybe someday—I'm not foolish enough to make final statements any more.

I certainly hope all is well with you, and that if there is anything I can do for you, you won't hesitate. Please write.

I love you brother, Chuck Radlow

Midnight, Salt Lake City

July 2

Some more sad news for me (on top of Chuck's letter)—found a note from Elder Pullins at the apartment this evening telling me to pack my things. I'm being transferred and will be working in the neighboring district of Ermita with Elder Carl Mason, a transplant from Gordon's mission, as my new senior companion. I had been counting on at least another month with Elder Merkley, so the change comes as a particularly unwelcome surprise. In the short thirty-nine days we have been together I have made tremendous strides forward on all fronts. Elder Merkley has been an example in dedication and a daily reminder to better myself. We never had a disagreement or misunderstanding. There has always been a good spirit present between us and we have bonded closely together as companions and friends. May I keep the fires going that we both helped to light.

PART FOUR

∾

Seniorship

Introduction:
The Structure of Mission Field Promotion and Mobility

As a consequence of time and experience in the field, many Mormon missionaries acquire attitudes typical of military combat veterans. That is, they generally become more realistic in their conception of the glory of the cause and the heroism of their participation. To some degree, the missionary enterprise is de-glamorized, but the ability to carry out duties efficiently is increased.[1] Most significantly, missionary veterans in the field narrowly learn to orient themselves to the plausibility structure of the mission organization. They learn to function in a missionary culture, and many (particularly males) seek recognition and advancement in LDS missionary ranks in much the same way that combat veterans become assimilated into military life and seek promotions in military rank.[2]

As we approached a year spent as junior companions in Mexico, we had become well integrated into the patterns of LDS missionary life. Gary had worked with six senior companions in Mexico City and Guadalajara, and Gordon had been assigned to eight seniors in four mission locations. By this time we were both becoming increasingly eager to exercise greater responsibility and independence through promotion to senior companion.

The Religious Reward System

The progressive development of young Mormons' capacity to perform the missionary role is complemented by the mobility structure of the LDS proselyting system. In turn, advancement in the mission organization is a preview of and, for many Mormon youths, an induction into the mobility structure of the LDS Church. Once missionaries are assimilated into the routines of missionary life, the mission organization, and hence the LDS Church, overwhelmingly becomes their dominant reference group. And, given a certain amount of experience and identification with the role, all other obligations are subordinated to one's missionary status. Thus, the religious socialization of many Mormon youths culminates in the mission field as commitments to the LDS cause are routinized and identification with the church is secured, at least for the time-being.

Any voluntary organization must provide incentives for members to participate, and among the most powerful that religious organizations offer are what Stark and Bainbridge (1980) call "supernatural compensators," including life everlasting and the hope for ultimate salvation from human suffering. In addition, there must also be more immediate rewards connected to people's everyday lives and self-concepts. An important strength of the LDS Church lies in its organizational ability to meet the needs of large numbers of ordinary people to belong and participate through a complex network of lay offices and group obligations. To be a faithful and active Latter-day Saint means to accumulate a repertoire of callings and positions in the church. It means becoming embedded in an intimate authority system in which one alternately instructs and is instructed, delegates responsibility and is delegated to, supervises and is supervised, and leads and follows. It is a system that provides status and recognition for advancements and performance. Mormonism could scarcely function without such participatory incentives for its members, and the same types of incentives are apparent in mission field organizations.

Like most Christian religions, the LDS Church preaches against self-pride, purely personal ambition, and "unrighteous dominion" in religious callings. First and foremost, Mormons are supposed to be devoted to doing God's work rather than promoting their own institutional careers in the ranks of church organization. But without a career mobility structure it is unlikely that lay religions such as Mormonism would continue to flourish from one generation to the next. The LDS Church teaches and promotes leadership qualities and aspirations as prime values, and promotions to positions of greater ecclesiastical authority activate the status system.

In the mission field, many young Mormons (especially males) become meaningful participants in the authority structure of the LDS Church for the first time. They are given significant responsibilities and held accountable for their performances by church leaders. Youthful, idealistic religious motives are channeled by organizational discipline. Personal motives and aspirations are expanded by the reward system of the mission organization. The esteem and plaudits of adult ecclesiastical authorities and peers motivate many young

Mormons and stimulate them to attain recognition through leadership positions in the mission organization. Informal conversation among missionary companions and missionary storytelling sessions provide important channels for articulating prestige motives.

In ways that are somewhat analogous to combat experience, certain exceptional missionaries emerge and, in their response to the trials of missionary life in the field, they may demonstrate unusual aptitude and personify the organizational ideals of valor, devotion, selflessness, and cool-headed competence in the face of adversity. In some cases, their deeds may become legendary, and they are celebrated as heroes and exemplars in both the rhetoric of church leaders and the folklore of mission culture.[3] The mythologized exploits of missionary heroes provide idealized standards of success and kindle the passions of ambition and emulation. As new missionaries, for example, we were treated to stories at the LTM, and later on in the field, about the legendary Benjamín Para, a Mexican whose missionary assignment preceded ours by several years and who was reputed to have baptized nearly seven hundred converts during his tour of duty in the late 1950s.[4]

In addition to heroes, stories circulate in the mission field about "bad" missionaries (who, because of their faithlessness, harm not only themselves but also the Lord's work) and even anti-heroes or "tricksters," who find clever ways to violate chaffing mission rules but nonetheless manage to be effective missionaries. William Wilson, a Mormon folklorist, concludes that missionary narratives "are instruments of socialization, helping assimilate missionaries into the way of life they must adopt in the coming months. . . . One becomes a missionary by learning the canon of missionary stories and eventually by passing them on to others. . . . The ability to take an active role in the storytelling culture is one of the markers separating the seasoned missionary from the novice" (1994, 209). Informal missionary narratives help to inculcate in missionaries "the rules on which both their individual success and the success of the missionary program will depend" (1994, 216). Although we recorded few, if any, popular field tales, we did document the personal qualities and exploits of our peers, both the good and bad as we perceived them, highlighting contrasts that reinforced our ideals about missionary performance.

Ambitious striving in the mission field can become a source of tension and invidiousness—characteristics more than familiar to competitive corporate organizations but often inconsistent with such basic religious values as modesty, humility, compassion, and harmonious sharing. Competitive mobility systems often generate resentment and ill-will for those not promoted and those for whom the advancements and recognition bestowed on others may seem unfair and arbitrary relative to their own perceived merits. Both of us experienced a certain amount of ambivalence about our ambitions for personal success, and we were frustrated by our long gestation as junior companions. Later, we (especially Gordon) worked with junior companions who registered all the signs of status aspiration and frustrated ambition. Even though we had relatively little contact with sister missionaries, we surmise that mobility aspirations in LDS mission field organizations are more likely to create tensions for young males as they strive for promotions to supervisory positions. In spite of (or perhaps even because of) a lack of competitive pressure for leadership positions, sister missionaries are often more effective proselytors than their male counterparts in many LDS missions.[5]

Punitive Mission Field Sanctions

Hand in hand with mission field incentives and rewards, punitive sanctions also control deviation from missionary norms. Such sanctions almost always entail denegration of a missionary's perceived moral character and range from the stimulation of private guilt over secret failings to the public disgrace of an early or dishonorable discharge for unwillingness to comply with minimum commitment standards. In cases of transgressions such as adultery, fornication, or homosexuality, the threat of instant excommunication is the most severe mission field deterrence (something we witnessed on several occasions in our own field experience). Mission presidents vary in their use of discretionary authority in sending home problem missionaries who have lost the desire to work or have chronic problems getting along with others.[6] We have no precise data on the overall number of Mormon missionaries sent home annually from the field, but we also have no reason to believe that it is a large percent of the missionary force, certainly not as great as the 7 to 11 percent attrition rates documented in a RAND Corporation report for the all-volunteer U.S. Armed Forces during the 1980s, summarized in an Associated Press release on October 10, 1988. Our missionary presidents in Mexico constantly warned their youthful charges to guard against letting devotional and personal standards slip, but in practice they seemed to bend over backward to accommodate occasional problem cases. They were also relatively lenient in reprimanding most missionary offenses, as shown, for example, in the way in which President Leroy Hatch dealt with Elder Throgg in Guadalajara and President Seville Hatch demonstrated forbearance with the volatile Elder Granger in the Veracruz Mission.

Although excommunication for sexual misconduct occurs relatively infrequently in the mission field, a certain amount of flirtation invariably takes place, and occasionally romances blossom to distract some missionaries from their proselyting assignments. We discovered that mission field romances could be, and occasionally were, a major problem for some, but they rarely involved elder-sister pairings. More commonly, romances tended to flare up between elders and young Mexican females (as with Elder Throgg and Neome Velazco in Guadalajara). The usual remedy was a transfer of the errant missionary to a new locale and/or a demotion in missionary rank. The reputations of missionaries who were transferred for disciplinary reasons typically suffered a significant decline, especially in the eyes of mission leaders, who were in a position to reward or withhold future status advancements within the mission hierarchy.

In our mission organizations in Mexico, promotions in rank were a function of both seniority and reputation; variations in the rate of personnel turnover created (or sometimes delayed) opportunities for advancement. In foreign-speaking countries, a longer gestation period may be required for junior companions to learn the ropes before they can be promoted, whereas those who speak the language may be advanced to senior companion more quickly, especially if they show missionary aptitude. That was true of elders in our missions (for example, Elders Martineau, Whetten, Hatch, and Orozco) who had grown up in the Mormon colonies of northern Mexico and already had Spanish-speaking skills as well as LDS backgrounds in, and familiarity with, Mexican culture.

In our missionary experience, the most important factor in mobility was the size and proximity of the preceding cohort group. For example, the cohorts who occupied leadership positions when we arrived had entered the field when the mission had just been divided in two, and relatively few experienced missionaries were ahead of them. Of necessity, many in the group had been advanced by the mission president after being in the mission only a short time. In our case, however, a relatively large cohort of missionaries had entered the field just ahead of ours, creating a blockage in the normal arteries of mission mobility. For many of us, that temporarily proved frustrating to personal ambition. We wished to be recognized by our peers through advancement in missionary status as we became increasingly disgruntled with subordinate positions as junior companions. Following our long-anticipated promotions to seniority, we were determined to enhance our reputations as able, dedicated missionaries.

A reputation, of course, requires time to develop and in the long run becomes an increasingly important variable in personal development. In the Mormon missionary organization it is primarily through the periodic reassignment and circulation of companions that reputations—for better or worse—are established in mission news and gossip. Eventually, a few of a missionary's former senior companions are likely to ascend to supervisory and leadership positions and are then able to recommend others for promotion. After several of our former senior companions (Pullins, Bayer, Robison, Martineau, and Rencher) became assistants to the president, the fortunes of our missionary careers began to rise. Ultimately, our efforts were rewarded with advancements to supervisory positions. After three and a half months as a senior companion, Gordon was promoted to supervising elder (district leader) in the state of Chiapas. Subsequently, Gary bypassed the usual step of supervising elder to become an *orientador* (zone leader) in Mexico City.

Changes in mission status were accompanied by a corresponding transformation in our perceptions of missionary work and companion relations. We became directly responsible for what we did or did not accomplish. We were no longer able to second-guess the judgment of our senior companions or knowingly shrug our shoulders when the work seemed not to progress well. Problematic junior companions now became a persistent theme in our letters and journal accounts. Although we made occasional cynical comments during this phase of our missionary careers, our rhetoric became more pious and platitudinal as we assumed positions of authority and increasingly identified with the formal structure of the mission organization. Our disdainful, impertinent comments about the religious beliefs and stubborn practices of those whom we were trying to convert also increased; we had to assume the lead role in prodding investigators and battling with both Catholic and Protestant detractors.

Sustained conversion rates in missionary religions such as Mormonism are likely to occur only in places where significant segments of a population are unattached to (or are dissatisfied with) existing religious institutions. In our Mexican experience, these conditions were most likely to prevail in urban centers, especially in and around Mexico City. Although clearly a necessary condition, the availability of a susceptible religious market alone does not produce conversions. Even where there are religiously dissatisfied people (a few of whom actually may be engaged in a conscious, active search for religious alternatives), they must still be contacted somehow and persuaded to make new religious commitments. That fact corresponded closely to our self-conceptions as divinely commissioned messengers of the gospel. We viewed our specific assignment as seeking out the pure in heart, who, we believed, would be intuitively receptive to our message. Thus, our efforts to convert people to Mormonism could only commence after willing listeners had been found, and the searching and finding process (for us, usually through tracting) preoccupied much of our daily work. There was, however, considerable variation among our peers in their conscientious willingness to search for new investigators. And once investigators were located, there was also variation in missionaries' persuasive manner and teaching abilities. As a rule, those who consistently worked the hardest at cultivating an extensive set of listeners and were also effective teachers had the greatest amount of conversion success over the long run.

We, like other ambitious missionaries, regarded official work norms as representing a minimum standard of acceptable performance and routinely pushed ourselves to exceed them. Thus, for example, the prescribed mission norm was to work a seventy-hour week. As senior companions, however, we attempted to average eighty-hour weeks of proselyting labor. Such extra effort was sanctioned by the informal, peer-supported criteria of missionary success that we employed to define and evaluate our status as dedicated workers. We were motivated to excel and maintain our reputations, and, consequently, self-respect, by tracting and teaching eleven to twelve hours a day, day after day, seven days a week. From similarly motivated companions we learned that it was dedicated consistency that would pay off in the long run, and we were willing to make the necessary investments of ourselves in order to be successful. Such an orientation closely approximates the ascetic religious attitude Max Weber (1958) celebrated as the Protestant Ethic: the psychological reciprocity of believing one's self to be chosen of God and the relentless compulsion to devote one's resources in a sober, calculated effort toward the accomplishment of a sacred cause.

It was this kind of devotion that we often identified as spirituality. When in our journal accounts or correspondence we spoke of being guided by the Lord or having the Lord's Spirit, it was the rhetoric of high morale, exhilaration, and happiness in the cause despite (or occasionally because of) some degree of deprivation and adversity. We experienced spirituality when achieving unity of action with companions, and, perhaps most important, as a growing self-confidence in our ability to do missionary work—especially in our ability to speak and act from both experience and spontaneity in coping with problematic situations.

As we moved from our missionary apprenticeships to become senior companions, we tended to devote more attention in our journals to the progress investigators were making toward baptism in the Mormon Church. This was particularly evident in Gary's writing, because he and his companions attracted large numbers of investigators in Mexico City, and the status of senior companion increased personal responsibility for success or failure in the work. Typically, the most effective teaching missionaries were those good at keeping prospective converts on track in the lesson sequence and able to get investigators to make and keep key promises in the process. Such commitments prominently included promises to read the religious literature left by the missionaries, especially the Book of Mormon; to pray for divine guidance in making their religious decisions; to comply with the health requirements and prohibitions of the Word of Wisdom; to attend LDS religious services on Sundays and during the week; and, for investigators with Catholic backgrounds, to forswear their ritual devotions to Catholic saints, especially the Virgin of Guadalupe. Perhaps most important, effective proselytors were able to encourage investigators to regularly reiterate their agreements to be baptized by a specific calendar date if they successfully concluded the six-lesson sequence. Our cryptic references to the numbered lessons we were giving to various investigator families were simply an abbreviated way of indicating their degree of progress toward the ultimate objectives of conversion and baptism into the church. Our journal practice of narrating investigators' progress through the standard lesson sequence was, in effect, an assessment method in which we often evaluated perceived obstacles and thereby kept ourselves consciously focused on the commitment process.

NOTES

1. For a classic study of the attitudes of combat veterans in World War II, see Stouffer (1949). See also Moskos (1970), who analyzes soldiering attitudes during the Vietnam War.

2. There are significant gender differences in the experiences of male and female missionaries serving LDS missions, particularly with respect to promotion and status aspiration within the mission hierarchy and mobility system. Thus, most of the generalizations we make in this section are more applicable to the experiences of young male missionaries than to sister missionaries. Because women cannot be ordained to the Mormon lay priesthood and are therefore excluded from making ultimate doctrinal decisions or formulating ecclesiastical policy, the institutional religious careers of Mormon women are usually much less visible than those of Mormon men (Cornwall 1994; England 1990; Hanks 1992; Newell 1985). That is also true in the mission organization. Without priesthood authority, sister missionaries cannot perform religious ordinances, including the rite of baptism, and must depend on male missionaries to interview prospective converts and perform baptisms. Nor can sister missionaries organize and officiate in small mission branches or call members to accept lay assignments, all of which elders, under the direction of the mission president, are able to do. In many ways, LDS mission organizations are microcosms of the larger ecclesiastical structure of the LDS Church. Historically, this organizational parallel has reinforced Mormon patriarchal authority in the mission field as well as in the church at large. To what extent, if any, future male LDS ecclesiastical offi-

cials will be willing to alter traditional conceptions of gender role authority remains to be seen.

3. For studies of Mormon missionary folklore, see Knowlton (1994) and Wilson (1974, 1981, 1988, 1994).

4. Para became the first Mexican mission president in the history of the LDS Church in Mexico when he was called to preside over the Veracruz Mission in 1972, six years after we completed missions in the same region. Since then, official emphasis on developing local leadership has led to many of Mexico's rotating mission presidents being Mexicans who, like Para, are returned missionaries and have advanced through the lay mobility structure of the LDS Church.

5. Although we lack systematic statistical data, several former mission presidents with whom we have talked agreed that many of the best proselytors were women. They concurred that sister missionaries tended to be better educated, more mature on average, and often more sensitive to investigators' needs and problems than were young male missionaries. Elders whom we interviewed tended to agree that sister missionaries were often more effective in converting investigators. That concession was mixed with the invidious perception that they did not work as hard as elders (for example, they put in fewer hours or tracted less often) and were more likely to express personal problems or seek guidance from mission leaders. These characterizations are similar to those reported by Embry (1997, 129–31) in oral history interviews with mission presidents, many of whom concurred that sister missionaries exerted a "refining influence" on youthful male missionaries and added a "spiritual element" to missions. They also maintained, however, that the women were ill more often than males and experienced a disproportionate number of distracting personal problems.

6. One pair of U.S. missionaries whom we interviewed in the field said their president had earned the nickname of "Send'm Home Homer" for his crackdown on missionaries who were not working.

10

⁓

"The Biggest Responsibility I've Ever Had":
Gordon's Story as Senior Companion
in Villa Flores, Chiapas

Promotion from junior to senior companion was a major transition for Gordon, which, in conjunction with his assignment to open the isolated Chiapas town of Villa Flores to Mormon proselyting, produced mixed feelings of exhilaration, optimism, apprehension, a sense of inadequacy, and rededication to his missionary calling. In Villa Flores, Gordon quickly discovered a heretofore unrealized ability to speak fluent Spanish and developed greater confidence in his capacity to teach investigator lessons. His first junior companion was a mature, well-prepared missionary who had almost as much experience in the field as Gordon. Companionship with the new junior was a source of both invaluable support and some friction, which developed gradually in the context of authority issues and competitive ambitions.

Both Gordon and his companion unreservedly committed themselves to their work (like Gary and Elder Merkley in Mexico City, often to the point of near exhaustion), relentlessly tracting the streets of Villa Flores in search of listeners sympathetic to their message. But in spite of their diligent efforts and a certain amount of initial curiosity by the residents, ultimate recruitment results in Villa Flores were scant. Almost immediately the two were confronted with an organized anti-Mormon campaign orchestrated by the head priest of the local Catholic Church. Later, they encountered small but vehement Protestant groups that were disposed to engage in scriptural battles and had little interest in investigating a new religion. People who consented to listen to presentations in their homes were wary of attending religious meetings at the missionaries' apartment in the center of town. Failure to attract a consistent gathering of investigators at Sunday services became a persistent source of frustration, and Gordon began to fear that they would succeed in baptizing only a few people and then be forced to leave Villa Flores as a failed experiment. That apprehension proved prescient. Although disappointed, Gordon also emerged from his Villa Flores experience as a much more capable and polished missionary, prepared to serve as a supervising elder in his next assignment.

In the meantime, Gary remained in Mexico City with a new senior companion who was a steady worker but whose proselyting style and personal relationship with Gary were significantly less stimulating than Elder Merkley's had been. Nonetheless, missionary work continued to be productive, with more baptisms and promising investigators. Like Gordon, Gary's confidence in his missionary capability had increased considerably. His morale began to sag, however, as time passed and there was little prospect for promotion to senior companion. He felt "strangled by the robes of juniorship." Letters received from Gordon as senior companion in Villa Flores were both a source of pride and invidious comparison. Gary's feelings were not enhanced by the demise of his relationship with Kathy Dempsey, who suddenly surprised him with a Dear John letter after months of writing about marriage plans. His spirits were soon revitalized, however, by a mission conference at which he was inspired by the prophetic utterances of LDS apostles from Salt Lake City and, more than anything, by his belated promotion to seniorship after spending more than half his mission as a junior companion.

Veracruz, July 10, 1965

Good mail day. Everybody decided to write me at the same time. Gary has been unexpectedly moved again (but is still in Mexico City) and says that Chuck Radlow has defected from the church (holy hell!). Dave Lingwall wrote that he went through with his July 4 wedding, and Mike and Karen Mitchell had a baby boy on the 29th of June—Mike sent a note and a big *cigar*. Some of this is pretty hard to believe. In fact, the only plausible news is Gary's transfer. On the subject of transfers, some *nuevos* from the Language Training Mission are supposed to arrive this week, which means that some promotions to senior companion will have to be made. If fortune smiles it could be my turn to go to bat.

LETTER FROM GARY

Gord: Sorry about the slight delay in writing. We were going at it pretty hard there, and I've incurred the wrath of various ones for failure to write more often. It just hasn't been possible.

Right in the midst of milk and honey, I was shocked with a change. As near as I can tell, they prematurely broke up a good team due to a scarcity of juniors in our mission. Also, Norm Morrison (remember the curly-headed kid who worked with you at Sudbury's Foodtown in Salt Lake?) needed some quick cheering up after a disastrous stay in one of the real holes of the mission, so as a form of therapy he was paired up with Merkley (who also just happens to be Morrison's cousin). By the way, Morrison is one of the better missionaries around, but he had been in a place that was rent with apostasy, strife, and black-painted rumors tacked onto the missionaries by certain branch members. An unenviable experience for him, and he lost twenty-five pounds. Anyway, I was moved just down the street into the neighboring district of Ermita.

My new companion is Carl Mason, a transfer from your mission. Don't know if you knew him at all. He's heard of you but never eye-balled you. He's short, blonde, slight of build, cheerful, and a likable guy. He's also a good worker by reputation—not spectacular, but steady. We should get along well on all levels. He's probably more self-effacing and unoffending than I am.

But let me tell you how my last month with Merkley ended—not bad, I modestly admit. We baptized seven outstanding families. We worked hard for success and would have had an eighty-hour-per-week proselyting average, but we both got a little sick towards the end and so ended up with seventy-five. I feel I made progress of a personal nature, but I also came to realize with greater clarity how much I lack. There were various occasions when I was forced to feel ashamed of my puny efforts and glaring weaknesses right in the face of immeasurable goodness and blessings from the Lord. I hope I'm on the road to whip some of these shortcomings and that I can keep the fires going. Meanwhile, it may be the end of August before seniorship calls for me to step forward.

You must have done pretty well yourself last month. Transplants Ionelli and Hatch from your mission are always pumping me full of praiseworthy reports about you. I just took Ionelli's place here in the District of Ermita, and he seems to think you'll eventually be made assistant to the prez (if they ever get around to making you senior). Apparently your scripture recital with Elder Rencher is common knowledge down there. I think these guys are trying to make me feel bad or something, but they're shooting at the wrong mark. I couldn't be prouder. Besides all that, I very much envy your Tuesday baseball. I figured those days were over for me. I'd sure like to dig into the old batter's box and take a couple of good swings at a fast ball.

Career-wise, I'm still fuzzy. Law is a long road but a worthwhile one, one that I'm sure we could both walk. If I wind up marrying Kathy (she's planning on it, and I haven't given her much room for wondering), and you the same with Beckie (?), part of our eventual decisions about five to eight more years of school would have to take into account responsibilities to wives and children (!). By the way, I think I should tell you that I recently got a letter from Chuck, who has been going through a religious crisis this summer. His prospects for serving a mission have been dashed and he has rejected the church. I'll send you his letter so you can read the details.

I tried to eradicate the last botched photo of myself with this new attempt herein enclosed, but you see the smirking results. You will notice, though, how cleverly the ever retreating hairline is covered up.

Agreed. One day, a year from this August, I'll meet you in El Distrito Federál with *Seleciones* [a proselyting pamphlet] in hand to fulfill both of our dreams of doing a little missionary work together as companions before going home.

Your brother, Gar

July 12

Great day in the morning! I couldn't be more anxious or excited. The time has finally come to see if I've learned anything from my missionary apprenticeship as a junior companion. I've just been made a senior AND I'm being sent to open up Villa Flores, a town situated four hundred miles from mission headquarters in the Chiapas Mountains where Mormon missionaries have never been sent before. My junior companion will be Elder Paul Heber, who is reputed to be one of the most ambitious and able new elders in the mission. I got the word at a baptismal service tonight at the chapel. Elder Rencher (my former senior companion in Minatitlán) and Elder Zuñiga, the two new assistants to the president, had been down to Chiapas a few days earlier, checking out the possibilities for sending missionaries to open up Villa Flores. I knew that and I also knew that I was a candidate for being made a senior companion. So when Elder Burch came in during the middle of the baptismal service and told me that Rencher wanted to see me outside, the little wheels of premonition clicked in my head and I knew exactly what he was going to say.

I've not quite sorted out all of my thoughts and feelings yet. To be honest, I must admit that I've stagnated a bit personally since coming to Veracruz. Perhaps I've just been overly anxious to strike out on my own as a senior companion and resentful of my subordinate position as a junior. At any rate,

I will need to humble myself and do a lot of spiritual stretching in order to do what is expected of me in Villa Flores. It will be sink or swim and I'll need the Lord's help in every way possible. I just hope I prove strong enough to do my own part.

Villa Flores, July 14

I left Veracruz yesterday with Elders Zuñiga and Rencher—my escorts to Villa Flores. Unfortunately, with night descending and Elder Zuñiga at the wheel, we ran smack into a cow sitting on the road and practically demolished our Volkswagen, not to mention the cow. I was the only missionary casualty with a cut under my right eye. A group of *campecinos* [peasant farmers] quickly congregated at the wreck, but nobody claimed the cow. Apparently this kind of accident is not uncommon around here. Grazing lands are not fenced in and livestock are frequently on the roads, creating a real hazard for motorists.

Nothing could be done for the cow, which was killed at impact, so we shifted our attention to the car. We had to remove the front fender and change the tire before we were able to limp into Tuxtla Gutiérrez, capital of the state of Chiapas, arriving well after midnight. We spent the rest of the night at the missionaries' house, which is one of the nicest in the mission. Elder Smith is stationed in Tuxtla as director of the Chiapas Zone, and it was great to see him again—first time since I left Minatitlán. He's back to being his old self and appears fully recovered from his bout with appendicitis.

We borrowed Elder Smith's car and left early in the morning for Villa Flores, gingerly picking our way over a rocky dirt road (and fording an occasional stream—no bridges!) that winds through the mountains. This place is really in the boonies. But, in spite of our rather inauspicious beginning, I feel enthusiastic and optimistic. We spent the remainder of the day making arrangements to show "¿Qué Es Un Mormón?" [What Is a Mormon?] and *Man's Search for Happiness* [a film made for the Mormon Pavilion at the New York World's Fair] at the local *cine* as a way of introducing ourselves to Villa Flores. Everyone so far has been very helpful. Now we're just waiting for my junior companion Elder Heber to arrive.

July 15

Elders Rencher and Zuñiga have gone and she's all ours. Elder Heber blew in late this morning on the bus with his pet cat (against mission rules), double-necked, twelve-string guitar (which he built himself), and notebooks of poems (which he writes and puts to music). It would be easy to conclude that Heber's a bit unconventional, maybe even eccentric, but he is also ambitious, aggressive, speaks confident (if not flawless) Spanish, and is by all accounts a hard worker. Heber's tall, rawboned, and a little older than most of us (he served four years in the air force, where he converted to the church). He has over eight months in the mission, so he's no greenie. He should supplement me in some of my weak areas and vice versa. I think we'll do some good together.

We gave the films another showing in town and then took our show up the road this evening to Villa Corso, a little pueblo where some investigators contacted by Rencher and Zuñiga live. To our great surprise a standing-room-only crowd of over one hundred people showed up for the free show in Villa Flores. Everything was going beautifully until a sudden thunderstorm knocked out the electricity and brought our production to a premature close. We had managed to get through most of the reel, however, and our audience was friendly and seemed favorably impressed by the presentation. I think we're off to a good start.

July 16

Heber and I are temporarily quartered in a small but decent hotel until we can find an apartment of some kind. This will be about the biggest responsibility I've ever had. The two of us represent the church in Villa Flores, and what we do or don't do here in the next few months will determine how the gospel is accepted by the people. If we are successful in winning a sufficient number of converts, a branch of the church can be established and, if I'm still here, I would have to assume the additional duties of a branch president.

My companion is a poetry-writing, song-composing sort who sings his own compositions à la Bob Dylan while playing his elaborate twelve-string guitar. He is, I must admit, pretty darn good. And his knowledge of the scriptures is as good or better than any previous companion that I've had. I immediately informed Elder Heber that as far as I was concerned we would function as co-seniors, sharing equal authority and responsibility for planning our work and making decisions. Heber is already a capable missionary and doesn't need a boss or tutor. We have several appointments set up for tomorrow and a number of referrals to check out, obtained from people who attended our film presentations. Our hopes and spirits are high.

July 17

Things seem to be progressing well. We just returned from presenting two lessons, one in Villa Corso, where we were introduced to the town's doctor, and a second to another doctor and his family in Villa Flores. These are precisely the kinds of people we most need to gain influence with if the church is going to be established here. My ability to speak Spanish has improved dramatically.

The lessons we gave today were the best I've ever presented. Elder Heber tends to be a little windy though, and departs markedly from the lesson outline when it's his turn to teach. As a result, the lessons were much too long, and in my opinion lost some of their coherence. I intimated my concern to Elder Heber and suggested we stick more closely to the logic of the lesson plan. He disagreed, or to be more precise, maintained that we shouldn't be overly concerned with making polite impressions on people, but should allow ourselves to be led by the spirit when we teach. To avoid making a mountain out of a molehill, I neglected to point out that my interpretation of where the spirit is trying to lead us might be a little different from his.

At any rate, we've made ourselves known, established some contacts, and found an apartment to our liking, which is big enough to also serve as a *capilla*. It's situated in a central location, about one block from the town plaza, and is adjacent to the local bank. We've also purchased or had made (all billed to the mission home) some necessary furnishings: beds, desks, chairs, table, benches for the *capilla*, etc. We even had a local carpenter make us a set of sacrament trays out of wood, and we bought some whiskey shot glasses so we can pass sacramental water to investigators once we commence holding religious services in Villa Flores. Up till now we've been living in a hotel and taking our meals at a downtown cafe. Something else I suppose we'll need to secure are the services of a maid to take care of our wash and prepare meals. There are no laundromats here and we don't relish the thought of taking our dirty clothes down to the river to beat clean on the rocks, as is the native custom.

July 20

Maybe the apple of Villa Flores won't be quite so juicy as we were led to believe by our first few bites. We will be challenged here, no doubt. But our companionship is rapidly gaining strength and we're in high spirits. It's almost 10:00 P.M. and we just finished having a *clase de compañero* by candlelight (electricity is out again due to some spectacular lightning last night).

The guy who was supposed to rent us the apartment (he owns, among other things, the local distributorship for Carta Blanca Beer) has not proved to be very reliable. He failed to move his own belongings out of the apartment as we had agreed and, consequently, we were unable to move in. We had to spend half the day looking for him and finally located him at his girl friend's house. He was a little sheepish, but claimed that he now needed to keep the apartment for himself. Instead, he offered us the entire second floor of the same building which, for the same rent, we agreed to take for 700 pesos a month [about $56]. Actually, this is a better deal for us. It will give us a much larger area, with a big separate room that can be used as a *capilla* once we get some investigators coming out to church. It includes a bathroom and a shower, but no hot water.

Our investigator family over in Villa Corso has apparently been scared off. Someone in town has been putting pressure on them and they no longer want to continue our discussions. The man told us he was concerned about his job and status in the community. And last night I just missed getting beaned in the head with a rock heaved at us by some little street urchin while we were walking downtown. Then today we had a real battle getting my check cashed at the bank and were forced to waste a lot of time before we finally got things straightened out with the manager, who personally agreed to endorse all of our checks from now on. At least we've found a good maid (whom we encountered while tracting) who has agreed to prepare our meals and do our wash. With most of our domestic arrangements now settled, we're ready to roll up our sleeves and concentrate our energy on bringing the church to Villa Flores.

P.S. I just received a letter from Gary overflowing with congratulations on my good fortune. Too much praise makes me feel like a phoney for not having deserved it. As usual I will need to keep a watchful eye on my self-pride and the "all is well" attitude of smugness and complacency that often precedes a fall.

LETTER FROM GARY

Gord: Way to go! That was a real thrill for me. Yes, thrill, I say! I had already received the news before your letter arrived. I got it straight from the mouth of your President Hatch while he was visiting our President Hatch here a few days ago. I almost startled him speechless when I walked up and shook his hand—he thought for a crazy instant it was you. When he finally found his tongue he said something like: "It's a good thing you're really not your brother, because I just made him senior and have sent him to open up a little town so far away you can't find it on a map. Gordon is one of our greatest missionaries, and we know we can expect terrific things from him. Some of his senior companions have never really let him go, but he came on a mission to do a job and has dedicated and greatly prepared himself." Those were his words, as closely as I can remember them, and they left me shivering with excitement and bursting with pride. Afterward, my companion, Elder Mason, added to the recitation of praise, once again relating the story of your scripture session with Elder Rencher, with Rencher telling Mason later that you were the best companion he had ever had, and that he felt somewhat small in his capacity as your senior. Such comments and news are a steady inspiration, and you could hardly be aware of the strength I have drawn from your high example and unflinching standards.

I can vaguely imagine what a broil of work and activity these past days have been for you. With all the details of getting set up and organized, it still sounds from your letter like you're off to an impressive start with the actual missionary work. I'll be anxious to hear how things are working out and pray for your success and happiness in the meantime. As for me, I'm still waiting with about equal measures of hope and despair for promotion out of the ranks of apprenticeship. I may have to stay patient for another month or so. No one really seems to know when the next batch of newcomers will be arriving, although Keith Flake (who you may recall was in the cohort behind us at the LTM) was just jumped ahead to senior over at least ten of us who are in line.

By the way, a significant transition just occurred in our mission a few days ago: Our President Hatch (Leroy) completed his three-year calling and was released. He is not as gregarious a man as his brother, and I did not develop a feeling of personal closeness to him. But I've admired his cool competence; under his direction we have become probably the highest-baptizing mission in the church. Our new president—Jasper McClellan—seems to be a very down-to-earth person (his wife even more so). Like the Hatch brothers, President McClellan is a product of the Mormon colonies in Mexico, so he already speaks Spanish and has a knowledge of the culture.

Meanwhile, Elder Mason and I have been working steadily. We've baptized a young Protestant bachelor plus a divorced school teacher and her three children, who are really exceptional. And we're currently carrying a lot of good investigators. My companion and I are getting along as pleasantly as can be in our personal dealings, but sometimes in our work Elder Mason can be pretty obnoxious and offensive in his presentation of lessons to investigators if their responses deviate much from the ideal. He also tends to waste time baiting and arguing with people at the door when we're tracting. In short, he displays a mild Jekyll and Hyde-type personality, because he's always very unassuming and diffident with me. Oh well, I sometimes actually learn more from what I consider flaws in my companions. Mason murders the subjunctive tense (although his Spanish is fluent enough), and catching his mistakes to myself strengthens my own Spanish (which, by the way, is improving a lot).

Earlier this past week the districts of Ermita and Churubusco held a joint *día de campo*. We played football on a slippery field for more than two hours, and I thoroughly enjoyed myself. It was flagball rules, everybody except Mason was an athlete, and the play wasn't too gentle. I got skinned in a few places and my clothes were all muddied up. There were a few soreheads among the group, but the crabbing (and bragging) didn't have much effect on the fun we all had. After football we piled ten in a Volkswagen and returned to Ermita chapel for several hours of basketball. Played until we could barely stand, then my companion and I came home exhausted and already feeling a little sick. The next morning we were sore and stiff from head to foot, literally had to shuffle around like a couple of old guys during our tracting rounds for the next several days.

Two weeks ago I received a depressing letter from Kathy in which she fired off a volley of complaints and criticisms against parents, friends, and me. I sent her back a reprimand of sorts and told her to quit griping. Haven't heard from her since. I did receive a letter today from Linda Booth [a girlfriend from high school]. Don told her that you had been killed by a mob, and she believed him. Shook her up for awhile, I'm afraid, until she called Mom. Speaking of Don, I assume you've been informed about him joining the Federal Reserves. That will be a bad deal for him come basic training this November. It will be a bad deal for us come Vietnam in a year or so when we return home.

One thing I've always meant to ask: Are you still keeping up your journal? There have been periods in my mission when I've let it go, but in general I've kept an almost daily record that I know will be of keen interest later on. I'd get a kick out of reading a similar record of yours.

Work hard but be careful. Don't convert Don's tall tales into truth and get yourself boiled in oil or something by outraged fanatics.

Your Brother, Gar

July 21

Batten down the hatches! Dig the trenches! The adversary has gone on the warpath. The first rounds of the battle were fired tonight in the form of a loudspeaker attack from the towers of the Catholic Church. The broadcast could be heard all over town and served notice to the people of Villa Flores to beware of the Mormon foreigners who have come as wolves in sheep's clothing to deceive them. As I stood listening in front of the little store, where we had stopped for a *refresco*, I couldn't quite believe what we were hearing. Here was a professed Christian, a Catholic priest—a supposed minister of the Lord—

spewing half-baked *falsedades* [falsehoods] to the people and warning them to avoid us, even publicizing where we lived and castigating by name the man who is renting to us. There was nothing new in his ideological attack, just the usual garbage about José Smith who made a career of tricking people with his gold plates. He said we had been well trained to deceive, that the people should deny us any chance to cast our spells, and ended with the standard clamor about the sanctity of the Virgin, saints, pope, etc.

Prior to the priest's public bombardment we had what we considered to be a pretty good day (in spite of having to retire early because of another electrical outage). We managed eleven hours of solid missionary work, presenting a first and second lesson that were both very promising, and obtained entrance into eight of eight houses tracting. We'll see what happens to our batting average after tonight's little demonstration. Actually, maybe it will help us weed out the vineyard. The kind of people we're looking for to accept the gospel won't be intimidated by Catholic priests.

July 23

I'll see how much I can write in my journal tonight without falling asleep in mid-sentence. I'm bone-tired by the time we turn in at night after ten to twelve hours of daily tracting. Actually, I haven't felt so good mentally and spiritually in a long time. Elder Heber and I are fast becoming friends and, in spite of our different styles, we're working well together. I've discovered that I can express myself quite well in Spanish and find myself in steady command of the discussions we have with investigators. If I don't continue to progress here, with all the challenges and opportunities before us, then I'm a worthless dud. I hope we continue worthy of the Lord's help.

Today was another profitable one, although again cut short this evening by the lack of electricity in town. Before nightfall brought a halt to our efforts we had totaled over ten hours of tracting and were invited into sixteen of nineteen homes. We even coincidentally knocked at the priest's private residence, one of the bigger homes in Villa Flores. He was aghast to see us standing in his doorway and vigorously shook his finger at us while retreating back inside the house, mumbling incoherently. He acted like he'd just seen the devil incarnate.

We haven't heard any more broadcasts yet, although I'm sure we stirred up a hornet's nest of Catholic concern today. In addition to our encounter with the padre, we kept bumping into a group of U.S. Catholic youth workers who are down here on their summer vacations performing church service. We finally chanced upon the adult director of this youth group and went a few theological rounds with him in English. I give the decision to Elder Heber, who really knows how to argue his way through the scriptures.

Later on in the day I discovered that I had left the key to our apartment locked inside the room. Our foolhardy solution to the problem was for me to inch my way along a narrow ledge two stories above the ground and attempt entering our room through an open window. I clung to the bricks in the wall with every ounce of strength I could muster in my straining fingers and toes. I became momentarily convinced that I was doomed, even though Elder Heber was supposedly anchoring me from the roof with a rope tied around my armpits. When I finally made it safely into the window, Elder Heber tells me that a cheer went up from a group of spectators congregated in the street below.

July 24

The work continues well. People are willing to talk to us and we've been engaging in a lot of preliminary discussions. Our main problem is to get someone seriously interested in the church and on the road to baptism.

Elders Rencher and Zuñiga stopped by for a short visit yesterday on their way to see the missionaries in Arriaga. Elder Rencher generously insists that I keep his leather briefcase, which I borrowed when I first came down here, rather than go to the expense of buying myself a new one. He says he no longer has any use for it in the mission home and would be embarrassed to be seen with the old thing when he returns to school at BYU. The truth is, I think, that it has a good deal of sentimental value for him and I'm complimented that he wishes me to have it. They also brought us a supply of Books of Mormon and hymnals which, I trust, we will soon be able to put to good use.

Elder Heber and I continue to get along great. I've felt the spirit of the Lord helping us in many of our discussions with investigators, and my confidence and ability to speak Spanish have continued to blossom. For the first time in my mission I feel like I really know what I'm doing, that I'm in control. The only thing I feel pressed on is time for letter writing and, of course, personal study has fallen way behind. Also, the burden of responsibility weighs and I'll likely lose some more precious territory off the fading hairline. But all in all, these have been the best days of my mission.

July 29

We're in the groove now, working with steady consistency. Our tracting average getting into peoples' homes is hovering around 100 percent. In the afternoons our appointment card is filled with follow-up visits from 3:00 to 9:00 P.M. Not all of these come through, of course, but it looks like most everyone in town will get a chance to hear our message. But we do need to break the ice. We need to find a good, strong man who is willing to go through all of the lessons and consent to baptism. We've given a lot of first lessons but have had much less luck with follow-up lessons. It's a clannish town. People are afraid of gossip, of what José Gomez, their *compadre,* will say if they get mixed up with the Mormons.

July 31

We were just getting ready to leave this morning when Elder Smith and his companion, Elder Carbine, showed up from Tuxtla to work with us. Elder Smith said he envied us the chance to open up a new town to missionary work and was anxious to see how things were going. We got a lot of tracting in, but didn't turn up any promising new investigators.

It appears that the fanatical Catholic fringe has reentered the fray. Elder Smith and I quickly discovered at virtually every place we stopped that the town has been flooded with a rather scathing, anti-Mormon propaganda sheet that isn't very complimentary and which intimates a few vague threats. Apparently the Catholic brass have succeeded in stirring up a little excitement against us. We can sure feel a lot of eyes played on us as we walk down the streets. And then there are the little kids who run after us yelling *"Mormones!"* But on the whole I don't think people will pay that much attention to the priest's warnings. Here's a copy of the anti-Mormon sheet being circulated in town, with my translation into English:

ATTENTION

People of Villa Flores

A week has passed since groups of two and four American individuals wearing ties have presented themselves in the city of Villa Flores and colonies. With more cunning than courtesy, they ask for five minutes of conversation in Catholic homes. It is the first attempt to communicate the MORMON doctrine. The Mormons have arrived! They are Protestants! These pretenders seduce the very ignorant in the faith, the wayward and sentimental visionaries, those who need a psychiatrist, the very credulous. The Mormon doctrine is based on the ridiculous stories of its founder, Joseph Smith, who organized Mormonism in 1830. Smith, a neurotic laborer and visionary, died in the Carthage jail of Illinois in the U.S.A. the 27th of June, 1844. Brigham Young better organized the sect and gave it strength. Upon his death he left seventeen widows and fifty-six orphaned children. Polygamy is part of the morality of the Mormons, even though they deny it.

There are people who believe that Villa Flores is a people of conquest, weak or without religious convictions, but no! Engaged in struggle for various decades, we will not betray our faith, which was forged with sacrifices, faith received from the rock of Saint Peter, who has the keys to the Kingdom of Heaven, given to him by Christ, the Son of God. Our faith was not forged in that of the false visionary prophets of past centuries predicted by Christ. Villa

Flores has lived for the protection of God and the Virgin of Guadalupe. Don't sell your faith! Don't give it to the intruders! People of Villa Flores, be alert! Arise to defend the sacred treasure of your faith! You are not a people to be conquered. You are a united people that works for the dignity of the home and the good of the community. Let us raise once more the banner that El Cura de Dolores [Father Miguel Hidalgo, who exhorted his Indian and mestizo followers in 1810 to violent revolt against Spanish rule] unfurled—*La Guadalupana*, symbol of the greatness of Mexico and of liberty. Let us fight anew for independence against invaders of the faith. Long live the Virgin of Guadalupe! Long live Mexico! Long live Christ the King! Long live the Pope!
Acción Católica Mexicana
Villa Flores, Julio de 1965

LETTER FROM GARY

Gord: The BYU basketball team has just completed a two-night stand of exhibition play here in the City against an all-star team of Mexican Olympic hopefuls, and I thought you might enjoy a brief account. We were only able to see the second night's contest, but what a romp. The Cougars' starters were pulled after only ten minutes, and the second team played the entire rest of the game, grinding the so-called all-stars into powder (50-23 at the half, 96-53 at the gun). I had almost forgotten how good well-played basketball can be—it was a real pleasure to watch Dick Nemelka and company play such beautiful, lethal ball together. [Dick Nemelka, an acquaintance from West High School in Salt Lake City, became a consensus All-American at BYU and then played for the Utah Stars in the American Basketball Association.] After little more than a quarter's work, Nemelka had already potted twelve points while simultaneously showing his brilliance as a playmaker. I talked briefly with Dick after the game. According to him, their team tour through Latin America has lasted seven weeks. They've lost but one game—a close one to the Brazilian Olympic team—and have done a tremendous job as representatives of the church. This is the first time, for instance, that I've ever seen the *"Mormones"* publicly mentioned in a Mexican newspaper, and the reviews and comments have been excellent.

Other recent entertainments include a *día de campo* that took us first to the University of Mexico, reputedly one of the world's largest institutions of higher learning. It must certainly be among the most colorful, with gigantic murals depicting mythical Aztec figures painted on the sides of the ultra-modern buildings. We then traveled across the city to the famous Chapúltepec Park, a huge, lovely tract of lush foliage and walkways.

We spent most of our time wandering around "Maximiliano's Castle," home of the French puppet emperor prior to the Mexican revolution spearheaded by Benito Juárez in the 1860s, and then home of subsequent heads of state until the last Mexican revolution of 1910–20.

We've been working too. A week ago I baptized an attractive and intelligent young woman—Ana Lucía—who had been referred to us sometime ago by friends who were concerned about her emotional health. She had previously received psychiatric counseling but continued to feel no happiness in living and told us she would just as soon die. We did what we could to console and began teaching. It all clicked, and in spite of her professed fear of water, she calmly entered the font last week and emerged radiantly from her baptism, a happy and seemingly new person. I have more ambiguous feelings about another family (Chavez) we've been teaching. After completing all the lessons, we discovered that the husband and wife were not formally married. We arranged for this to be done, but the proceedings were highly irregular, to say the least. The old judge thought we were Catholic *sacerdotes* [priests], but we still had to slip him a 20 peso note as part of the deal. Anyway, Hermano Chavez stayed uptown to attend to some personal matters while the rest of us all piled into a taxi for home. The taxi then drove around the block just in time for us to witness the *hermano* pull out a pack of cigarettes and light up. A keen disappointment and an immediate resolution not to baptize him. But in a subsequent interview that evening, he swore to us that he was willing to obey the Word of Wisdom, and that he truly desired to be baptized. So he was, with his wife and two daughters.

On the personal front, extra-curricular reading at meals and whenever has taken me through four volumes of the *Comprehensive History of the Church,* by B. H. Roberts, plus a couple of other good books. My Spanish seems to vary a lot from day to day, but I read out loud a great deal whenever there's a chance. I'm also working harder on a larger mastery of the scriptures, and I took a suggestion from one of your past letters and am writing an outline of the *Articles of Faith* in Spanish. Keep me posted. The sparks from your work help me keep my own fires from going out.

Your brother, Gar

August 2

Today we glimpsed the possibility of a breakthrough. We presented the fourth lesson on Christ's atonement to a man by the name of Garcia, emphasizing the importance of baptism, and it looks like he's headed down the right road.

There are a few minor problems, however. His wife isn't very supportive (Catholic, of course), and he hasn't given up smoking yet (but I think he's making an honest effort). Also, the dentist in Villa Corso is a sincere man. I gave him my Bible, which he's never read, so that he could compare it with the *folletos* we've given him. If he ever got on the bandwagon he'd make a good branch president. All in all, we're optimistic about our eventual success here.

August 4

These have been the best days of my mission. Regardless of whether or not we are eventually successful in Villa Flores, I can honestly say we've been working as hard as we know how, and if we fail it will not be because we didn't give it our best effort. We've talked to many of the prominent men in town about religious matters. They say they admire our determination and hard work, but they appear to have little faith in God or genuine devotion to the Catholic Church. Membership in the Catholic Church is a tradition. Many of the men here are simply cultural Catholics who consider religion as something primarily for women and children. They certainly don't seem to take the priest's warnings about us very seriously. I suspect that in the long run religious indifference will be a bigger obstacle to our work here than fanatical Catholicism.

August 7

It rains almost every night. Last night was a downpour highlighted by a terrific lightening storm. The streets quickly become streams of swirling mud. Giant toads, attracted by the water and then flattened by traffic, sometimes look as big as deflated footballs. The only real inconvenience is the constant loss of electricity. This cuts down on our ability to work at night, although we've given several lessons by candlelight. At the apartment we use candles and an oil-wick lamp. I've been getting a little lazy at night, or maybe I'm just exhausted. At any rate, I haven't been doing much letter writing or studying after we've wrapped up a day's work. I'll have to stay up extra late some night soon to write Gary the letter I owe.

Tomorrow is Sunday and I'm starting to get butterflies. We will be offering our first religious services in Villa Flores and hope to get started on the right foot. We've acquired a set of two or three investigator families, including Garcia, whom we've urged to attend tomorrow. We've organized a Sunday school program for the morning and a sacrament service for the evening. I'm supposed to give a talk in Sunday school, conduct a Sunday school lesson, and then give another talk in sacrament meeting. When will there be time to prepare? It looks like I'll need to set an extra-early morning alarm.

August 8

Well, I feel pretty decent about the way things turned out today. We had three investigators out for our Sunday services this morning, and one person (Hermano Garcia) showed up for our sacrament service this evening. Not exactly a crowd, but they were good services. We felt the Lord's spirit with us. I had a feeling of decisiveness and confidence, which I've experienced before, I'm sure, but haven't always recognized as God's helping hand. As a result I was able to give a pretty good Sunday school lesson and credible talks without much preparation. I just wish the rest of our investigators had come. It's still a struggle for them to override their fear of gossip and persecution by the local scoffers and fanatics.

August 10

A grand total of five souls showed up for our MIA [Mutual Improvement Association] service this evening. Not bad, really, but the majority of our baptismal hopefuls didn't make it. I relaxed and Elder Heber gave the lesson. He also strummed his guitar afterward and sang a couple of songs in English, to the entertainment of our little group. Yesterday I received notice from the mission home that I'm to be one of the speakers at district conference Saturday in Tuxtla. My assigned topic is the importance of using the Book of Mormon as a missionary tool. In the meantime Elder Smith has made plans to work with us Thursday, and Friday we'll be taking a *día de campo* with the entire district. Should be fun. We could use a break.

Gary writes that, after all these months of marriage talk from Kathy Dempsey while she was in bed with rheumatic fever, she recently severed their relationship once she had recovered and was able to start going out. Ticks me off. Gary's original attitude of wait-and-see caution toward Kathy should have been maintained. As for me, Beckie's still hanging in there despite mailbunglings, two-month lapses in communication, and no insurance to go on in the first place. But I've got a feeling she'll be there a year from now. In the meantime, I know that Gary's too good a person, too strong in his character, to let this undermine his missionary commitment.

LETTER FROM GARY

Gord: Kathy didn't exactly swallow her sour grapes, as you suggested she might in your last communication. Instead, she has abruptly, efficiently,

and even gracefully severed our romance, my illusions, and maybe even a
section or two of my heart. Her letter arrived a few days ago after several
weeks of silence following my last letter to her, in which I was critical of
her recent complaints and looming restlessness. She sang my praises and
her *culpa* [blame], but was nevertheless quite terminal about our relationship. I was initially stunned and not quite sure how I felt. Hurt and foolish, for sure. Later, genuinely pained. Quite familiar feelings, all of them.
My original intention of playing things cautiously this time around quickly succumbed to what I thought was Kathy's need for me (and no doubt
my own need to salvage previously injured pride). But whatever she may
have needed from me seemed to diminish rapidly as she finally regained
her health. My own fault in many ways; common sense and better judgment took a good shellacking here. Still, I did love her, whatever that may
mean. In any event, I replied to her after giving a lot of thought to what I
wanted to say. I guess I'm surprised at the degree of bitterness I expressed,
but it's the way I felt. Returned her photos, etc., and that's that. In all of
this, I have, of course, also allowed my relationship with Natalie to become seriously jeopardized. She increasingly writes less often, with nota-
ble neutrality when she does, and I, in turn, cannot now play the hypocrite and begin to represent myself to her in false colors.

In spite of my feeling a little empty and listless the last few days, our
work continues well. We are turning up good investigators from tracting,
but some of them, I fear, are getting turned off when they attend meetings
at the chapel. Reverence is often disgraceful, and I am a little concerned
about a new church policy just being implemented that assigns a ward
member to teach the Sunday investigator class instead of the missionaries.
I think this is a mistake that will hurt us more than help. [In spite of a
chronic shortage of experienced instructors at the time, this was the beginning of the church's attempt to institute member retention programs
in Mexico. Rather than a mistake, systematically involving members in the
religious socialization of new converts has become a key aspect of the
Mormon missionary program.]

Last night I woke up sick twice, once with the runs, once with heavy
vomiting. Tried to get out this morning but was soon back in bed with fever, chills, body aches, and general dizziness and weakness. Seemed to
have slept it off, though, and am feeling much better tonight. My companion and I are getting along fine. No contentions whàtsoever, and we enjoy
each other's company. Mason can be kind of funny, and he laughs at my
rare wit too.

Your brother, Gar

August 12

We're getting ready to leave for our *día de campo* and conference in Tuxtla. This will be our first break from active missionary work since arriving in Villa Flores a month ago. I haven't had much time to organize my conference talk—hope I don't blow it. We should be back to Villa Flores in time for Sunday services.

August 15

The weekend was a taxing one. Friday we went to the beach near Arriaga on the Pacific Coast and wasted ourselves trying to play soccer in the hot sand. The trip with Elder Smith in his Volkswagen was lengthy and took us through some of the greenest, most beautiful mountain country that I've ever seen. But what torturous roads! Saturday we drove to San Cristobal de Las Casas with President Hatch and elders from the mission home, including Elder Rencher, who accompanied to attend the conference. San Cristobal is an isolated mountain city, high above Tuxtla Gutiérrez, where Mayan Indians have managed to maintain their native customs and identity [In January 1994, San Cristobal was the site of an armed Indian uprising led by Zapatista insurgents against the Mexican government.] We returned to Tuxtla in time for an afternoon conference. I gave a mediocre conference talk, but it was a great conference anyway. I bade farewell to Elders Rencher and Smith, who are both leaving for home in a couple of weeks—two of the mission's finest, whose examples of consistency and dedication I hope to emulate throughout the remainder of my own mission. Two other old companions, Martineau and Robison, will apparently both be going to Veracruz as the new assistants when Rencher leaves.

Earlier in the morning we visited an archaeological site just outside of Tuxtla where a team from BYU was digging. According to the guy we talked to, they are working on the hypothesis that Chiapas is the region where Lehi and his family first settled after their arrival in the New World from Jerusalem, as recorded in the Book of Mormon. Yesterday we were back in Villa Flores to conduct Sunday services. Only the Zepeda family (but without the husband) showed up, but they look more and more like good prospects. I don't know what happened to the rest of our investigators, but we still have high hopes. I've never been happier.

August 20

Can it be? Today marks my arrival in Mexico. A year has vanished away as though it were a daydream. I can see the progress I've made as a missionary, but much remains to be done. I must take advantage of the short time left to me.

These have been hard-spent days. We should wind up with about eighty-four hours of proselyting for the week. At night, after reading for about ten minutes, I usually surrender to a motionless state of petrified sleep. My only real complaint, however, is a constant nagging pain below the belt which causes me to make sudden and frequent trips to the bathroom. I've had a good case of Moctezuma's revenge for a solid month, at least. This can be pretty inconvenient when we're out tracting. Yesterday we were working in a neighborhood over a mile distant from the apartment when my intestinal tract urgently signaled an emergency. We walked *very* slowly and carefully back to the apartment so I could use the facilities. Close call—I was in a cold sweat all the way. In any event, if things go as planned we should have our first baptisms in Villa Flores next week. We've been teaching two young men, Raúl and Eduardo, who have come along very quickly—perhaps too quickly. I have my doubts as to whether they're ready, but they're enthusiastic and say they want to join the church.

August 22

Sunday services were a little discouraging today. Hermano Garcia was the only soul to show up for my Sunday school lesson on the *santa cena* [the sacrament]. Nobody came to sacrament meeting tonight, but Elder Heber and I decided to conduct the service anyway. We sang a hymn, voiced a prayer, partook of the sacrament, and bore our testimonies to each other. At that point one of our new investigator families, the Coutinos who live down by the river, showed up. Rather than start over again we decided to give them the third lesson, which they seemed to accept well, except the old man's a smoker and did not come with the rest of the family. They are very poor (the father does some subsistence farming but is not in good health, and his wife peddles *liquado* [fruit juice] drinks and other odds and ends in the market) but are generous in spirit. The fact that they were willing to come all the way into town to our apartment for a meeting is a positive sign of their interest in our message.

August 23

Got a letter from Gary today in which, among other things, he expressed some concern for our safety in Villa Flores. Obviously the Catholics are not too pleased at our being here, but it's hard to believe that we're in any actual danger. Still, we've had several investigators tell us about the first Protestant missionaries who tried to enter Villa Flores thirty years ago. According to the stories, they were physically threatened and run out of town. One or two were supposedly hacked to death by irate mobs. Well, we've received a few sneers and some adverse publicity, but I haven't seen any lynch mobs forming. We asked our maid if she wasn't worried for herself because she has taken in *los Mormones* to eat in her home. She said, "Oh no, no hermanos" (which is what she calls us now). "Si al padre Católico no le gusta, qué se vaya al diablo!" [If the Catholic priest doesn't like it, he can go to hell!] Times have changed in Mexico and they continue to change. The Catholic Church still rules but not with the iron hand it once did. We have arrived and, while the priest may not like it, the fires of fanaticism no longer burn as brightly here as they did in the past.

LETTER FROM GARY

Gord: Click off one year; I'm not too overjoyed about it at the moment. I will now spend over half my mission as a junior companion. But although I feel fettered and frustrated right now, it can't be too much longer before my turn comes. My patience is apparently fathomless, because I still go around in a pretty good mood most of the time and I don't chew on my sour apples too often yet. Yeah, a year now; brought it home in kind of a funny way this afternoon. Elder Bronson [Gary's companion for a short time at the Provo LTM] now resides with us here, and the two of us went out to give a lesson together, because his companion has a broken ankle. I couldn't help but reflect, somewhat in shock, that just a seeming few days ago all of us were trying to stagger through the lessons with the *Escuchantes* at Provo. What we did today didn't seem real or possible then.

Gord, I can't begin to express my pride in you and what you are accomplishing. I know the Lord is blessing you now, and that he will continue to bless your efforts with eventual success in bringing the church to Villa Flores. The only thing that alarmed me on that foolish handbill you sent me was the hidden appeal to the righteous violence of religious fanaticism, at least instilling fear in your investigators if not resulting in personal danger to yourself and your companion. Any problems of this sort? I expect you'll keep me informed of all present activities and any interesting developments.

Elder Mason and I have a half dozen or so excellent prospects who are well on their way towards being baptized. We had just enjoyed a particularly good round of three different lessons with these investigators. But then a mess. We arrived with high hopes for a crucial showdown with a large family (the Fernandezes) that we've been working hard with for almost a month, and then sat for a solid hour and a half while my companion lectured, exhorted, argued, and rambled through all the scriptures he could think of. A through waste of time, and worse, irritating and antagonizing to the Fernandezes. Berating, cajoling, and table-pounding with intelligent people who lack conviction in what we are telling them is simply futile. The right orientation to our work, I think, was expressed by several missionary leaders at a recently held conference here in the City. Evident humility rather than ease of word or flashy aggressiveness was the common characteristic that most impressed me among those who spoke. The need for humility, at least for me, was the single greatest admonition that I took back to our apartment with me. That, and continued patience.

I was struck by a phrase from your last letter: "See you on top of the world." Hope you're right about that; I've still got some climbing to go.

Your brother, Gar

August 25

We failed again last night to conduct our MIA services. True, it rained, but we were still disappointed that nobody came. The Zepeda family always says they'll come but never do, and Hermano Garcia's wife has henpecked him into staying away (usually it's the husband who's the problem, not the wife). We looked up our two *jóvenes,* Raúl and Eduardo, who have been delinquent of late in showing up for meetings they have promised to attend. They said they're still preparing for baptism, but my doubts about their sincerity have increased, and we still haven't given them the lesson on tithing.

Yesterday we met a woman who invited us into her home, calmly listened to our presentation, and then really blasted us. She didn't rant or rage hysterically, but was pure icy venom. Among other things, she informed us that Mormonism is one of the most perverted and distant-from-God religions that exists, that in fact we don't even believe in God! Apparently the priest has been poisoning his congregation again with this sort of stuff. It also appears that we're being followed around town as we tract by some busybody Catholic women who make visitations to people after we finish talking with them. Little *hogár Católico* [Catholic home] signs always go up on doors the day after we pass through a neighborhood.

August 26

The Catholics are still lobbing occasional stink-bombs at us. The padre was on the airwaves again for awhile tonight. His performance seemed a little listless and uninspired this time, however, simply repeating the same old stuff from previous broadcasts. Some of our investigators may be intimidated.

There's always a certain amount of fear and cringing from the pointed finger of local public opinion. But in the long run I think the priest just cuts his own throat with propaganda attacks against us. While some people may be scared off, others are led to have a little curiosity and sympathy that they might not otherwise have. He accuses those who listen to us of being *nécios* [fools]. Surely that can't sit too well with many of the people who have been willing to talk to us. In the last two days our investigator dossier has blossomed with some new families that look promising. We've got our nets spread—hope we can draw them in safely.

August 30

I'm not sure what to think of our Sunday services yesterday. A crowd of eleven showed up for sacrament meeting, but nobody attended in the morning—Elder Heber and I ran through a twenty-minute Sunday school by ourselves, singing some hymns and partaking of the sacrament. In the evening some of our old investigators sent their kids (the Zepedas), but didn't come themselves. Hermano Garcia walked in just as we were getting underway, and about fifteen minutes before we finished the Coutino family from the river wandered in, making for the largest gathering that we've yet assembled. Nonetheless, church attendance, along with the town's bad glances, appear to be the major obstacles for most of our investigators. It takes courage for people in a town like this to ignore social pressure and prejudice. Raúl and Eduardo, our two *jóvenes,* are fading fast. For better or worse, we decided not to push forward with their baptisms last week.

August 31

Good MIA service tonight. We had ten in attendance and things seem to be looking up. I sat in the background while Elder Heber gave the lesson and sang a few songs for the entertainment of all. If we could just attract a similar crowd on Sunday, we'd be in business. One of our new investigators, a Protestant jeweler by the name of Vargas, stood up in the middle of the meeting to express his thanks to us for the work we are doing and gave an impromptu testimony of the divinity of Christ's mission. Perhaps he is the man we're looking for, one with leadership qualities who can set an example for others in Villa Flores.

September 2

I've got a bad taste left in my mouth after a tracting incident yesterday. We ran into a preacher of the Nazarene Church who was waiting for us in his house with a Bible on the table like a pistol drawn from its holster. He started firing arguments at us from the second we entered the door and never let up. We tried to defend ourselves with patience at first, but quickly gave in to the temptation to respond in kind, and we ended up on our feet in a shouting match with blood veins popping and fists shaking. It was an unfortunate scene. Our reputation could be badly damaged by such incidents. What really bothers me is that I sense an underlying competition between me and Elder Heber to score debating points when we get into discussions with people who want to criticize the church. This detracts from the true spirit of our message. I need to get better control of my personal pride, but then so does Elder Heber, who is sometimes overly zealous and insensitive to the consequences of his aggressiveness. Heber's personal method for retaliating against those who displease him is to shake hands when we leave and, with a cheerful grin on his face, crush their fingers to pulp. It's not true, of course, that Heber actually injures people, but he is six feet, three inches tall, has huge hands, the rawboned strength of a young Abe Lincoln, and a vicelike grip, which has left a number of antagonists wincing.

September 3

Took in my shoes for more repairs; second time since I've been in Villa Flores. When I complained to the *zapatero* [shoemaker] about the shoddy workmanship he said: "What do you expect? You fellows do a lot of walking." And I said: "Precisely, that's why we need to have good work done on our shoes."

I regret to say that, in spite of our shared commitment to missionary work in Villa Flores, a few strains have developed in my companionship with Elder Heber. Because of a recent reduction in the number of elders in our mission, President Hatch has been forming co-senior pairs. Elder Heber, with ten months accumulated as a junior, is green with the symptoms of ambition. Heber wears about the same size hat for his ego as Chuck Radlow and at times wears my patience thin with his occasional carping and not so subtle criticisms.

LETTER FROM GARY

Gord: A strong earthquake hit the City yesterday. Buildings, cars on streets, and every movable thing swayed as though on the back of some huge ocean vessel plunging through choppy seas. It lasted about five minutes and actually made me feel "seasick."

Let me tell you about a problematic situation with one of our visits that we've finally been able to bring into dock. Sometime ago, we stumbled onto a family (the Duráns) in which the wife (Alícia) said she was an inactive member. She was very sharp, started attending church again, and encouraged her husband, son, and mother-in-law to listen to us. Recently we baptized the three of them. Alícia then privately informed us that she might have been excommunicated from the church some years back for having premarital sexual relations and an illegitimate child with her present husband while he was still married (though separated many years from his first wife). She wasn't positive about the official outcome, and her account of the procedures by the then branch president of Ermita indicated several irregularities which cast some doubt on the legality of her treatment. I was able to track down the report of the church court, which was on file at the ward, and although an attempt was made to act correctly, it seemed to me that the affair was botched and that a miscarriage of justice was perpetrated. For instance, there were not any witnesses and no defense presented for Alícia. Moreover, the charge was adultery, but she had no knowledge of her now husband's marital status and was induced to engage in intercourse by promises of marriage and her own love for him. Although fornication is a grave offense, it should not be construed as adultery nor made grounds for excommunication.

In any event, Alícia had sincerely repented of her sin, held no bitterness against the church, was instrumental in bringing her family into the church, and desired to become active again in the church herself. Formerly she was president of the Ermita Branch Mutual, held various offices in other church organizations, and even lived in Provo, Utah for eight years while attending B.Y. High School and college at BYU. I hashed all this out with President McClellan at the mission home. In the end he gave us the go-ahead to use our judgment concerning the sincerity of her repentance and to rebaptize her if we felt she was worthy of renewed membership in the church. We did so believe, and this morning I rebaptized her in cold water almost up to my armpits. She is extraordinarily grateful to us and should be a terrific addition to the ward.

Yesterday we learned that Elder Mason is going to be transferred out to Guadalajara and will be replaced by Elder Ronald Struhs, who will be the new supervising elder here and my senior companion. Rumors are flying about other changes that are in the works, and I'm desperately hoping that I'll be included in them. I'm fighting hard against mounting frustration, but the robes of juniorship are beginning to strangle me. Struhs is a good elder, but I want nothing more than to prove that I am also a good elder. Four seniors are all finishing up their missions within the next week or so—four chances to see if there isn't an opening for me to squeeze into. Speaking of releases, Ray Throgg went home about a week ago. Elder Bayer spoke for him at his *relevo,* and Tim's remarks were more realistic than most at these affairs. Throgg apparently worked pretty well his last couple of months after being brought back into the City, shed a lot of excess weight, and his girlfriend (who had been dating other guys) decided to wait for him (I don't know what happened to Neome back in Guadalajara).

We spent the bulk of today giving Elder Mason a chance to do some sightseeing before he leaves tomorrow. My most pleasant moments were spent with the Setina family, who we looked up while I was showing Mason the Unidad Nonoalco. It's been almost a year ago exactly that Elder Wilkes and I first found them, and it was wonderful to be with them again. However, it's a source of real hurt that they've fallen inactive after Wilkes and I left. Finer people couldn't be found, and I never dreamed their enthusiasm for the church would wane. I'll do what I can to reactivate them with gentle urgings and future letters. They gave me a little lamp made out of gourds with my name on it that they've been saving all this time. Ended this evening with a nice steak dinner. Elder Mason's a pretty good guy. We enjoyed a lot of fun times together, and with him I've also enjoyed some of my finest missionary experiences.

Your brother, Gar

September 5

Esperanzas [hopes] were deflated yesterday morning when no one showed up for Sunday school, only to be pumped back up again when a fairly good-sized group appeared for sacrament meeting, including a young couple (Francisco and Ayda Gomez) whom we just met for the first time yesterday. We can't seem to maintain any consistency. Good new investigators keep popping up, and with the old ones on our list, it's hard to keep track of everyone. But at this point we still have no one ready for baptism, and it's hard to say if any will be willing to make the necessary commitments.

We worked eighty-five hours this past week and still didn't have enough time to visit everyone we should. We've been systematically tracting-out Villa Flores, from the center of town outward in concentric circles. As we reach the poorer and less central neighborhoods, we are coming across a greater number of Protestants, who usually prove even more obstinate and less hospitable than the Catholics.

I've been taking Pepto-Bismol for my case of the runs and, thankfully, it seems to be doing some good. I've never been sick much in my life and I'm unaccustomed to taking medication for ailments. Usually I just endure until I feel better. This has not proven a very effective policy in Villa Flores, where I've been tormented with intestinal problems ever since arriving.

September 7

Elder Heber's been getting my goat lately and, apparently, I his. The other night he acted exasperated when I decided we should check up on some investigators rather than turn in early for a change. On the way he followed behind me and criticized my "leadership" skills in choosing a path to avoid puddles in the road (it was raining). Symbolic criticism I suppose, since Heber takes pride in himself as a poet. I told him he was welcome to choose his own puddles. And then there are the preachy little sermons he offers me every morning when we share testimonies. His weekly reports to the supervisor regularly show a little more proselyting time than mine, a little more time spent in personal study, and even a little more time spent in companion study! He's intent on squeezing the maximum for himself out of every statistical report he can. I think he takes offense at the laudatory letters addressed to me from Elder Treanor (supervisor in Tuxtla), praising our work in Villa Flores, but which appear to give me most of the credit. Undoubtedly the problem is that Heber lusts to become senior companion, which I can fully appreciate. But come on! Some of this is just plain petty and ridiculous. I've not been dictatorial, in my opinion, and do my best to share authority. Heber will not be satisfied until he's completely in charge.

September 10

A good day (after several that have been a bit strained between me and my companion). We gave an exceptionally good second lesson on the Book of Mormon to a nondenominational Protestant type, who is well versed in the scriptures, and the spirit of the Lord helped us to deliver our message.

On our way to the next visit we were stopped by a man, obviously intoxicated, whom we had tracted a couple of weeks ago. He asked us to go with him to his house because his father had died, and he wanted us to conduct a small funeral service. We went, but hesitantly because of his reeling condition. No representative of his own church had come. At the house were a few scattered relatives and neighbors milling around in a disorganized state. The old man's corpse was lying on a straw cot with his hands and feet strapped down and a crude mask over his face. We went outside, arranged some benches, and then had everyone sit down in front of us. I directed the service. The two of us commenced with a hymn ("O My Father") and Elder Heber offered the opening prayer. I then arose and gave a talk as good as any I've ever given. My thoughts flowed easily and the right words with which to express them materialized with little conscious effort. I spoke to them of the mission of Jesus Christ and the meaning of his resurrection, which opened the gates of eternal life. Heber then emphasized similar themes as well as I've ever heard him speak. We finished with another hymn ("Come, Come Ye Saints"), and I gave a closing prayer, once again the words flowing easily and fluently. I'm sure that Elder Heber and I got more out of the experience spiritually than the bereaved family members, who were a little unruly at first in their grief, but grateful for our help. The rift developing between Heber and me over the last few days appears to have closed.

September 19

Received a letter from Gary today with news that at long last he's been made a senior companion in Mexico City, which has added greatly to my own renewed spirits. What a tingling shot in the arm the strong testimony of his words imparted as he related the events of a recent missionary conference with Apostles Brown and Romney. I have no doubt that Gary will quickly become one of the most outstanding and respected missionaries of the Mexican Mission.

LETTER FROM GARY

Gord: Sorry about the mail delay, but seniorship finally beckoned to me last Thursday, and I haven't had much spare time since. At long last! Still in the City, in fact back to Churubusco again, scene of my best month in the mission with Elder Merkley. My first junior companion is John Barlow from Cache Valley, Utah—a greenie with just three weeks in the mission stashed behind him. He's quiet and shy, but I hope to apply some confidence raising principles on him that occurred to me during the months I moldered under the oppressive mantle of juniorship.

The elder I replaced here didn't leave me a lot to go on, just a few references and tract-outs that we X-ed off pretty quickly. Still, I'm happy, you can imagine. I knew I would get socked with a good personal revitalization when the day came and that's what has happened. I too have dragged out fair Spanish from dark and dusty recesses. My self-confidence halted its dismal plummeting and has soared back to where it belongs: to a practical recognition of what I'm capable of and where my limits end, with a sure knowledge that I will receive the extra help I need if I push to the confines of my ability. I feel we have already been greatly blessed in these few short days of hard tracting. Every day seems to bring us one good family and we're hoping to make October a memorable month.

I don't know if you guys were recently graced with a visit from Apostle Romney and President Hugh B. Brown, but our joint missionary and stake conferences with them here (just before my promotion to senior a couple of weeks ago) resulted in never-to-be-forgotten days for us. President Brown was the concluding speaker at our missionary conference and he bore the strongest testimony that I have ever heard. The entire hall filled with missionaries was completely mesmerized. Every heart and eye were focused on the presence and words that fell from a prophet of God, for that afternoon President Brown spoke as a prophet of God. The prophecy he made was this (and when he spoke it a thrill went through my whole body): "I dare not say all the things I know. . . . There is someone sitting among you this afternoon who will become a member of the Council of the Twelve. Others will be called as bishops and presidents of stakes. And this prophecy will come true for those persons as they merit it with their worthiness."

Both President Brown and Apostle Romney addressed stake conference the next day, with about two thousand people jammed into the Roma chapel to listen. President Brown said he knew he had only a few years left to live. But with full knowledge of this, realizing that whatever he said now he would be held strictly responsible for and would take to the grave, he proceeded to bear the strongest possible testimony imaginable regarding the reality of the Father and the Son, that this is their church and their work. In a few short hours of powerful witness and wisdom spilling forth from both these chosen men the entire mission was measurably buoyed and strengthened, especially me as I was forcefully brought to realize how far I miss from hitting the right mark.

By the way, I also ran into one of your old companions that same conference Sunday: Elder Splinders. Don't ask me what he was doing up here, but he almost dropped his cookies when he saw me. He literally filled the air with your praises; to be concise, that you're the best down there. He even seemed to be a pretty good guy himself.

I finally wrote a reply to Chuck not long ago in response to his disaffection from the church. Didn't try to devise any defenses or throw any mud at him. Just told him how I feel about a few things. He hasn't written back yet, but I'm curious to know what his reaction will be.

Needless to report, I'm proud and pleased by your good work in Villa Flores. I envy you for the experiences you're having and the resulting personal growth that is yours. Unlike you, I've never been stationed in a pueblo. But I imagine that the major part of this coming year will find me out working in the boonies. I'm anxious to hear from you soon. I'm hoping you've got your foot finally and firmly wedged in the door, and that the floodwaters of success are bursting the crack. Keep me posted on how things go so that I may be in constant contact with your many times badly needed good influence.

Your brother, Gar

September 22

If I'm not mistaken we should have some baptisms in a couple of days. The Coutino family that lives down by the river appears set to go (minus the old man, who hasn't been able to give up his smoking yet). We promised Hermana Coutino that we would find her some white material so that she can make baptismal clothing for the children. Maybe I should also mention that Heber and I have become addicted to dining on street tacos every night before turning in. They're the best I've ever eaten but, along with the silt in the *água de limón* [lemonade] that we get at our maid's house for lunch, they undoubtedly add to my frequent intestinal problems. On the other hand, Elder Heber seems to be able to throw anything he cares to down his craw without any ill effects whatsoever.

September 24

Well, we've got fifteen *metros* [meters] of white cloth that I hope will come in handy sometime. The Coutino family decided to back out of their baptismal commitments for the time being. The family will follow the old man, who refuses to give up smoking as a requisite for baptism. And Raúl and Eduardo have split—haven't seen them for weeks. We're doing the best we can, but our lack of results after nearly three months in Villa Flores is a little discouraging.

September 28

We put in an enjoyable day yesterday working with the supervisors: Elder Udall (the new zone supervisor from Minatitlán) and Elder Treanor (the supervising elder from Tuxtla). However, a rather disturbing thought was injected into our present situation. There seem to be plans afoot in the mission home to close down Villa Flores because of its apparent infertility. To be truthful, this possibility has weighed on my mind since first arriving. My fear is that we'll end up baptizing a handful of good people here and then be forced to abandon them.

In another three weeks or so we will have completely tracted-out Villa Flores. We've done a fairly thorough job of contacting the majority of people in town. On the other hand, things could break loose for us at any time. We're teaching an impressive number of investigators who, if they were to pan out, would put us on the mission map. (We do have two people preparing for baptism this week, Francisco and Ayda Gomez, who have accepted all of the lessons.) Time is running out though. I've got a feeling that the mission home will give us just another month. According to Elders Udall and Treanor, my own time here is limited for sure. In a couple of weeks a number of missionaries will be finishing their missions and heading for home. When this happens, I'm supposed to be transferred somewhere as a supervising elder.

We were a little chagrined by not having any toilet paper in the apartment for our visitors. Had to make a quick trip to the store down the street for a couple of rolls. Elder Heber and I are supposed to take turns buying such household items but Heber blissfully neglects to take his turn. I got tired of paying all the time, so just quit. When we ran out of paper I figured Heber would take the hint, but no. He's cheaper than I am. Unbelievably, as a substitute we've been tearing off pages from the *Church News* (after we read them), which the mission home sends us periodically.

October 1

Another setback. The Gomez couple preparing for baptism isn't married. I could kick myself for not having inquired sooner about their marital status. Now we'll have to postpone their baptism and get them married. I must admit, though, that they've been willing to accept our teaching without any doubts. The simplicity of their faith has been a breath of fresh air to us. I'm optimistic that the delay involved will only be temporary.

As daylight hours become shorter around here, water for morning showers in our apartment is getting to be icy cold. Takes your breath away. I can only bear to jump in for a few vigorous seconds before toweling off. We've been eating well at our maid's home every morning (typical breakfast of *huevos rancheros* with *salsa picante,* refried beans, sliced avocados, tortillas, hot milk, and bananas), but I'm not regaining any of my lost weight.

Catholic fanatics seem to have retreated into their cellars—we've heard nothing from them for weeks, maybe because we've spent most of our time recently tracting on Protestant turf. I usually get rather blustering when lay preachers try to dispute us, but Elder Heber is pretty good at scriptural combat (as a convert himself, he's very familiar with all the usual biblical arguments) and most of the time we've emerged bloody but victorious. We need to be able to defend ourselves but, at the same time, self-proclaimed scriptural victories are not winning us any converts.

Interesting encounter on the outskirts of town yesterday when we knocked on the door of what turned out to be a brothel. The madam called all of her available girls into the dining room, where they listened politely to our tracting message and accepted *folletos* on "Chastity" by Apostle Mark E. Peterson.

October 6

New faces keep turning out for services, especially at our Tuesday night MIA meeting. Maybe it's Elder Heber's singing and guitar playing that brings them out.

In many ways the country here in the Chiapas Mountains is like the old Wild West. We've heard reports of shootings and blood feuds between different families in the area. Men often carry guns when they go out into the *campo* [countryside]. One of our investigator families appears to be locked into a particularly bitter feud. About a year ago the woman's husband and son were both shot to death over a land squabble. Her other sons took revenge on the assassins, killing several members of another family, and then moved into town for safety. Just the other day her oldest son and son-in-law were bushwhacked in the field where they farm. The son-in-law escaped with minor flesh wounds, but her son is in grave condition with a shotgun blast to the back and shoulder. Elder Heber and I were shocked to learn of these events when we went to teach them the fourth lesson on the resurrection and atonement of Jesus Christ for the sins of the world.

October 11

Our hopes keep bobbing up and down like a top in a tub. We could produce some baptisms any time if the Gomez couple would stop fiddling around and get married. As our tracting takes us closer and closer to the edge of town, we've attracted more investigators to teach than we're adequately able to keep track of. I hope something comes through for us before I'm transferred. It rained hard last night, but there were a few hardy souls who ventured over for Sunday services, and we had a good sacrament meeting. I felt relaxed and gave my first decent talk in several weeks on the topic of baptism.

October 12

Barring any quickly descending and/or unforeseen calamities, we should get three months' pay tomorrow in the form of two baptisms. Francisco Gomez and his common-law wife, Ayda, have made up their minds to get married. Elder Heber and I have contacted the local civil authorities and we will pay the required license fee. If everything works out as we hope, there should be four Mormons in Villa Flores by the start of the day tomorrow. This morning we went down to the river looking for a spot to perform the baptisms. The current is fast and the water muddy from the rains, but it will do.

October 13

All's well that ends well. In spite of past frustrations and an uncertain future, we are for the moment satisfied and happy with our success in converting Francisco and Ayda. The marriage proceedings dragged along painfully slow, tangled up in the usual red-tape *reglamentos* [regulations]. But at last things ground to an official conclusion and we were able to go forward with the baptisms. We went directly from the Palácio Municipál [municipal palace/ city hall] to the river. Hermana Coutino helped out as a *testigo* and also gave us the use of her home near the river as a place for changing into our baptismal clothing and conducting the baptismal service. The Coutino home is nothing more than an adobe hut with a dirt floor, but we were grateful for its use. After a hymn, prayer, and brief talks by both Elder Heber and myself, we all went down to the river to a place we had selected the day before. A line of boulders formed a pocket of protection right at the current's edge where we performed the baptisms in water that was surprisingly warm. From the river we returned to the Coutinos' little shack to confirm Francisco and Ayda, husband and wife, as new members of the Church of Jesus Christ. Later we went to their home in town for dinner. They are good people and will make good members of the church. I can only hope that others in Villa Flores will follow their example.

October 18

Elders Treanor and Carbine made an unexpected visit yesterday to observe our Sunday services and say goodbye before Elder Treanor leaves for home. According to Treanor, I'm to be shipped out of here in a week, for parts unknown, as a supervising elder. Heber, I assume, will stay in Villa Flores as senior companion. We started sacrament meeting with just the four of us present, but were quickly joined by our new converts, Francisco and Ayda Gomez, and two other investigators whom we've been teaching for the past several weeks. Following sacrament meeting we talked to our two new investigators (Elias and Dolores Masa), and it suddenly appears that we've got two more baptismal candidates. Former *Testigos,* they said that they're convinced by our teachings and want to become members of the church. But damn! We're stymied by the same old problem: they're living together but aren't married. We plan to see the judge first thing tomorrow morning and will try to make all the necessary arrangements. With a little luck we might be able to slip them in the water before I have to leave Villa Flores.

October 20

No such luck. We received a telegram bomb this morning from headquarters in Veracruz, exploding my hopes for the future of Villa Flores. BOTH Heber and I are being transferred immediately, and nobody is being sent to replace us here. Elias and Dolores are scheduled to be baptized in three days but missionaries are being withdrawn from Villa Flores—permanently, for all I know.

I suppose the occasion calls for some inspired statement, but the truth is, I'm just a little sad. I don't feel as though we failed in Villa Flores. We worked hard, had some success, and the future was beginning to look hopeful. What is to become of the Gomez and Masa couples now?

TELEGRAFOS NACIONALES

CAMBIÁMOSLES. HEBER A VERACRUZ. SHEPHERD A TUXTLA COMO ELDER SUPERVISÓR. [We are changing you. Heber to Veracruz. Shepherd to Tuxtla as supervising elder.] E. Seville Hatch.

11

∾

By Our "Sincerity and Earnest Conviction":
Gary's Story as Senior Companion
in Huítzilac Churubusco, Mexico City

Having spent more than a year as a junior companion, Gary was motivated to catch up with Gordon and other missionary peers in his new role as senior companion. His junior companions included a shy newcomer to the mission and his subsequent replacement, an extroverted arrivé of Mexican descent from the Language Training Mission whose exuberance appealed to many investigators but whose clowning also had to be reined in from time to time. Starting with virtually no inherited investigators, Gary and his companions gradually began to cultivate a sizable set of prospective converts, who ranged from the former mayor of Tulancingo to school teachers, college students, professional singers, and evangelical Protestants. Among the many obstacles to conversion for these investigators, Word of Wisdom restrictions (such as use of tobacco, alcohol, and coffee) and strong attachments to Catholic icons, especially the Virgin of Guadalupe, figured most prominently. Both Mormon members and investigators turned to youthful missionaries with their personal problems for pastoral aid and counsel, as well as material support. The dilemma of fraternization with converts, especially attractive females, continued to be a matter of concern, and Gary also increasingly understood the problems of convert inactivity and defection as major issues for the church in Mexico. After three months as a new senior companion, Gary suddenly was elevated in missionary rank to the position of *orientador,* a mission supervisory position of that era (now a zone leader), which jumped him ahead of the conventional promotional step of supervising elder (district leader).

Overlapping with Gary's appointment as senior companion, Gordon assumed the position of supervising elder in Tuxtla Gutiérrez, the capitol city of the state of Chiapas. In Tuxtla, Gordon's supervisory role was complicated by the need to help bolster the ecclesiastical organization of a struggling branch, concern for the future well-being of his handful of converts abandoned in Villa Flores, and, most of all, by a tempestuous junior companion whose violent temper and volatile mood swings were particularly frustrating. As supervising elder, Gordon's branch and proselyting routines in Tuxtla were punctuated from time to time by bus journeys over the Sierra Madre Mountains of Chiapas to work with missionaries in several towns and cities along the southernmost reaches of Mexico's Pacific Coast.

∾

Mexico City, September 9, 1965

At last! The day I've been waiting for so long finally arrived. We went over to the Roja's for lunch as usual and she had a note for me from President Mc-Clellan, making me a new senior companion. My first spot? Back to Churubusco in the City, but this time at the Huítzilac house. My first junior companion will be John Barlow, a new missionary with about three weeks in the mission. I'm excited, exhilarated. I don't want to talk about plans and expectations, I just want to get to work.

September 10

My first day as senior produced a lot of tracting and checkup visits but not many fireworks. Lunched at a member family's that Elder Morrison baptized (the Martinezes')—real nice people. We'll be eating with them regularly at mid-day, and Hermana Martinez will also be doing our laundry. We continued tracting in the afternoon without finding a thing, then spent the rest of the night looking up the remainder of the visits that Morrison left. None of them are at all promising. Guess we'll have to start from scratch. Elder Barlow is quiet but we get along fine. His Spanish pronunciation is actually pretty good, but he needs a little work in pounding home the lesson plans. He lacks confidence more than anything, but I have some good classes planned to handle it. We're living with Elders Flake and Kunz, but they're working out in Tlalpan and are only around the house in the morning. Also, we're practically within shouting distance of the Guerro family. I'm happy.

September 11

Our second day of work left me satisfied. We tracted with success in the morning, picking up four or five returns. One family (the Avilas) looks especially good, with twelve kids and quite a bit of manifest interest. We'll pick them up for church tomorrow. Checked the remaining two visits left by Elder Morrison; X-ed off one and set a date for a second lesson with the other one. It's not a lot to start with, but as I said, I'm pleased with the tracting results, and I know the Lord will bless us if we continue to serve him diligently.

September 13

Tracted all day and most of the evening until 9:00 P.M. Found one family (the Lemoses) that impressed us both as highly promising. Stopped by the big Avila family to see what they thought of church yesterday, and the supposedly wandering father was home—quite friendly, somewhat phony. Anyway, we gave him the tract-out lesson, and he said he'd be present for our scheduled lesson tomorrow. No real reason for worry yet, but I feel uneasy about them.

September 14

My uneasy premonitions about the big Avila family came true tonight. The husband started cranking out an unfriendly spiel that quickly put us on the defensive. Among other things he told us that Mexicans have a natural aversion and distrust of North Americans and therefore have a tendency to dislike anything that has a connection with gringos. He said the U.S. has badly abused Mexico in the past and continues to try dominating the world in any way it can, including through religious movements such as Mormonism. I was angered by such hogwash, but managed not to return the venom. The conclusion of our conversation was that the rest of the family could listen to us if they want, although he doesn't. Fine, but the mom and oldest girl are leaving on a two-week trip, so that shoots us down for at least awhile.

September 15

Worked hard but not too effectively today. People were preparing for the big national holiday tomorrow (Mexican Independence Day), and many were not at home. Crowds walked the streets, many apparently heading for the traditional *"Grito"* [shout] at the *Zócalo* tonight. A huge throng joins the president of the Republic who, standing on the balcony of his residence, shouts "Qué viva La Revolución! Qué viva Mexico!" [Long live the Revolution! Long Live Mexico!] Firecrackers, rockets, etc., spluttered sporadically as we made our rounds. Our fixed visits fell, and tracting was proving equally fruitless when we turned up what might be an outstanding family at the last door we banged on. My companion did most of the talking (he's improving a great deal). It's a big family (the Amadórs), with lots of teenaged girls. They all seemed very interested. We packed lunches back at the apartment for the missionary district *día de campo* tomorrow.

September 16

We arose this morning at 4:00 A.M. Met everybody at the chapel and then traveled out to Amecameca, where we arrived at sunup, near the base of Popocatépetl and Ixtacíwatl. Haggled with all the *camioneta* [small bus or truck] drivers in town to take us up to the hiking point, but they all wanted 200–240 pesos [$16–$19] for the twelve of us. Then a church member from Moctezuma happened along in his truck on a visit to his relatives, so we talked him into hauling us up the mountain. Just as we started off, a ranger out of some little off-the-road hamlet pulled us over and said we couldn't go any further in the truck, that we would either have to continue up in one of the tourist *camionetas* or turn back. He was obviously in cahoots with the chauffeurs, who were angered at losing out on their anticipated fees. Tempers began to rise, but the issue was settled in the usual way—50 pesos [$4] for the ranger, and we were on our way. Set out hiking as soon as the road gave way. The high altitude took one's breath away, clinging volcanic sand made walking extremely difficult. From a high vantage point, Mt. Orizaba in Veracruz was clearly visible rising out of the far-off bank of clouds to the Southeast. And somewhere beyond, completely invisible on the horizon, were the mountains of Chiapas, where Gordon is at work in Villa Flores.

September 17

Started paring off some of the fat today—X-ed off three sets of investigators who show little interest. We've got a lot of visits set up now, so we'll have to start being more selective. Gave two good first lessons: one to an *evangélica* family (the Novelos) and the other to a family we tracted-out a few days ago (the Lemoses). La Señora Lemos is a little afraid to let go, but I get the feeling that they've been waiting for us. My companion can only help me out on a few pages of the lesson plan, but we're trying to do the best we can. I know the Lord will bless our honest efforts.

September 18

After tracting and checking back on return visits all day, we were caught in a driving cloudburst and were drenched to the skin in a matter of seconds. Returned to the apartment to change clothes and wait out the storm. Nearly killed myself trying to run through an ankle-high chain that I didn't see stretched across an alley. Which reminds me: I can't believe how clumsy

I have become lately. And careless and forgetful? I embarrass myself each day with the silly little mistakes and *tonterias* [stupidities] I commit. I'm sure that my companion must consider me a great oaf. Mainly, I suppose, I'm a green senior, and I'm still breaking in the shoes. Anyway, left the apartment again about 7:30 P.M. and delivered a first lesson to the big Amadór family. Highly pleasing. The old man is about the biggest rambling windbag I've ever seen, but when I could steer him back on track the lesson sailed along beautifully. Señor Amadór owns a construction company and used to be very involved in politics (so he says, as the mayor of Tulancingo, when he was the idol of thousands and best buds with the Archbishop of Mexico).

September 23

The days have shot past and I haven't had much time to account for them here. At this point we have five families up to the third lesson with everything so far looking good. We're tracting a lot every day, but aren't finding as much return success as at first. We've completely tracted one area out and are starting on a new one. Joined with the Guerros for a family night and invited the Ibarras to attend with us—the wife is a member, the husband not, and we're trying to teach him. Most frustrating. He has an *evangélico* background and loves to argue irrelevant points. Actually, he's previously heard all the lessons from other missionaries, attends meetings regularly, loves to be with us, gives us reference visits, but refuses to submit himself to the ordeal of the *pila*. Anyway, we're working hard, and although September will soon shut us out, we're hoping for good things in October. All of our visits right now could go either way, but we'll keep plugging. I feel a great need to humble myself and seek more earnestly for the help of the Lord.

September 24

Some hidden problems have popped up with the Martinez family (where we eat lunch and take our laundry). Among other things, they're in a desperate financial condition, and the *hermana* needs an operation that will be quite expensive. We had been thinking about hiring a maid here at the apartment so we wouldn't have to waste so much time coming and going for meals and laundry at the Martinezes'. But when I learned about her situation we forgot about that plan, and I'm going to see if Flake and Kunz would be willing to send their clothes to Hermana Martinez for washing too. She enters the hospital tomorrow morning, so we're going to have a fast starting this afternoon and ending tomorrow afternoon on her behalf. They're fine people.

Hermano Martinez is a worthy husband and Hermana Martinez has a great deal of common sense, coupled with a great deal of faith. She depends on the elders for spiritual support, and we'll give her all we can.

Our investigators are all progressing well. The Novelo *hermanas* go through the lessons like champs, but they were singularly unimpressed with church services last Sunday. Irreverence and poor speakers are hurting us. The big Amadór family is talking like they're already members, but I have a feeling that the Word of Wisdom is going to cause trouble after the third lesson tonight. During the lessons so far, Señor Amadór starts off by relating half the political history of Mexico to us, then immediately conks out in a dead sleep for the rest of the lesson while his five husky teenaged daughters answer all of the questions.

September 25

We got caught again in a rainstorm this afternoon, getting wet and wasting some time. Then showed the filmstrip to the Lemos family and couldn't have asked for a better reaction from them. They're wholesome people, and if we baptize anybody next month, they should be the first. And the Amadórs accepted the Word of Wisdom a lot better than I anticipated, so their promise is beginning to brighten, too.

September 27

Elder Merkley worked with me all day in his new capacity as *orientador* for Mexico City missionaries. Long hours, but enjoyable ones, with a lot of catch-up talking between door-knockings. Had a very good fourth lesson with the Novelo sisters, although the younger one seems to have cooled off some. The fourth with the Amadórs got hung up on their baptismal commitment for this Saturday—my fault, mostly, for not stressing it enough before and now they're balking (I don't want to push anyone into the water, though, if they're not ready). Hermano Amadór kept dropping off to sleep during the lesson and, with people constantly coming in and out, general disorder prevailed. Also gave a fourth lesson to the Lemos family. They're ready and should be baptized this Saturday.

September 29

In all, a pleasing day. Presented a first lesson to a Señora Robleda and some *jóvenes*. She turns out to be a formerly well-known singer and, although now in virtual retirement for the past few years, is recording for Walt Disney as the dubbed-in Spanish singing voice for a character in an upcoming animated film. After the lesson (which seemed to interest her a great deal) she sang a song for us at my request. Doggone good, and it pleased her no end because of our appreciation.

Also held a very good fifth discussion with the Novelo sisters. Only one problem: the older sister has been on vacation, but now will be starting back to work and will not arrive home until late at night. Their baptism is scheduled for this Saturday and they indicated readiness. Had my first glimpse of their incredibly ancient, (supposedly) 130-year-old, great-great-grandmother. They claim she was born in 1834, which would be just four years after the founding of the church by Joseph Smith! She certainly looks ancient enough, but the claim they make for her age would probably make her the oldest person in the world.

We showed the film at the Amadórs' and also at the Liras'. Impressive both times, especially at Liras'. They're becoming more animated on each occasion we see them. I'm still uneasy about the Amadór family, and it's most doubtful that we'll baptize any of them this week.

Elder Flake was transferred to Irapuato this morning. He's sharp, no doubt about it. He was the only junior to be made senior companion ahead of me, and I was initially dubious of his merit. But not now. He has all of the right qualities: excellent Spanish, dedication to the work, love for the people, good common sense, and a cheerful personality.

September 30

Engaged the youngest Novelo sister in a little talk. The older one never did return home from work to see the film we were hoping to show. And in fact, her long hours at work might hurt our hopes for baptism this weekend. At least the younger one seems more willing now. They're both intelligent young women and would make excellent additions to the church.

October 1

Today ended on a somber note. In a frank interview after showing them the filmstrip, the Novelo sisters told us that they were not yet ready to receive an honest baptism. They want more time to be sure; they don't yet have a sincere conviction. I fear a delay is only an excuse for a day that will never come. We were finishing up with the sixth lesson last night with the Lemos family, after Hermano Lemos had made arrangements at his work to stay in the City until next week, when we caught up with the Second Commandment. The *hermano* is unable to overcome the inculcated tradition of his parents and could not promise to take down his *imágenes* [images/saints]. The hour we spent explaining and discussing was painful. Both of them are sincere and desire to be baptized, but this last vestige of pagan custom in Catholicism holds powerful sway. We asked them to pray together tonight and ask God to help them in their decision. We'll go by early tomorrow to find out what it is.

October 4

Busy days gone by. Finished last week with seventy-seven hours. The Lemos couple put off a decision about joining the church. They want to continue studying and praying on their own. Meanwhile, we've picked up some new visits that might pan out: a couple of young women (the Grovases), a young married student (Perez), and an *evangélico* family (the Floreses). We started a first lesson with the Flores bunch last night, but before we could really get under way the señor insisted that the Bible is the only word of God that can exist, that there can be no prophets in these modern days, and that Joseph Smith isn't mentioned in holy scriptures. I shocked him somewhat when I was able to show him where he was quite mistaken on all points. We then left them with that much to chew over, lacking enough time to finish the lesson. We presented the sixth lesson to the Amadórs, expecting more stalling, but surprise! They've made the decision to go ahead with their baptisms.

October 6

We filled out baptismal papers last night for the Amadór family, but were practically shot down later by the Liras. Tension was immediately apparent upon entering their house, and we had barely begun the fourth lesson when a familiar problem popped out. We had previously mentioned the falsity of worshiping or venerating images, and over this point the Liras revealed their disbelief in the principles we have been teaching them. I took time out to show them where idolatry is condemned in the Bible and then left them a strong testimony to think about until we visit them again.

Today we wound up baptizing three of the Amadór girls. The rest will wait, for various reasons, until Saturday or Sunday. I don't feel completely good about their being baptized. Somehow they don't seem sufficiently prepared, although they've had all the lessons plus extra discussions and the films. Also gave the sixth lesson to Aguirre and filled out papers for him—his wife, no. He's a worthy candidate and has gained a testimony. The big factor in deciding him was the Book of Mormon.

October 7

We baptized Alberto Aguirre this afternoon, a really fine guy. He trusts us implicitly and is grateful for the emergence of the gospel into his life. I baptized, conducted the service, and gave the usual short talk. His wife remains short of conviction, but has never given us full attention either.

October 9

Had a talk with Lambero (our school teacher investigator), answered some of her questions and told her she would have to come to her own decision now—a highly intelligent and cultivated person. I don't think we'll see a harvest, but as she herself said, we've planted good seed. We also held a little conference with Hermano Amadór. We're supposed to baptize him tomorrow between Sunday services and the rest of the family on Monday. While we were chatting I munched up half a taco filled with cow brains before they informed me of the contents. Reminded me a little bit of stale tuna fish.

October 10

Finally got Hermano Amadór into the water along with his ten-year-old son, Ramón, but not without complications. The baptism was set in the afternoon between church services, but when we arrived the water was only ankle deep in the *pila*. The lazy janitor was napping on a cot when I burst in on him, and when he refused to help us fill the font with buckets, I blew my stack—accomplished nothing, however. I ended up filling the font alone by hand, one bucket at a time. Later, while we were waiting to begin the service, Hermano Amadór unloaded some of his problems (business and financial) on me. Declared himself to be almost desperate and wants help. He's even unrealistically thinking of writing a letter to President David O. McKay in Salt Lake City for advice. I told him I would accompany him to Licenciado Lozano's office tomorrow to see what kind of legal aid we could secure. The *hermano* and his son were both cheerful upon coming out of the water.

Earlier in the day we had traveled over to Roma to inform Elder Morrison of our planned *día de campo* with the Ibarras and to invite them to come along if they can make arrangements. (Morrison had previously taught Hermano Ibarra before my arrival.) He wasn't in, but old friend Tim Bayer was as new *orientador* and companion to Elder Merkley. A very good move. Elder Cardon is now in the mission home as a new assistant to the president with Elder Peterson, and I understand that Elder Garza's new companion as the other assistant will be Elder Hatch, previously an elder in Gordon's mission. Elder Garza will probably be the dominant figure in the mission home for the remainder of his time—almost a year more. He's a native Mexican with an American education who is a supremely self-confident leader.

October 11

We had a baptism scheduled for Hermana Amadór and her two remaining daughters, but they failed us again. Mom wasn't home, Lourdes doesn't want to do it, and Rebeca wants to put it off. Later, we went up to Lic. Lozano's office with Hermano Amadór and his wife. They didn't bring along any of their documents, so we just got them acquainted with Licenciado Lozano and then set another appointment for them Wednesday.

October 14

Hit with a surprise change this afternoon. Peterson and Cardon dropped by about 3:00 P.M. with a new companion for me. He's Richard Silva, a just arrived greenie, from Las Vegas. Elder Barlow was on his way to Tlanepantla in short order. Barlow and I got along well but didn't get too close during our brief companionship—he's a timid sort, never took much initiative. My new companion looks like he'll be able to help out a lot more. His Spanish is sometimes halting but pretty blinking good, really. He seems to possess a lot of personal drive and is not afraid to give everything a good shot in the arm.

October 15

We started work in the new tracting area today and turned up a few prospects. Planned on a film and a sixth lesson with Hermana Robleda and family, but got shot down from all sides. First, her son had a bloody nose and the *hermana* went all to pieces as though he had been mortally wounded. A doctor was called, injections were administered, etc. After the tumult finally died down, we figured to at least have time for the film, but after everything was set up we discovered there was no rewind reel. Not frustrating at all. But we did deliver a good third lesson to Perez. So far I see no obstacles here. Dropped by the Amadórs' after a stretch of evening tracting. Hermano Amadór is all animated about bringing new people into the church and tomorrow he's going to show us an area he considers ripe for proselyting. Tomorrow, for sure, we baptize his wife and the remaining two daughters.

October 16

Hermano Amadór drove us out to a new *multi-familiar* [housing complex] he's all excited about as a promising new area for us to work. It did look pretty good, but it's in Moctezuma District. We then baptized Hermana Amadór, Rebeca, and Lourdes (the *hermano* decided everybody in the family would have to be together) in the afternoon. Later Hermano Amadór also drove us out to see a family he's talked to about the church. A humble home, nice people, but this time way up in Roma District—we'll pass the visit to Elder Merkley. Returned in time for a visit with the two Grovas sisters, but friends and relatives were present so I didn't try to give a lesson—just reiterated the Joseph Smith story and answered some questions about the Book of Mormon. The oldest girl (Carmen) behaved quite strangely. From a stream of odd, mystical comments she made at the beginning of the discussion, I thought she was going to try and weave a spell or something. She apparently feels herself to be in close touch with supernatural forces. Both girls are quite intelligent and interested in religious topics. We plan to pursue further discussions with them.

October 17

Hermano Amadór keeps bubbling around. Now I'm supposed to get in touch with the man in charge of church construction in Mexico to see if we can't hustle up some work for the *hermano*'s business. Following Sunday school this afternoon we strolled through a nearby historical museum: The Convent of Churubusco, where Mexican forces defended against the invasion of American troops just prior to the more famous battle of Chapúltepec and the fall of Mexico City in 1847. Smack dab in our tracting area.

October 18

Biggest news of the day was that Hermano Ibarra has finally agreed to be baptized. So, after three different sets of missionaries, three months of lessons, films, family nights, *días de campo,* and practically perfect attendance at all meetings, he finally succumbed. I have a suspicion, though, that he has enjoyed all the attention he has received. He's been ready for baptism for a long time, but appeared to greatly enjoy arguing and putting off his decision. He wants Elder Morrison, who was the first missionary to begin teaching him, to be present for the occasion.

October 19

We anointed Hermana Martinez this morning. She's been weak and listless since her operation. Saw her again at Mutual this evening, and she seemed vibrant as ever. The Robledas want to put off their baptisms awhile to think things over a bit more carefully. Hermana Robleda said she'd have a decision by Sunday.

October 20

A lot of tracting today but not many results. We knocked on the door of a

German man, a professor of religious history at the University of Mexico and pastor of a Lutheran Church in the Lomas de Chapúltepec, with degrees (he says) from Vienna, Harvard, Yale, etc. We visited with him for a few minutes, then parted with a mutual agreement not to waste each other's time. More of the same later when we engaged in a brief go-round with an intellectual agnostic. Left him with a copy of the Book of Mormon, which he declared he would not read.

October 21

Nasty weather, rained hard all day. We tracted a couple of hours in the morning and then called it quits. Went on a little shopping expedition and I purchased a couple of shirts and some socks. Most of my original wardrobe has been worn down to the bare threads and I haven't done much to rehabilitate it.

Hermano Lemos has finally returned. We spent some time talking to his wife this afternoon, but didn't get to see him. I'm worried that his three-week absence might have cooled him off some. His wife and the rest of his family would present no problems otherwise. We baptize Hermano Ibarra tomorrow. Elder Morrison will be on hand to witness and help out.

October 22

Left early in the morning to get things set up for the Ibarra baptism. I conducted the services, Elder Morrison baptized, and I confirmed. Hermano Ibarra was visibly moved, as were family and friends who were present. We were then invited to a very good celebration dinner with the family.

October 23

We finally had another lesson with the Grovas girls and their mother. Good. The oldest girl, Carmen, is a little strange (she almost always becomes mystical-emotional whenever we talk) but I think they'll make it now. Then we grabbed a cab and motored way over to Camerones where a special ceremony was being held to initiate the new work phase on construction of the stake center (which has been held up now for almost a year). Our purpose in going was to connect Hermano Amadór with Brother Baker (who is in charge of Camerone Construction) and see what kind of work arrangements can be made. Apparently they have worked out something, although the *hermano* keeps coming to me with more problems.

October 24

No investigators showed for Sunday school, but we had a goodly turnout for sacrament meeting. Then wound up getting hurt by a few thoughtlessly sarcastic remarks about the Catholic Church made by a visiting member of the stake high council. The Liras didn't like it, and neither did the Grovases. Hermano Lemos showed up just before service ended, and from his manner I anticipate a fall. He was smoking earlier this afternoon when we passed by. Tuesday my companion and I will have a fast on their behalf and then a once-and-for-all visit with them. We gave a good fourth lesson to the Grovases after church. I'm quite sure they'll be baptized, but not this month.

October 25

Might have turned up a few good prospects tracting today. Enjoyed a visit with the Robledases. The *hermana* played some of the records she's recorded—really pretty. We're not going to push them in the water this month either. Hermana Martinez is sick in bed again with a liver ailment. She's a wonderful person. Wish we could help her more. As it is, though, she's not going to be able to do our laundry anymore.

October 26

Fasted all day for our visit with the Lemos family this evening, but their decision about baptism is no—at least for the time-being. In our discussion some serious problems, unknown to me beforehand, came up. Behind Hermano Lemos's difficulties with his *imágenes* and the Word of Wisdom are some weighted reasons. He works for a tyrannical boss, and social drinking makes up an integral part of their business dealings. The boss becomes offended and angry when Hermano Lemos refuses a drink with him or customers. This is a common enough problem in the States, but here it could very easily cost a job, and that's what he fears. He told us that he took his *santos* [figurines of saints] down last week, but things become unpleasant last Sunday when all his relatives came over and noted that the holy objects were missing. Hermano Lemos was accused of betraying the memory of his parents, who had given him these things as gifts, and now Hermano Lemos fears that the weighty disapproval of his family will lead to alienation from them. Perhaps I am shirking my responsibility, but I don't intend to push these internal problems to a head. They must make their own decision, weighing the consequences on both sides. But we did have a good fifth lesson with Perez. He seems ready and waiting for baptism this Saturday.

October 27

Not many scheduled visits today, so a lot of tracting instead. We might have stumbled onto a good return when checking on a previous tract-out. I rang the wrong doorbell in an apartment, so when a strange woman (Señora Para) answered I gave her our regular door approach. She invited us in, we gave her a tract-out lesson, and she turns out to be quite interested. A long fifth discussion with the Liras was thought-provoking for them and shed light on many of their questions and doubts. They'll be leaving on a short vacation over the weekend, but I asked them to have a final decision for next week.

Doggone blinkety cold these past days. Doing a lot of extracurricular talking with my companion—a pretty good guy. Elder Silva is of Mexican descent, and although he never thoroughly learned Spanish at home, he's rapidly becoming fluent now. He has tendencies to be a wiseacre, but not in a mean-spirited way; just fond of having a good time. The rock 'n' roll tapes he plays loudly around the apartment sometimes make me cringe. He says the Beatles are not fading in popularity but are bigger than ever.

October 29

Elders Castañeda and Christensen worked with us half the day—tracted all morning. Castañeda and I paired off, and I ended up on the listening end of an incredible story. Elder Castañeda is one of eighteen children in his family. His early years in California were a succession of school changes and slum life. Later he got involved with a gang, used dope, and was in and out of trouble, reform schools, and jail. His mother was thrown in the pokey, too, for smuggling heroin across the border. He was finally placed in a foster home. The foster parents turned out to be good Mormons, he was converted, began taking an active interest in studies, and was eventually elected student body president of his high school. But he says he's always had an inferiority complex and, in trying to succeed, he seems to alienate different groups of people. Same thing in the mission. He's worked inhumanly hard, racked up a lot of baptisms, and now many elders resent him, considering him a "numbers man," out for glory. (I don't concur in this assessment.)

Perez wasn't home for the sixth lesson, and we're supposed to baptize him tomorrow. We may have turned up some gold with the new family (the Paras) that we accidentally found, ringing the wrong doorbell. They're a young couple, plus the wife's brother. Sailed through an extremely well-answered first lesson—they gave the impression that they've eagerly been waiting to hear the message we brought them.

October 30

All four of us pitched in and gave the apartment a good cleaning this morning. The good old *hermana* from Churubusco house will be here to work as our maid next Monday, and I didn't want her to be welcomed by the pigpen this place has become. Dropped over to Perez's later on, found him home, had a sixth lesson, and then baptized him this afternoon. He's a law student at the University of Mexico, plays second string on the varsity soccer team, and is a real good guy.

October 31

A young married couple who live in the Unidad near our apartment introduced us to some friends who also live there—a good family of five by the name of Pierdánt. We gave them the Joseph Smith story, then stayed to chat and answer some of their questions (they have many). Then went on to present another excellent tract-out, this time with a family called Azoto— three young ladies (two of them in their twenties) and an older brother. November is being ushered in with a very promising look about it. Must see how we'll shape up personally to meet it. Meanwhile, I'm pleased with our results in the month gone by. We've baptized some good people, worked pretty hard, and received a lot of blessings maybe we didn't deserve.

Gord's most recent letter shows that his hunches about a move and promotion to supervising elder were right. It's a shame that the Villa Flores Branch is being suspended, but being the first to carry the gospel to a new place will always remain as a lasting satisfaction. I envy the invaluable experience Gordon is racking up in the little hamlets where he's spent most of his time. City life can be pretty soft, and I've been spoon-fed on pablum practically all my mission. But no complaints; I'm very grateful.

LETTER FROM GORDON

Gar: I've just been made supervising elder of the Chiapas District and will reign from the city of Tuxtla Gutiérrez. My domain will stretch from Tapachula, bordering Guatemala, to Arriaga, along the Pacific Coast. What ever ego-expanding satisfaction might have been derived from my new calling, however, was virtually annulled by the closing of Villa Flores. That was a shock. Elder Heber was called to Veracruz to become a new senior companion but no one was sent to Villa Flores to take our places, as I had hoped would happen. I suppose the mission home was becoming impatient (although we did have a couple of baptisms), but the real problem is that nearly half of our missionaries are ending their missions and departing for home this week. There's just a simple shortage of troops at the present time—not enough to staff every little town like Villa Flores, I'm afraid. My hope is that Villa Flores can be reopened as soon as an adequate number of replacement missionaries arrives from the LTM. I talked to

President Hatch by phone and he pointed out that I could make trips from time to time, but it's a five-hour journey from Tuxtla to Villa Flores by bus. Realistically, I could never maintain investigators and a new branch of the church there under such conditions.

Fact of the matter is, though, I'm in Villa Flores right now with my new companion. We just arrived after a kidney-pounding journey by bus over the mountains from Tuxtla. We'll hold Sunday services tomorrow and stick around Monday to splash two more good people who were set to be baptized when Heber and I were pulled out. That will make four Mormons in town and a lot of big, deflated hopes.

In the meantime, I've got to get myself squared away to assume my new *cargo* [load] as supervising elder. Among other things, my junior companion, Timothy Granger, is the current problem child in the mission, and I'm supposed to pacify him or he might get sent home. Actually, I have a strange liking for him—he reminds me a little bit of Dave Lingwall. Physically, he's right along the same lines: stocky, muscular, and even looks like Dave, with *rubio* [sandy] hair. He lacks Dave's mental capacity and sense of humor, however, and his manners and impulsive actions are about ten times as coarse and unpredictable. I knew Elder Granger four months ago in Veracruz. My most vivid recollection of Granger is of him and his companion coming close to getting into a fistfight at a movie theater. Elder Treanor, his most recent companion, told me of several brawls and near brawls he had with Granger in Tuxtla. Treanor is six feet, three inches tall, played football his freshman year at BYU, and is big enough to sit on him. I'm not. I suspect we'll get along though.

Also, the branch in Tuxtla is apparently in chaos—badly weakened by quarrels and bickering among the members, inept leadership, scandals (including several cases of adultery), etc. The branch president is desperate for our help to keep things alive, further curtailing my thoughts of working in Villa Flores over the weekends. To give you an idea, President Hatch just wrote me, saying: "I realize you're short-handed there, but there is one more very necessary part of your assignment to bring to your attention. Branch President Esponda needs your help. Please support him in every way possible. This does not mean to work just with members, although you will need to do a lot of this until we are able to send some additional help. May the Lord be with you in carrying out all your many responsibilities." Unfortunately, few of the Tuxtla members seem too anxious to lend *their* help, and I'll probably end up teaching priesthood, Sunday school and Mutual classes. The Lord's been blessing me with problems and I hope I'm worthy to stand. I won't complain too much, though, because if we can help get the branch back on its feet, missionary success should also improve through better support from members. [In 1988 Tuxtla Gutiérrez became the headquarters city for a newly designated LDS mission in Chiapas. By 1994 a stake center and nine wards were functioning in the Tuxtla area, with approximately six thousand members.]

A week later: I didn't get this off in the mail last week while in Villa Flores, so I thought I'd add a few more lines. Tonight we visited a woman and her teenaged son who was partially blinded with steel fragments in his eye from an industrial accident at his job last week. We gave the young man a blessing and were then taken next door to a neighbor's home where we were introduced to a macabre and depressing scene. The neighbors' infant child died yesterday and had not yet been buried. Her body was lying on the kitchen table, illuminated by candles in the darkness, with small wads of cotton stuffed in her ears and nostrils, supposedly to prevent evil spirits from possessing her. We were asked to give the weeping parents a blessing, which I did, promising them that the child's sinless spirit already had returned to her Father in Heaven and not to "limbo," as the Catholics teach.

The Tuxtla Branch continues to teeter back and forth on the brink of disaster. Sunday school services yesterday were about the worst I've ever attended. Sacrament meeting was vastly improved, however, with a fairly good turnout and a more congenial spirit. I was one of the *predicadores* [speakers], and actually gave one of the best talks of my mission. Sometimes I fail pretty miserably to say much of value, while other times I truly seem to speak with the power of my convictions.

Sobre todo [above all] there's Elder Granger, a rare specimen. With a gritting of teeth, there have been no major explosions between us so far. This boy, however, has had more than his share of problems and will undoubtedly continue to have them unless he somehow learns to manage his temper, which is like a time bomb ticking away. For example, yesterday in a tracting visit he boiled over when the guy whose home we were in kept interrupting him to say he didn't want to hear anymore. Granger sputtered for a minute and then slammed his fist down on the table, abruptly stood up, knocked his chair over and stormed out the door. I was left behind to apologize to the speechless man. In addition, Granger appears to have declared war on the bees of Tuxtla, especially a variety of red wasps that are everywhere this time of year. The wasps are attracted to water and, whenever we pass the fountains in the central park, Elder Granger springs into action, smacking wasps out of the air with my "La Historia Mormona" book or the flannel board. Instead of studying at lunch time when we're home, he spends almost the entire noon hour attacking wasps in our backyard with a fly swatter. The most constructive thing I can say about this odd behavior is that it appears to be a way for Elder Granger to channel hostility and let off steam.

Speaking of unpredictable behavior, what's Chuck's newest theory? Do you really think he's departed from the church for good, or was his letter to you this summer just another intellectual tantrum? By the way, I got a recent letter from Elder Rencher, my former senior companion in Minatitlán, who has returned home and is now teaching Spanish at the Language Training Mission in Provo while attending school at BYU. It's a seducing thought. I think we could get in the LTM program. Another thing: I never thought I'd ever learn Spanish but surprised myself. With one language comfortably digested, it might not be such a bad idea to try for another. I suppose you would be inclined to the guttural tongue [German, which Gary had taken for a year in high school]. How about French?

All those padded reports you've received about me make me cringe a little because I know, in truth, that I regularly fall short in meeting my responsibilities. Keep frequent communication coming so I'll know what to do to keep my suspenders hitched up and on the right track. Keep yourself on full-throttle and we'll be side by side all the way.

Your brother, Gord

November 1

Presented an extremely well-understood first lesson to Hermana Robleda's sister. Then traveled over to the ward for a choir practice—we've been hooked into singing with a choir that is being organized to perform at stake conference later this month. Carmen Grovas (who studied music and has a trained singing voice) wants to participate, on condition that we join with her.

The Azoto bunch turned out even better than we had anticipated, but we have yet to talk with mama. Hustled back over to the Grovas sisters to give them and their mother a fifth lesson. They accepted it well enough, in fact it contained answers to many of their unexpressed questions. Carmen still lapses into strange moods at times when talking about religion. She started to cry towards the end of the lesson after recounting some of the dreams she has had which seem to carry great religious import for her. One of her dreams had to do with life after death, and our lesson material reminded her of it.

November 2

Spent a good chunk of the morning with our new reference visit, the Pierdánt family. The lesson was well understood and seemingly well accepted.

The questions and answers before and after the lesson show them to be highly hopeful prospects. A second lesson with Hermana Robleda's sister was also pleasant, but now Alfredo, Hermana Robleda's son, has a bad cold and the doctor forbids even a bath, so they want to wait until he is sufficiently recovered before being baptized. Hermana Robleda says our "sincerity and earnest conviction" have had a telling effect on her from the start.

November 3

We indulged in a slice of morning tracting and made some scattered visits, including Hermana Lemos and Hermana Martinez. Hermana Martinez is out of bed now and starting to slowly get better. The family still has an overabundance of problems, and she leans on the missionaries as confidants. She also told me that Olívia Muñoz (who is somehow related) has gotten pregnant by some worthless punk. Rather a shock, as the Muñoz family—and especially Olívia and her older sister—were always so close to Elder Mason and me over in Ermita.

November 4

A very encouraging round of visits today. A third lesson with Hermana Robleda's sister went over without a fuss, although she smokes and had claimed beforehand that she wouldn't be able to quit. We gave a second lesson to the Paras and they're so ready and comprehending that it's a pure joy to teach them.

We topped off the evening by showing "¿Que es un Mormon?" to the Pierdánt family. We ate a good dinner with them before the film and enjoyed pleasant small talk. The propriety of Alícia's (a teenaged daughter) continued enrollment at a Catholic "normal" school was brought up. I phoned President McClellan in the morning about the problem that might exist here and received some good advice—that she consider enrolling at the church's excellent new secondary school at El Arbolío—but I'm going to save the suggestion for her until she knows more about the church and can make a fair decision. We also touched on tithing, polygamy (Catholics are still taught down here that Mormon men keep harems), and the missionary program. Just before leaving, the father casually mentioned that they would be ready for baptism on the sixteenth, as though they had already made their decision.

November 6

Turned up an unusual tract-out visit this morning: a young engineering student who speaks quite good English, has attended Stanford University, and comes from a well-to-do family of Spanish descent. A very affable person and quite curious about us. He invited us for lunch next week at his parents' home, after we make a presentation of the first lesson.

The fourth lesson with Hermana Robleda's sister pretty well decided baptism for the whole family. All were present and all manifested a desire to be baptized, which I hope can be accomplished next week. A real love has grown between all of us, and it's always a pleasure to be with them. They've already invited us to have Christmas dinner with them.

Engaged in a prolonged third lesson with the Paras, but although they both smoke a little, no real problems were revealed. We engaged in a lot of extra explaining and they're still as good as gold. We weren't able to drop off a second lesson with the Azotos—the sisters arrived late, one by one, and the brother wasn't there at all, so we just enjoyed some interesting conversation instead. We did have a successful second lesson with the Pierdánt family. They always talk of their baptisms as an almost accepted reality. We snacked and chatted with them after the lesson until late. One small concern: We'll have to guard against Alícia—an attractive teenaged girl—getting overly friendly.

November 7

A very busy Sunday. Lots of lessons scheduled, but in the end only one delivered: a fifth to the Robledas. While there we finally settled on this Wednesday as the baptismal date for the *hermana,* Alejandro, and Patrícia. The *hermana's* sister may not be ready by them—she hasn't yet been able to completely give up smoking. Instead of a regular lesson with the Grovases, we ended up answering a variety of questions and talked about the temple, using some beautiful color interior photos of the temples to illustrate. But something isn't exactly right when they're all together, so we'll give Carmen a sixth lesson separately from the others. We had a good turnout of investigators at church, although testimony meeting right after Sunday school always produces such confusion that I often feel we lose ground on fast and testimony Sundays rather than gaining it.

November 8

The third lesson with the Pierdánt family on the Word of Wisdom produced some hesitant moments, but all in all it's going well. The younger kids love us. They hardly let us leave when we have another visit to get to. Received a surprisingly swift response from Steve London to the letter I sent him last month. Hang in there, Steve—you could shame us all if you were just able to put into heartfelt action what you know in your head.

LETTER FROM STEVE LONDON TO GARY

Dear Gary,

It was more than gratifying to receive your letter and learn that an especially coveted, if physically neglected, friendship has been resecured. I am grateful. Perhaps you should know that your writings have a profound, provocative, and arresting effect upon me as few things I have ever read. I thrilled too upon reading your journal account of President Hugh B. Brown's prophecy at your conference in Mexico City. It's implications are only all too frightening. Once, in one of my common lapses of wisdom, I asked an apostle a rather inappropriate question. His answer has proven hard to live, but it is undoubtedly the truth. You can guess the query. His reply he illustrated with two true stories. He said he once knew a man—if I remember right, the son of a president of the church—whose father had told him he would become an apostle. Well, the man never quit thinking about that, looked continually for it, and finally died a crushed and broken-hearted soul who missed by leagues the apostleship. He told me also of his own son, whose mission president had told him he would sit with the Twelve, as his father had, and the advice given when his son came to him with the promise: He told him to forget it or he would never, ever become a prophet. And so, as I contemplate blessings, and prophecies, and promises, I raise occasionally these thoughts in my own still terribly proud, vain head and they temper, or perhaps more accurately, condemn the vanities and indulgences. President Brown concluded that "this prophecy will come true for these persons as they merit it with their worthiness," and that frightens even more as a man asks himself a thousand questions.

Something Gordon wrote you also struck me rather hard: "I'll see you on top of the world." As I see you both rapidly getting there, the desire to follow is strong. In the long run the Lord seems to help those who help themselves. I know assuredly that merely calling on him will not avail. He simply will not carry a man very far, if at all. Nevertheless, each short experiment with personal effort has brought a promising measure of success, and I've come closer to catching fire here in Tierra Blanca than ever before. It's so easy to become lethargic, sleepily eating up the days in one of those Satan-authored and disastrous stupors. For all you have to do is pick some minor event a week or so away, and just sort of drift along to it, forgetting the opportunities and precious moments of the present. Your comments on the ghostly appearance in yourself of the insufficiencies of old companions I am finding true too. For a week your old companion has been one of those things you make someone who has too much time in the mission to be a junior, but whom you just don't quite trust to be a senior—a *co-mayor* [co-senior]. The slightly added responsibility is exposing. At least more of the things are being said that I've always thought should have been said, and the general climate is less stifling, freer of friction.

My Spanish is fair on grammar, acceptable on pronunciation, weak on vocabulary, but nonetheless a source of unrighteous pride. Plans for afterward are nil. Lots of school. The future hangs deadly in the balance. The rest of my mortal life, the life of my family, and later the sure eternities, depend, I believe, on my performance in these remaining few months. We'll see who's equal to the task and who not.

As ever, an admirer and friend, Steve

November 9

Relevos were given this morning at the mission home for Elders Carl Mason (my old senior companion in Ermita, with whom I enjoyed some excellent experiences) and John Martz. While leaving the mission home I bumped into President Seville Hatch of the Southeast [Mexican] Mission, and I again heard pride-popping news from him about Gordon. I also asked about Elder London. Happily, hints of progress in yesterday's letter were amplified, namely that Steve is finally starting to get to work and just happens to speak the best Spanish in the mission—so well, in fact, that President Hatch thinks he will have London translate for the general authorities when they come to speak at conference.

A sixth lesson with Hermana Robleda's sister in the afternoon confirmed that we won't baptize her tomorrow, but we will do the rest of the family. An evening sixth lesson with Carmen Grovas (didn't actually give a formal lesson, just talked) also confirmed that there are problems to be resolved here before baptism can occur. Carmen is somewhat of a mystic and has frequent dreams which she feels are in the nature of visions. When her mother was gravely ill awhile back, Carmen prayed and made personal vows to fulfill certain conditions if her mother's life was spared. Apparently the major promise was to go with her mother on a pilgrimage to various holy places in Mexico and South America. We didn't have time to review all the details, but I am concerned about some of the implications. We also delivered a fourth lesson to the Paras, and they had a bushel-full of questions, most of which seem connected to themes that we will be presenting in the fifth lesson—that should be the crucial session for them. We started a lesson with Hermano Quiróz, but my companion suddenly felt sick and retreated to the bathroom to puke, so we postponed the visit. Elder Bayer will be coming over to work with me tomorrow for two days. Elder Silva can get some bed rest if he's still feeling sick and I can augment an increasingly strong friendship with Elder Bayer. A district fast also starts tomorrow.

November 10

All the district missionaries were at the chapel to start the fast this morning. Then Elder Bayer and I tracted all morning without success almost up to baptism time for the Robledas. We traveled over to Roma for the services so that Alejandro could be baptized in warm water. I baptized and gave a small talk. Hermana Robleda's pre-baptismal jitters turned into bubbling excitement afterward. She insists we not stop seeing them occasionally, just because they're now in the fold. I better understand now the dilemma between wanting to sustain relations with people with whom you've worked so closely before baptism versus the need to devote as much time as possible to finding and teaching new investigators.

November 11

Elder Bayer and I gave a quick second lesson to the two younger Azoto sisters earlier this morning. Their reaction was only mediocre. At 2:00 P.M. we knocked off for a luncheon engagement with the well-off young engineering student that Elder Silva dug up a few days ago. But he had not yet returned when we arrived, so while we were waiting, his father (a professor of surgery at the University of Mexico) showed us around their beautifully modern home. He brought us out some vermouth, but we settled for ginger ale. Finally, the young man phoned with apologies about an unexpected examination at the university that would prevent his being with us. However, he invited us to stay and eat lunch with his parents, which we did. All of the family spoke English, which we mostly conversed in. The mother was gracious and refined. The meal was excellent: roast chicken, meat *sopes,* tossed salad, green squash, string beans, large glasses of cold milk, lemon pie, and assorted fruits. We touched lightly on many general subjects and also explained a little bit about Mormonism. All in all, a very different afternoon from the usual.

Carmen Grovas invited some of her friends over to listen to us this evening, but in a confidential aside informed me that we shouldn't start out with the Joseph Smith story and other first lesson topics. I told her nix, best to start out from the beginning. As a matter of fact, her friends were pretty incredulous, but if people won't accept the basics, there's not much point in wasting time with a lot of fancy explanations about other details.

November 12

We ate lunch with the Ibarras after a fruitless tracting stint in the morning, then showed our film to the Paras. They've got me a little worried now. Hermano Para hinted slightly at communist sympathies and the *hermana* is still smoking, although she's cut down a lot. The Pierdánt family is definitely planning on their baptisms next week after we completed tonight's fourth lesson. But my companion needs to cut back on his clowning while presenting the discussions. It's vital that we impart a certain spirit to our investigators, and that spirit cannot be present if we aren't serious in what we're saying and doing.

November 13

Tracted all morning and found nothing. Left off a second lesson with Carmen Grovas's friends, Berta and Lília, that went a little better than the first one we gave. Then over to the Paras' for an important fifth lesson that wound up being partially botched. The discussion developed into a confused mélange of far-ranging questions and we spent a long time trying to wade through them all. It had to be done this way though, I think. Both of them are quite intelligent and have ideas and doubts that one would expect most thinking people to have. We weren't completely successful in satisfying them, but we did manage to pare away some of the problem. They won't be ready for baptism, however, until we are able to clear up a few other points. Hermana Para was down to one cigarette today.

November 14

The Pierdánt family invited us over for dinner this afternoon. Afterward, we taught them the fifth lesson and took them to church. After sacrament meeting I had an interview with Carmen Grovas about her proposed pilgrimage. We talked seriously and frankly, and in the end she agreed that she could not herself participate in the religious activities of the excursion while simultaneously seeking baptism as a Mormon. However, she feels obligated to go because part of the vow was directly to her mother, and they have already made arrangements to sell their car to finance the trip. She promised she would travel only as an observer in order to fulfill the obligation to her mother. I told her to pray sincerely about the matter in order to receive direction in her course.

November 15

Hermano Quiróz's wife is in town for a couple of days, so we went over this morning to see what arrangements could be made for getting them married. But he scuttled off as soon as we arrived, and indications are that he hasn't been entirely sincere with us in his professed desire to be baptized.

Went by the Grovases' this afternoon to see what the result of Carmen's prayers had been. She evinced no trace of emotion this time, just assured us that she wouldn't take active part in any religious ceremony. We stayed awhile to talk and ended up in an impromptu Spanish-English lesson. Carmen is starting to *"tú"* [the intimate/informal mode of address in Spanish that missionaries were supposed to avoid, especially when talking to young women] everybody in sight, so careful.

We were supposed to have a question-answer period with Paras, but the *hermana* was sick, so we just chatted awhile with Hermano Paras. Left for a family night with the Pierdánts at the Guerros'. The result was a bit chaotic with what seemed like a thousand people crowded into the apartment and hordes of children initiating a reign of confusion. But *ni modo* [nonetheless], some new friendships were struck up between families and that's all I really wanted to accomplish.

November 16

Back to the Grovases' again to show some films and give Carmen's friends Berta and Lília (who, by the way, are progressing surprisingly well) a third lesson. Had our final lesson with the Pierdánts in the evening and the usual *cena* [supper] afterward. Hermana Pierdánt has a bad cold, but decided to be baptized tomorrow with the rest anyway, in warm water at the Roma *capilla*.

November 17

Elders Merkley and Bayer helped us out with the Pierdánts' baptismal service. Hermano and Hermana Pierdánt seemed deeply touched by the events of the day. They had already prepared dinner for us before leaving for Roma, wanting us to celebrate afterward with them. So we postponed another scheduled visit and enjoyed a warm occasion. However, as with others before, we will need now to cut back a bit on the time we spend with them. Realizing this themselves, they offered us a standing invitation for lunch every Sunday, which we accepted. This makes it possible to get together on a modest but regular basis at a time that won't subtract from our regular missionary work.

November 19

Made our visit with Carmen Grovas's friends. They had to leave at an early hour, so we were only able to get through half of the fourth lesson—very good so far. Tomorrow, the Grovas family leaves on their pilgrimage, so we won't be able to talk to the girls until next week. We rechecked an old, almost forgotten tract-out visit and discovered a potential gold mine, a family called Belmón. They're good, humble people and they went very well through the first lesson.

Adding to my good feelings was a new letter from Gord, even though his own present situation is marred by serious companion concerns. I know what he means about no *ganas* to write letters. (Sometimes it's like an in-class English theme that has to be written—no buts about it—and meanwhile you sit there trying to sweat the lard out of your brain while precious time ticks relentlessly away.) But my current aversion to sitting down and scribbling off a few lines cannot be credited, *grácias a Díos* [thank God], to a Neanderthal companion like Gordon's.

LETTER FROM GORDON

Gar: I owe you, but this letter most likely will be a miserable effort. I just don't have *ganas* to communicate on paper. My last letter home was a laborious affair and I haven't written in my diary for days. I don't know what to credit this to—most likely it's the spirit of apprehension and amazement that lingers here, triggered and augmented every time my companion pops off. I'm embarrassed to have classified Elder Granger in my earlier description alongside of good old Dave Lingwall. Granger belongs to an uncouth category of uncontrolled belligerence that is all his own. We haven't had any large personal blowups between us yet (if we weren't on a *mission* together, I'd tell him to go to hell), but I have tread unsuspectingly on his super-sensitive feelings several times and, unheralded, he'll snap out at some careless act or word from me. Granger's self-control is the equivalent of an eight-year-old. He's not really malicious, just lacks tolerance and a sense of humor, is mistrustful of people, has little or no ability to deal with frustration, and strikes out impulsively at those whom he blames for his troubles. To make matters worse, Elder Granger is agitated and depressed by letters from home. His father is unbelievably insensitive and cruel, demanding to know why his son hasn't been made a senior companion yet and accusing him of being a failure. Actually, compared to his past record, Granger's improved monumentally. Our zone supervisor passed through the other day and related to me a story that made my hair curl. According to him, Elder Granger's first place in the mission was Huixtla, Chiapas (reputed to be a sweltering hole in the jungle), where there was a small branch of forty to fifty fairly faithful members. All missionaries were pulled out of Huixtla shortly after my companion's departure, and *hoy día* [today] there is no branch; there are barely one or two souls there who claim to be Mormons. The horrendous part is that the *caida* [fall] of the church in Huixtla was blamed principally on the shenanigans and misbehavior of you-know-who. One of Elder Granger's juicier outbursts was this: He became enraged at the maid over some trivial matter, resorted to the impulse of brutality, actually struck the maid several times, and had to be pulled off by his companion, but not before attracting a crowd of curious onlookers at the door. The story spread from there all over town, and as bad as the facts were, the incident was bloated and swollen out of shape, and the name of the church was greatly stained. Well, that was the past, and I was shocked to hear about it. Granger seems to have grown up a bit since then, and I haven't witnessed anything quite so spectacular so far. I will not further enumerate the irritations, however.

In addition to branch and proselyting chores here in Tuxtla I've had to make several trips as supervising elder to work with the other missionaries in the Chiapas District. Last week we headed out to visit the elders stationed in Tapachula on the Guatemala border, but made the mistake of taking a bus *de secunda clase* [second class] out of Tuxtla. It was standing room only for four hours all the way over the mountains to Arriaga on the Pacific Coast, with passengers, baggage, and livestock of every description crammed on board. We staggered off the bus in Arriaga at midnight, hoping to catch a first-class bus bound for Tapachula. We ended up waiting four more hours in Arriaga for another bus, shivering in the wind, and napping sporadically on some hard benches outside the bus depot. Once on board I kept slumping asleep against the passenger sitting next to me and drooling on his shoulder. He didn't seem offended and I couldn't seem to help myself. It was after 8:00 in the morning before we arrived in Tapachula, just in time to have breakfast and go out tracting with the elders there.

After two days in Tapachula we left for home, stopping again in Arriaga, only this time to spend the night at the missionaries' little rented house. I woke up the next morning with a million bedbug bites and almost regretted we had not gone straight through on the bus. We tracted with the elders in the morning, then caught a *camioneta* for Villa Flores to check on our new converts and have our chapel and apartment furniture put in storage until the mission home can send some new missionaries to reopen the town. The trip from Arriaga to Villa Flores is through country even more wild and desolate than the ride from Tuxtla. We spent over three hours peering nervously into deep gorges while climbing over mountain crags on a narrow, winding dirt road that was often washed out and nonexistent in places. We were only able to stay two hours in Villa Flores before catching the last bus to Tuxtla. We took care of the storage business and said a quick hello to our two convert couples. I feel like a rat for leaving them alone with their new faith but no church to sustain them.

Gar, what I'd like to know is, what's your recipe for baptizing regularly? Anything special you've learned to do? We've always got *bastante* investigators, but most seem to eventually peter out. Sometimes I feel like I'm not doing my job properly. I've been bragging you up. Everybody down here wants to know how many baptisms you've had so far.

And what's wrong with studying French? I'm all for going to the University of Utah too, but we'll need some finances quick when we return home. Getting a job teaching Spanish at the LTM could help us get started. Give it some more thought.

Your brother, Gord

November 21

Stake conference today at the Roma *capilla*. The conference theme was the missionary program of the church, and great emphasis was placed on Mexican members preparing their worthy young people to take on greater responsibilities and to qualify for mission calls. The war in Vietnam has caused a shortage of American missionaries and this increases the need for more local contributions. The Azoto sisters surprised us by coming to the morning session.

November 22

Checked out a reference visit (the Balboas) in Santa Cruz this morning—first time I've been out there since Merkley and I split. The visit might be good. Balboa is the son-in-law of a member woman who just moved here from another town. Stopped by the Quebedos (whom Merkley and I baptized in June) while we were out there. They have fallen inactive (although they did just attend conference) and Hermano Quebedo is smoking again. We talked pleasantly together and, while he doesn't gush repentance, he's willing to try a little harder. The rest of the family would be fine with the *hermano*'s leadership. Came back to a very good second lesson with the Belmón family. They exhibit that certain quality that usually predicts future members of the church.

November 23

Solid tracting throughout most of the day. We may have turned up another good family (the Campos). The mother might prove out of it, but the teen-aged girls look sharp. Had a mediocre fourth lesson with the Azoto sisters. The main problem is that, while they have come out to church a few times, they haven't engaged in much serious thought or study. While going through the discussion with them my jaw tightened, and I could barely spit out my words. It's puzzling to me why every once in a while I suffer this sort of relapse in my Spanish, which normally flows without any difficulty whatsoever.

November 24

More hard tracting. We've practically finished with our current hunting grounds, but haven't really found too much. Traveled out to Santa Cruz again in the evening to see the Balboa man. Found him home, talked a few minutes, and set a date for Saturday. He seems like a nice enough guy, but his wife loudly *mandars* [gives orders] in the house. We returned for a third lesson with the Belmón family, which went over fine with all of them except the mother, who doesn't think she can give up coffee. The Word of Wisdom is a little tricky in presenting to people who have stubborn problems, and I wish that I had given the last half of the lesson rather than my companion, who rushed it through too fast.

November 25

Today was Thanksgiving in the United States, but the only thing we did to celebrate was play touch football with the district elders in the morning. Fun, but nobody exactly starred, and our team got soundly trounced. Left off play at 11:00 A.M. to tract and then worked straight through until our last (and only) visit at night. We were supposed to give the fifth lesson to the Azotos, but the oldest sister hadn't arrived from work, and while we were waiting, Maritza brewed up a cup of coffee, drank it in front of us, and declared that she can't give it up (which actually she hasn't even tried to do). Neither of them have put out much effort to study the *folletos* or the Book of Mormon, pray, or attend church.

November 26

The president's assistants, Elders Peterson and Cardon, stopped by the apartment this morning just before we left to tract. It looks like November will be low on baptisms throughout the entire mission, and they asked me my opinion of "how come?" I said that I didn't think we could assign any particular reason for it when everyone is generally working hard. After all, monthly *metas* are merely arbitrary periods of time as we set them and don't necessarily have to coincide with what was accomplished at the same time last year. The value and effectiveness of our work can't really be measured by analyzing short, statistical periods. Rather the story will tell itself only over the long run.

Aches and pains from yesterday's football game made for listless tracting this morning. Completed the last half of the fourth and all of the fifth lesson with Berta and Lília at the Grovases'. They're thinking of stalling, but we emphasized next Wednesday as the day for their baptisms. Struggled through a long, drawn-out fourth lesson with the Belmón family, mostly trying to re-hack the Word of Wisdom. The mother seems barely willing to even try it, and although there's not much problem with the rest and they're all fine people, the rosy hues we at first perceived are beginning to turn a tad grey.

November 27

We've about run out of good tracting area close by. We did tract-out a couple where the wife is an indifferent Catholic and the husband an agnostic and avowed Catholic despiser. They seemed nice enough people and were interested, so we gave them a first lesson. My companion took the last half and prolonged us an extra forty-five minutes with needless explanations. He still lacks discipline and experience in controlling the lesson so that he's in charge and not the investigator.

Bussed out to Santa Cruz and gave a well-done first lesson to the husband and little daughter of the Balboa woman. They're living with some relatives, and just after we had finished the lesson in a small side room, the señor of the house came in roaring drunk. Learning of our presence, he shouted outside the door that we couldn't escape, and that he would kill us all with his machete. We waited a few minutes for him to calm down, walked out of the bedroom where we had conducted the *plática,* said goodbye to the family, including the snockered-up old señor, and left.

November 28

I left early this morning to pick up a family (the Quinteros) for church. We tracted them out some time ago but have never taught them because the mother works about twelve hours a day. They surprised me by being ready, and they seemed to enjoy Sunday school a great deal. After services we gave a second lesson to the Balboa man and his daughter in one of the classrooms—almost like re-teaching members, since they already knew a lot about the church. We also gave a first lesson in the afternoon to the Campos family. A very "moosey" [mission slang for an attractive, flirtatious girl] daughter made it fairly hard to concentrate on things spiritual, but we managed all right and the lesson was pretty good. This day was especially enjoyable because of the good people—many of whom I have helped bring into the church—whom I had a chance to see and converse with at the *capilla*.

November 29

Had a dinky district class this morning that was soon adjourned in favor of a football practice. We're supposed to play Roma and Ermita this Saturday. Elder Cardon and my old companion Elder Haney from Guad (who has become mission secretary—he seems to prefer desk work much more to knocking on doors) stopped by and stayed to play. Cardon, an ex-quarter-back from his high school days, winged me some good passes in a short but fun contest.

We got waylaid at the Pierdánts' for a couple of hours waiting for the *hermana*'s sister to show up for a *plática*. The sister never did make it and it's evident that the Pierdánts wouldn't mind having us over more often. Could be that Alícia Pierdánt is after my companion. And speaking of plots, I am not unaware of a quiet campaign being waged at me by the Guerros on behalf of their oldest daughter, Consuelo.

Good news at the Belmóns'. The coffee problem appears to be nearly vanquished and a general enthusiasm about membership in the church pervades the whole family. The *hermana* had a little experience Sunday night that she considers a sign of sorts. She was retiring to bed and in the darkness, on her dresser where she usually keeps a small lamp or candle, were two perfectly formed stars—a small one above a larger one—that lit up the corner of the room with their brilliance. She called in her two sons and they also saw the stars, but when she turned on the lights, nothing was there.

November 30

Spent a lot of the day tracting, accompanied by my companion's and my Christmas caroling as we went along. While at Mutual tonight Hermano Guerro informed us that his oldest son (Guillermo) and his wife would like to talk with us at the Guerro house, so we went over and found out that they would both like to be baptized this coming month. November hasn't been as statistically good a month as I had planned, but then I'm becoming less and less impressed with statistics. We brought some good people into the church and that counts for a lot of satisfaction. A smaller number of quality converts should rack up as many gold stars as pushing a whole tribe of Indians into the pond, only to have them all head for the hills again after their baptisms. Another observation along these same lines: Many of us who have spent most of our time in Mexico City have accumulated some fairly impressive baptism totals compared to the guys stationed out in the *pueblitos* [small towns]. But certainly their worth as missionaries is not measured by mere numbers. I'm grateful for the many fine people I've been privileged to see come into the church, but at the same time I also envy Gord for the vast experience and growth he has gained from working out in the countryside, where adversity stokes a much hotter refiner's fire.

December 1

At last we were able to have a sixth lesson with Carmen Grovas. Her mother and her two friends—Berta and Lília—were also present. Carmen wants to be baptized this Saturday. The rest of them are willing but want to wait. However, I'm happy enough with Carmen's decision. All the extra time we've spent with her has proven worthwhile.

December 2

Followed a long morning's tracting with a trip out to Santa Cruz to teach a third lesson to the Balboas. They all claim bad health but seem chipper enough in the lessons. Another good lesson with the Belmóns in the evening—the fifth. Looks like they've completely conquered *café* [coffee] and are serenely contemplating baptism next week. One more hurdle to skim, however, with the old First and Second commandments. Their back rooms are plastered with *santos,* virgins, and other assorted religious gewgaws.

Tomorrow, bright and early, we go to the mission home for a conference and personal interview with President Theodor Tuttle of the First Council of Seventy.

December 3

Churubusco and Moctezuma districts spent the morning at the mission home. While President Tuttle individually interviewed each missionary in a small drawing room, the rest of us stayed in the living room and passed away the time by giving extemporaneous talks (pull a subject out of a hat procedure), and by having different sets of elders present parts of the discussions for criticisms on technique. My own interview with President Tuttle was not very searching—more of a pleasant little chat. President Tuttle is a warm, friendly man and we talked about my pre-mission activities, Gord, school, career plans, and even touched a little on missionary work: Do my companion and I get along? Are we working hard and enjoying our work? etc. I asked him just exactly what our responsibility is when people accept baptism but we can see that they are not really good membership material and are likely to become inactive. Although I feel that one of the greatest problems facing the mission is the large percentage of inactivity and falling away among new members, President Tuttle said to go ahead when people express desires to be baptized on the theory that it will be much easier to work with and help them once they are within the church as members.

After our interviews we traveled back to the district to fill out baptismal papers for Carmen Grovas. But she informed us that her declaration of wanting to be baptized this Saturday was only to impress Berta and Lília. We talked about the situation for awhile, and she promised unconditionally for next Saturday. I asked her to sing for us before we left, which she did, and, indeed, she has a beautiful voice—a mezzo soprano, if my musically untutored ear does not deceive. Finally, we dropped by the Guerros' to visit with Guillermo and his wife, reviewing much that they have already heard and explaining that which they haven't been exposed to in an improvised combination of the third through sixth lessons. I still want to go over the first principles of the gospel a little harder with them, emphasizing fé, arrepentimiento, bautismo y el Espíritu Santo [faith, repentance, baptism and the Holy Ghost]. I'd like Elder Merkley to be present for their baptisms, if possible, so I'm waiting to talk with him before setting the date.

December 4

Our anticipated football game with Roma and Ermita districts was aborted, as was a last-minute attempt to play against Moctezuma. Just as well. It rained all morning and the temperature wasn't exactly tropical. I felt it was a propitious time to address some Christmas cards and take care of some backlog letters, so we didn't stir out of the apartment until afternoon. Later we wanted a showdown with the Paras but the *hermano* was unable to get off work, so we watched a little TV and talked to the *hermana* for awhile. She's really a remarkable person. Just a few years ago she was a prime candidate for a berth on the Mexican Olympic team in gymnastics, but her husband opposed.

December 5

Had a frank little talk with the Paras. It's not going to work. In spite of their focus on more abstract questions during most of our sessions, it's really the basics (apostasy of the primitive church, prophetic calling of Joseph Smith, restoration of the gospel, etc.) that they can't accept. I'm very disappointed, but I still feel as though we've sown some fruitful seeds.

December 6

The continuation of conference this morning was prefaced by a highly amusing (but this time in good taste compared to past irreverencies) skit put on by Roma District and the mission home staff. As usual, the conference itself began with missionary testimonies in English. Then the rest of the time was filled by President Tuttle, who answered questions, lectured, exhorted, and bore testimony all afternoon. The conference finally drew to a close about 5:30 P.M., over *seven* hours in all. We gobbled down a couple of hamburgers, then grabbed a cab for visits with the Grovas family (supposed to talk with Laura, who didn't show up) and Hermano Quiróz and his wife (who must be one of the biggest stone-brain Protestants of all time).

December 7

The Belmóns fell tonight. We got half way through the sixth lesson when things started bogging down and it was soon apparent that they were not yet ready or willing to receive baptism. They're fine people, but old traditions usually die a slow, hard death, and they were honest enough to want a deeper-felt conviction before engaging in a good-faith embrace with the church. They cited the case of a young neighbor girl who was an active, enthusiastic Mormon. She always tried to interest her family in the church and accepted her religious obligations faithfully. But later, after marriage, she fell away, divorced her husband, took up smoking and drinking, and reentered Catholicism, bringing her children with her. The Belmóns say they want nothing like that to happen to them and wish to wait until they are sure it never could. They expressed a willingness to keep coming to church, so we'll just have to see what happens from here.

December 8

Went out to a little *rancho* with the Belmóns this afternoon for a wedding feast in honor of one of their relatives—humble surroundings, but a lot of good people enjoying themselves. We managed to wind up seated right at the head of the table, next to the bride, and ate well on turkey *mole,* rice, *refrescos,* bread, and roast pork. Appointment conflicts forced Silva and me to split up visits this evening. I went with Elder Kunz (who had no other pressing business of his own) to see Berta and Lília—they're on the brink of accepting baptism but have problems with family.

December 10

Highly enjoyed a *día de campo* today. Eight missionaries and about thirty members traveled to a picnic area halfway to Toluca. Just a pleasant feeling all day long being with close friends, former companions, and people I have helped bring into the church, including the Guerro and Pierdánt families. During the day, Elder Bayer mentioned that a movement is underfoot to make me Elder Merkley's replacement as *orientador* and companion with

Elder Bayer. I can't think of another elder in the mission I'd rather work with. Bayer is a top friend and top missionary. As *orientadores* we would be the equivalent of zone leaders in other missions. Our job would be to provide direction for all the missionaries in Mexico City, while finding and keeping our own investigators on the side.

December 11

I baptized Carmen Grovas this afternoon. Her friend Berta and my companion were the only others present to observe. Carmen was apprehensive and trembling, and the cold water scared her, but she was happy and contented afterward. After working so hard with Carmen it was especially pleasing to bring her into the waters of baptism. She is an attractive, energetic, and talented young woman.

December 12

Carmen Grovas invited us over for lunch after Sunday school, and we spent a pleasant time eating good food, taking pictures, and engaging in light conversation. Carmen is eager to become active in the ward and thinks she can help out the music program a lot. Also had a sixth lesson with the Balboas and, although I could have strangled the *hermana* for disanimating and criticizing her husband, we finally set next Saturday as their baptismal date.

December 13

Rumors were fulfilled today. This morning at district meeting Elder Peterson informed me that I will be taking Elder Merkley's place as *orientador* with Elder Bayer as my companion. I'm very happy about the move. I've always wanted to work with Elder Bayer, both because I regard him as one of my closest friends in the mission and because he is a very polished and effective missionary. I also know that I'm far away from deserving the position. *Quién sabe* [who knows] why I was chosen. I imagine Elders Merkley, Bayer, and Morrison all had more than a little to do with it by putting in good words for me at the mission home. But at any rate, here I am, and I know that the Lord will help me out if I can humble myself and try to be more worthy of his aid. I move Wednesday night and I'll be leaving some highly promising investigators behind. The important thing, of course, is for these people to become baptized, regardless of who does it. Elder Silva made a good companion for me, although there were also times when I felt like shaking him for his occasional cocky immaturity. But on the plus side, he's enthusiastic, ambitious, and helped to win a lot of good will among our investigators. If he can gain a little humility he should prove to be a very successful missionary.

December 15

Elder Silva and I worked hard yesterday, tracting and giving some lessons. But I spent today packing and saying goodbye to a lot of wonderful people whom I've come to know and care for greatly during the last seven months: the Guerros, Pierdánts, Duráns, Amadórs, Martinezes, Robledas, Grovases, Aguirres, Ibarras, and many others. The day passed by quickly, and then it was 10:30 P.M. and I was at the Roma apartment, where I snoozed on the floor waiting for Merkley and Bayer to return.

PART FIVE

Leadership

Introduction:
Leadership Consequences of LDS Missionary Activity

In addition to its manifest function of recruiting new members to the LDS faith, the mission field organization also constitutes a proving ground for the putative best of each new generation of Mormons. The winnowing effect of the mission mobility system does not just separate the most dedicated or able young missionaries from their less zealous comrades into positions of greater and lesser authority. By its comparative and evaluative nature the process also entails certain risks for all who undergo it. These risks are not primarily physical in nature, although physical danger is certainly a possibility that must be acknowledged, especially in foreign environments. Missionaries may contract serious illnesses, are injured through accidents and occasional assaults (all of which we experienced or observed during our own missionary tours in Mexico), and sometimes die.[1] But the more prevalent apprehensions for most Mormon youths in the mission field are cognitive, emotional, and social. Missionaries' identities, personal feelings of esteem and self-worth, and post-missionary lay careers in church callings are potentially at stake. That is implicitly understood by church officials, parents, and the missionaries themselves.

Encouraged by our family's missionary tradition, and mutually supportive of one another, we were highly motivated to become successful missionaries and, for the same reasons, were anxious not to fail. The LDS Church has taken steps to reduce some of the negative elements of achievement pressure and the competitive spirit—especially in the MTC phase—but still makes emphatic the severe personal and religious consequences, both objective (excommunication, disfellowship, and dishonorable release) and subjective (guilt and unhappiness), that may follow from serious deviations in the discharge of missionary obligations. In our missionary experience, we were to witness several cases of excommunication and more than a few cases of missionary guilt and depression. But the principal consequence of confronting challenges and risks in the field for most Mormon missionaries is the eventual adaptation to a sacrificial pattern of institutionally regulated duties and assignments.

Upon completion of their missions, thousands of young Mormons, seasoned by their field experience, annually return to their religious communities with at least strengthened religious convictions if not greatly increased zeal for committing their lives to the service of the LDS Church. It is not by coincidence that the majority of Mormonism's general authorities commence their ecclesiastical careers as successful missionaries. The administrative ranks of the LDS central bureaucracy, as well as leadership positions at all levels of local church organization, are stocked with returned missionaries (a point not lost on either of us or Steve London in reaction to President Hugh B. Brown's Mexico City conference address). Whatever their socioeconomic or national backgrounds might be, they share the organized experience of the missionary crusade. Each new cohort of returned missionaries constitutes a revitalizing pool of young adults—whose field experience has systematically exposed them to exercising religious callings through active participation in a corporate authority structure—from which the LDS Church replenishes its ranks of devoted followers and lay leaders.[2]

With roughly one-quarter of our missions left to complete, both of us—first Gary and then Gordon—were surprised (in spite of our partisan boosting of one another) by administrative assignments to serve as assistants to the president in our respective missions. Assistants to the president are supposed to be exemplary missionaries who have earned the respect of both their missionary peers and the mission president. Their task is to assist the president in planning, coordinating, and supervising proselyting efforts throughout the mission as a whole. In some respects, the role of assistant to the president is like that of a general staff officer in military organizations in contrast to the roles enacted by line officers in the field. Within military ranks the officer corps may be divided between those who aspire to staff positions and those who itch for a field command. In times of war it is common for some staff officers to become restless with bureaucratic duties and agitate for reassignment to field combat positions. To some extent, these same patterns of promotional aspiration, leadership preference, and status ambivalence had analogies in our missionary careers, especially once we were inducted into the administrative routines of the mission office.

In the Mexican missions during the 1960s, much of a mission president's time was encumbered with the administration of ecclesiastical affairs in branches and mission districts. With the mission president's attention divided between member problems and missionary concerns, the role of assistants, his representatives in dealing with other missionaries, was correspondingly increased. As assistants, we were trouble-shooters for the presidents, and we traveled widely throughout the mission to settle companion squabbles, convey new policies or proselyting strategies, welcome and orient newly arriving missionaries to the field, and explore the possibilities of opening new towns in the mission to proselyting.

More routinely, we also were responsible for publishing our missions' monthly periodicals (*El Clarín* and *El Faro*); recommending companion assignments, transfers, and missionary promotions; and organizing and speaking at missionary conferences. (Here again the mission organization is a microcosm of the larger ecclesiastical structure of the LDS Church. Periodic conferences and interviews with visiting authorities are a standard institutional practice worldwide for bolstering local morale, reorganizing personnel assignments, inaugurating new policies, and supervising the implementation of standardized church programs.) As assistants to the president, our most significant influence in the lives of other missionaries was undoubtedly through our recommendations concerning promotions, transfers, and companion assignments. The presidents made all final decisions but, at least in our experience, relied heavily on the reports and suggestions of their assistants.

By the time we became assistants in our respective missions, the regimented work ethic we had adopted as field missionaries was well ingrained in our self-conceptions of moral worth. We took our perceived responsibilities seriously yet also experienced a drop in esprit de corps as we attempted to adjust to staff and administrative duties. We sometimes felt sheepish about enjoying the "soft" life and living conditions of the mission office environment and the perquisites of transportation and travel, hotels, restaurants, and freedom from the routine structure of daily proselyting. But we also quickly learned to use the resources and influence connected to our positions to bend certain mission rules. For example, we arranged a semi-surreptitious reunion in San Martín and plotted our mission releases so we could spend time together in Mexico City and tour the country with our parents when they came down to pick us up.

Before becoming assistants to our mission presidents, we were promoted to supervisory positions in the field, which meant that we continued to be responsible for our investigators and proselyting areas while also assuming responsibility for monitoring the efforts of other missionaries in the districts or zones to which we were assigned. Gary bypassed the usual mobility step of supervising elder (or district leader) to become an *orientador* in Mexico City. After working several months in Tuxtla Gutiérrez as supervising elder, Gordon was transferred to become supervising elder of the Puebla District. Subsequently, Gary's tenure as an assistant to the president was segmented by an intervening assignment to open Manzanillo—a small port town on the Pacific Coast—to Mormon proselyting, as Gordon had done earlier in Villa Flores. Gordon was to spend his last five months in Mexico working as an assistant to the president out of his mission's headquarters in Veracruz.

NOTES

1. On several occasions in the late 1980s LDS missionaries were singled out as convenient targets for assassination by nationalist, anti-American terrorist groups in Latin America who associated Mormon proselyting with American imperialism and even as a front for CIA operations. Consequently, Mormon authorities withdrew all North American missionaries from Bolivia and Peru, leaving its missions in those countries to be staffed by a local force (Knowlton 1989, 1992).

2. The missionary experience is neither a necessary nor a sufficient condition for continuing adult activity in the LDS Church. Many individuals who do not serve LDS missions go on to participate in the lay structure of church organization, whereas a certain fraction of LDS missionaries—for a variety of reasons—become ambivalent, alienated, or indifferent and abandon their previous religious commitments. Some studies have estimated the inactivity (or dropout) rate of returned LDS missionaries in the United States to be about 10 percent (Madsen 1977). More recent figures have not been published, and, to our knowledge, the inactivity rates of returned LDS local missionaries in Mexico and other countries have never systematically been studied.

∾

12

"Knocking on Doors for Nine and Ten Hours a Day": Gary's Story as Orientador in Tacuba Roma, Mexico City

From this point forward, Gary was to be teamed almost exclusively with other motivated and successful veteran missionaries with whom, with rare exception, he was able to work harmoniously for the remainder of his time in Mexico. As *orientadores,* Gary's and his companion's own proselyting efforts were integrated into a schedule of regular supervisory visits with other missionaries throughout Mexico City. One such visit resulted in another strange episode that was perceived as an expression of supernatural forces opposing LDS missionary efforts. On another supervising excursion, Gary and his companion were the objects of an attempt by a gang of teenagers to do them physical harm.

Gary's journal accounts of other missionaries reveal a range of talent and dedication from those whose efforts he greatly admired and praised to others whose apparent lack of sincerity or commitment provoked criticism. He and his companion assumed responsibility for organizing district conferences, preparing instructional speeches at supervisors' meetings, and contributing editorial articles to the mission periodical. As was the case in his previous location, it was necessary for Gary to start from scratch in developing an investigator pool. Consequently, he and his companion spent long, arduous days tracting the urban neighborhoods of the city and seeking people willing to listen to them. Again (in contrast to Gordon's comparable exertions in the generally less receptive towns of southern Mexico) their persistence eventually began to pay dividends as they attracted a number of promising convert families with whom to work. Gary also maintained close contact with previous converts, including the Guerro family, whose new religious faith and activity in their local Mormon ward had never wavered. With re-

gard to Mexico City wards, Gary's occasional contact with local ecclesiastical officials stimulated both praise and criticism of their leadership. After two
short months in his role as *orientador,* Gary received another surprise promotion: to the mission home as an assistant to the president.

In Tuxtla, Gordon's emotionally troubled junior companion sank into
ever-deeper despondency until he received a transfer and promotion to co-
senior, which temporarily brightened his spirits. A short time later, Gordon
also received a transfer and moved back to Puebla as the supervising elder
in that city. Before that, at a supervisors' conference in Veracruz at Christmas, Gordon reestablished contact with Steve London, Gary's old LTM companion, whom Gordon had not seen since their arrival in Mexico as novice
missionaries.

Mexico City, December 16, 1965

First day in my new role as *orientador* and also farewell day for Elders Merkley and Morrison—a couple of the best missionaries and friends that I've ever
known. There was a packed house at the mission home to see them off.
Emotions ran high and I felt a little foolish in joining the boo-hooing, but
couldn't seem to help myself. My feelings and respect toward Elder Merkley
approach brotherhood and Elder Morrison isn't far behind. Elder Bayer and
I tracted the afternoon away without finding much, then went out to the
airport to see Merkley and Morrison off. A lot of people were there, along
with President McClellan and the rest of the mission office staff.

December 17

Worked pretty hard all day, about eight hours' worth of tracting. Didn't find
much. In fact Elders Bayer and Merkley hadn't been able to locate much of
anything during the last month or so and we're destitute of visits. There will
be a lot of door-pounding ahead to rescue January. Tomorrow is supervisors'
meeting, and presidential assistants Peterson and Cardon will be gone, so Elder Bayer and I are supposed to take charge. Bayer will convene the elders and
I'm to say a few words to the lady missionaries at their separate meeting.

December 18

I blurbled out a few unprepared remarks to the lady missionaries this morning at the mission home, then retreated back to the supervising elders' meeting in the president's office. We planned a Christmas party for the city missionaries and the president bawled us out, more or less, for going over to the

airport Thursday. He wants to calm down the *relevos* so they don't waste so much time. But hey, the biggest news of the day is that Elder Bayer will be the new assistant to the president when Elder Peterson goes home next Monday. He's the obvious, most capable, missionary for the job. Elder Bayer and I have always wanted to work together as companions but it looks like four days is all we get. We'll still work pretty closely together, though. My new companion as *orientador* will be Elder Doyle Judd—lifted out of Colima, where he's been doing an outstanding job in a real difficult place.

December 19

A take-it-easy-day. Elder Bayer packed and took care of some other last minute matters. Dave Manookin, an old friend from high school days and just released from Gord's mission, came to Sunday school this morning. Dave previously had dropped by Friday at noontime, and we had a pleasant conversation then and also this morning. There is always an element of unreality when we run into someone down here whom we knew well in our premissionary days. Anyway, Dave had the usual good things to say about Gord's reputation in the South. Seems to think Gord will wind up as assistant to the prez. It was a little exasperating that Manookin had just talked to Gord a couple of days ago while it will be another seven or eight months before I get the same chance. I'm still counting on us spending some missionary companion time together here in the City next August prior to our own releases.

December 20

Packed Elder Bayer up to the mission home, then stayed for Elder Peterson's *relevo,* whom Bayer is replacing as assistant. Afterward, I met with Elder Cardon and Bayer and with my new companion, Elder Judd, to go over some of our duties and also to plan for the supervising elders' conference next week. My companion and I will have to deliver talks. It also looks like the mission home is delegating us more responsibility generally as *orientadores.* Elder Judd and I haven't really had a chance to get acquainted yet, but the grapevine says he's very good. I like his looks: tall, rawboned, and sincere, with a gentle sense of humor. This afternoon he and I traveled over to Churubusco to make arrangements for Guermo Guerro and his wife to be baptized.

December 21

I gave a little talk this morning in district class, relating the meaning of Christmas to missionary work. We went on to tract hard all morning, then all afternoon. Set several visits, but we're still hurting pretty badly for investigators. Elder Judd is from Coalville, Utah, was student body president of his high school, was on a scholarship at BYU, and ran some for the track team. He's a fine person and dedicated missionary. We're already good friends. Arrived home a little after 8:00 P.M. to begin work on our conference talks.

December 22

A long, hard day of tracting, with little result. We're into a richer area of town now and running into a lot of Jews, who automatically seem disinterested in anything smacking of Christianity. Traveled over a fair hunk of our new district looking for a couple of reference visits in the evening. We did manage a first lesson with a middle-aged couple (the Romeros), who have had quite a bit of previous contact with the *Testigos*. The woman accepted well, but the man resisted the baptismal commitment.

December 23

We're knocking on doors for nine and ten hours a day with no success. Christmas makes it hard to find people home, and when they are in they're too busy with parties and all the other holiday distractions. Presented a second lesson to the Romeros, spiced with innumerable interruptions.

December 24

The day before Christmas and we tracted hard all morning with the same results: found nothing. During lunch hour I dipped into the extra holiday funds Mom and Dad sent this month and purchased a 340 peso [$27] suit. It's not exactly nineteenth-century black broadcloth, but it is pretty sober. I was beginning to look a little bum-ish. That blankety-blank grey suit from English Tailors in Salt Lake City was hanging in tatters at wrist and ankle, with both cheeks patched. Same with the old blue job from high school. Also bought a new pair of shoes.

Traveled over to Churubusco in the afternoon to smooth over details on baptism with Guermo and his wife and—surprise—we'll do it tomorrow, the last official baptismal day for December and a worthy way to celebrate Christmas Day. We also stopped by for a few minutes at the Robledas', with whom we'll eat dinner tomorrow afternoon, and the Pierdánts', who wanted us to be with them tonight.

Finally, we made our way back to the mission home. Enjoyed a quiet, simple, very warm little party. Sang some Christmas carols, heard some readings, broke some piñatas in the back yard, and finished with a light snack. A better feeling could not have prevailed, and we all enjoyed a very pleasant Christmas Eve. We extended the occasion by arranging for Elders Bayer and Cardon to drive us back out to the Guerros' around 11:30 P.M. for dinner.

Again, a good spirit was present after the opening of presents; we even received a couple ourselves. For me, some after-shaving lotion and talcum from Hermano and Hermana Guerro, and a bottle of men's cologne (yikes!) from Consuelo. I do believe she's the prettiest girl I've seen during my whole mission—maybe even anywhere, anytime.

December 25

Christmas Day dawned for us about 7:30 this morning. It proved to be a good day, and I even felt a little Christmasy this year. We baptized Guermo Guerro and his wife in a simple service attended by the rest of the Guerro family. The family is now complete within the church and they were all happy. We enjoyed a big, arduously prepared Christmas dinner with the Robleda family. Elder Silva and Doug Peterson were also there. Again, the best of feelings prevailed and the *hermana* sang several songs for us before we left.

December 26

We're beginning a fast for the conference tomorrow and it will be hard, since we really haven't had anything to eat since yesterday afternoon at the Robledas'. We won't be eating again until tomorrow afternoon after the supervisors' conference.

December 27

The conference of supervisors began at 8:00 this morning and lasted until about 1:30 this afternoon. Perhaps some of the talks were unnecessarily long (mine must have been the shortest—about ten minutes), and some confusion reigned on a new method of filling out supervisor reports, but on the whole the conference proved excellent for reevaluating fundamental purposes and instilling a renewed desire to better comply with responsibilities. The new mission program is a good one because it puts more emphasis on personal effort rather than on often misleading statistics. Numbers (competition for most baptisms, most proselyting hours, etc.) won't be as important as just doing what a missionary is supposed to do (dedicated consistency, effective teaching, etc.). The president's main message was to stay away from mere socializing with members as much as possible, spending that time instead to find new contacts. My own assigned speech dealt with the temporal or tangible duties of supervising elders: reports, district classes, etc. Not thrilling subject matter but I worked hard to prepare it and did a fair job of presentation. Best of the addresses, however, was Elder Garza's effort on the hard job of staying consistently committed to our work. When the speech-making finally ceased, we sat down to the mission home table and wolfed down the largest meal I've eaten since being in Mexico: huge steaks, mashed potatoes and gravy, salad, hot rolls, and chocolate cake. (A good thing too, since we were all starting to experience advanced symptoms of starvation from our fast.)

December 28

Gave a whole flock of tract-out lessons today while pounding on doors—four visits in a little over two hours during one stretch, and six altogether by day's end. We found the Miranda woman home and gave her a good second lesson (she's angry at her husband and they try to avoid being in the house at the same time). We also dropped off a third lesson with two members of the Romero family who weren't present at our last session. Most of the rest of the family gathered around anyway to hear it again. And a good thing they did. None of them are trying very hard to observe the Word of Wisdom, and they all have got a long way to go toward anything like baptism. A welcome letter from Gord contributed to my sense of a good day. Gordon's reported get-together with Elders London and Booth twinged me with envy. London's apparent level of admiration for us is a little embarrassing—it would be nice to be as good as he seems to think we are.

LETTER FROM GORDON

Gar: I'm penning this from Júchitan, Oaxaca. I'm sitting in a bus station waiting for the next bus to Tuxtla, which isn't scheduled until after midnight. I'm on my way home from a supervising elders' conference that was held at mission headquarters in Veracruz. All the nauseating symptoms of having run a 440-yard dash at full-tilt are gradually vacating my bod (despicable expression). I lugged my suitcase on a dead run all the way across town from the second-class bus station to the fancier Cristobal Colón. I couldn't drum up too much enthusiasm for continuing the tortuous trek on that other broken-down line. But mainly, I just missed their last bus out of town by fifteen minutes and was worried (mistakenly) that the same thing would happen at the Cristobal Colón station if I didn't hurry.

I wonder if things will ever filter back down to normal again? Upon returning to Tuxtla there's still the holiday madness to face, with branch and district fiestas. I got your rather *feísima* [exceptionally ugly] Christmas card just before I left for Veracruz at the beginning of the week. The *notícias* [news] of your promotion to *orientador,* however, were exhilarating. Way to go! It's about time your mission leaders saw the light.

I don't know if the Veracruz conference accomplished any great things but I must confess that it was a rather welcome break. I spoke, as did all the other supervisors. Most of the talks were mediocre, including mine. For some strange reason there was a noticeable pall of nervousness hanging over the meeting and most everybody arose with their knee bones knocking when it was their turn to speak (maybe because a lot of us are relatively new to the position). I conquered this old childhood feeling of dread before standing but it turned out that I didn't have much to say anyway.

Booth, London, and I got together for the first time since we parted ways sixteen months ago. Booth has just been made a supervising elder and, as I suppose you know, London has latched onto a mission home staff position as the president's personal secretary. I know that after such a period of time in the mission field many changes and shifts may be wrought in a person's outlook and philosophy but, for the most part, personalities and personal characteristics seem to persist. London was still the same old London of LTM days and Booth was still the same old Booth. It was great to be with them again. (Speaking of reunions with old friends, I spent a day with Dave Manookin in Tuxtla, just before he finished his mission. He stayed the night and I woke up about 3:00 in the morning to ask myself: What in the name of reason am I doing sleeping in the same room as Dave Manookin in the year 1965 in this far-flung and forgotten spot of the world in the Sierra Madre Mountains of Mexico?)

As late as my bus to Tuxtla promises to be, I'll probably still get more sleep tonight than last. I spent most of last night with London on the balcony of the missionaries' apartment in downtown Veracruz and we engaged in a talk-a-thon that endured until 5:00 in the morning. He was hungry to compare notes and we covered a million subjects. If Steve hasn't exactly kindled his spiritual fire to a white heat, he at least seems to have distinguished the iron rod and grabbed on to it [a Book of Mormon metaphor for religious obedience], and is working well in the mission office. The high esteem in which he seems to hold us is a little embarrassing. He especially thinks a great deal of you. I read some of the letters you wrote to him. He really prizes them.

Meanwhile, at the home camp in Tuxtla with my incendiary companion Elder Granger, fires have smoldered and even ignited in several anticlimactic puffs, but the BIG explosion, which I keep anticipating, has failed to go off yet. In fact the last week or so has been fairly pleasant (calm before the storm?). Maybe that's not entirely fair. Since a couple of slightly ugly incidents passed by a few weeks ago, Elder Granger has been behaving pretty well lately. There was a stretch there, however, when I just about didn't hack it. I came very close to writing the president. The worst incident was a blowup between Granger and our maid (who is undoubtedly the best in the mission). He'd been carping at her for some time over incredibly petty things, and finally began wildly accusing her of spying on him and violating his privacy (she unwittingly entered a room to put away the laundry and saw Elder Granger in his garments). The maid was mortified but scarcely guilty of any great crime. She was going to quit but thought better of it after I talked to her and she had a chance to calm down. The spirit of darkness reigned in the house for several days. Granger wouldn't leave for work and then, once out, he played deaf and dumb, refusing to give his part of the lessons. I was on the verge of blowing my own stack but didn't. It passed and he seems to have done a little thinking and settling down. I hope. I feel both anger and sympathy for Elder Granger. I'm trying to be as patient and as understanding as I can. But I have no training as a mental counselor, which is what I think Granger needs, and our missionary work has suffered greatly. *Quién sabe* what I'll go home to now? I've still got all kinds of time before the next bus comes along and a lot of things I wanted to tell you about but I'm truly shot and becoming incoherent. Man, this is going to be a long week.

Your brother, Gord

December 29

Judd and I finished up our joint article for the *Clarín* [the mission periodical] this morning. I wrote the first half, Elder Judd the second, then we stitched both parts together with a couple of rhetorical threads to achieve an illusion of coherence. Engaged in more heavy tracting throughout the day but this time we didn't get past a single door. Did give a couple of first lessons to previous finds, one to an intelligent school teacher (Veda), who went along with everything (perhaps just to see what we were leading up to).

December 31

I'm twenty-two years old today. We celebrated the occasion by working straight through until evening—mostly beating on doors tracting, interspersed with getting stood up on scheduled visits. These are difficult days for us to catch people at home. As soon as the holiday fogs settle down we'll be able to weed out our prospects. We started a second lesson with the Veda lady but only got as far as her declaration that she would never stop worshipping the Virgin. This one damnable doctrine binds more people in ignorance and has cost me more investigators than any other single factor during my time in Mexico. We came home about 7:00 P.M., my companion bought me a little birthday cake, I bought some ice cream, and we reflected a bit on our past, present, and future lives while eating. Greeted the New Year sound asleep in bed.

January 1, 1966

New Year's day found me directing the weekly supervisors' meeting this morning. We didn't deal with any special problems, just routine matters. Prospects for success in all the city districts this month look fair so far. Elder Judd and I flipped to see who would be traveling next week to make our supervising visits, and it looks like I'll go while Elder Judd stays at home to tend our own investigators.

January 2

A good day—almost fourteen hours' worth of effective work. About fifteen investigators showed up for Sunday school. We had the Quintero family bring the Romeros, which worked very well. But an irreverent fourth lesson with the Romeros after their return from church showed that most of them are still way off course. The Word of Wisdom is one of their problems. Checked up on an *evangélica* family (the Bautistas) whom we had previously tracted-out, and before we knew it we were sitting at their table eating a dinner of chicken, tossed salad and flan. Most of the children weren't home but a teenaged girl was (quite cute, I might add) and she unleashed a steady stream of chatter and amusing comments. When we left she accompanied us down the narrow stairs and grabbed Elder Judd's hand so he wouldn't stumble. He turned pink but didn't take his hand away. On to a quick second lesson with the Reyes. The husband is becoming more animated all the time and the pigpen they live in had even seen some efforts to tidy up. We finally found the Redorta family home, minus the papa. His absence, however, was filled in by several visiting relatives, including a liquored-up uncle who kept interrupting the lesson with noisy exclamations until finally Elder Judd had to take him into another room while I finished the first half of the *plática*. Aside from that, however, the rest of the family accepted everything quite well.

January 4

Turns out my first "orienting" visit was right back to my just recently departed Churubusco District. I worked with Elder Doug Peterson, who replaced me as senior companion to Elder Silva, and we put in a lot of tracting. In fact, we didn't give any lessons during my two-day stay. Those that Peterson had scheduled all fell through, so there was nothing else to do but knock on doors.

What happened to all the promising investigators I left to Peterson just three weeks ago?

January 5

Back to Roma to find that things have been going pretty well in my absence. We baptized Hermana Miranda in the afternoon. I interviewed her and Elder Judd put her in the water. A pretty good old gal. We gave three good lessons throughout the day: a second to Hermana Ercambrac and her son, a first to a promising family called Ágila (although the señor is an unstoppable windbag when he gets going), and a good second to the Redorta family, who are moving right along without any problems yet. Another thirteen-hour work day.

January 7

I've spent the last two days working with Elder R. D. Smith, supervisor of El Distrito Industrial. Elder Smith is a capable missionary and understands well his role as a teacher. Visits were scarce, however. We gave an aborted first lesson that we had to close off at the halfway mark because of the chaos being generated by five fiendish little children. Thursday night we waited at the chapel for some of Elder Smith's investigators who were supposed to be baptized, but after they finally arrived and were interviewed, Elder Smith uncovered some doubts and thought it best to wait awhile. Today was cold and rainy all afternoon and evening but we stuck it out, tracting most of the day. Elder Smith goes home in three weeks but is still working hard. We had several good conversations, with reflections on missionary work and how to do it better. I admired him for not pushing forward with last night's baptisms when he sensed they were not truly ready. My presence and the looming last days of his mission might have been arguments to do otherwise, but he didn't succumb.

January 8

Good days for lessons—a third with Hermana Ercambrac and her son, a second with the large Ágila family, and another first with a couple of frisky *jóvenes,* Santiago and Carmen.

Finally heard from Chuck today after a prolonged period of silence. His words are both offending and flattering and, ultimately, depressing.

LETTER FROM CHUCK RADLOW TO GARY

Dear Gary,

I can't believe how insane I'm driven by the letter writing enterprise. I want you to understand what's going on in my life and I feel an intense desire to somehow communicate it to you. Every once in a while I feel as though you should in some way know without being told these things. I can always sort of picture what and how you are doing. I find myself postulating at times in the middle of a walk or ride to class what Gary is doing at the present time, and it isn't too hard to create some kind of plausible context that you'd be moving in. After all there aren't too many things a missionary can do—especially the orthodox variety I take you to be. So you see, you have always been so constant and stable about these things that I've come to expect that you have the same understanding of what I'm like that I feel and have of you. So as I move from place to place and feeling to feeling, from despair to euphoria and back again to despair, there is a hidden assumption inside that you already know what's going on.

Enough of this prattle. So you want to hear the mundane details of my shaggy existence. I am at present in my utopian fraternity house after attending a lecture at the Union entitled "What Is God Like?" The question was far from answered tonight. About all that was said was that nothing could really be said, so I am left with the conclusion that the word "God" is an empty nonsense word devoid of any practical significance or meaning whatsoever. Seems that we might as well talk about glurg or schnarz.

My main concern of the last two days has been reconciling myself to the probable two years that I will spend in the army if things in Vietnam continue in their present direction. I suppose I have also been trying to convince myself that this horrible fate will never occur but secretly realize that it surely will. Well, I shall be a *good* killer. I am weary of the rat race around here at this moment—would like to escape from my books somewhere and close all people out. Or perhaps I would like to escape from my books and close all people in. My life seems to be a rerun of everything else that has happened to me in the past, except this time I have the lines all memorized and can anticipate the next movement and the end of the scene. I'll have to admit that it makes it tiresomely boring sometimes. But then I don't really mean this either. After all, the Great Sea Puss gets us all in the end.

I am playing business manager of the *Quad* [the Stanford University student annual]. It is hateful work, and I spend far too much time at it. I am thoroughly repulsed with the business world and dirty little men acting like the gods of Olympus in their stinking stupid empires built of greasy dollar bills. I think it's all a big joke on us and our inability to focus on what is truly valuable. What a joke this campus is. I see the great abnegators: those who have sacrificed the frail values of our decrepit civilization to wander around unwashed, unkempt, and uttering such a deal of stinking breath that it quite nauseates me. Oh but I love my neighbor, no matter the foolishness of his actions. We are all a fairly foolish mob. We put these rules down around as to how to act and react and feel and relate, and it's all too far away from our ability to act honestly and with a degree of integrity. I don't really believe this in most cases but I have met a few and it's pretty disgusting. I am sure that the world is basically good but I am also convinced that we are failing miserably in our stewardship in the long-range view. I feel in control of myself and the way that I feel. I am not in control of my fate in the external sense but no one can ever reach inside and change my basic feelings.

I appreciated your letter in the middle of my religious crisis this summer. And I am a dirty rat for not thanking you while the feeling of gratitude was still simmering. I read it to several people, so it has helped many. You are a wise person, Gary. Wiser and calmer than I shall ever be. I guess I am back in the fold. I am teaching Sunday school, but I haven't felt too close to God or the old religious symbols lately. I have a terrible feeling that it's the sin of pride in myself. It's the greatest sin and my largest fault. There are times when I feel my complete smallness in the face of events and an utter finitude and inability to face up to the problems of my existence. Goddamn these words. They get in the way of what I want to say. They are ugly, guttural symbols of what I want to say to you in my heart. I cannot put myself in a better frame of mind, however, in an artificial way, so you are doomed to ferret out the meaning of this trash. Absolute trash.

I am applying to graduate schools of education. I might go on a mission if I can get in a halfway religious mood. I'm a rat Gary. I can't communicate to you in letters or scribbled words. It is unnerving to me. Please have patience with me. I don't deserve it but I am eager to hear of your experiences.

As ever, Chuck

January 9

The Redorta family is really looking good. They all enjoyed Sunday school and a second lesson with them later in the afternoon was well received. Bishop Kaín had a brief conference with the Roma missionaries after morning services to assure us of his—and the ward's—desires to help us in our work. He's an excellent leader. We're working hard and receiving many blessings. There are times when I don't feel very worthy, but someone seems to be overlooking my weaknesses and I'm grateful. Elder Judd is one of the best around for sincerity and desires to serve the Lord.

January 11

Just completed two days working with Elder James Hill here in Roma, while my companion went over to Tacubaya to work with Elder Bronson. Bronson has somehow let himself become disanimated and is now merely co-senior. He and Elder Hill haven't been getting along very well, so we have recommended a companion change, which should be effected shortly.

Meanwhile, our own visits have given me both high hopes and some disappointments. We had a beautiful third lesson with the Redorta family on Monday night. That special spirit that people manifest when they are going to be baptized was present. We started what looked to be a great first lesson with a family called Chacón, but then hordes of relatives descended so we packed up the flannel board and will try again another day. This morning we had one of the best-answered fifth lessons I've ever delivered, with the Reyeses, and if the *hermana*'s pregnant condition permits they will be baptized this Saturday. We found a tract-out family at home (the Reynas) and gave what would have been a fair first lesson had it not been for the woman's three teenaged daughters all distractingly breast-feeding their wailing babies at different intervals throughout the lesson. A rough third with Ágilas—it's hard to control the father's love of windbaginess, besides his balking on a baptismal commitment.

January 12

We checked on people this morning who haven't previously been home. Discovered a messy problem with the *evangélica* woman (Bautista). A number of years ago she ran off with another man, leaving her husband and children. She's had one child by this man since, but no longer lives with him. She says she wants to be baptized but wants to remedy her personal situation first. Presented a second lesson with the Perez family that was measurably slowed down by the presence of some friends who hadn't heard the first lesson. The señora was telling us about an *espiritista* [spiritualist] religion called La Nueva Vida [the New Life] that features the "Maestro Divino" [Divine Teacher], who is really supposed to be Jesus Christ possessing the bodies of certain individuals and speaking through them. I would have laughed but Señora Perez probably believes this stuff.

We showed the film to the Reyeses and then to the Ágilas, where the *hermano* started blathering again without particular focus. He hasn't done much about the Word of Wisdom and still resists taking a stand on baptism. He's a nice guy (and his family is nice, too), but I'm beginning to wonder a little about his sincerity. Passed by the Romeros to talk things over but hardly anyone was there. Hermano Lemos and his wife were, however, and they were the ones in whom we had highest hopes. No longer though. They accept most things we've taught but won't curtail their devotion to the Virgin.

January 14

Yesterday, Elder Moser came over to work with me while Elder Judd went over to Moctezuma to work with Elder Goodmanson. A goof-off spirit is on the loose in the Moctezuma District. Some companion changes will be due. Elder Moser is probably one of the prime offenders there. He sure doesn't appeal to me much with his bluff, phony manner. He strikes me as lazy and prone to bask in the glory of his father, a prominent attorney and *politico* [politician] back in Salt Lake City. Secretly, he was taking a lot of time off from missionary work in order to indulge in flying lessons (!) at the Mexico City Airport, until President McClellan found out about it. He had hoped to convince the president that the mission should invest in a light plane to save traveling time for the mission home staff. Naturally, Elder Moser would be the pilot.

I gave the sixth lesson by myself to the Reyeses yesterday morning because Moser didn't get here on time. We'll baptize them Saturday. The Chacón family looks exceedingly promising after one full lesson and the Redortas are preparing themselves for baptism on next Tuesday. We had a little scare when Hermana Reyeses told us that her husband had gone off with a former drinking buddy, but he pulled through fine and nothing untoward happened.

January 15

I conducted the supervisors' meeting this morning at the mission home. The biggest part of the discussion dealt with the problem of so many missionaries leaving for home during the same period and the effect this drain has on the missionary work. President McClellan is greatly concerned about elders who stop working the last month or so, and his policy will probably be to send a missionary home early if there are indications that his last days will be spent partying. We also discussed the laxity problem that exists among the elders in Moctezuma. The president is not pleased.

We baptized the Reyeses later in the afternoon. They're humble people and were visibly happy. We were too. A crucial fourth lesson with the Águilas went surprisingly well. The *hermano* was quiet for once and now seems to be thinking seriously about baptism. My companion and I fell asleep going home late on the *tranvía* [trolley], traveling way out past our stop. We were awakened at an unfamiliar stop by a gang of punks on the platform who threw a rock the size of an Idaho potato that shattered the window where Elder Judd was sitting. Neither of us were cut, and in fact we didn't even wake up until other passengers began crowding around to gawk and see if we were hurt.

January 17

Traveled over to Tacubaya (Madero Ward) this morning to work with Dennis Smith, an all-around hero from Payson, Utah, where, in high school, he played first-string basketball, first-string QB in football, and held the BYU Invitational Track Meet record for several years in the javelin. He was also student body president and is a good student with a scholarship waiting for him right now at BYU. As a missionary he possesses great humility and a living testimony that motivates his work. He was just made senior and perhaps lacks just a little experience in handling his new role as effectively as he will later.

January 18

The Redortas' baptisms were today (the *hermana* and her two daughters). After waiting for an hour for the uncle to arrive (we didn't baptize him because of uncertain marital status), we performed one of the nicest services I've ever had a hand in. Elder Judd and I both gave good talks, he baptized, and I confirmed. A reverent, happy spirit was present during the entire procedure.

After the services were completed, a long-time member woman approached me with a rather grave personal problem. She's been submerged beneath a number of family and employment difficulties and, in a fit of recent depression, tried to take her own life by slashing her wrists (she showed me the still-fresh cuts). She asked me to give her a special blessing for spiritual comfort and strength in resisting a renewal of any such temptations. Just then Bishop Kaín walked in and I thought it more appropriate to go first to him with the problem, since she's a ward member. But he greatly surprised me by showing no sympathy and giving very little helpful counsel. My companion, myself, and Bishop Kaín then laid our hands upon her head to bless her, but the bishop's words were more reprimanding than comforting.

January 20

I'm working today and tomorrow with Elder McCranie, a convert from Texas who's a few years older than the rest of us. He's supervisor of Ermita, and we've been good friends since I've been in the mission. We tracted some, gave a couple of good lessons. Ate lunch with the Muñoz family. Olivia Muñoz is pretty pregnant (unmarried), but apparently is holding up fairly well under the circumstances. She wants to attend services at Roma until she has her baby in order to avoid the tongue-clucking of other members in the Ermita Ward.

I'm enjoying my stay with Elder McCranie. His Spanish still hurts in spots and he doesn't teach as well as many do, but he's constantly cheerful and the people love him for his kind heart.

January 21

Spent one of the worst nights of my life last night. At about 1:00 A.M. I was awakened by Elder McCranie's loud yelling from his room. It sounded like the baying of a hound on the hunt. Before I had fully regained my senses he crashed into my room and turned on the light. When he quieted down he told me that, from a deep sleep, he had been suddenly shocked awake by the most intense pain he had ever experienced. The pain was in his hand and felt as though he had grabbed a live electric wire and couldn't let go. Not knowing what was wrong, only knowing that he was being badly hurt, he sprang from his bed, ran and opened the outside door, then turned and ran back into my room, where the searing pain suddenly left him. We both retired again after talking for awhile, and I was in a semi-state of sleep when I was suddenly aware of a giant pressure forcing my entire body down into the bed. I wanted to shout and jump up but was held completely helpless for a number of seconds until, finally, a freezing chill coursed through my entire body and I lay free again in a cold sweat. Thinking that it had only been a nightmare, I attempted to sleep again. But not much later, when I once more hung at the halfway point between consciousness and sleep, I was again overpowered by that same dark force and was unable to move or cry out as pressure was exerted on me until the same cold chill swept me free and I lay drenched in sweat. At the same instant I heard Elder McCranie scream from the other room, so I leaped out of bed and went in with him. He was awake and said that he didn't know why he had shouted. After talking a minute we knelt to pray beside his bed in the midst of a tangible atmosphere of fear and depression. The rest of that long night was spent tossing and turning, with unpleasant dreams liberally sprinkled during periods of fitful dozing. We arose in the morning, not very refreshed but grateful for the sunlight.

January 22

The supervisors' meeting this morning was brief and routine. On the whole the mission is climbing back up the ladder towards a pretty good month for convert baptisms. After we adjourned, President McClellan called me into his office for a little talk and interview. His questions led me to believe that he's casting his net around for someone to become the new assistant when Elder Cardon leaves next week. He mentioned Elder Judd as a likely candidate, and I sincerely concurred on Elder Judd's fine qualities. I would truly feel inadequate for the job myself. Elder Keith Flake was already selected as one of the other new assistants, becoming Elder Garza's companion out in Guadalajara.

We went over to the Roma chapel, where Carmen Grovas's mother had requested that I baptize her. The *hermana* couldn't, because of stiffness, bend backwards in the water. So, to immerse her, we both knelt down in the *pila* and she went under face-forward with no problem. I also baptized the Reyes's little boy, Roberto. We finished off the evening with a good second lesson with our two *jóvenes* (Carmen and Santiago), followed by a faltering at the Ágilas'—a long but unproductive discussion with the *hermano*.

January 23

We had a big turnout of our investigators at Sunday school—about twenty of them. Elder Judd and I personally went by to pick up the Chacón family. Held a couple of lessons after morning services. Both the Bautistas and the Perezes look pretty certain for baptism next Wednesday. Visited briefly with investigators in the evening. Stopped by at the Bautistas' again, and the *hermana* had a tasty chicken dinner waiting for us. A good thing, too. We had barely eaten all day. Worked fourteen hours straight through.

January 24

Tracted all morning after a district missionary class in which Elder Judd and I gave instructions on how to give the first lesson more effectively. Dropped by the Ercambracs' to cross her off our list as an active investigator, but she melted us with the situation in which she finds herself, mostly due to a no-good, drunken-bum husband. Which reminds me: The Redortas are now having problems with their señor, who is being prodded along by a worthless, leeching brother into drunkenness and opposition to the church (previously, he had no objection to his wife and daughters' conversion). I often wonder why so many of the men down here seem so out of it. We also had a very happy fourth lesson with the Chacón family. All of them brim with intelligence and have firmly accepted their baptismal commitments.

Gordon's been changed again, to Puebla this time, which is just a mountain pass away from Mexico City. What would it take to get together while we're as close as this?

LETTER FROM GORDON

Gar: I started a letter to you well over a week ago. I seriously doubt that I'm any busier these days than in the past. I fear I'm just becoming less efficient with my time. I owe everybody letters and seem to have lost my touch for writing them.

To conclude the last episodes of the Tuxtla drama before I moved to Puebla: More and more, Elder Granger was becoming a missionary version of Dr. Jekyll and Mr. Hyde. Life with Granger was like playing in a yo-yo tournament, and we finally went spinning down to the end of our string. He declared that until he was made senior, he wasn't going to do anything. He blamed me for an admonitory letter from President Hatch, warning him to shape up, and then said he didn't like the way I smiled—it reminded him of his father (God forbid). He correctly read the anger I couldn't conceal in my face, and we had a tension-filled talk (during which he started to cry). The very next day Elder Granger received a telegram sending him to Oaxaca as a co-senior. And thus came the parting of the ways. Elder Granger moved his darkening shadow from Tuxtla the next day and was gone. From time to time I felt compassion and even fondness for Elder Granger in his more peaceful moments, but also literally trembled with anger at his childish shenanigans. I have genuine doubts about his emotional (and possibly mental) stability and grave concern for his future. I probably got along with him better than any of his previous companions and we were headed for disaster. (While packing, Granger told me he would miss me, that I had been his best companion. Heaven help him.)

As a replacement, they sent me the new up-and-coming goofy guy of the mission (Elder Sherlock)—a completely different sort than Elder Granger (daffy rather than violence-prone), but nonetheless exasperating. He woke me up his first night at 2:00 A.M. with the news that we had neglected to have our companion prayer before retiring. Sherlock has been in the mission three or four months, but didn't know any of the investigator lessons and could barely do the tract-out presentation. He's terrified of dogs (which was a problem because there are millions of them in Tuxtla that snapped at our heels whenever we walked down the street). He's obsessed with his camera and has tons of slides that he's taken everywhere he's been in Mexico. I told him to put away the camera until he learned the lessons from The Plan. I then began working with him on the discussions, and he progressed from not even being able to present the Joseph Smith story to handling reasonably well the first lesson. In addition to his lack of self-discipline, Sherlock's primary problem was a lack of self-confidence. Previous companions were apparently unwilling to trust him with investigators for fear he'd screw things up. But I told him he would be given a regular teaching role with material we rehearsed in our *clase de com-*

pañero, that he should present as much as he could to investigators, that I would cue him whenever he hit a rough spot, but that I would also let him keep carrying the ball instead of banishing him to the sidelines and taking over for him. I nodded assurance as long as he got things right, fed him a line when he forgot a point in the lesson, and fielded responses from investigators that stumped him. And by George, it worked. If I accomplish nothing else on my mission, at least I can say I helped Sherlock learn how to teach a missionary lesson.

I received my own change to Puebla a scant week and a half after Sherlock's arrival. As usual, left a bunch of prospective converts behind in Tuxtla that we were finally beginning to cultivate in spite of all the distractions. Well, after six months in the Chiapas wilds, returning to Puebla, the biggest city in our mission, offers its share of modern comforts and attractions (running hot water, dependable busses, etc). True, missionary work hasn't been overly productive as of yet. Tracting results have been about as profitable as mom trying to get us to root out dandelion weeds in the yard back home. Nevertheless, I've experienced some of the most stimulating work of my mission. For one thing, I've got a darn good junior companion this time, by the name of Dale Smith. For another thing, we're not talking to illiterate Indians here but to a more highly educated class of people who constantly challenge us left and right. Our present list of investigators includes several medical students who are attending the University of Puebla.

I haven't spent too much time thinking about it but I still see law in the crystal ball. The only hurdle to school for us when we return home will be finances. We won't have any savings and neither will the folks. Teaching Spanish to new missionaries at BYU might do the trick for us financially for a term or two. Don't be so proud. When is your release date? Mine has been set for the fourteenth of August. Let's continue planning a way to get together before we leave Mexico. And let me know how you're fitting on your new responsibility as *orientador.* I'm proud, as always, of your accomplishments.

Your brother, Gord

January 26

Went to Roma *capilla* with Hermana Bautista this morning to help her get her youngest daughter enrolled in the *primaria* [elementary school], operated by the church in the chapel during the week. Her older daughter, Clementina, is all set to begin school at the church-operated *secundaria* [secondary school], often referred to simply as "El Arbolío." We checked up on our investigators the rest of the morning, principally the Romeros, where some of the girls have expressed desires to be baptized. Got them all together and presented a brief review of all the lessons. We may baptize Sara and Lisa over the weekend.

Later: We did baptize Hermana Bautista and Clementina this afternoon. They were both happy and will make good members. Afterward, we traveled clear down past the *Zócalo* to drop off a third lesson with the Micas, then came back up for a fifth with the Chacóns. Surprise and goodbye twenty baptisms this month. It's not that they're unwilling but Hermano Chacón was suddenly called by his work to be out of town for a week or two. We gave the lesson anyway but a few more problems popped up. Mainly, Ana Luisa plans on marrying her creepy boyfriend in the Catholic Church, because he won't have it any other way. He's always present for the discussions but has accepted nothing. After the lesson we had a good discussion about marriage. Anyway, it turns out that Ana Luisa will find it difficult to be baptized very soon, and the rest of the family wants to wait until Hermano Chacón returns.

January 27

Haven't had a real break for a long time, so we took a half day off in order for Elder Judd to see some of the city sights he's not previously visited: Chapúltepec Castle, Museum of Anthropology, the National Palace. Looking at exhibits for hours was a little tiring but interesting anyway. Neither of us said anything about the assistant to the president position that opens up tomorrow with the release of Elder Cardon. Maybe Elder Judd has an inkling that he's on deck as the heir apparent, and this is the reason why he was particularly interested in getting in a little sight-seeing time today before being uprooted tomorrow.

January 28

It's difficult to believe but I'm now in the mission home as an assistant to the president instead of Elder Judd. Elder Cardon took me aside this morning before breakfast at our apartment and told me to get my things packed, but I wasn't really sure until I talked to President McClellan this afternoon. We had about a half-hour interview in which the president explained his decision and my role and filled me in on some projected plans. I'm companion to Elder Bayer and couldn't be happier with the prospect of working with him once more. (Although, as before, I'm sad to leave behind the good investigators that Elder Judd and I have cultivated; I'll also miss Elder Judd, whom I truly like and admire.) I'm fully aware of my own weaknesses in assuming this position. The Lord continually blesses me, even though I am often undeserving. May I do the very best that my abilities permit.

February 1

Received a telegram from Gord in response to the note I sent, advising him of my move to the mission home.

FROM GORDON, TELEGRAFOS NACIONALES

GAR, I'LL SEE YOU ON TOP OF THE WORLD.

13

∾

"Against a Wall of Religious Complacency":
Gordon's Story as Supervising Elder in Puebla, Puebla

As supervising elder of the Puebla District, Gordon was to enjoy a respite from the companion tensions and branch problems of Tuxtla Gutiérrez. Situated not far from the Federal District of Mexico City, Puebla is a major Mexican city and traditionally strong in its Catholicism. One of the oldest centers of Mormon activity in the Republic, Puebla supplied some of the early leadership for the nationalistic Third Convention movement of the 1930s and 1940s. At the time of Gordon's mission, Puebla supported two sizable LDS branches entirely staffed by Mexicans and boasted of one of the few LDS chapels in that part of Mexico. (As of 1994, there were twenty-five wards in the Puebla area.) Gordon divided his time in Puebla with two junior companions, the first a rising talent who contributed substantially to the missionary effort, and the second an affable novice from the Language Training Mission.

Stimulated by a set of challenging investigators, including a number of medical students and an evangelical preacher, Gordon perceived that his language, teaching, and debating skills were being pushed to new levels of competence. While working in Puebla, he experienced a gratifying reunion with branch members in neighboring San Martín, the locale of his first mission assignment in Mexico. He also was forced, in conversation with a former Mexican missionary, to reflect on the ethnocentric tendencies of North American missionaries in Mexico and, in turn, was reminded of anti-American sentiment in Mexico as Puebla students protested the Vietnam War.

In Puebla, Gordon experienced a resurgence of intestinal problems—and for the first time in his life he found himself questioning the wisdom of admonitory advice given by a general authority of the church at a missionary conference. He also received news that Beckie Jones, his girlfriend (and future wife), was preparing to accept a mission call. And finally, like Gary before him, Gordon was surprised by a call to become an assistant to his mission president, Seville Hatch, in Veracruz.

As an assistant to the president in Mexico City, Gary briefly was reunited as companion with his best friend in the mission. In his initial briefing with President McClellan, he was dismayed to learn that some general authorities in Salt Lake City believed that masturbation constituted a significant problem among field missionaries and that they apparently expected mission officials to crack down on offenders. Gary was introduced to the routines of the mission office and conference jaunts to districts outside of the capitol city. His stay in the mission home was highlighted by an exploratory trip to Arcélia, an isolated mountain village in the state of Guerrero, to scout the potential for sending proselyting missionaries there. Shortly thereafter, Gary was transferred to Guadalajara to function as one of the president's assistants over the mission's northern districts. He formed a strong working relationship with the other assistant in Guadalajara who soon was to become one of his best missionary companions.

Puebla, January 8, 1966

Will wonders never cease. I've been transferred to Puebla, my spawning spot in the mission. Elder Manhart has been promoted to zone director and I'm taking his place as supervising elder of the Puebla District. In some ways it was a rather surprising change. I was anticipating a move and even figured Puebla was the most likely place, but not for another month at least. Anyway, I received my telegram Thursday afternoon and left Tuxtla Friday morning. In between time I went around to say goodbye to everyone and was the guest of honor at a farewell party that had been quickly arranged by the other elders and celebrated by the branch members. The spontaneous warmth that the members demonstrate on such occasions always makes me regret having to leave a small branch like the one in Tuxtla.

It was a seventeen-hour journey to Puebla by bus and it was 4:00 in the morning when I finally arrived. My new companion is Elder Dale Smith, a sharp rookie with a little over three months in the mission. His Spanish is already good and it looks like I'll finally have a companion who can really contribute to the work rather than being another problem to deal with. We'll have to start from scratch without a single investigator. Tracting today resulted in nineteen visits, which were mostly quite good, but we were unable to make any return appointments. Nonetheless, my spirits are high. If I'm not mistaken we'll have a little *éxito* [success] here.

The Puebla District over which I have supervising responsibility has shrunk to two cities: Puebla and Oaxaca. Missionaries have been withdrawn from the smaller towns of Tehuacán, Atlixco, Apizaco, and San Martín, all of which were previously part of the Puebla District when I first arrived in the mission. This means a lot less traveling for me, thank goodness. There are currently eight elders working in Puebla and two in Oaxaca (including Elder Granger, whom I will undoubtedly see again soon when I make my visit to check on their work. I hope things are working out for Elder Granger as a co-senior but I wouldn't hold my breath). Also, the missionaries here in Puebla have changed their residence and now live in a new apartment complex across the street from the *capilla* (in contrast to the old place, which was a big house sitting in the middle of nowhere on the outskirts of the city). This makes it a lot closer for us to our tracting areas.

January 10

Things are going well. Elder Smith is an excellent companion—dedicated to the work, intelligent, sensitive—he's well on his way to becoming an outstanding missionary. And Puebla is a great place to be, a big city which has maintained much of its old Spanish colonial appearance. I've been working in the jungles and mountains of southern Mexico since July. Good to be back in civilization. It's hard for me to realize that I'm less than a hundred miles from Gary again, who's still stationed in Mexico City. Not a day passes that I don't think of him.

At Sunday services yesterday I ran into the first family (the Cruzes) I baptized with Elder Orozco after arriving in Mexico. They're all faithful members of the Puebla Branch and seemed as happy to see me as I was to see them. We've been invited to dinner at their house Wednesday night. During sacrament meeting I was called out of the audience to say a few words. Having nothing prepared, I resorted to an old talk on the principle of faith, which I prepared for the first time in San Martín over a year ago and which, with numerous modifications, I've delivered various times since.

January 14

The work here is *duro* [hard] but rewarding. People are more set in their Catholicism and less easy to approach. We're only slowly starting to gain some investigators. Nonetheless, our tracting has provided me with some of the most stimulating experiences of my mission. We've been working in a wealthy area of town where people are well educated and capable in religious discussions. Fortunately, my Spanish has never been better and my ability to answer people's objections and explain the gospel has increased. We've had the spirit of the Lord with us and have given some of the best lessons to investigators that I've participated in since coming to Mexico.

January 15

Chalk up another scripture battle of empty honors. I suppose that if someone had been keeping score, we would have been crowned with the victory but, as usual, little more than the experience was really gained. Our visit was set up with a young couple whom we had tracted and made a return appointment to see this evening, but there to meet us was the proverbial wolf in sheep's clothing (the young woman's father), licking his chops and anxious to devour us Mormon innocents. He wasn't an ignorant man—to the contrary, he was well studied in Catholicism—BUT, he nevertheless possessed the most disagreeable attributes of ignorance, namely: a loud mouth, constantly interrupting without regard to the other person's right to speak, always greatly diverting from the subject, preaching without making recognizable points, and refusing to accept logic and truth when they contradicted his views.

We struggled through the Joseph Smith story, testified, and tried to leave. But unfortunately I ended up bowing to the temptation to correct some of his misstatements about Mormonism and the fight was on. I gave him a volley of all the apostasy scriptures I could think of and followed with a round on the restoration of the gospel as prophesied in the Bible. He wasn't looking for the truth and didn't see the connection. He even denied the principle of prayer as a means for understanding the truth. He finally tried to pull his age, experience, and education on us, telling us that we were just a couple of boys with a lot to learn. True, no doubt, but this scripture came to mind and I couldn't resist reciting it to him: "But there is a spirit in man, and the spirit of the Almighty giveth them understanding. Great men are not always wise; neither do the aged understand judgment" (Job 32:8–9).

January 17

Yesterday was a busy day. I was asked to take charge of a baptismal service for Elder Cory, who had to be in Apizaco, so we started at 8:30 A.M. by filling the baptismal *pila* and heating the water, then worked straight through the rest of the day without so much as a break for a bite to eat until 9:30 P.M. After taking care of the *pila* we attended Sunday school and I taught the investigator class. Immediately afterward I interviewed Elder Cory's converts, then directed the baptismal service, gave one of the talks, and confirmed two of the new members. From there we hustled downtown on the bus to give a first lesson to some new investigators and then made it back to the chapel just in time to be late for sacrament service. As a finale to the day's efforts we were asked out to a member's home to give a blessing to a sister who was suffering from a severe earache.

January 19

The work continues uphill but exciting. I've never had to talk to so many sharp people who constantly challenge us with penetrating inquiries. The Lord continues to put words in our mouths and we've managed to hold our own. This afternoon we gave the first lesson on the restoration and organization of the church to several medical students and they made some of the keenest objections that I've yet encountered. They were polite, serious, and held strong convictions. But I think we made a good defense of our own views. Whether or not they're interested enough in our message to hear more remains to be seen.

In addition to the conventional missionary work, we've also been teaching English classes two nights a week in downtown Puebla. This is a scheme hatched some time ago by previous missionaries here as a way of making contact with new investigators. But as far as I can see that rarely happens. We teach the classes and that's that. The one who seems to be profiting most is the woman who offers the courses that we teach. She pays us 100 pesos [roughly $10] a week for our work and we turn over the money to the Puebla Branch president as a budget donation, but I just don't believe it's a proper use of our time. I told the woman that we would only continue teaching until the end of the month.

Next week there will be a missionwide conference celebrated here, with President Theodore Tuttle (representing the general authorities of the church as a member of the First Council of the Seventy) presiding.

January 25

The work is progressing. Slowly but surely our investigators are increasing in number. Our medical students (plus some of their friends) are difficult to find at home, but still seem interested and want to continue the discussions. They are fine young men.

Friday we had a missionary conference with President Theodore Tuttle. In my interview with him President Tuttle told me to keep working in the upper-class neighborhoods of Puebla, that when conversions are made there the potential for local leadership is greater, and that local priesthood leadership is what the church needs most today in Mexico. President Tuttle spoke to all the missionaries for almost four (!) straight hours, emphasizing the need to work with entire families and to concentrate our efforts on bringing successful business, professional, and community leaders into the church. (He also reaffirmed that business suits are required missionary attire, even down here, and that light colors are prohibited. Unfortunately, my light tan suit is the only decent article of clothing that I have left—my dark suit was stolen last year in Minatitlán. Truth is, it's only in the Puebla region during December–February that missionaries in the Veracruz Mission bother wearing suit coats of any kind. Most of the time it's just too hot.)

President Tuttle also admonished us about our goals and priorities when we leave the mission field. Our highest priority, he said, was marriage and a family. He admonished that we were not to postpone having children or limit the size of our families for selfish reasons. Concern for schooling and careers should not deter us from having families of our own right away. He said that to do otherwise would thwart God's plan of salvation in the last days. Frankly, I was a little taken back to hear such advice, reminiscent of nineteenth-century preaching. (President Hatch typically encourages missionaries to get a decent education first so they can support a family when it comes.) President Tuttle also blasted a former missionary who returned to Mexico a couple of years ago and has become interested in the teachings of the Church of the First-Born [an apostate Mormon group which practiced polygamy and whose founders, Joel and Ervil LeBarron, were originally from the Mormon colonies in northern Mexico]. President Tuttle told him that he was on the road to apostasy and that his church membership and salvation were in serious jeopardy if he continued to associate with this group.

In between conference sessions a group of us missionaries were gossiping and laughing outside the chapel when I spotted Noé Rivera, a former native missionary who was such a big help to the Tuxtla Branch a few months ago, arriving with some other members. After much searching Noé finally found work here and is now a member of the Puebla Branch. We greeted each other warmly and then I thoughtlessly kidded him about his *lujoso* [fine/costly] clothing—he was dressed in a new suit. With a pained look on his face he said, "You know, Elder, this is the one thing I don't like about you North American missionaries. You get together and talk English and leave the Mexican elders out. And you make joking comments that make us feel small." He said he knew we didn't intentionally mean any harm but that we needed to be more careful in our speech and to mingle with the members more, instead of congregating together at conference. I've never felt so small myself as I realized the truth of his criticism.

Later that evening after district conference for the members, I ran into a group who had traveled from San Martín to attend. It was a joyful reunion. Tony Bennett may have left his heart in San Francisco but, *después de todo* [in the end], I seem to have left mine in San Martín. The good people there want me to pay the branch a visit as soon as possible.

January 28

We've been banging our heads against a wall of religious complacency the last couple of days, trying to break down the rock-hard objections of many of our new investigators who seem willing to argue religion but are unwilling to make any commitments. Two observations are worth making. First, I'm getting a better idea of what it's like to be guided by the spirit. The Lord's help doesn't come without some genuine effort on the missionary's part. I've studied the standard works of the church and memorized hundreds of scriptures during my mission and, although my knowledge of the gospel is still relatively shallow, it isn't entirely lacking either. Nonetheless, I've been utterly amazed when entering into religious discussions at how clear my thoughts have been. As I've showed our investigators various passages from the scriptures, they have been opened up to *me,* and I've been able to apply them with a greater understanding than I've ever had until that moment. But although I believe that the Lord's spirit has been aiding us, alas, my second observation. For all the truth and understanding the scriptures provide, people are still capable of remaining unmoved. From the outset they are determined to defend their cherished traditions at all cost—sadly, it would seem, even that of the truth. Taking this position, they practically forfeit any spiritual communication and our message fails to penetrate. After all is said and done, only honest desire and prayer will lead a person to religious truth. This is a step so many of our investigators refuse to take.

January 30

Just got back from San Martín. We left Puebla right after a baptismal service for several of Elder Porter's investigators, at which I had been asked to speak, and arrived by bus in San Martín in time for sacrament service. The members there are still some of the most wonderful people under the heavens. When we walked into the *capilla* I was practically mobbed and embraced by one and all, including some bear-hugs by the old *hermanas.* Hermano Osnaya, who is now branch president, asked me to be the evening's orator. Even though I am not usually a good extemporaneous speaker, I was pleased by the chance to talk to the good people of San Martín and was complimented afterward by those who still remembered me as the bashful *nuevo* who came to their town with barely enough ability in Spanish to converse with small children. I'm amazed myself. It's only been a year since I left San Martín. As long as I'm in Puebla I should be able to return for an occasional visit.

According to President Osnaya, Elder Splinders, my former senior companion in San Martín, returned to Mexico last summer and *married one of his nieces*(!) in Mexico City—"Now we're relatives," he said, shaking his head in exaggerated disbelief. Actually, Hermano Osnaya seemed somewhat pleased by the irony. He and Splinders did not hit it off well when Splinders was here as a missionary presiding over the San Martín Branch. But times change, and when I reflect on my own experience with Elder Splinders I regret my intolerance and lack of appreciation for many of the efforts he made in a difficult situation.

February 1

Despertád! Cantád! Moradores del polvo! [Awaken! Sing! Dwellers of the dust!] I just received a note from Gary informing me that he has been called as assistant to the president in Mexico City! I almost burst a blood vessel in excitement when I read the news. May God bless him and help him to carry out his responsibilities.

NOTE FROM GARY

> Gord: I've been trying for two days to get a telegram sent off to you but there's a foul-up somewhere in the office. Anyway, I am now in the mission home as an assistant to the president. I can't believe it either, and I needn't go into great detail about my anxieties concerning my inadequacies and general unworthiness. I'll have to humble myself greatly before the Lord and depend on him to see me through this. Very briefly, I'm companion to Elder Tim Bayer, my old best buddy and former companion of five days as *orientador*. I'd like to give you some more details, and I will as soon as time permits, but I've got to close this for right now. I need your prayers and moral support.
>   Your brother, Gar

February 8

Still working with the medical students. We have them up through the fourth lesson so far, but their exams have hindered our ability to maintain regular contact recently. Once their exams are finished they plan to leave on vacation and we may lose them. The other day while visiting them the conversation turned to baseball, and when they learned I had played a little when growing up they got out their gloves and a hardball for a game of catch. I took off my tie, rolled up my sleeves, and we had a lot of fun. Unfortunately, I tried to show off by pitching a curve ball that wound up going wild and broke a window across the street. *Qué verguensa* [what embarrassment]. I tried to pay for the damage, along with a profusion of apologies, but the students refused, saying it was their fault, that they should have caught my wild pitch.

On the way home we passed the University of Puebla and found ourselves in the middle of an anti-American parade. The students were demonstrating against U.S. military forces in Vietnam and we were greeted by such chants as "Gringos! Cabrones! Váyense de Vietnam!" [Gringo bastards! Get out of Vietnam!]

LETTER FROM GARY

Gord: I'm happy with my new job and feeling a little guilty for all the blessings I receive. The rise to the big house on the hill was rather rapid and not altogether deserved. Actually, I'm not sitting on the throne yet. What I am is companion to the assistant. (The other assistant and his companion—Elders Garza and Flake, respectively—are stationed out in Guadalajara.) I am maybe, but not necessarily, heir apparent to Elder Bayer when he finishes up towards the end of March. Whatever, the two of us practically run most of the affairs of the missionaries in this mission. I still haven't acquired a firm idea of what is and what isn't expected of me. But while I'm learning, I couldn't ask for a better companion than Elder Bayer. Our friendship has that high-quality understanding and acceptance that is often only reached through years of association. Besides that, his wit keeps me in stitches all day. By the way, Elder Bayer wants to be a partner in our (fantasy) law firm. [Bayer did go on to become a corporate lawyer in Salt Lake City.]

President McClellan has been systematically interviewing all of the missionaries, and it came my turn shortly after taking up residence in the mission home. The interview was rather searching. Afterward, President McClellan informed me that about half of the elders so far interviewed have confessed to masturbation problems. He's not sure how seriously this should be regarded, but evidently some general authorities are communicating heightened concerns to mission presidents on the subject. This is about the last thing I can picture myself inquiring of anybody should it ever fall to our lot as assistants to interview missionaries. If people are working hard and producing good results, I guess that should speak for itself. If they aren't putting out an effort, the only way I would see masturbation as a possible factor would be through guilty feelings or as a symptom of other, more important problems.

After spending my first few days hanging around the mission home polishing off the *Clarín* and some other paperwork chores, we took off into the field to attend a joint member and missionary district conference in Iguala (a little north of Acapulco). Elder Bayer was called upon to speak in the afternoon session before an audience of several hundred people. He responded well, but I felt secretly relieved that I was not also asked to speak. I've never been good at talking off the top of my head, although I know this is a skill I will have to cultivate in this position.

The next day, Elder Bayer and I headed out with President McClellan to Arcélia, a remote mountain-top village from which a Protestant minister has been corresponding with President McClellan about the possibility of bringing his small congregation into Mormonism. The road was a dusty, narrow, dangerous, chuckhole-filled, mountain-climber all the way. The skeletal remains of buses and trucks scattered about far below in sheer gorges at several points along the route bore witness to the treacherous footing. We took turns driving and lulled away the long hours with interesting conversation. President McClellan is highly human, not at all stuffy or pious. The drive was marred only by a wave of carsickness on my part.

Arcélia is so isolated and primitive that basic supplies usually have to be flown in by small plane. The one "hotel" we found in town was in reality almost a *vecindad* [set of small, connected dwellings, typical of poor neighborhoods]. We immediately ran into our minister friend and did a little preliminary sparring with him over some greasy enchiladas in a ratty-looking cafe. Back at the "hotel," there was no running water but there were foul-smelling, filthy public toilets at the end of the corridor. Elder Bayer sent the cockroaches scurrying out of the bed when he turned back the covers.

The next morning, after breakfasting on *mandarindas* [tangerines] purchased at the local outdoor marketplace, we accompanied the minister to an even tinier outpost where most of his congregation dwells. They live in mud and bamboo huts, about as poor as I've ever seen, but they seemed to be good people who welcomed us hospitably wherever we went. Two men—carrying a large, freshly shot iguana tethered between them on poles—were taking their prey home to prepare for eating and invited us to join them later. These people aren't hooked up with any particular religious organization, and missionaries could probably achieve some success among them. But under existing conditions, a branch organized in Arcélia would be extremely difficult to regulate and maintain properly. With this as the main objection, along with some doubts about the minister's real motives, President McClellan decided to let the matter ride for a time, being satisfied meanwhile to distribute some *folletos* and Books of Mormon, and leave a good impression.

After returning to Mexico City, I indulged in some extremely interesting scanning of mission files on the LeBarron and Bautista cases. These guys were missionaries in Mexico back in the 1940s, developed some crazy ideas on polygamy, etc., were eventually excommunicated, and started up an apostate group known as the Church of the First-Born. If I have my facts straight, they had only paltry success in converting Mexicans but have established a still existing polygamist colony somewhere along the Utah-Arizona border. [The community is incorporated as Colorado City, Arizona.]

Thanks for the telegram—see you there [on top of the world]. Your brother, Gary

February 13

It appears that I've got another good case of intestinal *bichos* [bugs]. My case of diarrhea is as bad or worse, if that's possible, than it was in Villa Flores. For the past week I've been spending more and more of my spare time looking for bathrooms. I've been vomiting daily—sometimes before we leave in the morning, sometimes while we're out tracting. It's getting to be a real hindrance. I finally wised up enough to get some prescription medicine. We'll see if it does any good.

Received a letter from Elder Baron today, who has been the lone assistant in the mission home since January, advising me that there will be a district missionary conference in Puebla with President Hatch next week, which I am to direct. Because of all of the conferences lately, I'm going to postpone my trip to Oaxaca until April. Reports indicate that Elder Granger is having problems (brawls and fistfights) with his companion again. No surprise there. We'll see what President Hatch wants to do this time. Also, Gary forwarded a poetic but depressed letter from Chuck Radlow that he had forgotten to include with his last letter.

NOTE FROM GARY

Gord: There were so many other things to run through in the letter I just sent that I forgot to include Chuck's most recent epistle; I expect you'll be interested to read it. Keep shining your candle so I can keep the blankety heck on the right road.

Your brother, Gar

LETTER FROM CHUCK RADLOW TO GARY

Dear Gary,

I have found myself repenting of the somewhat nasty letter that I sent
you last month. It was written in one of my high points of frustration.
Sometimes I want very much to be able to communicate with you but I just
can't seem to get words to hold the feeling. Words have always been pretty
cheap with me. I throw them out to impress while I hide in the meaning-
lessness that underlies them. But it's even more than that. I have a kind of
block when it comes to writing you. Perhaps it's that you are doing what I
should be but just can't quite. Or perhaps it's the feeling that I really don't
have anything to contribute to your life. It's been a long time, Gary. The different seas and suns have changed us and although we might initially recognize one another, I wonder how much there is left to talk about.

I enjoyed the picture of your "flock." They look like beautiful people
and I can only have a kind of pride that you are doing a good thing in their
lives. As I have said before, I try to picture what sorts of things you are doing
and how you are feeling, but it's all so very far away. I see you knocking on
the doors and giving the lessons and conducting the classes. I think I can
sense a little of the love that you may have for the people you are with. In
many ways it is a beautiful world. Perhaps you ought to return to Mexico
one day and teach, after we have gotten through fighting the crazy war in
Vietnam. The decision point is coming and, in spite of criticism, it looks like
a widening of the war, calling up of reserves, and increased draft calls. It all
looks very ugly and hopeless right now but still we go on.

I have applied to the Peace Corps and eleven graduate schools. For
your information they are: Harvard and Stanford (education); Harvard,
Yale, Pennsylvania, and Brown (American civilization); Stanford (history);
and Harvard, Chicago, Princeton, and Union Theological Seminary (divinity). I have no idea where I will be admitted or where I will go if I am
admitted. Much of the future depends on Uncle Sam's desire for our bodies in Vietnam. My relationship to the church is ? and there is little else
that can be said at this point. I should send you a copy of the statement I
sent to Union Theological Seminary [where Chuck did attend graduate
school] that should give you a few insights. Meanwhile, I just finished thir-
ty-two pages of photo-essay for publication in the Stanford *Quad*. The
concluding poem goes like this:

One Man
who reaches out to hold and mold
One life

that can never be alone, but is
One world
that can never be quite done
but is becoming
One.

Gary, in many ways I guess I am just tired. Tired of working and thinking and depression and the whole silly mess. I'd just kind of like to run off somewhere for awhile and get to know what it's like to be alive. When I was writing last year about the feeling that permeates my life, I put it this way: A soft sadness is the way I would put it. A soft, lingering, unknowable sadness that cushions itself into tiny folds and valleys of our composure. The opposite of ecstasy, it bewilders a soul wishing to wing, but bound by—no smoothed, perplexed by sadness; alone, alone and swathing the mind's picture into blues, canceling out points of light and color and hushing them. The squeals of yesterday's joys—hush them now—they are gone as friends are gone with the stuff of memory trace lingering the image slowly on. But it too is blue and soft, so soft. That is its blasphemy, for its pain is quiet and its evening is calm and its death is blackness. Only blackness and one's own soul alone. Well, as the maudlin old poem says: "Life must go on—I forget just why."
Your old buddy, Chuck

February 17

In our casting around for investigators we've hooked on to what could be a major catch—or perhaps just an old tire. In any case, we're going to have to reel long and hard to bring him in closer for inspection. To switch metaphors, we've encountered a genuine old lion of a Protestant minister, complete with flowing white mane and roaring speech. We knocked on his door and were invited in for something less than a successful first visit. He fumed and argued so much that we never even got through the Joseph Smith story. He's broken away from the Seventh-Day Adventists and formed his own church, but still firmly adheres to their sabbath teaching and wouldn't talk about anything else. We left in a flurry of words but also left behind the *folleto* "Una Discusión Amigable" [A Friendly Discussion] for him to read.

I quickly forgot about the incident but when Sunday arrived, who should appear at the *capilla* but Reverend Sanchez and his wife. He praised our *folleto* to the sky and claimed that it didn't contain a single error, that it was the pure gospel of Jesus Christ (there was no discussion in the *folleto* of the sabbath day, however). We made an appointment to see him again during the week and steered our way through a lengthy first lesson on the organization of Christ's church. Reverend Sanchez is a little windy and loves to relate stories and quote scriptures. But after the smoke cleared I was heartened to discover that he had not contradicted any of the points in our presentation, with one major exception: Reverend Sanchez is not willing to accept Joseph Smith's role as prophet of the Restoration. He sputtered and fumed at this but finally allowed me to show him some supportive scriptures from the Bible, which seemed to calm him down a bit. He said he would read another pamphlet on the Restoration, which we left with him, and would pray about it. I think we put a thorn under his paw when we talked about the need for divine authority to organize Christ's church. He bellowed and is undoubtedly padding around a little wounded, since he is the founder, without any such authority, of his own church. We've made an appointment to see him again next week.

February 20

Conference time again. Yesterday we had the missionary session, which I directed. I also spoke and managed to give the best talk of my career as supervising elder. I wish I could just routinely get up and speak when I need to without hours of anguish and preparation. News from the mission home is that Dale Smith's days are numbered here as my companion and that within a week I'll be getting a new junior companion fresh from the Language Training Mission. My companionship with Elder Smith has been relatively short but I think mutually beneficial. I know I've gained a lot from him at a time when I needed a good companion.

We should have some baptisms soon and Dr. Sanchez is showing the right kind of interest. The other day he kept saying, "Now suppose I accept your message, what . . . ?" Our answer was that he would be baptized and ordained to the priesthood. Meanwhile, our medical student investigators have left Puebla on vacation and I miss our stimulating discussions with them. Hope they'll let us know when they get back and accept our invitation to attend church.

February 22

We had an interesting conversation today with one of the old-time Puebla members (Hermano Narciso Sándoval) who apparently took a leading part in the so-called Tercera Covención [Third Convention], a native movement that broke away from the church back in the 1930s and 1940s. As I understand it, hundreds of members from the Puebla area and little towns around

Mexico City petitioned church authorities in Salt Lake City for a native Mexican mission president. When the petition was rejected there was a split in church ranks, and a large number of Mexican members declared their independence and formed a native Mexican church. There was division and hard feelings for a number of years around here and excommunication of the leaders of the protest faction, including, I take it, Hermano Sándoval. [Narcisco Sándoval, a prominent Mexican leader of the Third Convention rebellion, later reconciled with Anglo authorities and was reinstated as a member of the church in good standing.] The *convencionistas* followed church doctrines and practices but operated their own program for about ten years. Things were finally ironed out when President George Albert Smith made a personal visit from Salt Lake and the protesters were brought back to full fellowship in the church. The issue was over authority and Mexican leadership. There are still no native Mexican mission presidents, but the old-time members remain strong in their belief that, as missionary success continues, new wards and stakes will be organized and administered by native leadership all over Mexico. I hope they're right.

February 24

Elder Smith's change came through today. He's been assigned as junior companion to good old Elder Booth in Poza Rica. My new companion is already here: Elder Silver, a strapping, wide-shouldered, thick-armed, curly-haired, fun-loving sort of kid from Idaho who's still in the throes of repenting from (according to him) a rather riotous pre-missionary existence. I've taken an immediate shine to him and I think we'll work well together. I recall my own first bewildering days in the mission and know Silver will have adjustments to make, but I think I can help him off to a good start.

We have continued to meet with our Seventh-Day Adventist preacher, the Reverend Sanchez, and the inevitable showdown in which we'll have to lay our pistols on the table and battle the Sabbath-day issue is fast approaching. Today we left him with a copy of the Book of Mormon, which he agreed to read and digest in the next two weeks. We hope that he will read with seriousness of purpose and put Moroni's promise of spiritual knowledge through prayer to the test. My words alone will never persuade him and he knows the Bible a lot better than I do. Only a spiritual confirmation will convince him of the truthfulness of our message.

Somehow, somewhere, I've lost my glasses. Can't see worth beans. I'll have to buy a new pair just when I thought I might be able to save a little money for a change. Blast it! Also, I just received word that Gary's been changed as an assistant in Mexico City to assistant in Guadalajara. The administrative organization of Gary's mission has always seemed a little strange to me.

Gord: Maybe you noticed the new return address. Just arrived in Guadalajara and wanted to let you know what the story is. Two of the assistants—Santiago Garza and his companion, Keith Flake—have been stationed out in Guad for several months in order to more effectively run the northern affairs of the mission. But Elder Garza (he's been assistant since last May) now wants to return to Mexico City to work awhile, so I'm going up north to work with Elder Flake. There's a possibility that I might come back into the City when Elder Bayer goes home the end of next month, or I might be permanent in Guad. Or there's the possibility, with so few missionaries here now (less than seventy), that the extra assistants might be done away with when Elder Bayer leaves. That would probably mean me. *Ni modo* [it doesn't matter], must wait and see.

Meanwhile, I'm sorry to be parting so quickly again from the company of Elder Bayer. I was enormously enjoying our companionship. And I suspect that Tim is a bit miffed over the new arrangement that will team him up with Elder Garza. Tim is senior in mission time to Garza, but Garza has been an assistant to the president since last summer and has developed tremendous influence. Even President McClellan seems to pay him deference. On the bright side, I am looking forward to the greater independence and reduced office work that are part of the Guadalajara assistant's position. And my new companion, Elder Flake, (who hails from the quaintly named town of Snowflake, Arizona), is as sharp as anyone, anywhere. [Snowflake was established as a Mormon colony in 1878 and named in honor of two men: Keith Flake's great-grandfather, William, the town's founder, and the pioneer Mormon apostle Erastus Snow, a direct ancestor of Lauren Snow, Gary's future wife.] In him, I will be blessed with one of my finest companions.

Had an odd little experience tonight after our arrival in Guad. The two lady missionaries who are stationed out here invited us over to their place for a home-cooked spaghetti dinner, and we gabbed over our meal until late. Nothing wrong with this, I suppose. But I must confess feeling a little like we were having some sort of illicit date. [Mission regulations now expressly prohibit such get-togethers.] We meet in homes and elsewhere with female investigators all the time and never think a thing of it. But this is the first time in almost two years that I have been in the exclusive company of young (not to mention quite attractive) women my own age for a purely social, non-missionary activity. What a thought to go to bed on.

Your brother, Gar

February 27

It's been a long time since I last stepped into the water but today we finally celebrated a baptismal service. We baptized a *joven* by the name of Marciál Juan, who has been meeting with us at the chapel for discussions and has already been attending services with unfailing regularity. Following the baptism we went downtown to the First Methodist Church of Puebla with Elder Porter and his companion. Porter had been invited by some of his investigators to visit a Methodist youth league conference. We were unsure of what to expect but guessed that we would be called upon to introduce ourselves. As it turned out, the *joven* who is president of the group invited me to stand and explain to the conference of several hundred people who we were and what we did. Surprisingly, I was not the least bit nervous and spoke fluently, using the best Spanish of my career in an extemporaneous summary of the church's basic teachings and its missionary program. Following my little speech we answered a number of questions from the audience and distributed *folletos*. We were treated kindly and with respect, and I think we succeeded in making a favorable impression.

March 10

Yesterday we sparred a round with Dr. Sanchez, our evangelist minister, in which we finally began to grapple with the seventh-day issue. For the most part it was a wary, jabbing-type of encounter with no haymakers delivered and at the end of blows the score was still 0-0. The key, I think, still lies in the Book of Mormon which, unfortunately, he has not yet read. When we see him again next week I'm going to try to maneuver the conversation back to a discussion of priesthood authority.

We've also spent many hours this week working with the branch missionary committee in translating a church film into Spanish for a special Sunday program. The film is entitled *Every Member a Missionary* and emphasizes the role that members should play in helping missionaries find investigators to teach. After the dialogue is translated, various members of the Puebla Branch will read and record parts to synchronize with the film.

March 14

Well, that's over, thank goodness. Saturday night we worked from 8:30 till 4:00 A.M. recording the film dialogue in Spanish and dubbing it on to the sound track for Sunday's program. It wasn't perfect but not bad either, considering our means. Last night we presented the program to the two Puebla branches combined. It was a large and restless audience and I've certainly given better talks in my life but, all in all, the film went over well enough and most of our good investigators were there to see it. Maybe by the end of this month we'll start reaping some baptisms. Every place I've been assigned as senior companion I've had to start virtually from scratch, with few or no investigators whatsoever to inherit from previous missionaries, only to be transferred to a new assignment once my companions and I have begun to cultivate a respectable crop of new prospects.

March 15

Borrowed some money ($15) from Elder Silver and bought myself a new pair of glasses. I'm not too confident in the accuracy of the prescription, however. Like me, most of the missionaries in Puebla have been having problems with the well-known revenge of Moctezuma. The exception is Elder Silver, who eats like a horse and hasn't had so much as a twinge of queasiness yet. It isn't fair. I've been paying my dues for a year and a half. By now you would think I would have developed some sort of immunity. Sadly, not so. I've steadily lost weight and routinely feel half sick since coming to Puebla.

Elder Manhart, who has been zone director of the Poblana Zone, is leaving for home this week, so I suppose it's possible that I might be moved into his position. In the meantime I got a letter from Beckie, who hasn't written in a long while, informing me that she has decided to accept a mission call from the church. She doesn't know where she's going yet but will probably leave in June, two months before my release from the Southeast Mexican Mission. This means I'll not see her for another two years.

March 19

We showed the film *Man's Search for Happiness* to Dr. Sanchez in the sanctuary of his little church this evening. The film's powerful message brought tears to his eyes but he's still unbudgeable on the seventh-day issue and cannot accept the Book of Mormon. He remains convinced that only the Bible can be the word of God. That means we have a good and valuable friend but Hermano Sanchez will not be baptized into the church.

I paid back Elder Silver's loan on my glasses. Silver's language skills are still very limited but he's good-natured and provides good companionship. No promotion for me to zone director, which is just as well since directors end up having to travel more than anyone except assistants to the president.

I'm happy. We're working hard and I've never had more confidence in my ability to do the work.

March 23

My missionary career continues to take abrupt and unexpected turns. I'm packing my stuff tonight and will be leaving Puebla for Veracruz in the morning. In two weeks I'm to become assistant to the president. Elder Baron, current assistant to the president, and Steve London (whom I last saw just before Christmas) made a surprise appearance during Mutual classes last night with the news, and this morning we left early for Mexico City to get drivers' licenses for me and several other members of the mission office staff who had also come up from Veracruz. Unfortunately, I flunked the eye exam (with my newly purchased glasses, no less) and was not permitted to continue with the licensing procedure. I can drive for a couple of weeks on a tourist permit but apparently will have to obtain a new prescription for my glasses if I want a permanent license to drive. Unlike most field missionaries, assistants to the president have access to mission vehicles for their transportation. While in Mexico City we stopped off at the mission home in the Chapúltepec area, one of the richest neighborhoods in Mexico. Compared to our mission headquarters in Veracruz the place was a palace. I entertained an unrealistic hope that Gary might be back in the big City, but learned to my surprise that instead he has been sent out to open up a little town on the Pacific Coast called Manzanillo. I was disappointed not to see him but was also happy that Gary will have the chance, as I did, to open a new town to the teaching of the gospel.

Elder Baron has been assistant to the president since January. His release date to return home is not until July, so I, along with everyone else, assumed he would serve a lengthy tenure in the mission home. According to Elder Baron, though, he's anxious to return to the field as a working missionary and, in fact, wants to finish his mission here in Puebla. He says that he and President Hatch think I'm the best man to replace him, but I feel the same way I did when I was called to open up Villa Flores: anticipation and excitement are mixed with a fairly healthy dose of apprehension and concern about my worthiness for such a calling. God help me do my best.

14

∾

"They Expect Us to Handle It All": Gary's Story as Co-Senior Companion in Manzanillo, Colima

Following his first six weeks as an assistant to the president, Gary was called upon to open the small Pacific Coast city of Manzanillo to LDS proselyting. This interlude exposed him for the first time in his mission to the stress of complying with standard proselyting expectations in a place where relatively few people were interested in investigating a new religion while simultaneously being responsible for the functioning of an understaffed branch of the church that was perpetually on the verge of collapse. Gary's previous companion as an assistant to the president, Elder Flake, joined him in Manzanillo, and the two worked smoothly together in initiating domestic arrangements, organizing branch affairs, and introducing themselves to the community. Within a month of their arrival, however, Elder Flake was transferred. His replacement, an immature new missionary from the Language Training Mission, became an additional burden to bear.

In Manzanillo, Gary and his companions struggled to find new investigators through the tracting process, and, like Gordon in the generally less receptive areas of southern Mexico, they frequently found themselves in scriptural battles—primarily with Protestant detractors. The few LDS members who lived in Manzanillo seemed ambivalent about active lay involvement in the church, were occasionally ridiculed by their neighbors for being Mormons, and were weighted down by personal problems.

Gary and his companions sought occasional relief from the pressures of missionary life through get-togethers with the neighboring missionary pair in Colima to play basketball and, on one occasion, go body surfing near a tourist resort, an activity strictly prohibited by mission rules. In Manzanillo they also made numerous contacts with North Americans representing the secular outside world, from which they had largely been separated: sailors; the American consul; a former major league baseball player, Larry Doby; and—most improbably—the writer Ken Kesey and his counterculture band of Merry Pranksters. Before leaving Manzanillo to return to Mexico City, Gary was able to convert one promising investigator woman and several of her children. At the end of his mission he returned to Manzanillo to baptize her eldest son, who had caused his mother grief by his initial refusal to join with the others.

While Gary toiled in Manzanillo, Gordon enjoyed the relative comforts of office life and conference travel as assistant to the president in Veracruz. He worked closely with his old friend Steve London, who had become the mission president's personal secretary, and developed an appreciation for the mission president's relaxed manner, willingness to delegate responsibilities to assistants, and empathetic concern for the welfare of his young mission- ary charges. Although he liked being at the center of mission decision mak- ing, Gordon experienced some restlessness with office routines and welcomed occasional trouble-shooting assignments in the field.

Colima, March 6, 1966

Elder Flake and I arrived in Colima yesterday evening to work with Elders Hunt and Vance and to attend branch conference here. A pretty drive: sugar cane fields, mountain passes, palm trees, and the volcano of Colima. Send- ing Elder Vance out here appears to have been a good move. He was despon- dent and even thinking of quitting his mission a couple of months ago back in Mexico City. But I recommended Elder Hunt as a good match-up for him (they're both down-to-earth guys from neighboring small towns in Arizo- na), and they're working very well together in a tough place.

President and Sister McClellan also arrived last night on a tour of the northern branches. Unfortunately, hardly any members showed up today for the scheduled conference meetings, so President McClellan decided to post- pone things for a few weeks to allow for more preparation. He wants to get the branch more solidly organized around members, but Colima lacks almost any leadership material. [By 1994, Colima was a district headquarters, sup- porting four area branches with more than two thousand members.] So we just held a regular sacrament meeting, following which the president want- ed to drive over to Manzanillo, a couple of hours out of Colima on the coast, where two large member families are reportedly living. Manzanillo is a small, somewhat grubby Pacific Ocean port town, but it has beautiful beaches and promises to develop into a booming tourist attraction within a few years. We searched for and found the two member families: the Valdézes and the Preciados. After a short visit to the beach (where I was soaked to the knees misjudging an incoming wave) we held a short testimony meeting right at the ocean's edge. Our impromptu service was keynoted by the president's surprising, apparently spontaneous, decision to establish a branch and send missionaries to Manzanillo. Maybe he was contrasting member apathy in Colima with the enthusiasm generated by the two large families already here who do not have a church organization to sustain them.

Guadalajara, March 7

Elder Flake and I drove back into Manzanillo from Colima this morning. President McClellen sent us to locate a potential house to serve as both missionary quarters and a *capilla*. We found one right off the bat: large, fully furnished with stove, refrigerator, beds, tables, chairs, and utensils; and smack dab on the beach not thirty yards from the edge of the ocean. The owner is a woman whose main residence is in Guadalajara. She'll rent it to us for 1,200 pesos [$96] a month, so we'll sign a contract as soon as President McClellan sends us a check.

Spent the entire five-hour drive back to Guadalajara in conversation with Elder Flake covering a multitude of subjects; a good friendship is growing between us. We talked some about the prospects of opening Manzanillo, and then I told him that I would like to be one of the missionaries sent to do it. I've been giving our positions as assistants in Guad quite a bit of thought and can frankly find no compelling reason for our being there. The number of missionaries in the mission has shrunk to about seventy in number (compared to the hundred or more who are usually on hand), and there just isn't that much work to occupy four assistants. My plan would be to send Elder Flake to Mexico City as companion to Elder Garza again when Elder Bayer goes home (making just two assistants), and then have me go to open up Manzanillo with a new junior companion. Being honest with myself I have to recognize that Elder Flake is more qualified for the mission home job, and I wouldn't feel badly to get back to regular missionary work with my own investigators, etc. Anyway, Flake counter-proposed himself as the one who should be released as assistant and sent to Manzanillo. So I guess we'll have to haggle it all out with Garza, Bayer, and President McClellan. To facilitate this, we called the mission home to set up a meeting in Morélia with Garza and Bayer to discuss what to do.

March 9

Left for our Morélia summit meeting early this morning and arrived at the elders' house there right at noon. Elders Bayer and Garza pulled up immediately afterward from Mexico City. The first subject to come up was my idea to send me to Manzanillo and Elder Flake to the mission home. We argued pros and cons for some time without coming to an agreement. It looks like President McClellan will have to decide. Our second major agenda item was to work out a massive set of companion changes. There are nine or ten elders leaving for home in the next couple of weeks, with replacements from Provo on the way. We expended a great deal of sweat to make all the resulting changes work out right. Half of the missionaries in the mission were involved by the time our task was complete.

Manzanillo, March 11

We signed the house contract this morning. Packed and left for Manzanillo in the afternoon. I got carsick on the canyon drive, but after heaving at the side of the road I felt better. We got into Manzanillo about 10 P.M. and, after securing the key to the house, we slipped into gym trunks and washed off in the surf, wading and floating around for maybe a half hour. It was the first time ever for me in the ocean. The water was quite salty and very warm, and the waves were fair-sized. We'll have to draw the line from now on, though. We felt sheepishly guilty afterward. The mission rule is no swimming and we didn't—exactly—but the rule did get a good stretching.

March 12

Attended to odds and ends today. We arranged with a carpenter to make us a pulpit and table, had some handbills printed up to advertise the film we plan to show here Tuesday evening, etc. Visited briefly with the Valdéz and Preciado families to inform them of our presence, our plans, and to invite them to Sunday services tomorrow. In between times, we hung around the house, not wanting to begin tracting until we have shown the film and the town is a little better acquainted with us. Night found us taking a stroll along the beach, wading and splashing a little.

March 13

Celebrated the first Sunday services in Manzanillo today. We drew straws to see who would teach what classes this morning—I drew adults and Elder Flake took the kids. Elder Flake also directed the opening exercises. My class wasn't much to rave about. Took it from old study notes on the nature of God. Hermana Preciado seems a little reluctant to get into the swing again. Her family was showered with a lot of difficulties for being Mormons while living in Colima. She didn't show up for Sunday school but did make it over for sacrament meeting in the afternoon. I directed the afternoon service: called upon four members of both families to give short talks, after which Elder Flake and I occupied the rest of the time. Elder Flake's remarks go down as about the best I've ever heard by a missionary. My own talk was much briefer and nowhere near as effective. Attendance at sacrament was seventeen.

March 15

Attended to various chores yesterday, including the passing out of hundreds of handbills around town for tonight's film presentation of *El Pavellón Mormón*. And tonight? We were a roaring success! People were late coming but then they swarmed us in droves. We estimated a turnout of between 150–200 persons. We had to show the film three times to accommodate everyone who was waiting outside to get in. After each showing we asked interested parties to fill out little slips of paper with their names and addresses. In this way we have now identified seventeen families for future missionary contact.

Guadalajara, March 16

We were surprised by an unexpected encounter and resolution this morning on the way back to Guadalajara when we met Garza and Bayer coming around a curve in the road. They were heading into Manzanillo with a load of chairs for the *capilla* and some news for us about where Flake and I will be spending the next few months: *Both* of us will stay in Manzanillo to open the place up. When Elder Bayer goes home next week there will be just two assistants to the president, with Elder Colvin (of all people) stepping in as Elder Garza's new companion. I hadn't been expecting this. I was sure Elder Flake would go back into the mission home with Elder Garza, and that I would be left in Manzanillo with a new junior. I suspect President McClellan may have been worried about hurt feelings if one of us was kept on as an assistant and the other dropped. I know I wouldn't have felt badly—it was my idea in the first place. Oh well, we'll see where the wheel of fortune stops next time around. And Elder Flake and I do make, I think, a good missionary team. We're both excited about prospects in Manzanillo and continue to thoroughly enjoy each other's company.

Manzanillo, March 17

Packed up this morning after breakfast in Guad. Bayer and Garza then drove me and Elder Flake down to the bus station at noon on their way back to

Mexico City (we are now shorn of our Volkswagen). The bus to Manzanillo stopped over in Colima for a couple of hours, so we got off and bumped into Hunt and Vance on the street. We accompanied them on some of their visits and brought them up to date on current plans. We're forming a new district consisting of Colima and Manzanillo, with Elder Hunt as supervisor. We finally arrived in Manzanillo late at night, grabbed a cab out to the beach, and went directly to bed upon arriving at the house.

March 18

Back in the trenches again as a pair of glorified co-seniors—we did our first real tracting in Manzanillo this morning. We're going slow and giving everybody more than a fair chance when we talk to them. In the afternoon and evening we looked up addresses obtained from our earlier film showing. Some of the people we found look pretty promising.

March 19

Gave a fair first lesson to a Señora Amézcua and her teenaged son in the afternoon. Then looked up more film references in the afternoon without turning up anything too spectacular. Our custom-built pulpit was finished and delivered today. We're still waiting on blackboards and a sacrament table.

March 20

President McClellan and President Alvarado drove in this morning about an hour before conference was due to begin, bringing with them sacrament trays, *folletos,* baptismal clothing, manuals, and branch reports. Their purpose in coming was to organize the Manzanillo Branch by selecting and setting apart branch officers. Our new branch president will be Hermano Valdéz. His counselor and secretary will be Eric Vicente, a young man who has been a member for six years, but hasn't been to church for three years, having lived during this latter time in Manzanillo with no branch to attend. Auxiliary organization positions in the primary and Sunday school are now filled by the Valdéz and Preciado kids. We had a good conference, with everything running as smoothly as though the branch had been in operation for a long time.

March 21

Today's tracting attracted one or two worthwhile visits to check back on. We also looked up more references from the film presentation, but we're now missing most of the paper slips containing names and addresses of the viewers who indicated an interest in hearing more about the church. After a thorough search of the house, our only conclusion is that the woman caretaker may have snagged them up when she came over the other day.

Started a second lesson with the Amézcua woman and her son. It was after midnight before we finally left, but they continue to look promising. Buses are scarce here and the walk of several miles into Manzanillo and then back to the beach is killing our car-accustomed feet. Elder Flake's excellent Spanish and lucid teaching ability sometimes make me sound like simple Simon, but I don't really mind. We're getting to be great friends and are both gaining from this experience.

March 22

Mutual at our beach house this evening was late getting underway but eventually proved to be a success, thanks to Elder Flake, who has a real knack for organizing group activities. We didn't give a class; just built a fire on the beach, sang songs, played games, roasted hot dogs, and made popcorn. None of the Preciado family came, but the Valdéz family brought their Baptist neighbor, Señora Godina, and her three kids. Several other Baptist *jóvenes* with whom we've been talking recently were also in attendance.

March 23

Almost finished tracting-out the Unidad—a relatively small but nicely constructed neighborhood of family dwellings on the south side of town. Didn't turn up much. We did run into a retired American Negro. Stayed and talked to him for some time. He loaned us a religious magazine entitled *The Plain Truth*, which is, I believe, a *Testigo* publication. Finally finished the day with a lesson at the Amézcuas' home to their rather block-headed neighbor. He listened to the second lesson last night, but it took us close to two hours to stumble through the first lesson with him tonight.

March 24

We bumped into another possibility for the *capilla* while tracting this morning—a large hall, with old office partitions, on the third story of a building that overlooks the main plaza. (President McClellan would prefer that missionary quarters be separate from the chapel.) We talked to the owner who said he would rent it to us for 600 pesos [$48] a month.

We waited at the house in vain this afternoon for the Baptist *jóvenes* to show up for an appointment. Disappointing also was a scheduled third lesson with the Amézcuas which fell through when the boy, Samuel, never made it back from school. But I did receive a telegram from Gordon this morning that has kept me floating around all day. He's been called into his mission home as assistant to the president. It's a move that I knew would come sooner or later—every person who has ever wandered out of the Southeast [Mexican] Mission and passed through Mexico City has left a prophecy about this happening. So I wasn't at all surprised, just filled with pulsating excitement and happiness for Gord. He fully deserves his position and will bring honor to it.

FROM GORDON, TELEGRAFOS NACIONALES

ME LLAMAN A LA CASA BLANCA EN VERACRUZ. SALGO HOY. [They're calling me to the White House in Veracruz. I leave today.]

March 25

We were finally able to reach President McClellan by phone this morning about renting the large room we found for a *capilla,* but he decided no. It wasn't clear why he opposed—it was his suggestion that we be looking for another place.

My self-confidence absorbed a shaking tonight when I started a first lesson and my Spanish and composure both seemed to desert me at the same time, creating a nightmare feeling that I haven't experienced since the early days of my mission. It was as though my jaw were wired shut and my tongue plastered with thick peanut butter so that I could barely talk. What's going on here? I closed the lesson down and we left, Elder Flake demonstrating a level of sympathy and understanding that I appreciated very much. We gave another lesson that went a lot better to an *Adventista* [Adventist] woman and a young friend of hers, who is studying with the Church of Christ. So far, more Protestants than Catholics have been willing to listen to us (which is the opposite of what usually happens).

March 26

We tracted in the neighborhood around the house this morning, but it's mostly tough going. The Catholic priests have already warned the faithful against having anything to do with us. We attempted a slightly irreverent first lesson with Esteven Peregrina (one of our Baptist *jóvenes*), a couple of his friends, and his nonsense-blathering mother. He at least remains hopeful. We lost the Barretos when we went back for a second lesson. Their family and Catholic friends turned up the pressure when they found out about us, and Señor Barreto decided it was more important to appease them.

March 27

Sunday services today were fair, but the Preciado family is dragging us down.

They're always way late for meetings and sometimes don't make it at all. Antonio Preciado is supposed to be Sunday school superintendent, but he's gone to Colima, so I directed. My companion took the adult classes and I took the kids. I later blew a talk for sacrament meeting that I had not taken time to properly prepare. Someday I'll learn that I'm no orator and that I must ready myself before speaking. Before the meeting started I went over to pick up the Amézcuas. They would never have made it over on their own gumption. Our hopes for Esteven Peregrina disintegrated this afternoon when he came over to the house with a cynical *amiga* [girl friend], and they engaged us in a short, irreverent battle over our beliefs. Then Elders Hunt and Vance surprised us with a late visit just before bedtime. They want to plan a *día de campo* with members from both the Colima and Manzanillo branches. They lingered, gabbing, and didn't depart until well into the wee hours.

March 28

Practically finished tracting-out the Las Brisas [The Breezes] neighborhood this morning. Tough going. We made a deal with the proprietor of El Sombrero, the restaurant right next door to the house, to eat our meals there for 15 pesos [$1.20] a day each. This arrangement should save us a lot of time and provide us with a better diet than the peanut butter and jam we've been living on.

A big American Navy oil tanker arrived in port today; sailors are wandering all over town. We talked to a couple of them for awhile, and they said they'd direct their Mormon mates over to see us if possible. We also had an excellent first lesson today with the Baptist family that the Valdézes introduced us to (the Godinas: a mother and her two teenaged sons and daughter). It will be a battle, but I know that they've been impressed with everything so far.

March 29

Spent all day tracting and in so doing found a family (the Quirózes) from Veracruz who heard the missionary lessons there several years ago. The señor wasn't home but, unless he's a complete bum, we may have stumbled onto our best prospects yet.

March 30

More long tracting hours until evening. This time we found a young Mexican sailor (Castellan) who has been a Mormon for about four years and his wife, who isn't a member yet. He bubbles with enthusiasm about the prospects of a branch of the church here and she shows high interest too. We stopped by to see the Quiróz family from Veracruz, but the husband was working late. The rest of them are fine people. Finally gave a ragged third lesson to Hermana Amézcua and Samuél. They're teetering on the edge of indecision, but I think they'll eventually make it.

Hermano Valdéz received a telegram from a Mr. Laughton, who is the American consul in Guadalajara, requesting that he reserve a hotel room for him and his family (they're Mormons) during Semana Santa [Holy Week]. My companion and I will have to help out on this; Hermano Valdéz is not sure what to do.

March 31

On our way into town this morning we found out that two American sailors became embroiled in a fight last night and both of them ended up in the hospital. One of them is not expected to live, having suffered critical knife wounds. Good show for the U.S. We dropped in on the municipal president of Manzanillo to see about securing a beach house for the American consul and his family during Semana Santa (every place in town has been reserved for weeks). We were tendered use of a police truck and a three-man squadron to try and turn something up. Drove out to the exclusive Santiago Beach area and checked the best hotel. They only had some bungalows left and, when we made a long-distance call, Brother Laughton decided to come down the week after the holidays when most of the tourists will be gone.

A second lesson with the Godina family, who showed some signs of waning enthusiasm, but they're still hopeful. We visited the Quiróz family, who had investigated the church in Veracruz, and finally met the señor, who speaks pretty good English but waxes a little philosophical. It will prove a tough chore to get him baptized. He did invite us to eat with them.

April 2

We paid a visit to the two American sailors in the San Pedrito Hospital this morning. The critically wounded one has somehow managed to pull through, although his condition is still grave. He's lost a lot of blood and his internal organs are pretty perforated. He's a good-looking, athletically built kid from Iowa. He would doze off every few minutes, but was completely coherent when awake. We were able to talk to the nurse for him about his condition and medical treatment, etc. His assailant was a scrawny kid from Philadelphia, who received a slight wound in his rib section and then went through the unnerving experience of watching his victim struggling for life for three days right across the aisle from him. He related his version of what happened: both were drunk, got into an argument, he lost control of himself and attacked the other with a seven-inch switchblade. Now he's worrying that the Mexicans are going to prosecute him here and throw him into jail forever. The American consul is trying to get him out of the hospital and out of the country before that happens. Both sailors were glad to talk to Americans. We'll drop by sometime next week to see how they're getting along.

The afternoon and evening wound up being completely washed out. We waited at the house for the sisters to show up for their Relief Society meeting, but no one came. Finally, we walked over to the Amézcuas' to ask the *hermana* if she would let us use a bungalow she owns in Las Brisas during Semana Santa. The owner of our beach cottage is coming down for the holiday, and we had previously agreed to vacate for the time she'll be here. Hermana Amézcua was graciously agreeable. Returned to the house for Mutual but suffered a repetition of this afternoon's fiasco: the only ones who made it over were the young Mexican sailor and his wife. The Manzanillo Branch is obviously weak. We have to depend primarily on two families for everything, and one of them is completely undependable. None of the newly set-apart branch officers appear to have taken their responsibilities seriously. They expect us to handle it all. We will have to do something—take more time from our missionary efforts, I suppose, and devote it to strengthening our branch members. Still, we can only do so much in this regard, with just two member families to work with.

April 3

We ran Sunday school and sacrament services consecutively this morning so we could be out of the house before the landlady and her family arrived from Guad. We just started to get all our stuff packed away when the family swooped down on us. Actually, they're nice people, so we aren't too worried about leaving things behind for the week. The little Amézcua place in the Brisas will be all right for us to stay in, except it has no running water. This will mean nightly rinsing off in the ocean and pumping water into buckets for flushing the toilet.

April 4

No problem with the Godina family on the third lesson today. They are naturally all *de acuerdo* [in agreement] with the Word of Wisdom; prohibitions against smoking and drinking fit nicely into their Baptist background. Waited until almost 10:00 P.M. at the Amézcuas' for a fourth lesson, but once we finally got underway it was ragged and spiritless. Samuél doesn't pay any attention and can't answer the simplest questions. Neither he nor his mother are very close to becoming members at this point.

Colima, April 6

We put in some long hours yesterday but they didn't prove very effective. We had a second lesson with the Quiróz family from Veracruz, but not before first eating dinner with them and engaging in a marathon talking session. A fourth lesson with the Godina family today told us that it won't be easy for them to break off old religious shackles, but they're still in the running. We changed into jeans after finishing work for the night, then struck off for Colima, thumbing for a ride on the highway. A couple of *jóvenes* picked us up. Elder Flake spent the entire trip arguing with one of them, but I conked out before we had gone very far. The car broke down just outside of Colima, so we walked in the rest of the way. I spent the night fitfully suspended in Elder Hunt's hammock.

April 7

Up and out of the house bright and early this morning to begin our *día de campo*. We hitchhiked rides out to Cuyutlán, a beach resort where the surf is famed for its emerald green color and the size of its waves. The place was swarming with a holiday crowd, and we had to walk a mile down the beach to escape the mobs. After finding a less populated area, we took our shoes off to do a little wading and gradually ended up where the waves were breaking, about fifty yards out from shore. They were gigantic, at times swelling to heights of fifteen to twenty feet before crashing down in a violent roar of foam and turbulence. The thing to do was to catch a wave just before it broke and let it shoot you along like a surfboard while swimming for dear life down the edge of the curl. Or dive under the wave just as it began to break and then find yourself popping up behind the surf line in deep ocean. Not exactly sticking to missionary rules and more than a little dangerous, I suppose, but a lot of fun. After our clothes dried out we hitched a ride back to Colima, cleaned up, and went to the movies. The last show was late, so Flake and I stayed overnight again.

Manzanillo, April 8

We hitchhiked back to Manzanillo this morning and arrived in time to put in a couple of hours tracting before lunch. A first lesson with the sailor's wife (Castellan) went like a how-to-do-it model. She's in complete agreement with everything, and we could probably baptize her tomorrow if we wanted. When we came home in the evening we found Elders Colvin and Garza waiting on our step. Hunt and Vance had also come in with them, so Manzanillo should see a lot of tracting tomorrow.

April 9

We split up the tracting in three sectors this morning. I drew Elder Garza to work with. We hiked around the hills overlooking the bay, knocking mostly at poor hovels. I was concentrating on giving our pitch to an exceedingly porculent woman at one shack when both she and Elder Garza began snickering. I felt a gnawing sensation against the toes of my right foot and, glancing down, observed a scrawny goat diligently attempting to make a meal of my shoe. Later, as we tracted on, Elder Garza told me they are thinking about sending a new greenie down here sometime next week. If so, I imagine that I'll stay and Elder Flake will be moved to greener pastures. Our visitors all retreated back to Colima after lunch.

Our fifth lesson with the Godina family this afternoon was prolonged by a lot of extra questions. The boys had a reference book, published by a Baptist writer, that contained scriptural quotations supposedly in opposition to Mormon teachings. We got through most of the questions without any trouble, but they still are not committing themselves to baptism. Later we went by the hospital to visit with the American sailors, bringing along a few American magazines for them to read. But the American consul had pulled some strings, and both of them had been flown out a couple of days ago.

April 10

No Sunday school this morning due to the fact that our landlady and her family didn't leave the house for Guadalajara until afternoon. Brother Laughton (the American consul from Guad) arrived while we were setting up for sacrament meeting, which he and his family had come to attend. My companion gave his usual excellent address, and I managed a fair talk myself, on Christ and the Resurrection. Brother Laughton also spoke briefly, in a horrible gringo accent, as did his wife, who also sang a nice solo. After the service was over we replaced the meeting chairs and furnishings with the regular house furniture for the Laughtons, who are going to vacation here for the next week. But we may have a little trouble with our landlady. She walked in during sacrament meeting this afternoon looking for some bedding and became a bit huffy when she discovered we were holding a religious meeting in her house.

April 11

Elder Flake was sick all last night and this morning with the runs, chills, headache, etc., and I felt a little sickish myself. Lacking running water and most other amenities, this little shack we're holing up in this week would not be a good place to suffer through an extended bout of diarrhea and vomiting. Flake said he felt somewhat recovered in the afternoon and we ventured out. But neither one of us over-abounded in pep and enthusiasm. Conducted a listless sixth lesson with the Godinas, and it looks like they're going to put off baptism for awhile. I do feel that they'll eventually accept and be baptized. A couple of other scheduled visits fell through, so we came home relatively early. Actually Elder Flake should have rested the whole day. I'm starting to get a bad head cold.

April 12

I think the Godinas are going to make it. We had a little visit with the *hermana* and Rodolfo, plus an unexpected visitor in the person of a Baptist *joven* (name of Noé, supposedly a terror with the scriptures). Noé started to rip right in on the Book of Mormon, but Elder Flake handled him superbly, and with Hermana Godina and Rodolfo switching to our side, Noé ended up very flattened indeed. During the course of the discussion Hermana Godina practically committed herself to baptism. Such an event would be a tremendous boost to the Manzanillo Branch.

We noticed some very strange specimens wandering around town today. They appear to be Americans, I would guess mostly in their early to midtwenties, dressed in outlandish garb with decorative paint designs on their faces. They are undoubtedly connected with the wildly painted bus that has been parked on the beach between our house and El Sombrero restaurant.

April 13

Had more discussions with the Godinas. Today was the day we had initially set for their baptisms, but the *hermana* wants to wait. She says she will go ahead with it on Sunday, and I think Rodolfo and Flor will too, but I'm not so sure about Ramón. We went on to have a fairly decent fifth lesson with the Amézcuas in the afternoon, and there's a slight possibility that they might consent to baptism this Sunday too. Hermana Amézcua and Hermana Godina are old friends. They both teach school and they want to get together for a final talk before they make any final commitments.

While cutting through town this afternoon we bumped into a couple of the young American beatniks or hippies or whatever they're supposed to be and stopped for a good-natured chat. They invited us to drop by their colorfully painted bus for a longer visit, offering to let Elder Flake use their tape-recording equipment to play a tape he just received from his parents. We decided to take them up on their offer this evening. We walked over to their bus, which is crammed with electronic equipment and living gear. All told they appear to number about four couples—a pretty crazy crew. They call themselves the "Merry Pranksters" and seemed a little surprised that we had never heard of them. When we asked why we should know them, they claimed to have made a record and are now down here making a movie about themselves. They are adamantly opposed to the Vietnam War and other social evils, as they see them, back home in the U.S. They also said there's a cultural revolution going on back home (whatever that's supposed to mean), especially among college-age kids. After letting Elder Flake listen to his tape they were politely incredulous to learn more about what *we* are doing in Mexico.

After awhile, most of the conversation became confined to us and a slightly older, balding man by the name of Ken Kesey, who is evidently leader of the group—an intelligent, articulate person who, given the group's antics and general appearance, surprised me with his soft-spoken style. Other "Pranksters" were not so low-key. Ordinary conversation was routinely spiced with obscene language, and one of the young women, who was lying down in the back of the bus, seemed to be in a delirious state—moaning, cursing, and occasionally shouting that we should "get the blankety-blank off the bus." We declined an invitation for something to drink from some kind of large container and, thanking them for their hospitality, departed. It's hard to imagine a more incongruous comparison, but since they just live next door, I wonder how many people in town may somehow associate them with us— the crazy gringos on the beach. Not very good publicity for us, I'm afraid. [Unknown to Gary and Elder Flake, Ken Kesey was the author of the award-winning *One Flew over the Cuckoo's Nest*. In the early 1960s he was a bohemian writer and outspoken advocate of the recreational use of LSD, and he and his young associates (the Merry Pranksters) became icons to the emerging counterculture in the United States. The Pranksters' flight to Manzanillo, Mexico, to avoid federal drug charges in the United States is detailed in a chapter of *The Electric Kool-Aid Acid Test* by Tom Wolfe.]

April 14

More tracting—just about finished with the hill surrounding the town. We ate lunch with the Laughtons at midday, and afterward Brother Laughton took us for a tour of the bay in his speedboat. Good news: Ramón told us today that he definitely plans on being baptized with the rest of his family. Also talked with Hermano Quiróz about some of his "different ideas." It turns out that he is a Mason and has no intention of joining the church, although he hopes to stay friends. He gave us a peek at the supposedly secret handbook of Masonic rituals and also showed us some of his ceremonial vestments.

April 15

A startling turn of events: Elder Flake was gone today from Manzanillo by three o'clock in the afternoon, abruptly recalled to Mexico City as a regular missionary and assigned a new junior companion to break in. His replacement—and my own new junior companion—was sitting in the front yard of the beach house when Flake and I came home at noon. His name is Morton Remer and he just arrived in Mexico, dripping green from the LTM, the day before yesterday. He's short, somewhat chubby, amiable, and the few people he's already seen today seem to like him right off the bat. Elder Flake immediately made the rounds to say goodbye, then quickly packed and we saw him off at the bus depot. In my judgment Elder Flake is undoubtedly one of the finest teachers of the gospel in anybody's mission. We enjoyed a close and mutually beneficial companionship. His departure will certainly make it tougher for me to keep the precarious situation of the Manzanillo Branch from worsening, but I will do the best I can. It's also a special responsibility for me to make sure that my new companion receives the proper kind of initiation into missionary work.

After Elder Flake departed we dropped by the Amézcuas' for a frank talk, and they expressed themselves clearly against baptism, at least for the time-being. Their comprehension of the lessons has not been great, nor have they been receptive to acquiring a testimony through prayer. We went back to the Godinas', and the *hermana* was visibly shaken and upset that Elder Flake had been removed so suddenly. She's having second thoughts now about their baptism on Sunday and may want to wait again. I explained the situation as best I could, and when we left she seemed to be feeling better about everything.

Elder Flake and I had previously agreed to meet with Noé again for further discussion, but when my new companion and I arrived at his home we found that he had also invited the Baptist pastor, and they were both spoiling for a showdown. I foolishly allowed myself to be partially dragged into one. It was impossible to keep completely calm in response to the distorted remarks of the pastor. He attempted to attack the church on the usual grounds, but I managed to place him on the defensive instead. Still, after an hour and a half, we had accomplished nothing more than waste time.

The final flung brick of the day hit us when we went by Hermana Castellan, wife of our sailor member. She confessed to having pretended not being home the last several times we have come by, then broke out crying and sobbed that she was unworthy to become a member of the church. I tried to calm her down with a few *consejos* [counsel, advice] and she seemed to feel better. She wouldn't reveal the exact nature of the problem and I didn't try to pry. A very heavy day in all. Obstacles are suddenly starting to line themselves up, one after another. I know President McClellan is very concerned about the future of the Manzanillo Branch, and I also know that we'll need every bit of help we can get from the Lord to save it. A long letter from Gord with first tidings of his mission home experience was the only bright note in an otherwise dismal day.

LETTER FROM GORDON

Gar: This is way past due. Thanks for the hand-pumping, backslapping support expressed in your last letter. I felt the same sting of excitement for you back in February when I got your wire that you had been made an assistant. I feel honored and elated about the call, of course, but in the meantime the inauguration shouts have been somewhat silenced by a not very exciting apprenticeship in the mission home. The story is that Elder Baron, current assistant to the president, wanted to finish his mission working in the field and will be leaving tomorrow for Puebla now that I've been familiarized with all the routines and responsibilities of the position. Actually, there wasn't that much to learn. As I'm sure you're well aware from your own experience, my primary duties as assistant consist of putting out the mission magazine every month, recommending transfers and companion changes to President Hatch, attending and speaking at conferences throughout the mission, developing ideas to make missionary work more effective, and working with other missionaries from time to time. These are all important tasks but the constant, direct work with investigators is missing and in between official duties there's more leisure time and monotony than I'm used to. I can understand why Elder Baron is so anxious to get back into the thick of things in the field. I will need to look for ways to magnify my calling and not waste time. I know I will be looked to as an example so my most important task, I think, will be to maintain high standards of personal conduct, maintain humility, and allow my actions to be guided by the spirit of the Lord. I must guard against becoming cocky or complacent.

Already I've racked up a lot of travel hours in trips with the mission office staff that have carried me from Tapachula, near the Guatemala border, to Mexico City for a driver's license (I flunked the eye test on a newly purchased pair of Mexican glasses). While in the City we passed by your mission office where I met Elder Judd and your one time greenie companion from Cashe Valley, Elder Barlow, who was absolutely convinced that I was you. Both expressed nothing but the highest regards and respect for you. Also present was a brash and overly loud elder by the name of North, who deserved a punch in the nose for his disdainful predictions on the success of Manzanillo. Sorry to have missed you. I was hoping to surprise you with our visit, but I ended up being the one surprised when I learned you had been sent to open up Manzanillo.

Last week Baron, London, and I went downtown to watch a parade in honor of Díaz Ordaz, president of the Republic, who was in Veracruz to inaugurate some new buildings. We were almost trampled to death by the wild-eyed mob that was pursuing the presidential motorcade down main street. Ordaz was standing up in his limo, blowing kisses to the crowd while his bodyguards and the police were clearing a path with their billy clubs. During the excitement someone broke into our parked car and swiped my suit and my only good pair of pants, which I had just picked up from the cleaners. My wardrobe is getting to be pretty skimpy, not to mention threadbare, and I no longer have a suit to wear. Fortunately, suits are seldom required here during the hot seasons of the year, but I'm really ticked by the loss.

Now that Baron's leaving I won't have a designated companion, but I will have the daily companionship of the office staff, including Elder London who's been mission secretary since December. Grant Harris, who is serving in the mission home as secretary of mission records and statistics, is another elder I've enjoyed pairing off with from time to time. Elder Harris had previously always struck me as a wiseguy—brash, arrogant, disdainful of Mexicans, with a real complex about his Spanish and ability to effectively teach the missionary lessons. But I've since discovered that once you get past his sneering exterior he's clever, a hard worker, and a genuinely funny guy who provides good company. [Now, mission rules require that assistants to the president be matched with a regular companion and be assigned to a proselyting district and specific work area. When we were in Mexico, assistants were expected to do some ad hoc proselyting, when time permitted, and work with other missionaries but were given much wider latitude in defining their own agendas.]

I've been on Elder London to write you, and of course he faithfully promises to do so. Don't hold your breath. I don't know how Steve would be doing if he were a senior companion working in the field. There's never been any doubt about his potential and, given a challenge, perhaps he would rise to the occasion. At any rate, among the gringo missionaries Steve speaks far and away the best Spanish in the mission. I've heard some who have somehow managed a more authentic native ring in their pronunciation (like Elder Martineau, who grew up in Colónia Juárez), but none who are more precise or grammatically correct. My own Spanish already has suffered drastically from disuse since I've been working in the mission office. I'll rely on Steve to correct my numerous mistakes when writing for the *Faro*.

Gar, out of curiosity, how much do you weigh these days? I've perished away to around 62 kilos, which never much concerned me until I shockingly figured it out in pounds [approximately 135 pounds]. Two years ago I weighed 155. I went to see a local doc and it appears that I've probably had a mild case of amebic dysentery since at least Villa Flores. I'm now taking some pills that will supposedly cure me. By the way, have Mom and Dad indicated anything to you about coming down to pick us up? Do you know your release date yet for sure? Try to find out. If we work it right maybe you could slip down south to join me in Veracruz and then we could swing back together to Mexico City. Whatever the case, I still want us to have a working day together, if at all possible, before we leave Mexico. Keep me posted concerning the battle on the Manzanillo front. Elder North's pessimism not withstanding, I know that you and Elder Flake make a terrific team and, with the Lord's helping hand, will succeed in bringing the church to Manzanillo.

Your brother, Gord

April 16

Hermana Godina continues in her doubts about tomorrow's baptism, but meanwhile wants her daughter Flor to be baptized along with her brothers Ramón and Rodolfo, should they decide to take the step. Flor has attended Sunday services with her family but has only listened to one lesson. Today, therefore, we gave her a first lesson in the morning and a combined forth and sixth lesson in the afternoon. Now a new problem. Our Guadalajara landlady, who's still in town, made it very clear that she's not pleased with her house being used as a Mormon *capilla*. She expects us to start looking for another place to have our meetings, although she can't force us out of the house until our contract expires in August. I'll have to contact President McClellan again for his thoughts on the matter. I wish we had received permission earlier to rent the big place in town that Elder Flake and I ran across several weeks ago. Meanwhile we moved from our little Brisas place back to the big beach house this afternoon.

Mutual this evening started out almost an hour late because of tardy arrivers, but once underway turned out pretty well. I gave an informal class on the importance of developing *metas,* and we had fun playing games afterward.

The Godinas' baptisms are scheduled for tomorrow morning at 6:00 A.M. Hermana Godina said she planned to spend most of the night praying about her decision. She made a special plea that we add our prayers to hers, which we always do. Noé was at Mutual tonight and was furious at the idea that the Godinas might be baptized.

April 17

Sleep seemed to come only in snatches last night as I worried over the Godinas' baptisms. I finally arose at 5:00 A.M. to press the baptismal clothing and prepare for the service. The Godinas arrived at 6:30, having decided to take the step. I interviewed them all with satisfactory results and directed and spoke at a short service (both the Valdéz and Preciado families made it out of bed to be present). Then we all repaired to the ocean edge, back of the house, where I took Sister Godina into the water with me. The footing was treacherous, the tide was strong, and it proved difficult to perform the ordinance. I finally succeeded, however, in baptizing Sister Godina as a new member of the church and the first convert in the Manzanillo Branch. After returning to the knot of onlookers we decided to walk a bit further down the beach, where a peaceful cove promised an easier experience for the others.

When we arrived at our new spot I entered the water but was shocked when Ramón started backing away. I talked to him carefully for a few minutes, but he said he had changed his mind (quite apparently with the help of Noé, who had been talking constantly to Ramón as they walked along the beach). After his definite refusal I baptized both Rodolfo and Linda Flor, neither of whom professed similar qualms. Hermana Godina was heartbroken over Ramón's last-minute defection, and the morning that had begun so brightly dissolved into a long, dismal trudge back to the house. I consoled Hermana Godina as best I could and promised her that Ramón would eventually make the right decision, but her faith has been shaken and it will require time to mend the damage that has been done. In this afternoon's sacrament meeting I delivered a speech calculated to bolster her spirits, and it did seem to help somewhat. I feel almost as badly as she does.

April 20

The last few days have been mentally painful for me. I still feel badly about Ramón and concerned for his mother. The results from our hard tracting continue to be nil, while numerous other small problems press. We quit eating at El Sombrero restaurant after two solid weeks of fish head soup and now must confront the daily and time-consuming task of eking up enough decent groceries to live on (we're a stout walk from the nearest store). We've finished tracting in the hills and are now back in town again. We've given some first lessons to new investigators but they don't show much promise. We've seen the Godinas a couple of times and the *hermana* still wonders why the Lord has neglected her prayers in behalf of Ramón. So many problems seem to be thundering down on us at once that I almost feel I might have to be the first to pin a prophet's medal on Elder North (loud and brash as he is) for making such astute predictions to Gord in Mexico City a few weeks ago about the chances of our branch surviving here.

April 21

Had a horrible breakfast of botched, homemade pancakes this morning. Tracting went a little better, and Elder Remer is making marked progress. We gave a long, constantly interrupted lesson to a family out in San Pedrito. My companion about fell out of his chair when a young married girl started to breast feed her baby right in the middle of the discussion. He had been told to expect it, but it's not usually such an attractive young woman. Later I talked to Hermano Valdéz; his work situation is grave. He had been weeping and is a distraught man. All of the family want to go back to their home town in Monterréy and the pressure on him is mounting. About the only reason they're staying now in Manzanillo is because the *hermano* feels obligated to the branch (he had originally told President McClellan that they wouldn't leave until September). It would be the probable death knell for the Manzanillo Branch if they were to leave now. I'll wait until the president answers my letter before I try a phone call about the latest problems. Hunt and Vance were at the house when we returned home tonight. They just came over to visit and we talked till late. It was good to see them and made me feel a whole lot better about things in general.

April 22

We had some success tracting this morning. We're finding a lot of people home who weren't there the first time Elder Flake and I went past. Stopped by for a brief chat with Hermana Godina. She's feeling a little better (or at least is covering her feelings) about Ramón. She agreed to start teaching the Sunday school class next week. Tomorrow I'll talk to Ramón and see what he's been thinking about since last Sunday.

April 23

Engaged in a short but serious conversation with Ramón this morning. I told him it was his decision and that we wouldn't be coming around to pester him about it every *rato* [moment]. Then held an agonizingly long first lesson with a large group of mostly indifferent listeners. My companion took his half of the lesson almost through for the first time. Good, although the going is tedious. We stayed home in the afternoon for the children's primary classes, but nobody showed. I prepared my Mutual class, for which there was a good turnout in the evening, and everything went fairly well. Later, after everyone had gone home, my companion and I witnessed a Catholic religious procession, winding its chanting, candle-lit way out to some holy spot past our house. There were a lot of people in that line.

Colima, April 24

We had very good attendance for both Sunday services today—almost 100 percent for sacrament. At this moment our little branch appears to be regaining some of its health, especially now that Hermano Valdéz seems to have made satisfactory arrangements at his work, thus removing temporarily the immediate worry of their leaving. I had to take out the usual extra time early this morning to prepare the Sunday school lesson and in the afternoon to prepare a talk for sacrament meeting. Hermana Godina will begin teaching the Sunday school lesson next week, which will be a big help. My companion did comparatively well with a short talk I helped him to prepare, but he makes no personal effort to study unless I sit right down with him. Instead, he drops into a dead snooze in less time than it takes to tell about it. I hate to complain so much myself, but Elder Remer's almost daily whining about the hardships of missionary life in Manzanillo is starting to grind on my nerves.

Hopped a bus right after the conclusion of evening services—a long, hot, crammed-with-people ride. I wanted to pick up some Books of Mormon, Hunt's basketball, and also call President McClellan to fill him in on the branch situation and ask for some things we need to have mailed. Arrived in Colima too late to make the call to Mexico City, so we decided to stay over and try our luck in the morning.

Manzanillo, April 25

Ate breakfast with Hunt and Vance, then put through my call to Mexico City. Told the president about the house situation, asked him to have sent down the things we need, and discussed some of the Valdéz family problems. The president authorized us to find another house and otherwise just counseled us to do our best under the circumstances. Our bus back to Manzanillo didn't pull in until late morning, so we just checked on a few apartment possibilities, bought some groceries, and went back to the house for lunch. Engaged in a brief spat with my companion. His griping about everything in general and Mexicans in particular finally got my goat.

April 26

More tracting and fallen visits throughout the day. The best news is that the apartment we looked at yesterday seems to be everything we want. It's modern, furnished, has large rooms, located right in town, and the owner wouldn't object to our meetings. He wouldn't budge an inch lower than 900 pesos [a little over $70] a month, which is high but still 300 less than what we're paying now. We finally broke through with a lesson today—a couple of guys at a government *farmacia* [pharmacy] who invited us to come back. One was very sharp, the other very argumentative.

April 27

Played a little basketball with Ramón, Rodolfo, and one of their friends, but our play was eventually curtailed by the griping and boo-hooing of my companion. I was becoming too disgusted to play any longer when we got word that President Camacho (one of President McClellan's native Mexican aides) and his wife were in town looking for us. We bumped into them in the center of town, showed them out to the beach house, talked over some branch matters, and sent them back off to Colima. I phoned President McClellan about the apartment we found and he gave the go-ahead, also stipulating that we be on the lookout for yet another place as missionary living quarters that will be separate from the *capilla*.

Tracted all afternoon. We've almost finished off the Unidad Hidalgo for the second time. We again encountered the retired American Negro whom Elder Flake and I ran into when we first arrived in Manzanillo. As we were leaving today he revealed that he was Larry Doby, the former major league outfielder for the Cleveland Indians back in the fifties. Incredible! He says he loves it down here, away from the American potboiler of pressure and racial prejudice. [After Jackie Robinson broke the color line in 1947 with the Brooklyn Dodgers in the National League, Larry Doby became the first black baseball player in the American League.]

April 28

Our two investigators at the *farmacia* have interested a doctor friend into listening to us. We'll start with the first lesson again for all three of them. Also today we were stopped in the street by a young but prospering architect, who says he listened to most of the missionary lessons in Uruapan about a year ago. He invited us to his home, where we talked for some time. He's an intelligent, sophisticated, and very exacting man, who speaks quite good English. His self-professed primary interests in Mormonism focus on our philosophical concepts (the nature of God, the purpose of existence, etc.). I have just the thing for him to read: *New Witness for God* by B. H. Roberts. We'll have a general discussion with him some time next week to figure out which path would be best to follow.

April 29

Met with the municipal president this morning to see if he could help us secure a *fiador* [co-signer] for our apartment contract. He suggested we get Mr. Laughton to send us down his signature from Guadalajara, then phoned our prospective landlord and got him to agree to such an arrangement. We may have picked up a few notches of prestige with these maneuverings, and with the American consul's note of recommendation there shouldn't be too many future problems about renting to Mormons.

The appointment with our buddies at the *farmacia* turned out to be a snare set for us by the so called "doctor," who is really a representative of a Catholic propaganda outfit called the "Catholic League" of something or other. He wasn't very well versed for religious combat, however, and it was rather amusing to hear him parrot pounded-in Catholic concepts that had nothing to do with the questions being asked. Whatever ideas he had of refuting our teachings were rather squashed. We drew the lesson to a close at the half-way point. The hour was late, the "doctor" hadn't come to sincerely search for truth, nor was he willing to accept it if found.

April 30

Gave a poorly received first lesson to an otherwise friendly fisherman down on the edge of the lagoon. My companion blew his part, became ticked at himself and quit. After we left I vented a lecture at him on a few points that I've been wanting to hash over for some time now. It seemed to accomplish some good and, in fact, we've been hitting it off better the last few days. Good mutual service tonight—more animated than any other I can remember here. Teresa Valdéz, who's supposed to be the Mutual president couldn't make it, so I ran the whole show.

May 2

Hermana Godina brought a man with a truck out to the beach to help load our furniture, and we were moved into our new quarters in town by 10:30 this morning. We don't have a stove or refrigerator installed yet, and the hot water boiler is plugged up. Went over to the Preciados' in the afternoon to pick up the last of our clothes (Hermana Valdéz is going to start doing our laundry now). Our new landlord keeps putting off the signing of our contract, and I keep nagging him about it. Suffered through a real mess trying to finish up the first lesson to our *farmacia* friends. The Catholic-Leaguer was present again, and so was a Swiss guy, whose Spanish wasn't the best. I knew better than to try to wade through such a confused mélange, but I tried anyway, and the sad results were all that could be expected.

May 3

We finally had the apartment contract made up and signed today, but now we are told we have to have to mail it to Guadalajara for Brother Laughton's personal signature; a mailed note will not suffice. We had a general talk with our affluent young architect, Señor Cerda. Skimmed over a variety of subjects, dealing mostly with philosophical concepts. So far I see no theological problems that can't be solved. Elder Ron Crompton (my old buddy from Madero during the first days of my mission) was the missionary who taught Señor Cerda and his wife in Uruapan, and they still think very highly of him. Later, Elder Herrera came along as a replacement for Crompton and couldn't answer the questions they posed, so their interest gradually diminished.

May 4

Gave up on our landlord and made arrangements ourselves to have the stove installed. Also had a man come over and repair the boiler, otherwise we would be waiting for an eternity of *mañanas* [tomorrows] to get things done. Tracted in the morning, visited briefly with the Godinas in the afternoon. Ramón, Rodolfo, and some friends of theirs have made a steel guitar by themselves that works surprisingly well, just in time for the upcoming holidays. Every night until the middle of this month is going to be a party night in town. These are Las Fiestas de Mayo [May celebrations]. A rock 'n' roll band is going full blast right outside our apartment at midday and then again every evening until midnight. Speaking of revelry, I haven't seen the American Merry Pranksters in town of late. I wonder how their "movie" turned out. [The Pranksters—aware that they were under surveillance and about to be arrested by Mexican authorities—had returned to the United States, where Kesey was taken into custody on drug charges by the FBI.]

May 6

Another long day of tracting in the morning and afternoon. We've completely finished the main commercial sector for the second time; not seeing many glitters of gold. In the evening we finally got our long-delayed fifth lesson underway with Cerda, the architect. I modified it a little to mesh better with the irregular circumstances of not having gone through the other four lessons first. The plan of salvation and the principle of eternal progression, presented in simple terms, were very satisfactorily received. Deeper, more probing questions were saved and will be discussed at our next meeting.

Good to get another letter from Gord—like finally receiving an overdue issue of your favorite magazine subscription carrying the latest episode of an eagerly awaited serial story.

LETTER FROM GORDON

Gar: I've been on the road a lot since writing last, attending mission conferences in Tuxtla Chiapas, Villahermosa, and Mérida on the Yucatán Peninsula. It was good to be back in Tuxtla, although hard to believe that almost five months have passed since I was supervising elder there, trying to keep Elder Granger from running amok and the branch from disintegrating into chaos. (Things subsequently have calmed down and the Tuxtla Branch appears to be prospering again.) While in Tuxtla, London and I snuck out in the mission station wagon to make a quick trip over the mountains to Villa Flores to visit the two couples I baptized there last October. They were pleased to see us but also appeared bewildered as to what they should be doing as members of the church without a church to attend. I could only encourage them to continue living the principles of the gospel and offer them continued hope that in the future missionaries might return to Villa Flores to open a branch there. Secretly, I regret to say, I have some doubts about the prospects of opening up Villa Flores again—it's so damn remote and isolated from other towns in the region.

Speaking of Elder Granger, London and I recently paid a visit to him and Elder Sherlock (who also drove me to despair in Tuxtla as Granger's replacement) who are now working *together* as companions in Tierra Blanca, Veracruz. After he was transferred from Tuxtla, Elder Granger had major blow-ups (fistfights and blood) with two different companions in Oaxaca, and Elder Sherlock was a constant source of exasperation to his next companion after I left for Puebla. In desperation, President Hatch put them together in Tierra Blanca and, unbelievably, it seems to have worked. Granger admonishes Sherlock and bosses him around, but Sherlock doesn't seem to mind much and they've actually been getting some missionary work accomplished together.

Prior to the Villahermosa conference, President Hatch dispatched me to check on a missionary pair in Campeche, a charming port city situated on the Gulf of Mexico between Veracruz and Mérida. Their weekly reports had shown a significant decline in effort and effectiveness and the senior companion, a native Mexican by the name of Orellana, had written several very dispirited letters recently to President Hatch. We (Elder Harris, the mission office records secretary, was my companion for the trip) arrived unannounced and found Orellana and his companion at their apartment, half-dressed, lying around reading magazines and listening to music on the radio instead of out doing missionary work. Elder Orellana was obviously depressed and had some fairly serious doubts about his missionary calling. His companion was a little embarrassed by our unexpected arrival but is just trying to make the best of things as the junior companion. (How well I remember my own days with Elder Splinders in San Martín.) A bawling out and pep talk just didn't seem the right way to handle things. Instead we sat down and organized some visits for that night and made plans to tract the following morning. Orellana is intelligent and capable but is bogged down with concerns about family problems at home and low finances. I told him I would talk to President Hatch about getting some financial aid through the mission home and tried to encourage him to forget about outside problems and concentrate on missionary work. Brave words, easy for me to say in situations like that. I don't know if I was much real help or not.

Last week I was in Mérida for conference with Elder London (and gave a very unprepared talk, since London and I had spent the day making some arrangements for a doctor to see one of the Mérida missionaries who was later diagnosed with typhoid fever). Richard Martz, another elder, also accompanied us, and the reason for his so doing is worth commenting on. Elder Martz is due to go home shortly and always had desired to work in Mérida but never got the chance. President Hatch has a fondness for Elder Martz, who, even now, has limited language ability and has never been a supervisor or had a leadership position. It's another reflection of President Hatch's generosity and kindness that he asked Elder Martz to come along to Mérida with us on this trip.

After conference London and I did a little sight-seeing. According to Steve, when he was stationed in Mérida a year ago all three missionary pairs (including the lady missionaries) chartered a boat and went snorkeling off Isla Mujer [a tourist island resort]. Jeeez. Apparently President Hatch found out about it when one of the missionaries started feeling guilty and blew the whistle. There were reprimands and transfers aplenty. It reminds me of the story I heard about a pair of missionaries down here several years ago who hopped on a plane over the weekend for Miami Beach, Florida, which actually is a fairly short flight from Mérida. The ambiance of Mérida is so delightful and it's so cut off from mission headquarters in Veracruz, that apparently the temptation to play has been irresistible for some missionaries.

I spoke to President Hatch about Mom and Dad's plans of driving to Mexico in August to pick us up after we're released. Our mission policy on touring with parents seems to be that President Hatch not only condones it, he encourages parents to come (a number of other missionaries' parents have done so here in the past). So I should be free to follow whatever plans we're able to make. At your end we'll have to go by President McClellan's final decision, of course, but I'm confident that we can get things worked out.

Looking forward, as always, to hearing from you soon. Your brother,
Gord

May 7

Hunt and Vance dropped in on us late last night. Their main news was that Hunt and I will probably be receiving changes next Tuesday. The source of this information was a phone conversation with Elder Garza. Based on what Garza intimated to me the last time he was in town tracting with us, I could be headed back to the mission home as an assistant again to take Elder Colvin's place when he leaves for home. Will just have to wait and see what happens.

For the first time in my whole mission my finest Technicolor dreams at night are shifting to that unbelievable day in August when Gordon and I will part company with Mexico. I can't deny that anticipation of near-future plans and the beginning escalation of going-home excitement are crowding more prominently into my thoughts as the days race by. But I can also be sincere and say that such mixed feelings haven't introduced any conscious loafing or coasting; instead, my conception of missionary work continues to grow along with a desire to better fulfill my calling.

We obtained the architect Cerda's permission to be *fiador* for our apartment contract and got in a little tracting before lunch. Elder Remer and I practiced singing some songs in the afternoon for the talent night at Mutual. The program turned out pretty well, with almost everyone participating. Remer and I accounted for six songs ourselves (if only Mr. Willardson and the South High Acapella Choir could see me now!).

Colima, May 8

We held our first branch priesthood meeting this morning, with President Valdéz teaching the lesson. We also ordained Rodolfo Godina a deacon in the Aaronic priesthood. Eric Vicente had agreed to give a talk in Sunday school, in commemoration of Mothers' Day, but he ducked out the first chance when no one was looking, so I ended up doing it. I also gave a fair talk later in sacrament meeting on the topic of prayer. Attendance today seemed paltry with the absence of the Preciado family from both services. Remer and I thumbed a ride to Colima in the evening with a compulsive talker and a carload of his relatives. Looking forward to a little basketball tomorrow.

May 9

Played some good basketball with Hunt and Vance—needed recreation, lots of fun. We met a couple of guys at the playground and half agreed to play a benefit game against a group of Colima "all stars" to raise funds for a school remodeling program. I don't know how we'll work it out, with Hunt's and my transfers supposedly coming up any day. Hunt will try to make it over to Manzanillo tonight or tomorrow to let us know what he's worked out with the all-star benefit.

Manzanillo, May 10

No telegram for me today. Hunt didn't show up either. We tracted all morning and all afternoon. The hill shacks are all that remain in our second sweep of Manzanillo.

May 11

Farewell Manzanillo: Received my telegram this afternoon after a morning of tracting. Went around to say goodbye to everyone and packed my stuff. The telegram directed me to report to the mission home (without specifying what happens to me after that), but I'm on a midnight bus to Colima instead of Mexico City because I didn't want to leave Elder Hunt in the lurch with this basketball business unsettled. The Godinas came to see me off. The *hermana* was upset and feels doubly deserted now that Elder Flake and I are both gone. This should be a temporary thing that she'll get over, but I do agonize for the Godinas when, in a few months, the branch is likely to disintegrate if both the Valdéz and Preciado families move out of Manzanillo. That would leave the Godinas virtually alone, unless some new people can be found and baptized soon.

  I leave Manzanillo regretful that we were unable to accomplish more. But I also leave immeasurably enriched by the experience and personally strengthened by several crises that I managed to weather, when it seemed as though Satan was doing everything in his power to bring me down. On several occasions I found my soul stripped barer than I thought possible. Then, in my helplessness, I learned the power of God's hand as he imperceptibly, but surely, guides us through the crashing tempest to calmer waters. I'm profoundly grateful for the opportunity I've had to assist in the opening of Manzanillo to missionary work and pray that my replacement and others who follow will be able to advance what's been started. [By 1994 Manzanillo was a district headquarters, with jurisdiction over five branches in surrounding areas, with approximately two thousand members.]

Mexico City, May 12

I arrived in Colima at 2:00 A.M. only to find that Hunt and Vance had *both* left for Mexico City the previous afternoon. So much for benefit basketball games. I slept on the floor of the missionary cottage, then caught the first morning bus to Guad. From there I found the quickest bus leaving for Mexico and arrived in the City at 1:30 A.M. I climbed over the mission home fence, retrieved the key for the gate from its familiar hiding place in order to bring in my bags, and was in bed by 2:30 A.M.

May 13

I talked with President McClellan this morning about the problems that face the branch in Manzanillo and felt reassured when I learned that Elder Lewis—a very capable missionary with a lot of branch experience—is my replacement. I was also informed that I'm being called back into the mission home as an assistant, this time as companion to Elder Garza. And, appropriately enough, Elder Flake is also back in the saddle again as companion to Elder Colvin. A flood of new missionaries within the past little while (and more on the way) has made me and Flake practical again. All four of us will be working out of the mission home here, instead of one pair using Guadalajara as headquarters.

The other three assistants made it back this afternoon from an expedition to help four elders—led by Elder Judd—to get situated as the first permanently based Mormon missionaries in Querétaro. We immediately sat down with President McClellan to hash out our working schedules, responsibilities, lines of authority, etc. Theoretically, we'll all be co-equals in the discharge of duties. But as a matter of fact, and as common sense would dictate, Elder Garza will be the man with the last word. It's good to see Elder Flake again and to be in close association once more. It's also good to be back where the pulse throbs strongest. These last three months that presumably I'll spend working with Elder Garza can't help but be some of the most beneficial, stimulating times of my mission.

15

⚭

"Let the Record Stand":
Gordon's Story as Assistant to the President in Veracruz

Gordon continued the last three months of his mission at mission headquarters in Veracruz as assistant to the president. Having spent a month without a designated companion, he took advantage of a successful field missionary's hepatitis relapse to bring him into the mission home as a companion. This proved to be a boost to Gordon's spirits, but he also felt cut off from missionary fieldwork and began to worry about a declining sense of religious purpose in the mission office environment. President Hatch had to take several trips outside mission boundaries and was also much preoccupied with branch and district problems. During his absences, Gordon and his companion were left in charge of missionary affairs. Office routines (including processing weekly field reports for statistical publication in the mission periodical) were interrupted from time to time by conferences at which assistants were expected to speak, by influxes of new missionaries from the Provo Language Training Mission, releases of old missionaries departing for home (which occasioned reshuffling field assignments and making companion switches), and occasional reports of companion conflicts and missionary romances.

As new missionaries arrived and former companions ended their missions, Gordon was led to reflect with some ambivalence on missionary motives, work ethics, and ambitions for status. His last months in Mexico were highlighted by several disasters and near-disasters, including a nasty automobile accident, the excommunication of a fellow missionary for sexual misconduct, and a night spent in the Tapachula jail in Chiapas. It also befell Gordon to make one last trip to Villa Flores to dispose of church property and officially end the church's missionary activities there. Finally, Gordon was also able to work out a meeting with Gary at the border of their missions in San Martín, as the two laid plans to coordinate their mission releases so they could work together in Mexico City and, with their parents, tour the areas where they had labored.

Called back again to Mexico City as an assistant to the president after two months in Manzanillo, Gary alternated companions and made several supervisory tours of mission districts while baptizing investigators in Mexico City. His account of providing help to a visiting LDS tourist, who was having a nervous breakdown, once again illustrates how the mission president routinely delegated authority to youthful assistants. Gary was particularly heartened during return visits to Manzanillo to see a stabilization of branch problems there and prospects for a more optimistic future, as well as the continued faithfulness of a number of earlier converts in Mexico City.

Veracruz, May 12, 1966

Seven *nuevos* unboarded yesterday and the meshings of a missionwide series of changes have been thrown into gear. Over two dozen transfer telegrams have been sent out and there will be missionaries passing through Veracruz all hours of the day and night to their new assignments. To heighten the excitement we're trying to get the *Faro* to press, which seems to be taking forever. And just to keep nerve endings really shredded, we've received several reports that Elder Hildenberg has been carrying on a romance with a member girl in Poza Rica. I've notified Hildenberg to report to the mission home and he should arrive sometime today or tomorrow. The last thing we need is for our new missionary arrivals from the LTM to be exposed to this sort of hanky-panky on their first day in the mission field.

One of the new missionaries, Elder Rake, already has managed to make a negative impression—on me, anyway. He's smart but humorless and arrogant. He immediately announced his ultimate goal of becoming assistant to the president, which he seems perfectly convinced he will achieve. The desire to work hard, progress, and become an increasingly effective representative of the church is expected of every missionary. It would be dishonest of me to say that I have not been motivated by the possibility of advancements in missionary leadership positions as an indicator of personal progress. But Rake's type of undisguised, self-serving ambition is totally out of line. I've decided to recommend to President Hatch that Rake be sent as a junior companion to Elder Hyde in Córdoba. Heber, as I well know from our time together in Villa Flores, is another missionary who has had to struggle with his personal ambitions and self-pride (but who also has proven to be an effective proselytor with an enormous capacity for hard work). We shall see who out-competes whom for the glory, or if a deeper conception of missionary work emerges for Elder Rake.

May 16

Saturday, the fourteenth of May, I had one of the worst experiences of my mission. Elder Hildenberg and I were about twenty kilometers outside of Veracruz on the road to Jalapa. President Hatch had asked me to check on companion problems brewing between Elders Ross and Martinez, which had been reported several days earlier. Hildenberg himself was already in the mission doghouse for his romantic activities in Poza Rica and was waiting for President Hatch to return from Mexico City for disciplinary action. In the meantime I asked Hildenberg to accompany me on the trip to Jalapa, thinking it would be a good chance for me to hear his side of the story.

We were doing about sixty miles per hour and talking. A curve was coming up. Then, suddenly, a big ADO [Autobús de Oriente] bus loomed ahead, hugging the center line of the road. We were in a slight skid and dangerously close to the bus. I thought we were going to hit head-on, so I pulled the wheel to the right and the next few seconds passed like a nightmare. Our lightweight Volkswagen went into a series of uncontrolled spins. Forever etched in my memory will be the face of a passenger at a window of the bus, a frozen scream caught in her throat as we careened past within touching distance, the screaming of tires merging indistinguishably with our own. One of our back tires smacked into a small embankment off the side of the road and the car was flipped completely over several times, finally crashing to a halt on its top. I remember lying on my back, looking up at the wheels of the Volkswagen still spinning around. In the rolling process the passenger door had sprung open and Hildenberg was hurled out of the car and skidded along the ground, like a flat stone flung across a pool of water, until he collided with a picket fence.

I found myself pinned under the car, half in and half out of the passenger-side window. I knew instantly that I wasn't hurt and called out to Elder Hildenberg, asking him if he was all right. He replied in a shaken voice that he was hurt and couldn't move. I pulled myself free from the wreckage and went over to him. His back and arm were injured, possibly broken. A crowd of nearby villagers quickly formed and someone went to notify the Red Cross, which arrived about twenty minutes later. Hildenberg was taken by ambulance back to Veracruz and I followed later with a Mexican *federale* [federal police officer], who had arrived at the scene just minutes after the crash. By the time we got to the hospital, Hildenberg had already been examined and x-rayed—miraculously, no breaks or fractures were found. His injuries were painful but nothing more serious than lacerations and strained muscles. My only injuries were a slight knot on my forehead and a bruise high on my left thigh where the car had come to rest on me. How we escaped serious injury or death is a mystery. Surely the protecting hand of God was with us.

Yesterday we took Hildenberg to a private clinic and he appears to be on the way to making a rapid recovery. What remains is the legal red tape, including insurance forms and traffic fines. The *federale* at the scene of the accident proved to be a man of good will and tremendous help. In his written report he maintained that Hildenberg was the driver and not I. He told me he respected the Mormons and knew we were honest in our dealings but urged me to allow him to fudge the report so I wouldn't have to go to jail. He neither asked for nor seemed to expect a bribe in exchange for his help. Apparently, in Mexico, if an auto accident causes injuries to passengers or bystanders, the driver is supposed to be charged automatically and arrested to stand trial for damages. Unlike the United States, the law of the land in Mexico is guilty until proven innocent rather than the other way around. With Hildenberg designated as the driver and in the hospital, the whole affair should blow over with a minimum amount of legal trouble for me and the church.

May 20

Bills from last week's nasty car wreck total up as follows: $40.00 deductible on the mission's insurance policy and a $24.00 fine. Also, broken glasses will cost me another $15.00–20.00. All told, this puts me up the creek about $80.00, more than I would spend normally in *gastos* [living expenses] for an entire month. The costs, not to mention the injuries, could have been much worse, but they're still pretty steep and it will be an unexpected drain on Mom's and Dad's resources, which bothers me a lot. Reflecting now on the incident I feel a strange detachment, as though I was an observer at the event but not personally involved. How close to calamity we were, how close to death. And yet we renew our routines as though not very much had happened.

May 22

Just got back from the Poza Rica conference. It was a good one. There have been a lot of shenanigans up there lately, but with Elder Hildenberg gone and some other changes made last week, things appear to be pretty well ironed out. There was a welcome spirit present at the morning missionary session and I gave the best talk that I've managed for some time. The afternoon session with members was equally good but it was also the warmest, most sultry meeting I've ever had to endure. After taking my seat from speaking, perspiration seemed to burst from every pore in my body and I felt as if I had been drenched with warm sea water.

Elder Hildenberg has mended well and, when fully recuperated, will be sent to Campeche to work with Dale Smith, my old junior companion from Puebla days. Smith is an exceptionally well-prepared and able missionary who should help Hildenberg get back on the right path. Illness throughout the mission, companion spats, and some minor missionary romances have combined to make it necessary for us to plan a large number of companion changes for next week. In spite of everything though, it looks like another good month for overall mission baptisms. Last month Bill Porter and Mark Silver alone baptized close to thirty people in Puebla (including a number of my investigators that Porter took over when I left for Veracruz).

After talking with President Hatch it was decided that the mission will pay half of the $40.00 deductible for my car wreck. President Hatch also suggested that I take a loan from mission office funds to pay for my share of the costs, which can be repaid in small installments over the next several months. This arrangement relieves me of a lot of my mounting financial worries.

May 24

Office routines, weekly reports, London showing me how to use the printing press for the *Faro,* trying to teach myself how to type, etc. Yeeach. Anticipating a little trip tomorrow with President Hatch.

Arriaga, May 25

This has been a pleasant journey, traveling with President Hatch and conducting some mission business. We left Veracruz for Arriaga to give Elder Kimball a release from his duties as branch president and to install a native member in his place. This is the first time that a native Mexican has been called to serve in Arriaga and President Hatch is anxious to see how things work out. [By 1994, Arriaga was the district headquarters for six branches and approximately two thousand members in nearby towns.]

President Hatch kept us entertained the entire trip with a never-ending stream of stories about his experiences in the church and as an apple farmer in northern Mexico. President Hatch is a Mexican citizen, a descendent of the original Mormon colonists in Colónia Juárez. His gringo accent is sometimes pretty awful but he speaks fluent conversational Spanish and has a much larger practical vocabulary than most missionaries, due to the fact that we spend most of our time talking about religious subjects and not about topics or objects of everyday concern. I've come to like and respect President Hatch's relaxed, unpretentious methods and keen sense of humor. He's more interested in people than programs for their own sake. The chief concern he constantly conveys is for the physical and spiritual welfare of his missionaries rather than setting statistical records. He gives real responsibilities to those called to positions of authority in the mission and trusts them to use common sense and good judgment in the performance of their duties. I like that. Assistants to the president are not treated as mere figureheads or rubber stamps but have genuine influence in helping direct missionary activities.

May 28

That was a *triste* [sad] trip. Tuesday, Elder McCain (who has replaced Harris in the mission home as records secretary) and I drove all the way down to Villa Flores to perform the dirty job of permanently closing the place down. Essentially this meant disposing of all the furniture and furnishings that Heber and I had placed in storage with the hope that new missionaries would eventually be sent back in. President Hatch felt that with other priorities putting pressure on mission resources it was best to pull out and stop paying rent on an empty building. I agreed. The president is right but I still feel badly. I could hardly bear to give the discouraging news to our two convert couples there who have been waiting expectantly for our return.

We gave all the pew benches we had made for the chapel to the Church of the Nazarene—an evangelical group with whom Heber and I had numerous clashes over doctrinal differences and competition for Catholic souls to proselyte. The minister, with whom we once had a nasty argument, seemed stunned by the gift but was grateful. Most of his flock is dirt poor and they meet for worship in an adobe house with few furnishings. We distributed our old beds, tables, chairs, and *rompero* [portable dresser and clothes closet] among the Gomez and Toledo families and our former maid (who never wanted to investigate Mormonism but became very fond of Heber and me, tears rolled down her cheeks when we left). Hard to believe that in another month and a half it will be a year since Heber and I opened up Villa Flores. There was never any guarantee that we would succeed in establishing a permanent branch there, but neither would I have dreamed that I would be the one sent back to close it down almost a year later. [Full-time missionaries were not sent back to Villa Flores until the city of Tuxtla Gutiérrez was designated as the headquarters for a new Chiapas mission in 1988. Now, the small LDS branch in Villa Flores is under the jurisdiction of the Tuxtla Gutiérrez Mission.]

Upon our return to the mission home tonight I learned that Elder Janzen, junior companion to Elder Elison here in Veracruz, suddenly requested to terminate his mission and has been sent home. I don't know any of the details yet. His abrupt departure will make necessary some off-the-cuff shifting and companion changes that will foul up some of our earlier plans. President Hatch has gone up north on a business trip and won't be back for a week or so. I'll be in charge of the mission office until he gets back. Other tidbits: Elder Hildenberg is well enough to travel now and has already left for Campeche. In exchange, Elder Orellana will move here to take Janzen's place as companion to Elder Elison. Elison, whom I got to know well in Minatitlán, is probably the most stalwart and dedicated missionary in the mission, so the change could have a salutary effect on Orellana.

LETTER FROM GARY

Gord: Thought it high time to send you some *notícias* [news]. Elder Garza and I just returned to the mission home from a week-long tour of our northern districts, including Manzanillo. Hermana Godina became a little over-excited by my showing up again so soon and tried to pressure her son, Ramón, into getting baptized while I was in town. It put him on the spot, and he said yes to baptism sometime in the future but not now. Our next stop was Guadalajara for a combined member and missionary district conference. I was proud of the showing made by the Manzanillo Branch members who attended and also performed in the district talent show. Hermana Godina made a stirring declamation, Rodolfo sang and accompanied himself on his homemade electric guitar, and some of the Preciado and Valdéz kids performed a little dance number. I had brief opportunities to chat with old Guadalajara acquaintances, including Neome Velazco, who, I was stunned to find out, is pregnant and unmarried. I didn't pry about the particulars, and she seemed only moderately self-conscious about it.

Long traveling hours throughout the trip were highlighted by intriguing conversations with Elder Garza. He's a truly amazing person. He was primarily raised by his grandfather (his father, who was an American serviceman, abandoned his Mexican mother) in rural northern Mexico under the kinds of impoverished conditions that we see all the time in our missionary work. He migrated to California with an older brother as a young teenager; was initially placed in an elementary school because of English deficiencies; quickly broke through the language barrier and was moved up to his appropriate age group; became academically, athletically,

and politically prominent in high school (being elected student body president, governor of Boys' State of California, and finally president of Boys'
Nation in Washington D.C.). He was made an assistant to the president in
our mission after serving only six months as a regular missionary. He possesses great natural ability in virtually all areas of endeavor, is intensely
motivated to excel, yet conducts himself in a cheerful, easy-going way that
puts people at their ease while stimulating them to reach beyond their
normal limitations. He does love to go to the movies, if that can be counted as a flaw. The other night we went to see *Goldfinger,* with Sean Connery
as James Bond. I can see why these James Bond movies have become so
popular—racy excitement with a sense of humor. But probably not the
sort of stuff we ought to be watching right now.

Tonight the mission home has been filling up with elders coming
through en route to new assignments. Someone from Guadalajara reported that Elders Lewis and Remer have been arrested (!) in Manzanillo because of the film Flake and I showed to inaugurate our work. Apparently
the charge against them is showing a movie to the public without a permit, even though Lewis and Remer aren't the "guilty" parties. Could it be
that some of our Catholic opponents there are digging up whatever silly
excuse possible to impede the missionary effort? Or maybe just the brief
appearance of the "Merry Pranksters" in town this past April so upset the
authorities that they felt obliged to crack down on any other gringos who
might be construed as disrupters of the community. In any event, President McClellan has already contacted our church lawyer, who seems to
think he can arrange to have Lewis and Remer bailed out quickly with
minimum fuss. Stay tuned for further adventures.

P.S. Speaking of adventures, Linda Booth writes to say she slips in a
rezo [prayer] for us once in awhile at mass [she was Catholic] so her people won't stone us (Don has again been teasing her with outrageous tales
of our supposed exploits, which she half believes).

Your brother, Gar

May 29

Things have been exploding over our heads with regularity the entire month
of May. I was shocked this morning to learn that Elder Janzen was excommunicated from the church the day I left for Villa Flores. After months of
depression and guilt, Janzen came to President Hatch and confessed that he
had fornicated with a girl, the daughter of a women hired by the missionaries as a maid, while working in Villahermosa. Where the devil was his companion at the time? Companions are supposed to stay together precisely to

prevent this sort of thing from happening. But of course there are always opportunities to stray if one has a mind to. The president called Salt Lake City and talked to Gordon B. Hinckley (who heads the Church Missionary Committee) for instructions. The word was: Excommunicate the young man immediately and put him on a plane for home. President Hatch hastily assembled an Elders' Court, consisting of himself, the available mission home staff, and Janzen's current companion, Elder Elison. The formalities of a brief trial were observed and Elder Janzen was officially deprived of his priesthood, his missionary calling, and his church membership. [Mission presidents are now instructed to avoid using full-time missionaries on disciplinary councils that try their peers for serious transgressions of mission standards.]

Today we received an anxious, long-distance call from Elder Janzen's stake president in Boston, Massachusetts, wanting to know what was going on. Janzen has not yet arrived home. It appears likely that once he crossed the border into the U.S. he simply got off the plane in Arizona and disappeared. Dandy. What a disaster for him and his family. I can't think of a more crushing outcome to one's original high hopes and expectations after having accepted a missionary calling. Since President Hatch was gone, I was called to the phone. Unfortunately I was unable to provide much information to Janzen's understandably exasperated stake president, since I am just now learning for myself the details of this tragedy. London, who was on the court which excommunicated Janzen and knows more than I, got on the phone with the Boston stake president and gave him Janzen's flight itinerary.

I felt like shouting and cursing over the whole affair, but shortly afterward we received another long-distance call. This time Gary was on the line! (After I just received his letter yesterday.) My mood went instantly from stunned consternation over the Janzen case to exhilaration. It's been over twenty months since we last had a conversation. He was calling about the possibility of arranging a rendezvous somewhere in the Puebla area the next time I go there for conference—according to the mission schedule, that will be around the last of June. *Sí señor!* I don't think President Hatch will have any serious objections to bending mission rules so we can meet, but Gary might have to sneak over his mission borders in the context of performing some nearby official business. We'll see what can be arranged.

May 30

What next? Just returned from Villahermosa with Elder Bill Porter in tow. Porter has succumbed to hepatitis for the second time during his mission and he's pretty discouraged. President Hatch's home in Veracruz is a much better place in which to recuperate than the missionaries' quarters in Villahermosa. For the past several months Porter has been the most productive elder in the mission. He splashed twenty-seven baptisms in Puebla before going to Villahermosa to become the new supervising elder there. With just a little more than four months of his mission left, Porter is afraid that President Hatch might send him home early for health reasons. But I'm going to suggest to the president when he calls that Porter remain in Veracruz until he recovers his health and that he then be made my companion as assistant to the president.

On the way back from Villahermosa with Elder Porter, London and I stopped off in Coatzacoalcos to inform Elder Cory that he will take over Porter's duties as supervising elder of the district. At first, Cory thought we were joking. He's gone through some discouraging times, has not always worked to his capacity, and never thought he would be given a position of leadership in the mission. But he now has a good junior companion and has started to work effectively again. He's bright, has excellent Spanish, and with a little self-esteem restored through an increase in responsibility, should, I'm confident, quickly become one of the mission's top supervisors.

June 7

After last month's crises things have calmed down considerably. Elder Porter and I are working together in the mission office and just about have this month's *Faro* ready to go to press. Porter's spirits zoomed when he was informed of the plan to keep him in Veracruz as an assistant to the president rather than receiving an early release as he had feared. As it turns out, his case of hepatitis appears to be relatively mild and his strength and *ganas* to return to work have been steadily gaining. It's undoubtedly best that there be two assistants as companions in the mission home. The companion system can be a source of strength and support as well as occasional conflict to develop one's character. What is true in the field should also be true in the mission home. Porter and I have always hit it off well and, along with London's company, the occasional boredom of office work has been alleviated considerably.

Last night we were honored by a brief visit from Elder Marion G. Romney of the Council of Twelve. Apostle Romney has been down here looking over some property that the church is interested in buying (if the church continues to grow at its present rate, a lot of new chapels eventually will have to be constructed) and before departing by plane to Mexico City, President Hatch brought him to the office to meet everyone. Brother Romney didn't interrogate or put anyone on the spot—just a short, gracious visit with some words of encouragement. [By 1994, there were a dozen LDS chapels in the Veracruz area.]

June 12

President Hatch is in Mexico City for a mission presidents' conference, so Porter and I will stay put in the office and watch the store until he returns. Office routines more or less eat up the day. I'm getting restless. No missionary conferences scheduled for a couple of weeks. I'm looking forward to meeting Gary on the twenty-fifth of this month outside of Puebla. Rendezvous point: San Martín, on the border of our two missions.

Received an announcement of Beckie's missionary farewell. She's going to Wellington, New Zealand. Our correspondence has dwindled from a letter every week when I first arrived in Mexico to an occasional note every couple of months. But unlike Gary and Kathy, we're still in communication. I know Beckie will make a good missionary. She's determined and spunky. She'll be gone for eighteen months. Our last sister missionaries in Veracruz departed in December and the church has never sent any new ones to replace them. Supposedly southeast Mexico is too primitive for sisters. As far as I know, the ones here previously did all right. Also received a letter from home voicing doubts about the feasibility of Mom and Dad coming to Mexico. The problem seems to be a certain amount of coolness toward the plan by Gary's mission president, President McClellan. In contrast, President Hatch not only approves but encourages parents to come when possible. In his opinion, parents who have sacrificed and supported their sons and daughters on missions deserve the opportunity to meet the people their children have taught and brought into the church. President Hatch doesn't think it disrupts missionary work very much. In fact, he thinks it's good for the work because the members, especially the newer converts, are animated by the visits and, as a result, the mutual bonds of affection and appreciation are strengthened. I will continue to encourage the folks to come. One way or the other we ought to be able to work something out. [Mission regulations now allow parents to travel to their sons' and daughters' areas of missionary service upon their release from the field.]

June 13

We got blasted out of bed last night by an enormous lightning bolt that struck our apartment building in downtown Veracruz. I literally picked myself up off the floor, thinking that a hydrogen bomb had gone off in my brain. This did my feelings of well-being little good, since I was whipped earlier in the evening in a wrestling match with Elder Porter. We were horsing around some and Porter challenged me. On the one hand, we're about the same size, but Porter wrestled in high school. On the other hand he's had hepatitis, so I figured the odds were fair. I struggled mightily but was eventually pinned and forced to concede. I then went to the bathroom and threw up. There's little doubt that Elder Porter has recovered fully.

June 14

President Hatch is back from Mexico City and says he has a new traveling assignment for me and Porter. Thank goodness. I can only take so much of the office at a time. I sometimes fear for a loss of resolution and spirituality when things get too soft. Some of the mission staff thought it would be a good idea to take a little time every afternoon to lay out in the patio and get a tan, but I said nix. I can't imagine admonishing all the field missionaries to dedicate themselves to the work while we're lolling around getting suntans at the mission home. Then last night London put on an irreverent but hilarious performance at the apartment, imitating the pope with a beehive on top of his head and strumming "We Thank Thee O God for a Prophet" on his guitar to a hillbilly beat. Funny, but I dunno. I need to make sure the mission staff and I stay focused on our callings.

Tuxtla Gutiérrez, June 16

Back in the saddle again. President Hatch has sent Porter and me out to visit the Chiapas District, where we are to explain some new directives to the elders that were given last week at the mission presidents' conference in Mexico City. The church wants to emphasize more emphatically the teaching and conversion of entire families, not just individuals. Far too often *el señor de la casa* [the man of the house] gives consent to spouse and children to join but remains aloof himself. The church wants to strengthen family unity and the priesthood potential of Mexican men. We're supposed to begin developing a proselyting approach geared to these objectives.

Porter and I were on our way to Tapachula but only got as far as La Ventosa in Oaxaca, where we threw a rod in the Volkswagen. Fortunately, the first truck that passed by stopped to give us a helping hand. The driver towed us with a rope (!) about thirty miles to the nearest gas station—no mechanics, no parts. It was raining hard and we were on a twisty, mountain road. Continued towing was out of the question so we decided to try and boost the car up on the bed of the truck and take her all the way into Tuxtla Gutiérrez, the nearest city where we could find a Volkswagen dealer and, coincidentally, the trucker's destination. The truck driver pulled off the road into a little ravine.

We laid down the tailgates of the truck in drawbridge fashion, connecting the truck with the slope of the ravine, and then rolled the Volkswagen on as slick as a whistle. Our sense of impending doom was changed to elation. Our Good Samaritan truck driver was a cheerful, decent man who refused any money for his help. We arrived in Tuxtla around 6:00 P.M. and immediately took our car to the VW dealer. It's going to be awhile before they can order the necessary parts. Fine. We'll work with the elders here in Tuxtla a day or two and then, if the car's still not ready, Porter and I will catch a bus to Tapachula, so as not to waste time, and pick up the car on our way back to Veracruz.

In the meantime it's good to be back in Tuxtla, one of my favorite places in the mission. The climate's mild, the food's terrific (our old maid is still on the job), and the scenery is spectacular. Booth is now the supervising elder here and I look forward to working with him tomorrow. The two of us can only shake our heads in amazement at how far we've come since arriving together in Mexico in August 1964. The Tuxtla Branch seems to be prospering again, with optimistic expectations for the future.

Tapachula, June 19

I do believe this takes the cake. It's past one o'clock in the morning, we're in Tapachula, and it appears that I will spend the night in the Tapachula jail, with common criminals for companions. My offense was getting caught without a passport or travel visa in my possession. I should have known better. Tapachula is a border city to Guatemala. Black market activities and illegal border traffic of all kinds are common here, hence greater vigilance and enforcement of immigration laws. Most places in Mexico are pretty lax about foreigners carrying official credentials and I've become accustomed to leaving mine in Veracruz whenever I travel so as not to lose them in one of my common moments of carelessness.

Porter and I were on the bus from Tuxtla. Just outside of Tapachula our vehicle was stopped by immigration officials in military uniforms, who boarded the bus and asked to see everyone's papers. At first I thought I had fallen asleep and was having a bad dream. It was like a World War II movie about the Nazis searching for stowaway Jews or members of the Resistance, especially as their inspection brought them closer to us in the back of the bus. Porter had his visa with him, so was personally clear, then I explained to the inspector that mine was in Veracruz. I showed him my tourist driver's license, but that was insufficient. We were ordered off the bus and taken to the immigration office. It was late at night and processing of my case would have to wait until morning. Porter was set free to go find the Tapachula elders' apartment while I was transported by jeep to the municipal jail for detention.

Lovely place. Actually it appears that I've been put in the good cell. Everyone's asleep and all but a few of my fellow inmates have wood cots to repose upon. As for me, I will sleep on a chair. This about cuts the bottom out of our trip. I don't think they'll let me go until my visa is sent down from Veracruz. Porter will have to call President Hatch first thing in the morning with the news. I'm not exactly clear yet on what is to become of me. Eventually I'll be released, I'm sure. In the meantime I'll just have to regard the experience as an unusual adventure and make the best of things.

June 20

I judge it to be about 9:00 A.M. I spent a fitful night without much sleep. Shortly after being locked up last night, one of the prisoners next to me in the cell commenced moaning and wailing about cramps in his stomach until the guard came for him. He never returned so I took a chance and laid down on his cot for a little rest. There are a dozen or so men sharing the same cell. Some have created a measure of privacy for themselves by hanging blankets over ropes stretched across the room to partition off small areas around their beds.

Everyone was routed out early this morning for roll call. We were placed together with prisoners from other cells in a large room which I took to be the drunk tank—not much more than a bare concrete cave where men huddle on the floor without a single furnishing for comfort. Urinals consisted of big oil drums. The stench was pretty bad. Out in the yard an officer called out names in alphabetical order. When a prisoner heard his name he had to snap to attention and yell *"Presente!"* and then sprint from the drunk tank to his own cell. I got my share of looks. Not too many gringos dressed in white shirts and sporting neckties like me. Besides, the officer stumbled over pronunciation of my name, to the merriment of the men. No breakfast was served to the prisoners. Apparently, if you want to eat you must either depend upon friends or relatives to bring you food or buy from the street vendors, who are allowed into the prison yard. I saw vagabond kids, eight to twelve years of age, in the jail begging food from the adult prisoners. I went without. Not really hungry anyway.

I struck up a friendship of sorts with one of the prisoners in my cell, in fact, the one whose bed I borrowed last night. He's cheerful and gregarious this morning, apparently recovered from his agonies of the night. He claims to be a political prisoner but admitted he's been charged with sell-ing prescription medicine without a license. He also claims to be a Jehovah's Witness and preacher of the gospel. When he saw my Bible he wanted to read scriptures with me. I've been humoring him but at the same time I'm genuinely glad to have a friendly soul to pass the time with in this wretched place. If Mom and Dad could see me now they'd—well, I just don't know what they'd think.

June 21

I was released from jail yesterday and warned by the authorities not to leave Tapachula until my visa arrives from Veracruz. The *jefe* at immigration talked to President Hatch on the phone and was given assurances that I really was who I claimed to be. My visa is supposed to arrive here by plane tomorrow at noon. Porter and I will work with the Tapachula elders today, and if all goes well tomorrow with immigration, we'll catch an afternoon bus for Tuxtla. I feel chagrined about all the bungling on this trip. Hope we can make it up.

On top of everything else I almost lost my glasses. When Porter showed up to get me out of jail I searched everywhere but couldn't find them. I reported my loss to the jailer, who immediately returned to my cell and had them recovered in a minute. It seems my friend the Jehovah's Witness had swiped them. For what reason I can't imagine. He stuck his head out the bars and waved a vigorous farewell as I left with Porter and the immigration official.

Veracruz, June 23

Back in Veracruz. No admonitions from President Hatch about the fiascos of our trip to Tapachula. He simply told us he was relieved that we were home safe and sound and that we should start making preparations for district conference in Puebla day after tomorrow. This is a conference that I've been looking forward to for weeks. Gary and I have made arrangements to meet in San Martín Saturday afternoon.

The trip back from Tapachula passed without any additional *novedades* [accidents/unexpected events]. The Volkswagen was ready and waiting for us in Tuxtla but we got a late start after visiting with some of the branch members. By the time we reached the mountains around San Andres in the state of Veracruz we were so exhausted that both Porter and I took turns falling asleep at the wheel. For five or ten minutes I would battle off an overwhelming urge to conk out, then surrender the car to Elder Porter, who would immediately do the same. Finally we had to pull off the road to nap and didn't drag into Veracruz until 3 A.M.

Gord: I gather you've been on the road lately. Us too (us being me and El-der Flake). We're not officially companions again (yet), but an opportuni-ty emerged for us to pair up for an excursion to work with missionaries in several southern destinations and to wrap up with a conference on the way back. Our VW broke down on the highway to Chilpancingo. Ar-ranged to have it towed back to Mexico City, then set out thumbing. Caught a ride with three young American women who attend a Catholic girls' college in San Francisco and are vacationing down here. After an amiable ride in their new Impala convertible, they dropped us off a couple of miles outside of Chilpancingo, and we came in the rest of the way on the back of a construction diesel that had stopped for us to jump on. Two lady missionaries—Schnebbly and McInnerny—are stationed there; it's a nice little branch with enough active males to handle priesthood duties. We didn't have to do much, just spoke at sacrament meeting (with Elder Flake producing his usual magic from the pulpit).

After several days of productive work with elders in Iguala and Acapul-co, we returned to Chilpancingo to accompany the LMs by bus to the Cuernavaca conference. The bus was jammed and we had to stand for four hours in the steaming mass of bodies that wedged the isle. We arrived in a stupefied condition at Cuernavaca at 2:00 A.M. and wound up catching only a few hours of hard sleep on the *capilla* floor. The sisters didn't com-plain, though. They're both heavyweights, for whom the crowded stand-ing conditions on the bus must have been murder, but they're also both good sports and very good missionaries. I'm sometimes guilty of giving too little thought to the lady missionaries but, with few exceptions, they are typically reliable and effective workers. Even the occasional "problem" lady missionaries never seem to disintegrate to the low level of attitude and productivity that sometimes occurs among our worst elders.

Prior to this trip, President and Sister McClellan had been on a two-week leave of absence in Arizona. They left us assistants in charge of run-ning the mission, which kept us pretty much chained to administrative duties at the mission home. Elder Garza and I did make sallies into the City, tracking down references that come into the office from time to time. Among several other good prospects, we've been giving lessons to three sweet, elderly sisters who always insist on feeding us enchiladas and *sopes* doused in exceedingly chillied, bitter, greasy mole. Rather than offend them by not finishing, we wait until they absent themselves in the kitchen, then wrap and stuff as much of our meal as we can into my briefcase.

When they come back we profess fullness but great satisfaction with what we've eaten. We also recently welcomed and oriented a batch of new missionaries and then got them packed off to their first assignments. The workings of this process seemed quite mysterious to me my first full day in Mexico when I was matched up with Elder Pullins. Now I just wish these new guys well; it's not an easy transition.

One last incident to report: Apostle Romney and his wife passed through about three weeks ago. We were conducting a *relevo* for a departing missionary, but because of Apostle Romney's presence a large crowd was in attendance and the farewell developed into almost a regular Sunday service. He was called upon to speak, and I was asked to translate for him. I was caught off-guard and nervous but managed to keep my tongue wagging and did okay. He spoke for ten or fifteen minutes, but I was so intent on catching his words and translating them into reasonable Spanish facsimiles that I hardly noticed what he (or I) was actually saying.

Hearing your voice again on the phone after almost two years was unbelievable. Now the twenty-fifth of June is almost upon us, but I feel more like it's December, it's Christmas Eve, and I'm eight years old. See you shortly.

Your brother, Gar

Puebla, June 26

Conference in Puebla Saturday was excellent, featuring some of the best missionary talks that I've heard given anywhere. And though my own talk was reasonably well prepared, I found my thoughts wandering to contemplate the prospects of meeting Gary later in the day at San Martín. After conference ended, London, Porter, and I piled into the Volkswagen and headed out to the dusty little pueblo where I began my mission. How should I act? How should I feel? Unrestrained excitement? Tears and shouts of joy? Well, it just wasn't that kind of reunion. Both Gary and I characteristically restrain our feelings in public. But beyond this, our personal bond is so secure and mutually understood that it seems to transcend the need for such displays.

We met on the outskirts of San Martín and introduced our respective companions (Gary was with Elder Garza, the other assistant in Mexico City). I joked, with little room to talk, about Gary's receding hairline; he commented on my emaciated appearance (exaggerated I'm sure by London's navy blue suit—a size too large for me—which occasionally I borrow for conference apparel ever since losing my only suit to a thief in Veracruz). Past and present were quickly bridged as we drove into town, toured some of my old haunts, and discussed our release plans and the possibility of the folks coming down in August to pick us up. After an hour or so of pleasant conversation it was time to go. We all shook hands, exchanged *abrazos* [hugs], and pronounced our *hasta luegos* [see you laters]. Gary and Elder Garza got in their car and we watched as they turned north to Mexico City. We then headed in the opposite direction, toward Puebla and Veracruz.

June 27

Plans worked out yesterday with Gary are: I will go up to Mexico City for Gary's release, we'll spend a few days working together in the City, then fly to El Paso to meet Mom and Dad, turn in our visas and pick up tourist permits to reenter the country at the border, journey back down to Veracruz for my *relevo,* then tour our respective mission areas.

I have a big insect bite of some kind (London thinks it's a spider bite), picked up while in the Tapachula jail, which is still sore and has swollen my ankle up a bit. On reflection, some of the messes I've gotten myself into lately through my own carelessness are hard to believe. I've been lucky so far but I need to start being a lot more careful.

Veracruz, July 3

What a madhouse. Veracruz has been hit by an avalanche of at least half the elders in the mission. Eight are on their way home tomorrow after a mass *relevo* in the morning. Numerous others are passing on their way through as a consequence of the big mission change in assignments and companions that has gone into effect and, to top things off, the Orizaba District's in town for a *día de campo* tomorrow. It seems like every couple of minutes someone pounds on the door and bursts into the office with his bags and, in the midst of a din of shouting and salutations, begins a round of handshaking and back-pounding *abrazos*. Among those to be released tomorrow is Dennis Baron, former assistant to the president. It seems to me that Baron has spent the last few months of his mission mostly going through the motions. Maybe that's an unfair thing to say. Baron has had some baptisms and done some good in Puebla. But his weekly reports show a missionary who's working at less than full throttle—in my book a somewhat disappointing finish for someone of Baron's ability and past accomplishments.

Another former companion, Paul Heber, is in town as supervisor of the Orizaba District. I'm recommending to President Hatch that Heber be made companion to Porter as assistant to the president when I leave in August. I have mixed feelings about this and Porter is not exactly thrilled with the idea—he's never cared much for Heber. But based on his record and missionary accomplishments, no one is more deserving. Heber is knowledgeable, dedicated, and has baptized a lot of people in difficult places where other missionaries have had scant success. He also toots his own horn and doesn't always seem to mind stepping on people's toes in his ascent to the top. There's an element of ruthlessness in Heber's methods that has always bothered me, but he does have strong leadership qualities. The final decision, of course, is up to President Hatch.

Yesterday we met with President Hatch and all the mission zone directors in an informal but profitable session in which we hashed over mission policies. President Hatch wants ideas for a mission handbook to be distributed to new missionaries when they first arrive in Veracruz. Putting together this handbook is supposed to be our next project. In the meantime we've been working hard to get the *Faro* ready for press. Elder Porter is very good with the layout work. Elders Elison and Orellana are to be designated as missionaries of the month in this issue of the *Faro,* so that's one reshuffling of companions that has worked well. Orellana seems to have recovered his spirits and should be made a senior companion again soon.

Tapachula, July 9

Back in Tapachula for conference again, this time with visa in hand. The missionary conference in the morning was a success but we just received a wire from Juchitan, Oaxaca, where the *mesa directiva* [board of directors] is stuck with a shorn wheel-bearing. They've decided to go back to Veracruz on the bus. As a result the district conference for members has been canceled and we'll be heading back to Veracruz ourselves first thing in the morning. President Hatch joked about the Tapachula "jinx." As for myself, I decided against a nostalgic visit to the Tapachula jail.

Veracruz, July 16

Most of the day yesterday was consumed helping an American couple on vacation in Veracruz in their dealings with an unscrupulous auto mechanic. A couple of days ago they bashed in the side of their car in a collision across the street from the mission office. Some of the office staff, including London, went over to help. They translated for the Americans, negotiated with the police, and helped to find a repair shop. The couple was later shocked when they received the final repair bill, which was several thousand pesos over the original estimate, and phoned the mission office for help again. Elder London and I took a copy of their bill to another shop for an independent evaluation of the cost for parts and labor and discovered that they had been overcharged triple. We proceeded to the place where the car had been serviced, confronted the owner, and demanded a refund. The man played dumb and shrugged his shoulders, claiming he didn't understand what the problem was. I surprised myself by calling him a *mentiroso* [liar], but actually stayed cool-headed for once. London informed him in an impressive tone that we represented the gringo couple and that we were prepared to engage our lawyers to file suit. At this the man suddenly changed his tune and forked over a sizable refund, which we returned in good spirits to the American couple.

Gary writes that there may be a few kinks in our going-home scheme, but it looks like we can still work something out.

LETTER FROM GARY

Gord: Got your note late last night and just finished speaking with your President Hatch (on business in Mexico City) and President McClellan this afternoon. Your plan is good but can't quite be worked, I'm afraid. President Hatch says it's not possible for you to go to the border, turn in your visa and come back as a tourist before you're released as a missionary. In addition, my official release date has been set for the fifteenth of August, and President McClellan takes a dim view of any early releases that don't involve returning directly to school. President Hatch can't give you more than a one-week early release without permission from the Church Missionary Committee in Salt Lake. It would be nice to have the family present for your release—mine, too, for that matter—but I don't see anyway around these *obstáculos* [obstacles]. I imagine that President Hatch will have already talked to you before this letter arrives, explaining what can and cannot be done. Anyway, I think the original plan is still best. I'm still waiting for a reply from President Tuttle in Salt Lake about going down to Veracruz for your release (which I think he will approve). Then we spend three days or so here in the City until my *relevo,* which will be Sunday the fourteenth. We catch a plane out Monday morning and meet the folks in El Paso or someplace, exchange our passports for tourist visas, then all come back into the country together. If you can hatch another plot better than this, let me know. (Speaking of getting together again, our reunion in San Martín made for one of the most enjoyable afternoons of my mission, even if it did involve breaking a few more rules. No regrets about that.)

Both the June and July issues of the *Faro* arrived here a couple of days ago. Your article on "Dedication" was about the best I've ever read, by you or any other assistant to the president; your layout work picked up a notch too. I must say, though, that we wind up spending entirely too much time on producing the *Clarín* here in our shop. I see no good reason to go to such elaborate extremes of production as we have lately, wasting far too many potential hours of missionary work that might otherwise be engaged in. [In subsequent years, missions were officially discouraged from publishing and disseminating elaborate periodicals or newsletters. Now, monthly mission newsletters are not supposed to be larger than one piece of paper printed on both sides. And the mission president, not his assistants, is responsible for its format and contents.]

I've reached full assistantship now, whatever that's supposed to mean. Elder Colvin returned to civilian life last week, and President McClellan interviewed me as successor. I'm still of the opinion that Elder Flake is the more qualified of the two of us and told the president so. Anyway, Flake and I are now officially back together as full-time companions. I have great admiration for Elder Garza, but Elder Flake is no slouch in the respect department, and he and I have developed the kind of friendship that permits us to be at perfect ease with each other.

Elder Flake and I have a couple of more work trips planned for these last few weeks, and, actually, made a recent trip together back to Manzanillo following a conference in Guad. The primary purpose for doing this was to baptize Ramón Godina, who had reportedly informed the elders out there of his readiness. Hermana Godina was highly pleased to see both Flake and me together again, but Ramón said nothing of fulfilling his promise and the subject of baptism was never brought up. I told myself long ago that I would not play the role of pesky pleader; it will have to be Ramón's voluntary decision. We departed disappointed but hopeful for another day. Then, with Elder Flake driving and me asleep in the front seat, we hit a slick spot on the road as we came around a curve and almost replicated your recent smashup. The VW spun out of control past a steep embankment on one side of the road, then slammed into the face of the mountain on the other side, crunching up the rear fender, side door, and blowing out a tire. Neither of us were hurt. A truck came along and pulled us out of the ditch, we changed the tire, and went, with good fortune, on our slightly wobbly way.

Prior to our companion changes, Elder Garza and I enjoyed several additional rewarding experiences, including the baptisms of the three old ladies who press super hot food upon us when we visit. After coming up from the water, the oldest sister (Hermana Aldana) directly addressed me with a surprising and touching little thank-you speech. We also taught and converted a very intelligent, poised, and attractive young woman (Paula Cárdenas), who had found and read a stray *folleto,* mailed in a reference card for herself, and proved to be a textbook example of the ideal investigator. Her parents don't approve, but she's twenty-one, and it was a special pleasure to bring a person of her quality into the church.

It's also been a pleasure these last weeks, because of our ability to be very mobile, to have continued contacts with previous converts who are progressing in the gospel and invite us to dinner regularly. Hermano Guerro, for instance, was just ordained an elder. Carmen Grovas has charged into church activities with full fervor and just finished directing a youth musical production in her ward. Other converts remain active but have come to us for help with various problems. Hermano Pierdánt, for instance, has lost his government job for political reasons, and we are trying to arrange for him to obtain a sponsor to work in the U.S. And old Hermano Amadór asked us recently to anoint and bless his fifteen-month-old son, who was very sick. A violent thunderstorm struck just as we arrived at their home, and the rain beat down upon us in a solid curtain as we rushed to their door. By the time we got in we were completely soaked, the water running in rivers off our clinging clothing. We gave the child a blessing, although from his appearance I'm sure he must be mentally retarded. Afterward, we had hot *atole* and cookies with the family, listened for awhile to Hermano Amadór's familiar stories of Mexican politics and the good old days, and then retired from that cozy scene back out into the rainy night. I'll try to slip in one more letter before the last bell bongs.

Your brother, Gar

July 19

Some more companion problems appear to be brewing. I just received a letter from Elder Harris in Oaxaca, who reports that Martinez and Murdock have been brawling. According to Harris their differences have gone beyond mere grumbling and dirty looks; they've been beating on each other. One of them is going to have to be quickly transferred, probably Martinez, who has had his share of trouble since coming into the mission.

July 25

Just a little more than two weeks now remain before I'm to be released from the mission but it still seems like a distant and improbable event. This is good because I don't want to be unduly distracted from my calling by daydreaming about the future as a civilian back in the U.S. Gary and I seem to have most of the details worked out for leaving together, so I'm going to put it out of my mind until it's actually time to go.

Thursday another batch of *nuevos* arrived fresh from the Language Training Mission. President Hatch was in Mérida so Elder Porter and I were in charge of taking care of all their arrangements. We tried our best to make their first impression of the mission field a positive one. I've never quite forgotten the somewhat haphazard greeting given me, London, and Booth when we first arrived in Mexico, nor the initially poor impression we received of the missionaries' living quarters and level of spirituality. Porter and I picked up the new elders at the airport, helped them unpack, took the whole bunch to dinner at the Hotel Veracruz (courtesy of President Hatch's expense account), where we made some speeches to welcome them, praised them for the work they've already done to prepare themselves to learn the language and preach the gospel, admonished them to remain dedicated to that purpose, reviewed mission policies and regulations, and then informed them of their new companion assignments and field destinations.

I sometimes wonder what difference it might have made to Elder London in the long run if he had gotten off on a better footing when we first arrived in the Veracruz Mission together. In any event, London subsequently has become indispensable to the efficient running of the mission office. There will probably be a period of office chaos after he leaves for home.

August 5

I can't seem to put pen to paper any longer, but Gary managed to get one last letter sent off. I share his amazement at the thought of impending events.

LETTER FROM GARY

Gord: We'll be together again within the week, so I don't know why I'm doing this. Just nervous, I guess, and writing is soothing. Let me just relate three or four last, memorable experiences. For one thing, I'm getting to end my mission with a particularly satisfying baptism (and will perhaps have several more on deck by the time you're here with me in Mexico City). Elder Flake and I made one last journey north, which included a stop in Manzanillo. We first located Hermana Godina, and she told us that Ramón was ready and willing—on his own, for sure—to be baptized. We found Ramón, and he backed up his mother's hopes. We then collected Hermana Godina, Rodolfo, Flor, members of the Valdéz and Preciado families, a newly converted family (!) and Elders Lewis and Langston (Remer's replacement) and led a caravan to a quiet beach north of town for a baptismal service. After reaching our destination, Elder Flake and I both made brief remarks. Ramón and I then waded out a short distance into the ocean and I baptized him. His mother was overjoyed, but I think Ramón was even happier. He later said that he now wants to serve a mission himself, and I feel certain he will become a leader in the church. The little branch that Elder Flake and I founded is currently vigorous and active, with an increase in new membership. Lanky Elder Lewis—with his guitar and quiet, tolerant, perceptive ways—was the best choice in the mission to send out here. He has really accomplished wonders (in spite of being tossed in jail for Elder Flake's and my sins).

Back in the City, Flake and I became involved in a very different kind of situation. President McClellan received a long-distance phone call the other morning from a man in the United States whose mother was in Mexico City visiting friends. She had two small granddaughters with her—the man's own children. She had just made an incoherent phone call to him, and he feared she was having a nervous breakdown. The man and his mother are both active church members, and his first impulse was to call the mission home for help. He gave President McClellan an incomplete address where his mother might be staying, and the president in turn passed it on to us and asked us to try to track her down. We finally found her at a well-to-do house in a nice section of town. We introduced ourselves at the door, were invited in, and talked to her for about a half hour. Her name was Jane Sanderson, and she looked to be in her early fifties. Coincidentally, she had attended LDS High School in Salt Lake City during the same years as Dad. Furthermore, she also lived in Cowley, Wyoming, during the same years our family was there and may even have taught Don when he attended first grade at Cowley Elementary. Although she was nervous and a little rattled at our sudden appearance and implicit purpose, she seemed quite in command of herself, denied the existence of any problems, and resisted our efforts to be of any service. Finally we departed but left her the mission home phone number and encouraged her to call if any difficulties should arise.

No sooner had we arrived back at the mission home than I answered a call from Mrs. Sanderson in which she matter-of-factly requested that we return and pick up her and her grandchildren. We immediately borrowed the president's bigger car, and while waiting for Mrs. Sanderson and the two girls to finish packing, heard a strange story from the woman with whom Mrs. Sanderson was staying. Mrs. Sanderson was in fact apparently in the process of having a nervous breakdown. The previous night she had practically gone berserk, roaming the house at night in an undressed state, calling out and crying, and dressing and undressing her two bewildered granddaughters. Sandwiched in between moments of hysterical rambling, Mrs. Sanderson confessed out loud to having had a love affair many years ago with her friend's now-deceased husband. This woman was naturally alarmed, and after we had left earlier that morning she insisted to Mrs. Sanderson that she place herself in our hands for help.

Back at the mission home, everyone treated Mrs. Sanderson pleasantly and with complete normalcy. After she had given a somewhat scrambled account of what had happened to President McClellan, Mrs. Sanderson and her granddaughters were settled into guest rooms for two days while we arranged for their departure back to the U.S. Various staff members entertained the girls with games of Monopoly and kept Mrs. Sanderson occupied with sympathetic conversation. She had one emotional outburst of tears her first night and requested that Elder Flake and I give her an anointing and blessing. We did and she retired tranquilly. By the time we took her and the children to the airport two days later, Mrs. Sanderson seemed to be in perfect control of herself and happy to be going home.

Speaking of blessings, Carmen Grovas recently requested that we anoint her for relief of wracking body pains that appear to correspond with her menstrual periods. Her doctor had suggested that she get pregnant and never mind marriage. We told her to keep seeking a good *joven* who would make a good husband, then get married, then see about the pregnancy business. Several days later she seemed fine and presented me with a mariachi record, a nice set of cufflinks, and a tie pin as a somewhat premature farewell present and "token of her gratitude." I always feel sheepish on these kinds of occasions and probably did not adequately express my own appreciation and gratitude to her.

I fully appreciate President McClellan's concern about missionaries slacking off the last few weeks of their missions. But I don't believe that either you or I have been guilty of this at all. For over a year now a major desire with respect to our leaving the mission field has not been to party at the end but to work together for a few days as missionary companions. When we finally realize this goal a short while from now, I hope, among other activities, that you will be able to help me deliver a final lesson to (or even assist in baptizing) an extremely sharp young brother and sister pair who rank among the best investigators that either Elder Flake or I have ever taught. Medardo Torres is nineteen and a physics major at the University of Mexico. Carmen Torres is eighteen and a top student at a private girls' school. They seem to be each other's best friend, are impressively bright and eager, barrage us with questions, are intrigued (with parental

approval) by the possibility of becoming Mormons, and appear determined to finish the lessons before I leave Mexico.

So, both exciting and uncertain prospects loom. Everything seems
eerily unreal. Within days a major phase of our lives will come to a close.
Mexico will become a memory. Then what?

Your brother, Gar

August 9

My journal for the past two weeks has been sadly neglected. The imminent
end of my mission in Mexico has sapped my enthusiasm for writing. I suppose I should finish this chronicle with a grand summary and inspiring conclusion. But let the record stand as it is. If the account of my mission has not
already been adequately expressed in previous pages of this journal, so be it.

We had an unusually good supervising elders' conference today at President Hatch's home. The mission currently is being led by some of the most
conscientious and able young men that it has been my good fortune to know,
who lead most effectively by the excellence of their own examples.

President Hatch is calling Elder Heber into the mission home to take my
place as assistant to the president. Porter has requested to be sent back into
the field to finish the last two months of his mission in the little town of
Apizaco, near San Martín.

Elder London and Elder Booth will both be boarding a plane for home
next week. But first, London and I leave tomorrow for Puebla to meet Gary,
who will arrive by bus. We'll return to Veracruz for my farewell Thursday,
and then Gary and I will depart by bus for Mexico City to work together for
a few days prior to Gary's release. We will subsequently fly to the border to
meet Mom, Dad, and Susan, and will immediately reenter Mexico by car to
visit the places were Gary and I have labored for two years of our lives: Guadalajara, Manzanillo, and Mexico City in Gary's mission and San Martín,
Puebla, Veracruz, Minatitlán, Tuxtla Gutiérrez, and Villa Flores in mine. And
then the great adventure promised us two years ago will finally come to an
end as we begin the long journey home.

Postscript

Gary arrived as planned in time for Gordon's farewell service from the Southeast Mexican Mission. We then traveled together by bus back to Mexico City,
where, for several days, we realized our hopes of working together as missionary companions, including long hours of tracting and presentation of a
final investigator lesson to the Torres family. During this time we also read

each other's journals, conceivably germinating the idea to produce this book. The morning following Gary's release from the Mexican Mission, we boarded an airplane for El Paso, Texas, where we were greeted by our parents and younger sister, Susan. After surrendering our passports and then finding it necessary to bribe a Mexican border official for tourist permits to reenter the country, we drove back from whence we had just come to bid final farewells to the places and Mexican people who had touched our lives and left their imprint on our personalities. While in Mexico City, our parents and sister were able to witness Gary baptize Medardo and Carmen Torres.

Upon returning to civilian life in the United States, we recommenced our education at the University of Utah in Salt Lake City. Gordon married Beckie Jones not long after she returned from her mission to New Zealand. Gary dated Natalie Fletcher after her return from the Austrian Mission until the unexpected announcement of her engagement to be married to another returned missionary whom she had known in Austria. Approximately three years after completing his mission, Gary met and married Lauren Snow from Bountiful, Utah.

The discrepancy between the relatively enclosed missionary world we left behind in Mexico and the mass dissent and social upheaval taking place in the United States in 1966 and 1967 could scarcely have been more dramatic. Like many other youths of our generation, we had passively supported what had seemed to be the obviously justifiable moral and political goals of the civil rights movement. After our missions, we increasingly became disturbed by the church's apparently intransigent racial policy, which at that time was to withhold the LDS lay priesthood from people of African ancestry. We also came to oppose American prosecution of the war in Vietnam and, as with civil rights, passively sympathized with the anti-war movement then gaining locomotive momentum on college campuses across the country. These movements massively were calling into question the rightness of taken-for-granted authoritarian systems, and they had an impact on our thinking as we readjusted to secular life.

Perhaps most important, the university provided a new and stimulating outlet for our awakening intellectual interests, which had remained largely dormant during our missionary hiatus. Unconsciously and gradually, our missionary experience had contributed greatly to our intellectual maturation, as for the first time in our lives we disciplined ourselves to study and learned to concentrate systematically on a particular set of teachings for making sense of the world. The overall plausibility of those ideas had never in our experience been effectively challenged before. But now, at the university, removed from the intensive plausibility structure of the mission organization, and with much the same motivation to succeed as students as we had sustained while functioning as missionaries in Mexico, secular systems of thought and critical analysis gradually began to have more appeal for us than the theological doctrines of the Mormon faith.

Despite our missionary experience in Mexico, neither of us followed the Mormon norm of an active career of religious callings and organizational assignments in the lay structure of the LDS Church. We became interested in the study of sociology and pursued graduate degrees. Gary obtained his Ph.D. from Michigan State University, and Gordon received his from the State University of New York at Stony Brook. We have subsequently collaborated on research and writing projects of mutual interest.

Although we have become detached over the years from the religious commitments of our youths to the LDS Church, we have cultivated an active scholarly interest in the study of Mormonism. Many relatives and friends, both in the church and out, may see this as perverse, but we do not. In pursuing our own paths, we have never wished to injure the religious sensibilities of others. We continue to value our Mormon heritage and look back without regret on our missionary days as a time of challenge and growth in our lives and as a time of worthwhile struggle and accomplishment.

Nearly three decades passed before one of us returned to Mexico. In late March 1993, Gordon's eldest daughter, Lynne, completed an LDS mission to Costa Rica. He and another daughter, Pam, flew to San José to greet Lynne and spent several days touring with her in the areas where she had worked as a Mormon missionary. On their way back to the United States, the three had time to stop in Mexico City and make a brief excursion to San Martín, Puebla, where Gordon had been sent on his first assignment as a novice missionary in August 1964. By the time of his return visit with his daughters, a commodious Mormon chapel had been constructed and in service for more than fifteen years in San Martín, now a ward in the Nealtican Puebla Stake, one of five LDS stakes headquartered in the Puebla region. Several of the earliest members of the LDS Church in San Martín—who had united their faith at a time when the church was a struggling branch of fewer than fifty people holding religious services in an apartment over a cantina in the market place—still resided there, including the Hernandez, Vargas, and Osnaya families.

A telephone call was made to *la casa* Osnaya to say that visitors from the United States wanted to drop by to say hello. The Osnayas lived on the same street and in the same house—not far from the *zocalo*—that Gordon had entered many times as a young missionary for meals and evening conversations after Sunday services. A stocky man with dark, bright eyes and a drooping mustache opened the door, and Gordon stepped forward. "Soy Elder Pastor" [I'm Elder Shepherd], he said. "Yes, I know," the man replied, "pasen ustedes, pasen!" [come in, come in].

Gordon experienced a flood of recollection. The man at the door was Oscar Osnaya, who, when Gordon last saw him, had been a four-year-old terror whom his teenaged aunt had been assigned to keep corralled during church meetings. His grandfather was old Hermano Osnaya, who had been called to serve as branch president in San Martín shortly after Gordon was transferred to another assignment. Later, Hermano Osnaya became the first Mormon bishop in San Martín. Both he and his wife had died years ago. The head of the Osnaya household now was Dionísio, son of the Osnayas, who, to Gordon's surprise, had married María Vargas, who was a lively teenager at the time of her family's conversion and baptism into the church by Elder Martineau in 1964. It was María's younger brother, José Luís, whom Gordon had befriended and had done some occasional tracting with in San Martín when Elder Splinders was indisposed. Gordon now learned that several years later José Luís had died suddenly of an undetermined illness before he could realize his youthful dreams of serving a full-time Mormon mission.

As Gordon stood soaking in the long forgotten yet familiar contours and contents of the Osnaya living room, Pam tapped him on the shoulder and whispered, "Dad, look at this!" On a long wall above the couch hung a sizable frame that contained neatly arranged rows of old three-by-four-inch photographs. There were Bill Martineau, José Luís Lara, Cipriano Orozco, and Gerald Splinders, among many other missionary companions who had worked in San Martín. And there, almost in the center of the frame, was the smiling young face of Elder Pastor. Gordon and his daughters spent a night and a day partaking of the remarkable hospitality of the Osnaya family and other old-time members of the church in San Martín.

To his abiding regret, Gary has never returned to Mexico.

16

❧

Issues for a Missionary Church Facing
the Twenty-first Century

The primary purpose of this book is to document the process of religious socialization, to which Mormon youths are exposed as missionaries, and the
development of their capacity to perform organizationally defined religious
roles as they carry out proselyting assignments on behalf of a rapidly expanding international church. It would be unrealistic to conclude, however, simply because of this experience, intensive as it is, that the subsequent religious
careers of all Mormon missionaries are securely cast as they return home and
resume secular pursuits. Some, including those who were highly dedicated
in the field, like we were, lose their primal religious faith or develop other
commitments that take precedence to the LDS Church.[1] But it would be
equally erroneous to fail to acknowledge the powerful shaping effects of the
missionary experience on the subsequent lives of the majority who undergo
it and the important consequences for the continued growth and vitality of
the LDS Church.

In this concluding chapter we identify and comment on four thematic
issues that merit further study as a confident missionary church faces its
destiny in the twenty-first century: continued Mormon sectarianism; increased female missionary participation and gender authority issues; the
growth of a native, international missionary force; and the complex problems of lay activity, member retention, and native leadership.

The Missionary Experience and Mormon Sectarianism

Mormon scholars have expressed concern about institutional problems that
complicate the church's efforts to become a world religion. For example, in
his analysis of the dialectical tensions between LDS accommodation and

retrenchment within American society, Armand Mauss (1994a,b) concludes that modern Mormonism, both doctrinally and socially, is listing in the direction of Protestant fundamentalism and is in peril of losing its peculiar Latter-day Saint identity in the world religious economy. Mauss worries that retrenchment trends in scriptural literalism, corporate church governance, traditional gender role definitions, youth indoctrination, and political conservatism threaten to limit Mormonism's potentially universal appeal and make it more inviting to individuals who have a fundamentalist, authoritarian religious outlook. Consequently, he suspects that such individuals are being disproportionately recruited by the missionary enterprise and actively retained in the modern LDS Church.

In part, this analysis reflects the growing alienation of liberal Mormon intellectuals (always a small fraction of the Mormon lay community) from the institutional church. Yet it also indicates a selective market niche in the religious economy and a limitation on prospects for continued expansion. A key question to be answered, however, concerns the potential size of that niche. In the United States at least, LDS retrenchment has been in harmony with a resurgent national conservatism since the late 1960s, which no doubt has contributed significantly to Mormonism's enhanced appeal. There is no compelling indication that the popular ideological appeals of religious conservatism—or even authoritarianism—are about to wane.

The socialization and recruitment of Mormon youths into a disciplined missionary force has a profound affect not only on LDS retrenchment tendencies but also on Mormon sectarianism—on sustaining a crusade mentality for advancing the Mormon cause in the modern world. Increasing prosperity and social respectability among succeeding generations have frequently signaled the onset of worldly accommodation and a corresponding loss of sectarian fervor for successful religious movements historically (Johnson 1963; Niebuhr 1929; Wallis 1975; Wilson 1961). The demise of sectarian fervor is not, however, an inevitable consequence of generational succession. As long as religious movements are expanding through vigorous efforts at recruitment, they are likely to continue cultivating a crusade orientation that keeps them in tension with other groups in society. Committed missionary religions tend to resist liberalizing their basic precepts and continue to insist on the orthodox conformity of their members. It is when religions diminish or cease active efforts to convert the world that they become most susceptible to the pressures of compromise and accommodation (Stark and Bainbridge 1985, 363).

Clearly, the Mormons have prospered greatly in the twentieth century. Just as clearly, the LDS Church has modified many of its original beliefs and related religious practices, resulting in a significant degree of assimilation in

U.S. society and a corresponding reduction of social tensions and internal commitment norms for the lay membership, as Mauss has indicated. And yet every generation of Mormon leaders has continued to stress a variety of sectarian themes in its rhetoric and teachings, especially claims to exclusive possession of ultimate religious truth and the divinely appointed duty to carry this truth to the world in a relatively short span of time (Shepherd and Shepherd 1984a). Although it has become much more concerned with its image and with public relations in modern times, the LDS Church has never wavered in its commitment to growth through active proselyting. Indeed, Mormon leaders eagerly and systematically pursue effective public relations and a favorable corporate image to advance the ultimate ends of missionary work (Ashton 1977; Christensen 1982; Esplin 1977; Fletcher 1982).

Thus, the sense of mission in a sacred cause, which each new generation of Mormon youths receives, is similar to the crusade conception of earlier generations. In what we might conceive of as a "routinization of charisma," however, the zeal of new generations of Mormons is typically not fired by dramatic conversion experiences or persecution, as were the movement's original followers, but by inculcation in a lay system of religious service. Now, for the core U.S. membership, middle-class affluence is made compatible with dutiful sacrifice. Many LDS parents plan for the departure of children on missionary assignments with the same sense of prideful necessity that they have in sending them away to college. For many of the most active LDS families, such planning increasingly has come to include daughters as well as sons.[2]

Trends in LDS Missionary Participation by Young Women

Lack of official encouragement notwithstanding, single women have served full-time LDS missions since the turn of the twentieth century (Embry 1997; Evans 1985; Kunz 1976). Until the 1970s, however, females represented only a relatively small fraction of full-time LDS missionaries in the field. By the early 1990s their numbers had increased rapidly and, according to a personal communication from the LDS Church Missionary Department in 1992, accounted for nearly 20 percent of the total missionary force. This represents a major demographic restructuring in the Mormon missionary enterprise. In part, it has been necessary for young women to fill voids caused by the rapid expansion of LDS missions worldwide.[3] At the same time, trends toward marriage at a later age among Mormons in the United States reflect larger societal trends and help enlarge the pool of women in their early to mid-twenties from which Mormon missions can draw. More LDS young women pursue college educations and vocational training, and they also volunteer in larger numbers for missionary assignments than ever before. These trends indicate that expanding cohorts of LDS women, who have greater worldly experience than their predecessors, are willing to postpone marriage and family aspirations than customarily has been the Mormon norm.

LDS male authorities are ambivalent about the implications of these trends. Their response thus far to the dilemma of maintaining traditional Mormon sex role definitions while continually having to recruit for and staff an ever-expanding missionary enterprise has been to continue to emphasize young men's missionary obligations but not impose similar official expectations on young women.[4]

In what ways, if any, do the personal consequences of the missionary experience differ between women and men? And, ultimately, what are the consequences of a significantly increased rate of female missionary participation for the institutional structure of the Mormon religion? These are good questions for which we do not have particularly good answers. Our missionary accounts are devoid of any insight or empathy toward a feminine perspective of missionary life. During our time in Mexico we had only marginal contacts with a few sister missionaries, of whom we took relatively little notice. For awhile, sister missionaries were not assigned to Gordon's mission in southern Mexico, ostensibly because of difficult living conditions, less security in travel, and a greater likelihood for health problems in that region of the country.

Because female missionaries are typically required to work in a subordinate capacity to males, however, we surmise that a major consequence of their service is the reinforcement of a male-dominated priesthood hierarchy. As one informant expressed matters, "There are more non-traditional and progressive women now going on missions; but once they're in the mission, they seem to model themselves to the role and its limitations" (Hanks 1992, 328). But at least some sister missionaries—perhaps an increasing number as the volunteer rate of female missionaries increases—may find their assignments liberating. They demand duties outside of marital and family obligations, provide chances to exercise self-reliance and organizational skills, and strengthen self-confidence and a sense of sisterhood.

The growing number of LDS sister missionaries parallels the contemporary increase of female recruits into the U.S. armed forces. As *Newsweek* reported, "The sheer number of women in uniform suggests that a new era is coming. Fully 24 percent of all air force recruits in 1994 were women, compared with 19 percent for the army, 17 percent for the navy and 5 percent for the marines" ("The Military Fights the Gender Wars" 37). The ambivalence of many Mormon officials toward increasing numbers of young women volunteers for LDS missionary service is similar to that frequently expressed by government and military leaders trying to cope with changes in traditional gender role distinctions within combat organizations (Elshtain 1991; Gilmartin 1991; Rothstein 1991). "The services are still struggling with the implications of gender equality in uniform. . . . The Pentagon's 1993 decision to open selected combat jobs to women is even more critical. Command of a combat unit is the only promotion ladder to top echelon posts for officers—which means the new policy will eventually lead to a surge of women officers at the top of the chain of command" ("The Military Fights the Gender Wars" 35, 37). Similarly, most LDS mission positions in the field require priesthood authority and are therefore male-dominated. As Hanks observes, "Missionary possibilities for missionary sisters are generally limited to senior companion or area leader and mission office staff. Occasionally there have been all-female districts and zones of sisters with sister zone leaders and sister district leaders, especially in foreign countries," but these have been very rare exceptions to the rule "due to necessity, situation, or experimental policy" (1992, 326–27). As of 1994, separate districts or zones for sister missionaries were explicitly prohibited by the *Mission President's Handbook* (1990, 19).

Like military officials, Mormon male leaders seem reluctant to abandon stereotyped conceptions of women as the "fairer sex," whose physical nature might make them less able to overcome the privations and dangers of duty in the field. Of genuine concern is the potential danger of assault and rape, especially in urban areas that have high crime rates.[5] Church leaders are also concerned about distracting romances and sexual liaisons, which in military organizations can seriously interfere with discipline and morale. For Mormon officials, concerns about enlarging the sister missionary force are strongly associated with concerns about postponing young women's marital prospects. Officials are also hesitant because of problems that might arise from fundamental LDS ideals of sexual chastity and mission field celibacy at a time when young Latter-day Saint men and women are supposed to sublimate their sexual energies completely in service to the church.

The feminist movement has been identified by some leading LDS officials as a major threat to the integrity of Mormon institutions (Gottlieb and Wiley 1984; Mauss 1994a; Packer 1980; White 1985, 1989). Indeed, the modern LDS Church is not immune to the influence of large-scale social trends or to social change. The degree and eventual patterns of adjustment to the gradual growth of feminine consciousness within the church, potentially abetted by the increased missionary ideals and organizational experience of capable young women, should be one of the investigative areas of central interest for future observers of Mormonism in the twenty-first century.[6]

The Growth of a Native Missionary Force

A key factor in the international expansion of Mormonism and its prospects for continued development in the twenty-first century is the growth of the non-U.S. component of its missionary force. For a generation following World War II, almost all missionaries were North Americans. Since the 1970s, however, and concomitant with the development of LDS stakes, temples, and missionary training centers outside the United States, the number of local missionaries accepting full-time proselyting assignments has greatly accelerated. Now, approximately one-quarter of the LDS missionary force is made up of first- and second-generation converts from countries (especially Latin American countries) outside the United States (Hart 1993a, 3).[7] Assuming that the systematic development of local missionaries has become an integral part of the dynamics of modern Mormonism, it is conceivable that continued LDS international expansion in the twenty-first century will be accompanied by an increase in the number of missionaries not native to the United States, to the point where they surpass their North American counterparts as a proportion of the total missionary force.[8]

The close interdependence of several core institutional factors in LDS growth and development should be emphasized in connection with a growing international missionary force. The cultivation of local missionaries is largely contingent on the formation of local stake and ward organizations under the direction of local leaders and, subsequently, on the institutionalization of Mormon youth programs, especially seminary and institute courses, which channel young people toward accepting missionary assignments (Shepherd and Shepherd 1996). Mexico provides a prominent example of this linkage.

During our missionary tours from 1964 to 1966, Mexicans made up between fewer than 10 percent and no more than 20 percent of their country's LDS missionary force. Now, up to 90 percent of the staff in most Mexican missions is staffed by local missionaries (Wells 1990, 6).[9] Local missionary enlistments first began to climb in the late 1960s and 1970s in conjunction with the rapid formation of Mexican stakes and the associated youth auxiliary programs that began during the same period. Instituted in 1979, the Mexico City Missionary Training Center is the largest operated by the LDS Church outside the United States; thousands of Mexicans have been prepared for missionary service at that facility. The church in Mexico has also begun to export missionaries to other Spanish-speaking areas worldwide, including Hispanic barrios in southern California and the southwestern United States. Many Mexican missionaries attend LDS seminary and institute classes before entering the Mexico City MTC, and it has been reported that nearly 15 percent had attended Benemerito, the LDS Church college and preparatory school on the outskirts of Mexico City (Wells 1990, 6), which was instituted just before we arrived in Mexico.

Earin Call, a former mission president and director of LDS schools in Mexico, observed in a personal interview in January 1994 that church-sponsored education in that country has been critical to Mormon growth there. He credits the church's education system with producing a generation of Mexican leaders who typically have enrolled in church schools or seminary classes and then gone on to accept and perform missionary assignments before returning home to assume ward and stake leadership callings. Because of their youth and relative lack of ecclesiastical experience, some returned Mexican missionaries have faltered in leadership callings, but a large proportion have succeeded. It is doubtful whether the extensive complex of LDS stakes and wards in Mexico would function adequately without the sustaining presence of thousands of local members and lay leaders who have passed through the missionary experience. This is especially true in light of the problems associated with assimilating converts into the kind of active lay religious roles that the LDS Church requires.

Member Retention and Native Leadership Concerns

Because Mormonism depends on active lay involvement, LDS officials are acutely conscious of member participation rates and the problem of maintaining the allegiance of converts following baptism into the church. Member retention has become a major concern, particularly outside of the United States. According to one Mormon scholar, "Probably the most complex challenge we face in the internationalization of the church in the twenty-first century is this: Can we make changes in the way we organize and experience the LDS community that will reduce and contain the massive defections of recent decades?" (Decoo 1996, 113).[10]

Retention problems in Mexico (and elsewhere in Latin America) for the LDS Church have become increasingly apparent. Indeed, they were apparent to us as young missionaries in Mexico in the 1960s. As Tullis has noted,

> At the same time the phenomenal new baptismal rate was occurring during the 1960s, the church, preparatory to its eventually forming stakes and wards in numerous Latin American countries, was also rapidly transferring leadership obligations and opportunities to local members. . . . But there were relatively few men in the church at the time, and fewer still who were qualified for major administrative assignments. . . . The North American mission

president was operating for a maximum number of conversions to the faith. But he assumed little or no responsibility for what happened to the new members. . . . The new local leaders needed new members with at least minimum leadership capability. What the mission presidents delivered was a tremendous quantity of members who were mostly inexperienced by any relevant leadership standard. The enterprise simply broke down, with relations between local ecclesiastical authorities and some North American mission presidents becoming strained indeed. (1978, 103)

The LDS Church keeps extensive records of members' activity in local congregational units but usually does not publish such information. Reliable retention data is difficult to come by. Based on 1980 sources, Lawrence Young, a Brigham Young University sociologist, calculated that only 19 percent of adult Mexican males who were members of the LDS Church had been ordained to the Melchizedek priesthood. Because Mormon males must be active participants in the church for a period of time to demonstrate their worthiness for the priesthood, the percentage of Melchizedek priesthood holders is an important indicator of member retention. Approximately 70 percent of adult Mormon males in Utah held the Melchizedek priesthood in 1980, for example, indicating a predictably much higher member retention rate in the Mormon heartland than in Mexico (Young 1994, 57–58).

Limited data on weekly attendance at sacrament meeting in Mexican mission districts for 1991 indicated that average attendance for priesthood holders was 32 percent in contrast to 50 percent for women, with an overall average of 34 percent.[11] Consistent with these figures, Robert Wells, an LDS general authority and former Mexican mission president, reported in 1988 to a group of Brigham Young University alumni at the Benemerito school in Mexico City that "we normally get one-third of our people out to stake conference. We get about one-third of our people attending sacrament meeting. We have a challenge. One-third of our people are fully active always. One-third are lukewarm and one-third we don't see back in church a few weeks after they're baptized" (1988, 8).[12] Although these figures are probably no worse (and perhaps even better) than attendance rates in many other churches, they do represent a significant problem for LDS authorities who rely on Melchizedek priesthood holders to officiate in and administer the extensive lay programs of local congregations.[13]

LDS evaluation researchers in the 1980s confirmed that member retention problems in Mexico were frequently related to failure in rapid-growth areas to socialize and integrate converts (many of whom were accustomed to passive religious involvements) into the lay structure of local wards or branches. Interviews with members who had withdrawn from active participation indicated that the majority of Mexican adults who had converted voluntarily still identified themselves as Mormons and continued to profess belief in Mormon teachings even though they had become inactive or were alienated from other local members. Those who no longer identified themselves as Mormons were likely to have felt pressured into joining, or were children at the time of their family's conversion, and were never successfully socialized in church programs. In response to such problems, the LDS Church has instituted—with some degree of success—a variety of reactivation programs to encourage disaffected converts to return to fellowship; has concentrated on nurturing converts in their local congregations, both before and following their baptisms; and has developed a set of leadership training seminars for local leaders, especially new branch presidents, bishops, and stake presidents.[14]

Lay participation in the modern LDS Church, especially in leadership positions, presupposes a certain literacy level as well as the willingness to function in a bureaucratically regulated organization that stresses record keeping, reporting and supervisory systems, hierarchically imposed objectives, and standardized programs. Thus, Young (1994) characterizes modern Mormonism as guided by a managerial church well accommodated to the corporate structure of North American society but often out of touch with the social realities in other parts of the world, where many converts lack a formal education.[15]

At the same time, in an analysis of LDS organizational trends and prospects in Latin America, David Knowlton, a Mormon anthropologist, emphasizes Mormonism's appeal to rising segments of the middle class and the church's increasing dependence on that group to staff leadership positions: "Not only do most leaders in stake presidencies and higher fill middle-class occupations, but the majority comes from sectors with management skills, sectors relatively young and growing rapidly, as the Latin American economy changes" (1996, 171). Knowlton identifies another critical group from which the church recruits leaders in Latin American countries: salaried employees of the Church Educational System and the Presiding Bishopric's Office. "This is truer the higher the leadership level, and is especially true of regional representatives, mission presidents, and Latin American general authorities. This means that church employment is important for future high leadership" (1996, 172). Thus, in Latin American countries, especially Mexico, "certain socioeconomic sectors symbolically represent the church as its leadership. Though the majority of members might come from less affluent sectors, the character of the institution is symbolically represented by those from the management sector, including salaried church employment. This sector was virtually nonexistent in Latin America fifty years ago but has expanded massively during the same period the church has grown there" (172). Knowlton concludes that as the middle class continues to expand "as Latin America develops economically, the church is in a favorable niche for further growth, despite the simultaneous potential for class conflict" (174).

In Mormonism, the dual functions of expansion via recruitment and retention of members through participation in church programs are both served by the missionary system. The LDS Church, especially in high-growth regions of developing nations, has come to depend on local missions as socializing agencies for local missionaries. In many respects, the LDS mission field organization is an idealization and a microcosm of the institutional church. In the field, young missionaries are immersed in a managerial ethos of daily planning, reporting, and supervision. They are grounded in institutional procedures and groomed to assume local leadership positions on completion of their full-time proselyting service. It is in the mission field where a kind of "hybrid Mormon-American managerial culture" is most clearly modeled and transmitted.[16] Retaining the participation of a sufficient fraction of returned local missionaries, socialized and equipped to discharge organizational roles, is of central importance to the continued international development of Mormonism in the twenty-first century.

In Mexico, a lack of experienced leadership and member activity problems persist, but there can be little doubt that the LDS Church is on firmer footing than ever before. Of greatest importance to the future of Mormonism in Mexico will be the continued socialization of new generations, born into the church and prepared—many through experience as missionaries—to function in a lay Mormon ecclesiastical culture which, under local leadership, gradually is becoming better adapted to Mexican life. In the process, there undoubtedly will continue to be internal organizational problems and cultural conflicts, but a critical mass of sufficiently active Mormons already has been achieved to sustain the regeneration and expansion of the LDS Church in Mexico. How long it can continue to grow at its current rate is a question without a definitive answer. It is likely, however, that Mormonism is far from having exhausted its market appeal in the religious economy of modern Mexico. Despite the potential of religious market saturation for conservative religious values, convert member defections and inactivity rates, alienation of intellectuals, and even future national schisms, the LDS Church will continue to become a major presence in the world religious economy of the twenty-first century.

NOTES

1. For studies of LDS patterns of religious disaffiliation, see Albrecht and Bahr (1983); Albrecht and Cornwall (1989); and Bahr and Albrecht (1989). These studies are reminders that religious commitments seldom, if ever, can be understood as completely static attitudes toward life. To the contrary, most peoples' religious faith tends to wax and wane, and religious commitments change periodically, either increasing or decreasing in response to the changing circumstances of their lives. If that were not the case, it would make little sense to discuss changing patterns of religious recruitment, affiliation, and periodic revivals in society. It is precisely because religious commitments are subject to change that religious organizations such as the LDS Church simultaneously compete for adherents and become preoccupied with maintaining or strengthening the commitment of those members they have.

2. Based on a small, haphazard set of informal interviews with full-time church employees and administrators at LDS headquarters in Salt Lake City and the Provo MTC, we discovered that most had either supported daughters on proselyting missions or were encouraging them to consider missionary assignments. None said that they would discourage their daughters from considering full-time missionary service.

3. Because of continued institutional emphasis placed on traditional gender roles, Bennion and Young (1996, 23) speculate that any major increase in the size of the LDS missionary force must come from retired couples or the traditional pool of young men. The current 1-to-5 female-to-male ratio among single missionaries, however, represents a major historical increase in the number of young women serving LDS missions. We see no reason to think that the rate of female missionary enlistments will decline any time soon, and we surmise that their rate will slowly increase. Of course, if LDS authorities would change the required age for single sister missionaries from twenty-one to a younger age, or encourage young women to prepare for full-time missionary service with the same emphasis given to the socialization of young men, we would expect a dramatic increase in the size of the missionary force.

4. Embry (1997) has shown the historical ambivalence of LDS authorities toward recruiting females for missionary service throughout the twentieth century. At times, appeals were issued for more sister volunteers, especially those with office skills or experience in church auxiliary organizations. At other times, directives were given to local officials to consider only those young women without any marriage prospects or, on occasion, not to call any new sister missionaries at all. In contrast to the current 20 percent level of participation, Embry reports (112) that in the 1970s the Church Missionary Committee wanted to keep sister missionaries to under 10 percent of the full-time missionary force.

5. Embry cites oral history interviews with LDS mission presidents indicating that they are concerned about sister missionaries' tracting and having to knock on strangers' doors, and they are not in favor of sisters receiving assignments to "primitive" missions or "rough areas." We are unaware of any statistical data on the incidence of assaults or attempted assaults against LDS sister missionaries worldwide.

6. For a statistical analysis of changing definitions of women's roles in the LDS Church since 1950, see Iannaccone and Mills (1994).

7. Missionary enlistment rates are correlated with the infrastructural development of LDS stakes internationally. For a summary of the varied development of LDS stakes (and, by inference, local missionary involvement) in Latin American countries, see Knowlton (1996).

8. A dramatic increase in the number of non-North American missionaries is also true worldwide among Protestant and Catholic mission agencies. That trend is associated with the shift of Christian population centers to countries of the southern continents (Siewert and Kenyon 1993).

9. Although we lack systematic data for separate missions, we do possess 1993 documents for the Mexico Puebla Mission that show a total missionary force of 143, 75 percent of whom were Mexican. Of the total, there were twenty-seven sister missionaries (19 percent), all of whom were Mexican.

10. For a thoughtful analysis of LDS retention problems in Europe, see Decoo (1996). An earlier collection of prescient essays by both LDS leaders and scholars on the implications and problems for Mormonism as it becomes an international church can be found in Tullis et al. (1978).

11. These figures were obtained from the 1991 LDS World Missionary Report (copy in our possession).

12. Wells, who appeared undaunted by the problems of rapid LDS growth in Mexico, also said, "We'll just call the best men and let the Lord bless them and magnify them. . . . It doesn't bother me to see imperfect leaders. . . . We're plowing ahead without perfect leaders . . . I would rather see a mission baptize 1,000 a month and lose 333, but have 777 there, than baptize 10—like in some European missions, who also lose 3 to total inactivity. . . . The Savior said the kingdom is like fishermen who cast the net and bring in all kinds of species, and that's what we are doing—we're bringing in everybody that will promise to live the commandments, knowing full well that probably a third of them won't. But that doesn't bother me at all" (1988, 6, 7, 9).

13. According to a national survey, barely 20 percent of Protestants and 28 percent of Catholics regularly attend Sunday services in the United States (Hadaway, Marler, and Chaves 1993).

14. These observations are based on conversations with LDS Church researchers. Early efforts at instituting member retention programs in Mexico were occasionally noted with some ambivalence in our missionary journals, as local members were encouraged to interact with prospective converts by teaching Sunday investigator classes and accompanying missionaries as they delivered proselyting lessons in investigators' homes.

15. Facing even more discordant cultural situations in Africa, Bennion and Young report that LDS missionaries there have been instructed to focus on recruiting families in major cities who have "(1) literacy in [English or French], (2) some kind of employment, (3) transportation as well as proximity to an LDS chapel in the growth center, and (4) prospective Melchizedek Priesthood holders" (1996, 25). Such a pros-

elyting strategy conceivably could become a model for future LDS missionary efforts in other developing regions.

16. The term *hybrid Mormon-American culture* was coined by Gottlieb and Wiley (1984). It is the distinctly American character of Mormon organization and ecclesiastical practice that, according to Young (1994), has created image problems and conflicts for the LDS Church in nationalistic developing countries, where negative associations are often made to link the LDS Church with Yankee imperialism. Such critiques contribute to a more complex assessment of the consequences of the Mormons' centralized, managerial approach to missions. For similar problems shared by other evangelizing North American churches, especially in Latin America, see Howes (1991).

Bibliography

Adams, W. E., and J. R. Clopton. 1990. Personality and dissonance among Mormon missionaries. *Journal of Personality Assessment* 54:684–93.

Albrecht, Stan L., and Howard M. Bahr. 1983. Patterns of religious disaffiliation: A study of lifelong Mormons, Mormon converts, and former Mormons. *Journal for the Scientific Study of Religion* 22:336–79.

Albrecht, Stan L., and Marie Cornwall. 1989. Life events and religious change. *Review of Religious Research* 31:23–38.

Allen, James B., Ronald W. Walker, David J. Whittaker, Armand L. Mauss, and Dynette I. Reynolds, eds. Forthcoming. *Studies in Mormon history: A bibliography.* Urbana: University of Illinois Press.

Anthony, Dick. 1990. Religious movements and brainwashing. In *In gods we trust: Patterns of religious pluralism in America,* edited by Dick Anthony and Thomas S. Robbins, 295–344. New Brunswick: Transaction.

Arrington, Leonard J. 1958. *Great Basin kingdom: An economic history of the Latter-day Saints.* Cambridge: Harvard University Press.

Ashton, Wendell J. 1977. Mormon image: An interview with Wendell J. Ashton. *Dialogue* 10:15–20.

Avant, Gerry. 1994. Missionary training center expands. [Salt Lake City] *Church News,* March 19, 3, 11.

Bahr, Howard M., and Stan L. Albrecht. 1989. Strangers once more: Patterns of disaffiliation from Mormonism. *Journal for the Scientific Study of Religion* 28:180–200.

Beecher, Dale F. 1975. Rey L. Pratt and the Mexican Mission. *BYU Studies* 15:293–307.

Bennion, Lowell C. 1995. The geographic dynamics of Mormondom, 1965–95. *Sunstone* 18:21–32.

Bennion, Lowell C., and Lawrence A. Young. 1996. The uncertain dynamics of LDS expansion, 1950–2020. *Dialogue* 29:8–32.

Berger, Peter L. 1967. *The sacred canopy: Elements of a sociological theory of religion.* New York: Doubleday.

Berger, Peter L., and Thomas Luckmann. 1967. *The social construction of reality: A treatise in the sociology of knowledge.* New York: Doubleday.

Bergera, Gary. 1988. What you leave behind: Six years at the MTC. *Dialogue* 20:146–56.

Berleffi, Bobbie. 1987. A conversation with Bobbie Berleffi. *Sunstone* 11:45–48.

Bloom, Harold. 1992. *The American religion: The emergence of the post-Christian nation.* New York: Simon and Schuster.

Briem, Robert M. 1984. Relationship between locus of control, health, belief attitudes, and gastrointestinal diseases among missionaries. Ph.D. dissertation, University of Utah.

Britsch, R. Lanier. 1979. Mormon missions: An introduction to the Latter-day Saint missionary system. *Occasional Bulletin of Missionary Research* 3:22–27.

Bromley, David, and Anson Shupe. 1979. Just a few years seem like a lifetime: A role theory approach to participation in religious movements. *Research in Social Movements, Conflicts and Change* 2:159–85.

———. 1981. *Strange gods: The great American cult scare.* Boston: Beacon Press.

———. 1987. The future of the anti-cult movement. In *The future of new religious movements,* edited by David Bromley and Phillip Hammond, 221–34. Mercer, Ga.: Mercer University Press.

Bronfenbrenner, Urie. 1970. *Two worlds of childhood.* New York: Russell Sage Foundation.

Brown, Harold. 1978. Gospel culture and leadership development in Latin America. In *Mormonism: A faith for all cultures,* edited by F. LaMond Tullis, 106–15. Provo: Brigham Young University Press.

Buerger, D. J. 1987. The development of the Mormon temple endowment ceremony. *Dialogue* 20:33–76.

Burdick, Michael, and Phillip E. Hammond. 1991. World order and mainline religions: The case of Protestant foreign missions. In *World order and religion,* edited by Wade C. Roof, 193–209. Albany: SUNY Press.

Christensen, Bruce L. 1982. A light unto the world: Public relations is necessary and legitimate for the church. *Sunstone* 7:25–26.

Collier, George, and Eliazbeth Quaratiello. 1994. BASTA! Land and the Zapatista Rebellion in Chiapas. Oakland: Institute for Food and Development Policy, Food First Books.

Cook, Guillermo. 1994. *The changing face of the church in Latin America.* Maryknoll, N.Y.: Orbis Press.

Cornwall, Marie. 1987. The social bases of religion: A study of factors influencing belief and commitment. *Review of Religious Research* 29:44–56.

———. 1989. The determinants of religious behavior: A theoretical model and empirical test. *Social Forces* 68:572–92.

———. 1994. The institutional role of Mormon women. In *Contemporary Mormon-*

ism: Social science perspectives, edited by Marie Cornwall, Tim B. Heaton, and Lawrence A. Young, 239–64. Urbana: University of Illinois Press.

Cowan, Richard O. 1984. *Every man shall hear the Gospel in his own language.* Provo: Missionary Training Center.

———. 1992. Missionary training centers. In *Encyclopedia of Mormonism,* edited by Daniel H. Ludlow, 913–14. New York: Macmillan.

Cross, Whitney R. 1950. *The burned over district: The social and intellectual history of enthusiastic religion in western New York, 1800–1850.* New York: Harper and Row.

Day, Gerald R. 1992. Mission presidents. In *Encyclopedia of Mormonism,* edited by Daniel H. Ludlow, 914–15. New York: Macmillan.

Decker, Ed, and Dave Hunt. 1984. *The godmakers: A shocking exposé of what the Mormon Church really believes.* Eugene: Harvest House Publishers.

Decoo, Wilfried. 1996. Feeding the fleeing flock: Reflections on the struggle to retain church members in Europe. *Dialogue* 29:97–118.

Dow, James. 1993. Protestantismo en el campo: Causes materiales del Abandono de fiestas en la Sierra Oriente de Hidalgo. *Notas Mesoamericanas* 14:123–30.

———. 1997. The theology of change: Evangelical Protestantism and the collapse of native religion in a peasant area of Mexico. In *Explorations in anthropology and theology: New perspectives,* edited by Frank A. Salamone and Walter R. Adams, 113–23. Lanham: University Press of America.

Duke, James B. 1992. The weakness of strong ties: Measuring the influence of peers among LDS adolescents. Paper presented at the conference of the Center for Studies of the Family, Brigham Young University, Provo, Utah.

Elliott, Doris Williams. 1991. Women, the Mormon family, and class mobility: Nineteenth-century Victorian ideology in a twentieth-century church. *Sunstone* 15:19–26.

Ellsworth, George. 1951. A history of Mormon missions in the United States and Canada, 1830–1860. Ph.D. dissertation, University of California, Berkeley.

Elshtain, J. B. 1991. Feminism and war. *The Progressive,* September, 14–16.

Embry, Jessie L. 1997. LDS Sister missionaries: An oral history response, 1910–71. *Journal of Mormon History* 23:100–139.

England, Eugene. 1983. The dawning of a brighter day: Mormon literature after 150 years. In *After 150 Years: The Latter-day Saints in sesquicentennial perspective,* edited by Thomas G. Alexander and Jessie L. Embry, 97–135. Provo: Brigham Young University Redd Center for Western Studies.

———. 1990. On being male and Melchizedek. *Dialogue* 23:64–80.

Esplin, Fred C. 1977. The church as broadcaster. *Dialogue* 10:25–45.

Evans, Vella Neil. 1985. Woman's image in authoritative Mormon discourse: A rhetorical analysis. Ph.D. dissertation, University of Utah.

Finke, Roger, and Rodney Stark. 1988. Religious economies and sacred canopies: Religious mobilization in American cities, 1906. *American Sociological Review* 53:41–49.

————. 1992. *The churching of America: Winners and losers in our religious economy.* New Brunswick: Rutgers University Press.

Fletcher, Peggy. 1982. A light unto the world: Image building is anathema to Christian living. *Sunstone* 7:16–24.

Foster, Lawrence. 1979. From frontier activism to neo-Victorian domesticity: Women in the nineteenth and twentieth centuries. *Journal of Mormon History* 6:3–21.

Fox, Jonathan. 1993. *The politics of food in Mexico: State power and mobilization.* Ithaca: Cornell University Press.

The Gallup Report: Religion in America. 1987. Princeton: The Gallup Organization.

Gentleman, Judith, ed. 1989. *Mexico's alternative political futures.* San Diego: Center for U.S.-Mexican Studies, University of California, San Diego.

Gilmartin, P. A. 1991. Proposed policy shift on women in combat meets resistance. *Aviation Week and Space Technology,* June, 81–82.

Goffman, Erving. 1961. *Asylums: Essays on the social situation of mental patients and other inmates.* New York: Doubleday.

————. 1963. *Stigma.* Englewood Cliffs: Prentice-Hall.

Gottlieb, Robert, and Peter Wiley. 1984. *America's saints: The rise of Mormon power.* New York: G. P. Putnam's Sons.

Groesbeck, C. Jess. 1986. Thought reform or rite of passage? *Sunstone* 10:30–31.

Grover, Mark L. 1977. *The Mormon Church in Latin America: A periodical index, 1830–1976.* Provo: Brigham Young University Press.

Hadaway, C. Kirk, Penny Long Marler, and Mark Chaves. 1993. What the polls don't show: A closer look at U.S. church attendance. *American Sociological Review* 58:741–52.

Hanks, Maxine. 1992. Sister missionaries and authority. In *Women and authority: Re-emerging Mormon feminism,* edited by Maxine Hanks, 315–34. Salt Lake City: Signature Books.

Hansen, Klaus J. 1967. *Quest for empire: The political Kingdom of God and the Council of Fifty in Mormon history.* East Lansing: Michigan State University Press.

Hart, John L. 1993a. Local missionaries supported in service by international fund. *Church News,* November 13, 3, 5.

————. 1993b. Mexico formally registers church. *Church News,* July 17, 3–4.

————. 1995. Preparation: A key to success in serving full-time missions. *Church News,* June 10, 3.

Heaton, Tim B. 1986. How does religion influence fertility? The case of Mormons. *Journal for the Scientific Study of Religion* 25:248–58.

————. 1992. Vital statistics. In *Encyclopedia of Mormonism,* edited by Daniel H. Ludlow, 1518–37. New York: Macmillan.

Heinerman, John, and Anson Shupe. 1985. *The Mormon corporate empire.* Boston: Beacon Press.

Hicks, M. 1982. The aesthetics of the endowment: Some concerns about substituting film for live action. *Sunstone* 7:46–49.

Hill, Marvin J. 1989. *Quest for refuge: The Mormon flight from American pluralism.* Salt Lake City: Signature Books.

Hoge, Dean, and David Roozen, eds. 1979. *Understanding church growth and decline.* New York: Pilgrim Press.

Howes, Graham. 1991. God damn Yanquis: American hegemony and contemporary Latin American Christianity. In *World order and religion,* edited by Wade C. Roof, 83–95. Albany: SUNY Press.

Hughes, Richard T., and C. Leonard Allen. 1988. *Illusions of innocence: Protestant primitivism in America, 1630–1875.* Chicago: University of Chicago Press.

Hutchison, William R. 1987. *Errand to the world: American protestant thought and foreign missions.* Chicago: University of Chicago Press.

Iannaccone, Lawrence. 1990. Religious practice: A human capital approach. *Journal for the Scientific Study of Religion* 29:297–314.

———. 1992. Religious markets and the economics of religion. *Social Compass* 39:123–31.

———. 1994. Why strict churches are strong. *American Journal of Sociology* 99:1180–211.

Iannaccone, Lawrence, and Carrie E. Mills. 1994. Dealing with social change: The Mormon Church's response to change in women's roles. In *Contemporary Mormonism: Social science perspectives,* edited by Marie Cornwall, Tim B. Heaton, and Lawrence A. Young, 265–86. Urbana: University of Illinois Press.

Irving, Gordon. 1976. Mormonism and Latin America: A preliminary historical survey. Task Papers in LDS History no. 10. Salt Lake City: Historical Department of the Church of Jesus Christ of Latter-day Saints.

Jensen, Jay E. 1988. The effect of initial mission field training on missionary proselyting skills. Ph.D. dissertation, Brigham Young University.

Johnson, Benton. 1963. On church and sect. *American Sociological Review* 28:539–49.

Johnson, Clark V. 1977. Mormon education in Mexico: The rise of the Sociedad Educativa Y Cultural. Ph.D. dissertation, Brigham Young University.

Kanter, Rosabeth. 1972. *Commitment and community: Communes and utopia in sociological perspective.* Cambridge: Harvard University Press.

Kimball, Spencer W. 1981. *President Kimball speaks out.* Salt Lake City: Deseret Book Company.

King, Trancred I. 1983. Mormon missions and missiology. *Dialogue* 16:42–50.

Knowles, David. 1966. *From Pachomius to Ignatius: A study in the constitutional history of the religious orders.* New York: Oxford University Press.

Knowlton, David. 1989. Missionaries and terror: The assassination of two elders in Bolivia. *Sunstone* 13:10–15.

———. 1992. Thoughts on Mormonism in Latin America. *Dialogue* 25:41–53.

———. 1994. Gringo Jeringo: Anglo Mormon missionary culture in Bolivia. In *Contemporary Mormonism: Social science perspectives,* edited by Marie Cornwall, Tim B. Heaton, and Lawrence A. Young, 218–36. Urbana: University of Illinois Press.

———. 1996. Mormonism in Latin America: Toward the twenty-first century. *Dialogue* 29:159–76.

Kraemer, Hendrik. 1994 [1958]. *A theology of the laity.* Bellingham: Regent Publishing.

Kunz, Calvin S. 1976. A history of female missionary activity in the church, 1830–1898. M.A. thesis, Brigham Young University.

Latourette, Kenneth Scott. 1953. *A history of Christianity.* New York: Harper.

Leclercq, Jean. 1961. *The love of learning and the desire for God.* New York: Fordham University Press.

Leone, Mark. 1978. The Mormon temple experience. *Sunstone* 3:10–13.

———. 1979. *The roots of modern Mormonism.* Cambridge: Harvard University Press.

Levy, Daniel. 1987. *Mexico: Paradoxes of stability and change.* Boulder: Westview Press.

Lewis, Jim, ed. 1994. *From the ashes: Making sense of Waco.* Lanham: Rowan and Littlefield.

Lewis, Oscar. 1959. *Five families: Mexican case studies in the culture of poverty.* New York: Basic Books.

———. 1961. *The children of Sanchez: Autobiography of a Mexican family.* New York: Random House.

———. 1964. *Pedro Martinez: A Mexican peasant and his family.* New York: Random House.

Lofland, John, and Rodney Stark. 1965. Becoming a world-saver: A theory of conversion to a deviant perspective. *American Sociological Review* 30:862–75.

Lozano, Agrícol. 1983. *Historia del Mormonismo en Mexico.* Mexico: Editorial Zarahemla.

Ludlow, Daniel H., ed. 1992. *Encyclopedia of Mormonism.* New York: Macmillan.

Mabry, Donald J. 1982. *The Mexican university and the state: Student conflicts, 1910–1971.* College Station: Texas A&M University Press.

Mackey, Randall. 1985. The God-makers examined. *Dialogue* 18:14–15.

Madsen, John M. 1977. Church activity of LDS returned missionaries. Ph.D. dissertation, Brigham Young University.

Marquez, Viviane Brachet. 1994. *The dynamics of domination: State, class, and social reform in Mexico, 1910–1990.* Pittsburgh: University of Pittsburgh Press.

Martin, David. 1990. *Tongues of fire: The explosion of Protestantism in Latin America.* New York: Basil Blackwell.

Marty, Martin E. 1979. *Righteous empire: The protestant experience in America.* New York: Dial Press.

———. 1987. *Religion and republic: The American circumstance.* Boston: Beacon Press.

Marx, Gary T., and Douglas McAdam. 1994. *Collective behavior and social movements: Process and structure.* Englewood Cliffs: Prentice-Hall.

Mauss, Armand L. 1994a. *The angel and the beehive: The Mormon struggle with assimilation.* Urbana: University of Illinois Press.

———. 1994b. Refuge and retrenchment: The Mormon quest for identity. In *Contemporary Mormonism: Social science perspectives,* edited by Marie Cornwall,

Tim B. Heaton, and Lawrence A. Young, 24–42. Urbana: University of Illinois Press.

———. 1996. Mormonism in the twenty-first century: Marketing for miracles. *Dialogue* 29:236–49.

McAdam, Doug. 1988. *Freedom summer.* New York: Oxford University Press.

McCarthy, John D., and Mayer N. Zald. 1977. Resource mobilization and social movements: A partial theory. *American Journal of Sociology* 82:1212–41.

McLoughlin, William G. 1978. *Revivals, awakenings, and reform: An essay on religion and social change in America, 1607–1977.* Chicago: University of Chicago Press.

McMurrin, Sterling M. 1965. *The theological foundations of the Mormon religion.* Salt Lake City: University of Utah Press.

Merton, Robert K. 1968. *Social theory and social structure.* New York: Free Press.

Middlebrook, Kevin J. 1995. *The paradox of revolution: Labor, the state, and authoritarianism in Mexico.* Baltimore: Johns Hopkins University Press.

The military fights the gender wars. 1994. *Newsweek,* November 14, 35–37.

Miller, Scott D. 1986. Thought reform and totalism: The psychology of the LDS Church missionary training program. *Sunstone* 10:24–29.

Mission President's Handbook. 1990. Salt Lake City: Church of Jesus Christ of Latter-day Saints.

Moran, Gabriel. 1983. *Religious education development: Images for the future.* Minneapolis: Wisdom Press.

Moskos, Charles C. 1970. The American combat soldier in Vietnam. *Journal of Social Issues* 31:25–37.

Murphy, Thomas W. 1996. Reinventing Mormonism: Guatemala as harbinger of the future? *Dialogue* 29:177–92.

Neill, Stephen. 1964. *A history of Christian missions.* Baltimore: Penguin Books.

Newell, Linda King. 1985. The historical relationship of Mormon women and priesthood. *Dialogue* 18:21–32.

Newton, Marjorie. 1996. Towards 2000: Mormonism in Australia. *Dialogue* 29:193–206.

Niebuhr, H. Richard. 1929. *The social sources of denominationalism.* New York: Henry Holt.

Olmstead, Clifton E. 1961. Social religion in urban America. In *American mosaic: Social patterns of religion in the United States,* edited by Phillip E. Hammond and Benton Johnson, 139–48. New York: Random House.

Packer, Boyd K. 1980. *The holy temple.* Salt Lake City: Bookcraft.

Parry, Keith. 1994. The Mormon missionary companionship. In *Contemporary Mormonism: Social science perspectives,* edited by Marie Cornwall, Tim B. Heaton, and Lawrence A. Young, 182–206. Urbana: University of Illinois Press.

Poore, Ann. 1996. *The reality of abstraction: Painting in Utah, 1946–1996.* Logan: Nora Eccles Harrison Museum of Art, Utah State University.

Quinn, D. Michael. 1993. I-thou vs. I-it conversions: The Mormon "baseball baptism" era. *Sunstone* 16:30–44.

———. 1997. *The Mormon hierarchy: Extensions of power.* Salt Lake City: Signature Books.

Rambo, Lewis R. 1982. Current research on religious conversion. *Religious Studies Review* 8:146–59.

———. 1993. *Understanding conversion.* New Haven: Yale University Press.

Richardson, James T., Joel Best, and David Bromley, eds. 1991. *The satanism scare.* New York: Aldine.

Riding, Alan. 1985. *Distant neighbors: A portrait of the Mexicans.* New York: Alfred A. Knopf.

Robert, Dana L. 1994. From missions to beyond missions: The historiography of American Protestant foreign missions since World War II. *International Bulletin of Missionary Reserach* 18:145–62.

Roof, Wade C., ed. 1991. *World order and religion.* Albany: SUNY Press.

Roof, Wade C., and William McKinney. 1987. *American mainline religion: Its changing shape and ruture.* New Brunswick: Rutgers University Press.

Rothstein, L. 1991. War of words over women warriors. *Bulletin of the Atomic Scientists* 47:6–7.

Rubalcava, Boanerges. 1992. The church in Mexico. In *Encyclopedia of Mormonism,* edited by Daniel H. Ludlow, 899–902. New York: Macmillan.

Sandeen, Ernest R. 1970. *The roots of fundamentalism.* Chicago: University of Chicago Press.

Schlesinger, Arthur M. 1974. The missionary enterprise and theories of imperialism. In *The missionary enterprise in China and America,* edited by John K. Fairbank, 336–73. Cambridge: Harvard University Press.

Shepherd, Gary. 1976. Moral conformity in open and closed groups: A comparative study of moral decision making among Mormon, Catholic, and public school children. Ph.D dissertation, Michigan State University.

Shepherd, Gordon, and Gary Shepherd. 1984a. *A kingdom transformed: Themes in the development of Mormonism.* Salt Lake City: University of Utah Press.

———. 1984b. Mormon commitment rhetoric. *Journal for the Scientific Study of Religion* 23:129–39.

———. 1984c. Mormonism in secular society. *Review of Religious Research* 26:28–42.

———. 1986. Modes of leader rhetoric in the institutional development of Mormonism. *Sociological Analysis* 47:125–26.

———. 1996. Membership growth, church activity, and missionary recruitment. *Dialogue* 29:33–57.

Sherkat, Darren E. 1995. Embedding religious choices: Integrating preferences and social constraints into rational choice theories of religious behavior. In *Assessing rational choice theories of religion,* edited by Lawrence Young, 138–53. New York: Routledge.

Sherkat, Darren E., and John Wilson. 1995. Preferences, constraints, and choices in religious markets: An examination of religious switching and apostasy. *Social Forces* 73:993–1026.

Sherwood, Carlton. 1991. *Inquisition: The persecution and prosecution of the reverend Sun Myung Moon.* Washington, D.C.: Regnery Gateway.

Shibutani, Tamatsu. 1986. *Social processes.* Berkeley: University of California Press.

Shipps, Jan. 1985. *Mormonism: The story of a new religious tradition.* Urbana: University of Illinois Press.

Siewert, John A., and John A. Kenyon. 1993. *Mission handbook: A guide to USA/Canada Christian ministries overseas.* Monrovia, Calif.: MARC.

Snow, David A., Louis A. Zurcher, and Sheldon Ekland-Olson. 1980. Social networks and social movements: A microstructural approach to differential recruitment. *American Sociological Review* 45:787–801.

Snow, Leroy C. 1928. The missionary home. *Improvement Era* 31:552–54.

Sonne, Conway B. 1987. *Ships, saints, and mariners: A maritime encyclopedia of Mormon, 1830–1890.* Salt Lake City: University of Utah Press.

Stark, Rodney. 1984. The rise of a new world faith. *Review of Religious Research* 26:18–27.

———. 1994. Modernization and Mormon growth: The secularization thesis revisited. In *Contemporary Mormonism: Social science perspectives,* edited by Marie Cornwall, Tim B. Heaton, and Lawrence A. Young, 13–23. Urbana: University of Illinois Press.

Stark, Rodney, and William S. Bainbridge. 1980. Towards a theory of religion: Religious commitment. *Journal for the Scientific Study of Religion* 19:114–28.

———. 1981. Networks of faith: Interpersonal bonds and recruitment into cults and sects. *American Journal of Sociology* 85:1376–95.

———. 1985. *The future of religion: Secularization, revival, and cult formation.* Berkeley: University of California Press.

Stephen, Lynn, and James Dow. 1990. *Class, politics, and popular religion in Mexico and Central America.* Washington, D.C.: Society for Latin American Anthropology.

Stoll, David. 1990. *Is Latin America turning Protestant? The politics of evangelical growth.* Berkeley: University of California Press.

Stouffer, Samuel A. 1949. *The American soldier: Combat and its aftermath.* Princeton: Princeton University Press.

Sweet, Leonard I. 1979. Milennialism in America: Recent studies. *Theological Studies* 40:510–31.

———, ed. 1984. *The evangelical tradition in America.* Macon: Mercer University Press.

Talmage, James E. 1962. *The house of the Lord.* Salt Lake City: Bookcraft.

Tanner, Stephen L. 1982. We are all enlisted: War as metaphor. *Sunstone* 7:27–31.

Taylor, George T. 1986. Effects of coaching on the development of proselyting skills used by the Missionary Training Center, the Church of Jesus Christ of Latter-day Saints in Provo, Utah. Ph.D. dissertation, Brigham Young University.

Taylor, Marvin J. 1984. *Changing patterns of religious education.* Nashville: Abingdon Press.

Thomas, Darwin L. 1986. Afterwards. *BYU Studies* 26:99–103.

————, ed. 1988. *The religion and family connection: Social science perspectives.* Provo: Religious Studies Center, Brigham Young University.

Thomas, Darwin L., Joseph A. Olsen, and Stan E. Weed. 1989. Missionary service of LDS young men: A longitudinal analysis. Paper presented at the annual meeting of the Society for the Scientific Study of Religion, Salt Lake City, Utah.

Thomas, E. W. 1980. *Uncertain sanctuary: A study of Mormon pioneering in Mexico.* Salt Lake City: Westwater Press.

Thorp, M. R. 1977. The religious backgrounds of Mormon converts in Britain, 1837–1852. *Journal of Mormon History* 4:51–66.

Troeltsch, Ernst. 1960. *The social teachings of the Christian churches.* New York: Harper and Row.

Tullis, F. LaMond. 1978. Church development issues among Latin Americans. In *Mormonism: A faith for all cultures,* edited by F. LaMond Tullis, A. H. King, S. J. Palmer, and D. F. Tobler, 85–105. Provo: Brigham Young University Press.

————. 1980. The church moves outside the United States: Some observations from Latin America. *Dialogue* 13:63–73.

————. 1987. *Mormons in Mexico: The dynamics of faith and culture.* Logan: Utah State University Press.

Tullis, F. LaMond, Arthur H. King, Spenser J. Palmer, and Douglas F. Tobler, eds. 1978. *Mormonism: A faith for all cultures.* Provo: Brigham Young University Press.

Turner, Ralph, and Lewis M. Killian. 1987. *Collective behavior.* Englewood Cliffs: Prentice-Hall.

Tuveson, Ernest L. 1968. *Redeemer nation: The idea of America's millennial role.* Chicago: University of Chicago Press.

Underwood, Grant. 1982. Millenarianism and the early Mormon mind. *Journal of Mormon History* 9:41–51.

————. 1994. *The millenarian world of early Mormonism.* Urbana: University of Illinois Press.

Van Gennep, Arnold. 1960. *The rites of passage.* Chicago: University of Chicago Press.

Van Wagoner, Richard S. 1989. *Mormon polygamy: A history.* Salt Lake City: Signature Press.

Vogel, D. 1988. *Religious seekers and the advent of Mormonism.* Salt Lake City: Signature Press.

Walgren, Rawn A. 1975. A comparison of mission programs used in the three language training missions of the Church of Jesus Christ of Latter-day Saints. M.A. thesis, Brigham Young University.

Wallis, Roy. 1975. *Sectarianism.* New York: John Wiley.

Walls, Andrew. 1984. Christianity. In *Handbook of living religions,* edited by John R. Hinnells, 56–122. Harmondsworth, Middlesex: Viking Press.

————. 1991. World Christianity, the missionary movement and the ugly American. In *World order and religion,* edited by Wade C. Roof, 148–69. Albany: SUNY Press.

Walsh, Tad. 1993. Missions add to education: BYU's returned missionaries. [Provo] *Daily Universe*, June 10, 1.

Weber, Max. 1958. *The Protestant ethic and the spirit of capitalism.* New York: Charles Scribner's Sons.

Wells, Elayne. 1990. Centers prepare missionaries to be effective instruments. *Church News*, January 13, 6, 7.

Wells, Robert E. 1988. Untitled talk given to BYU alumni group at the Benemerito School, Mexico City, January 4. Manuscript copy in authors' possession.

White, O. Kendal. 1985. A feminist challenge: Mormons for ERA as an internal social movement. *Journal of Ethnic Studies* 13:29–50.

———. 1989. Mormonism and the equal rights amendment. *Journal of Church and State* 31:249–67.

Whittaker, David J. 1993. Mormon missions and missionaries: A bibliographic guide to published and manuscript sources. Special Collections and Manuscripts, Harold B. Lee Library, Brigham Young University, Provo, Utah.

Widstoe, John A. 1939. *Priesthood and church government.* Salt Lake City: Deseret Book Company.

Wilson, Bryan. 1961. *Sects and society.* Berkeley: University of California Press.

Wilson, William. 1974. And they spake with a new tongue. In *Conference on the language of the Mormons,* edited by Harold S. Madsen and John L. Sorenson, 46–48. Provo: Brigham Young University Language Research Center.

———. 1981. On being human: The folklore of Mormon missionaries. Sixty-fourth Faculty Honor Lecture, Utah State University, Logan.

———. 1988. Dealing with organizational stress: Lessons from the folklore of Mormon missionaries. In *Inside organizations: Understanding the human dimensions,* edited by Michael O. Jones, 271–79. Newbury Park: Sage Publications.

———. 1994. Powers of heaven and hell: Mormon missionary narratives as instruments of socialization and social control. In *Contemporary Mormonism: Social science perspectives,* edited by Marie Cornwall, Tim B. Heaton, and Lawrence A. Young, 207–17. Urbana: University of Illinois Press.

Wilson, Samuel, and John Siewert, eds. 1987. *Mission handbook: North American Protestant ministries overseas.* Monrovia, Calif.: MARC.

Wolfe, Eric. 1958. The Virgin of Guadalupe: A Mexican national symbol. *Journal of American Folklore* 61:34–39.

Wolfe, Tom. 1968. *The electric kool-aid acid test.* New York: Farrar, Straus, and Giroux.

Woodward, Kenneth. 1981. Onward Mormon soldiers. *Newsweek,* April 27, 87–88.

Woodworth, Warner. 1987. Brave new bureaucracy. *Dialogue* 20:25–36.

Wrong, Dennis. 1961. The oversocialized conception of man in modern sociology. *American Sociological Review* 26:183–93.

Yorgason, L. M. 1970. Preview of a study of the social and geographical origins of Mormon converts. *BYU Studies* 10:279–82.

Young, Karl E. 1968. *Ordeal in Mexico.* Salt Lake City: Deseret Book Company.

Young, Lawrence A. 1994. Confronting turbulent environments: Issues in the organizational growth and globalization of Mormonism. In *Contemporary Mormonism: Social science perspectives,* edited by Marie Cornwall, Tim B. Heaton, and Lawrence A. Young, 43–63. Urbana: University of Illinois Press.

Index

Mormon Studies from the University of Illinois Press

Prisoner for Polygamy: The Memoirs and Letters of Rudger Clawson at the Utah Territorial Penitentiary, 1884–87 *Edited by Stan Larson*

Joseph Smith III: Pragmatic Prophet *Roger D. Launius*

Kingdom on the Mississippi Revisited: Nauvoo in Mormon History *Edited by Roger D. Launius and John E. Hallwas*

Differing Visions: Dissenters in Mormon History *Edited by Roger D. Launius and Linda Thatcher*

Political Deliverance: The Mormon Quest for Utah Statehood *Edward Leo Lyman*

The Angel and the Beehive: The Mormon Struggle with Assimilation *Armand L. Mauss*

Mormon Enigma: Emma Hale Smith (2d ed.) *Linda King Newell and Valeen Tippets Avery*

Carthage Conspiracy: The Trial of the Accused Assassins of Joseph Smith *Dallin H. Oaks and Marvin S. Hill*

Science, Religion, and Mormon Cosmology *Robert Erich Paul*

Same-Sex Dynamics among Nineteenth-Century Americans: A Mormon Example *D. Michael Quinn*

Mormon Thunder: A Documentary History of Jedediah Morgan Grant *Gene A. Sessions*

Prophesying upon the Bones: J. Reuben Clark and the Foreign Debt Crisis, 1933–39 *Gene A. Sessions*

Mormon Passage: A Missionary Chronicle *Gary Shepherd and Gordon Shepherd*

Mormonism: The Story of a New Religious Tradition *Jan Shipps*

The Journals of William E. McLellin, 1831–1836 *Edited by Jan Shipps and John W. Welch*

The Saintly Scoundrel: The Life and Times of Dr. John Cook Bennett *Andrew F. Smith*

Mormon Lives: A Year in the Elkton Ward *Susan Buhler Taber*

Victims: The LDS Church and the Mark Hofmann Case *Richard E. Turley, Jr.*

The Millenarian World of Early Mormonism *Grant Underwood*